ADVANCED MATHEMATICS

BOOK 4

THE
SCHOOL
MATHEMATICS
PROJECT

ADVANCED
MATHEMATICS

BOOK 4

CAMBRIDGE UNIVERSITY PRESS

Published by the Syndics of the Cambridge University Press
Bentley House, 200 Euston Road, London NW1 2DB
American Branch: 32 East 57th Street, New York N.Y.10022

© Cambridge University Press 1970

Library of Congress Catalogue Card Number: 67-28685

ISBN: 0 521 08108 4

First published 1968
Metric reprint 1970
Reprinted 1973 1974

Printed in Great Britain
at the University Printing House, Cambridge
(Brooke Crutchley, University Printer)

THE
SCHOOL MATHEMATICS
PROJECT

When the SMP was founded in 1961, its main objective was to devise radically new secondary-school mathematics courses (and corresponding GCE and CSE syllabuses) to reflect, more adequately than did the traditional syllabuses, the up-to-date nature and usages of mathematics.

This objective has now been realized. SMP *Books 1–5* form a five-year course to the O-level examination 'SMP Mathematics'. *Books 3T, 4* and *5* give a three-year course to the same O-level examination (the earlier *Books T* and *T4* being now regarded as obsolete). *Advanced Mathematics Books 1–4* cover the syllabus for the A-level examination 'SMP Mathematics' and five shorter texts cover the material of the various sections of the A-level examination 'SMP Further Mathematics'. Revisions of the first two books of *Advanced Mathematics* are available as *Revised Advanced Mathematics Books 1* and *2*. There are two books for 'SMP Additional Mathematics' at O-level. All the SMP GCE examinations are available to schools through any of the Examining Boards.

Books A–H, originally designed for non-GCE streams, cover broadly the same development of mathematics as do the first few books of the O-level series. Most CSE Boards offer appropriate examinations. In practice, this series is being used very widely across all streams of comprehensive schools, and its first seven books, followed by *Books X, Y* and *Z*, provide a course leading to the SMP O-level examination. An alternative treatment of the material in *SMP Books A, B, C* and *D* is available as *SMP Cards I* and *II*.

Teachers' Guides accompany all series of books.

The SMP has produced many other texts, and teachers are encouraged to obtain each year from the Cambridge University Press, Bentley House, 200 Euston Road, London NW1 2DB, the full list of SMP books currently available. In the same way, help and advice may always be sought by teachers from the Director at the SMP Office, Westfield College, Hampstead, London NW3 7ST, from which may also be obtained the annual Reports, details of forthcoming in-service training courses and so on.

The completion of this first ten years of work forms a firm base on which the SMP will continue to develop its research into the mathematical curriculum, and is described in detail in Bryan Thwaites's *SMP: The First Ten Years*. The team of SMP writers, numbering some forty school and university mathematicians, is continually evaluating old work and preparing for new. But at the same time, the effectiveness of the SMP's future work will depend, as it always has done, on obtaining reactions from a wide variety of teachers – and also from pupils – actively concerned in the class-room. Readers of the texts can therefore send their comments to the SMP in the knowledge that they will be warmly welcomed.

1974

The S.M.P. advanced texts are based on the original contributions of

P. G. Bowie	G. S. Howlett	*G. Merlane
*H. M. Cundy	*A. Hurrell	*D. A. Quadling
*J. H. Durran	*T. A. Jones	G. D. Stagg
*L. E. Ellis	M. J. Leach	*B. Thwaites
*C. C. Goldsmith	P. G. T. Lewis	J. S. T. Woolmer

and are edited by Dr H. Martyn Cundy assisted by Miss E. Evans.

* Those primarily concerned with this book are indicated by the asterisk.

Many other schoolteachers have been directly involved in the further development and revision of the material and the Project gratefully acknowledges the contributions which they and their schools have made.

New editions of S.M.P. *Advanced Mathematics Books 1* and *2* have been published under the titles of *Revised Advanced Mathematics Books 1* and *2*, and a book of *Answers and Hints for Revised Advanced Mathematics Books 1 and 2* will be published during 1975. The old editions of *Advanced Mathematics Books 1* and *2* will be kept in print so long as there is sufficient demand for them. S.M.P. *Advanced Mathematics Books 3* and *4* complete the course begun either by the *Revised Advanced Mathematics* books or by the earlier unrevised editions.

CONTENTS

PREFACE

This book completes the main S.M.P. sixth-form course in Mathematics. While, like its predecessors, it strays occasionally outside the confines of the A-level examination syllabus, it seeks to draw together the various lines of development, and to round off a self-contained and unified course.

Most of the completely new work in this book is in the earlier chapters. There are two chapters on statistics—37 and 38—which introduce the continuous variate and the important problem of making estimates from samples. The student is encouraged throughout this work to be consciously critical of his basic assumptions and to probe more deeply than is customary at this level into the reasons behind many oft-recommended techniques. A fuller investigation of significance is left to the Further Mathematics book, but these chapters should bring a sound appreciation of the problems involved.

Chapter 39 shows the power of vector methods in constructing a mathematical model of the energy principle; the results are classical, and considerable attention is paid to the mathematical conditions corresponding to a conservative field of force.

Chapter 41 is mainly concerned with the practical technique of partial fractions and its application to integration, but it also points the way to a full theoretical treatment.

The remaining chapters summarize and amplify previous work: Chapter 36 collects together the work on integration by applying it to further geometrical and physical situations; Chapter 40 goes more deeply into mechanical and electrical dimensions and gives an introduction to dimensional analysis; Chapter 42 rounds off the linear algebra by showing the vital role played by the idea of linear dependence, and the relevance of the determinant in this connection. Finally, Chapter 43 ties up some loose ends and answers some questions about infinite processes: whether iterations converge to a limit; whether 'the more terms the merrier' is a good general rule for Taylor approximations; whether we can trust our intuition about what happens when numbers become large.

In all this we have kept in mind the needs of pupils preparing for examinations, and plentiful revision material will be found. Revision exercises are, as usual, scattered throughout the book, and in addition a chapter of Revision Projects has been added. These are prepared as collections of material, suitable for research by small groups, which cover much of the work of the course but also suggest developments which, it is hoped, will prove interesting. We should like the pupil to feel that he has the mastery of a core of mathematics which he can put to use in many different contexts.

The final set of revision examples begins with questions of the short A-level type, followed by longer questions arranged by topics. They are intended to be representative of examination questions. The miscellaneous exercises, however, at the ends of the chapters are often more difficult, and will be found in a number of cases to lead on to further study.

The fruits of our cooperative labours are thus made available to all. It may be felt that in the course as a whole some chapters are over-full; this is chiefly because we have attempted to provide, both in the text and in the exercises, sufficient extra material to stimulate the abler pupils. In this way we hope that the books we have produced will appeal not only to those preparing for A-level examinations, but also to those who wish to consider some of the deeper implications of the S.M.P. approach. Our pleasure is to have been engaged in a work of reformation; our confidence, to know that the work, in its turn, will be reformed; and our hope, that, when this happens, something will be found of use for the future fabric, and not too much which is merely a monument for mirth.

From 1973 onwards, it will be possible to have begun the S.M.P. sixth-form course in mathematics with either *Advanced Mathematics Book 1* and *Advanced Mathematics Book 2* or *Revised Advanced Mathematics Book 1* and *Revised Advanced Mathematics Book 2*. *Advanced Mathematics Book 3* and *Advanced Mathematics Book 4* serve to complete the course in both cases.

ACKNOWLEDGEMENTS

It is pleasant to record our thanks to Mrs K. E. Cundy for unstinted help given to this enterprise in preparation of diagrams, collation of proofs, entertainment of revision committees, tolerance of domestic confusion, and injection of cheerful optimism. We are also grateful to Mrs Elisabeth Muir for her typing of the MS with detailed thoroughness, often under difficulties.

We thank the Oxford and Cambridge Schools Examination Board for permission to reproduce questions set in the S.M.P. A-level examinations, and the Mathematical Association for allowing us the use of an occasional question from their Diploma papers.

Finally we would reiterate our gratitude to the staff of the Cambridge University Press, whose patience we have tried, but never exhausted.

A NOTE ON METRICATION

(i) All quantities of money have been expressed in pounds (£) and new pence (p).

(ii) All measures have been expressed in metric units. The fundamental units of the Système International (that is the metric system to be used in Great Britain) are the metre, the kilogram and the second. These units have been used in the book except where practical classroom considerations or an estimation of everyday practice in the years to come have suggested otherwise.

(iii) The notation used for the abbreviations of units and on some other occasions conforms to that suggested in the British Standard publications PD 5686: 1967 and BS 1991: Part 1: 1967.

GLOSSARY OF SYMBOLS

Additional to those in earlier books

ALGEBRA

$\begin{vmatrix} a & b \\ c & d \end{vmatrix}$ Determinant of matrix $\begin{pmatrix} a & b \\ c & d \end{pmatrix}$; $ad - bc$

det **A**   Determinant of matrix **A**

Δ General determinant, usually of

M   General matrix, $\begin{pmatrix} a_1 & b_1 & c_1 \\ a_2 & b_2 & c_2 \\ a_3 & b_3 & c_3 \end{pmatrix}$

M′   Transpose of **M**, $\begin{pmatrix} a_1 & a_2 & a_3 \\ b_1 & b_2 & b_3 \\ c_1 & c_2 & c_3 \end{pmatrix}$

A_1 Cofactor of a_1 in **M**, $b_2 c_3 - b_3 c_2$

B_1 Cofactor of b_1 in **M**, $-(a_2 c_3 - a_3 c_2)$; other cofactors defined similarly

K   Elementary matrix of type $\begin{pmatrix} k & 0 & 0 \\ 0 & 1 & 0 \\ 0 & 0 & 1 \end{pmatrix}$; one-way stretch

T   Elementary matrix of type $\begin{pmatrix} 0 & 1 & 0 \\ 1 & 0 & 0 \\ 0 & 0 & 1 \end{pmatrix}$; permutation of axes

S   Elementary matrix of type $\begin{pmatrix} 1 & 0 & 0 \\ k & 1 & 0 \\ 0 & 0 & 1 \end{pmatrix}$; shear

L   Linear transformation; satisfying
$$\mathbf{L}(k\mathbf{x}) = k(\mathbf{Lx}), \quad \text{and} \quad \mathbf{L(x+y)} = \mathbf{Lx} + \mathbf{Ly}$$

$\{f(i)\}$ The sequence $f(1), f(2), f(3), \ldots$

Σu_i The series $u_1 + u_2 + u_3 + \ldots$

CALCULUS

$\int_P \mathbf{F}.d\mathbf{s}$ Limit of the sum $\mathbf{S}\mathbf{F}.\delta\mathbf{s}$, taken over the curve P

PROBABILITY AND STATISTICS

r_i Relative frequency density over interval δx_i

$F(X)$ Cumulative frequency $\sum\limits_{-\infty}^{X} r_i \delta x_i$

ρ Probability density, such that $p(\mathbf{a} < \mathbf{x} \leqslant \mathbf{b}) = \int_a^b \rho\, dx$

ϕ Probability density function, such that $\rho = \phi(x)$

$\Phi(X)$ Cumulative probability $p(\mathbf{x} \leqslant \mathbf{X})$, or $\int_{-\infty}^{X} \phi(x)\, dx$

$\phi(x)$ Normal probability density; $(1/\surd(2\pi))\exp(-\tfrac{1}{2}x^2)$

$E[(x-\mu)(y-\nu)]$ Covariance of x and y

$\hat{\mu}$ Estimated mean

$\widehat{\sigma^2}$ Estimated variance

t 'Student's ratio'; probability function for $m\surd(n-1)/s$

MECHANICS

W $\int \mathbf{F}.d\mathbf{s}$; work done by force $\mathbf{F}$

P $dW/dt = \mathbf{F}.\mathbf{v}$; power of force $\mathbf{F}$

T Kinetic energy, $\tfrac{1}{2}mv^2$

$\mathbf{p}$ Momentum, $m\mathbf{v}$

c Velocity of light, 3×10^8 m/s

E Total energy, mc^2

ρ Density; mass/volume

η Viscosity; force per unit area/velocity gradient

λ Elastic constant; force which (if linearity held) would double the length of a string

$(\bar{x}, \bar{y}, \bar{z})$ Coordinates of centre of mass of a body

I Moment of inertia; Σmr^2, where r is the perpendicular distance of m from the axis

k Radius of gyration, such that $I = (\Sigma m)\, k^2$

CONICS

S Focus

e Eccentricity; SP/PM, where PM is perpendicular to directrix

AA' Major axis, of length $2a$

l Half-chord through S perpendicular to AA'; semi-latus-rectum

Note also full list of units and symbols in Table 1, p. 1245.

36

MORE APPLICATIONS OF INTEGRATION

In Section 3.4 of Chapter 22 (p. 615) we saw that the notation $\int$ for an integral was derived from a letter **S**, denoting a sum. It was pointed out that we can approximate to the area under a graph $y = f(x)$ over the interval $a \leqslant x \leqslant b$ by the sum of areas of rectangles of the kind shown in Figure 1, which we write as

$$\mathop{\mathbf{S}}_{x=a}^{x=b} f(x)\, \delta x;$$

and that the limiting value of this sum as the lengths δx tend to zero is the integral

$$\int_a^b f(x)\, dx.$$

We divide the region under a continuous curve into thin sections, over each of which we treat the variation in height as negligible. We thus get an approximation to the area by adding together the areas of these thin sections; the integral is the result of proceeding to the limit.

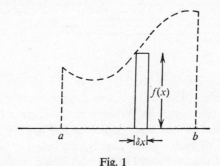

Fig. 1

So far we have applied this only to the evaluation of areas, but it has many other uses. We shall discuss some of them in the present chapter; but first the reader should put the book down and think of other situations in which the idea might be useful. Besides direct generalization, he may be able to think of applications in the fields of mechanics and probability, as well as many branches of physics.

1. CALCULATION OF VOLUME

1.1 Suppose that when a bath is filled with water to a depth x metres, the area of the surface of the water is A square metres. Then A is a function of x, and a knowledge of this function enables us to calculate the volume of water which the bath will hold.

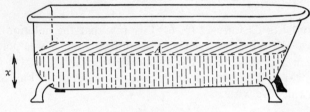

Fig. 2

An apparent difficulty in this problem is the complicated shape of the boundary of the water in contact with the bath; but we can make progress by following the method used in calculating areas, finding a region whose volume approximates to that of the bath.

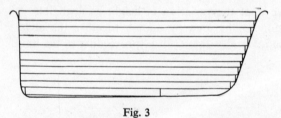

Fig. 3

Imagine the space inside the bath to be filled with sheets of cardboard laid horizontally, each piece being cut to the profile of the water surface at a different depth (see Figure 3). We suppose the edges to be cut vertically, so that a typical sheet has the shape indicated in Figure 4. This enables us to give the volume of such a sheet exactly, the formula being $A\,\delta x$. Then the total volume of the cardboard in the bath could be denoted by

$$\mathop{\mathbf{S}}_{x=0}^{x=h} A\,\delta x,$$

where h is the height of the rim of the bath above the plug-hole.

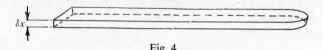

Fig. 4

The total volume of these layers of cardboard will not, of course, be quite the same as that for the water in the bath, since they do not conform to the profile of the bath at the edges. If, however, the cardboard is very thin, then the approximation will be very close. Following our practice in discussing areas, we therefore denote the volume of water which the bath will hold by

$$\int_0^h A\,dx.$$

For example, if the bath were 0·5 m deep and if the surface area when the depth of water is x metres were A m², where A is given by the formula

$$A = x + 5\sqrt{x},$$

then the volume of water would be V m³, where

$$V = \int_0^{0·5} (x + 5\sqrt{x})\,dx$$

$$= \left[\tfrac{1}{2}x^2 + \tfrac{10}{3}x^{\frac{3}{2}}\right]_0^{0·5}$$

$$\approx 1·305.$$

1.2 The justification for using integral notation in this example, and for carrying out the evaluation by finding a primitive of the area function, may be made along the lines of Section 3.3 of Chapter 22 (p. 613). In this work, however, we shall find it more convenient to use increment notation.

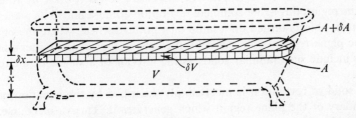

Fig. 5

Let V denote the volume of water in cubic metres when the bath is filled to a depth of x m (Figure 5). Then V, as well as A, is a function of x. When the depth increases by an amount δx m, the volume will increase by δV m³. The region shown in Figure 4, a prism with cross-section A and thickness δx, has volume less than δV (since the region with volume δV, shown in Figure 5, has sloping sides). Therefore

$$A\,\delta x < \delta V.$$

A similar inequality can be derived by considering another prism of thickness δx whose cross-section coincides with the upper surface of the shaded region in Figure 5. The area of this cross-section, at depth $x+\delta x$ metres, is naturally denoted by $A+\delta A$; and the volume of this prism is greater than δV. Therefore

$$(A+\delta A)\delta x > \delta V.$$

Putting the two inequalities together,

$$A\delta x < \delta V < (A+\delta A)\delta x;$$

whence
$$A < \frac{\delta V}{\delta x} < A+\delta A.$$

(This statement is strictly true only when A increases with x; how can the method be adapted to suit other cases?)

The argument is completed by considering the limits of the terms in this relation as δx tends to zero. Then δA tends to zero, so that $A+\delta A$ tends to A; and $\delta V/\delta x$ tends to the derivative dV/dx. It follows that,

$$\frac{dV}{dx} = A.$$

Thus the volume is calculated by finding a function whose derivative is A, as in the example worked out above.

1.3 Solids of revolution. An important special case is the calculation of volumes of solids of revolution. These are solids formed by rotating a plane region through a complete revolution about a line in its plane; for example, objects turned on a lathe or a potter's wheel, where the outline of the plane region is described by the cutting tool or the potter's hand. They include such familiar solids as the interior of a sphere or a circular cone.

A solid of revolution is most simply described by the equation of the boundary of the plane region which generates it. This is, of course, the intersection of the solid and a half-plane bounded by the axis of revolution. In particular, suppose that the region has for its boundary parts of the graph of $y = f(x)$, the lines $x = a$ and $y = b$, and the x-axis (Figure 6). Then the volume of the solid obtained by rotating this about the x-axis is given by

$$\int_a^b A\,dx,$$

where A is the area of cross-section perpendicular to the x-axis. Since this cross-section is a circle of radius $f(x)$, the volume of the solid is

$$\int_a^b \pi\{f(x)\}^2\,dx.$$

1092

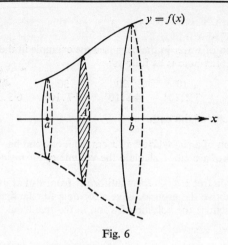

Fig. 6

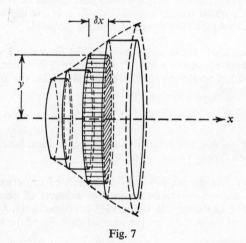

Fig. 7

In this case the solid can be regarded as the limiting form of a set of circular discs threaded on the x-axis. A typical disc (shown shaded in Figure 7) has radius y and thickness δx, so that the total volume is

$$\sum_{x=a}^{x=b} \pi y^2 \delta x,$$

or

$$\sum_{x=a}^{x=b} \pi \{f(x)\}^2 \delta x.$$

The limiting value of this volume is the integral given above.

Exercise A

1. The surface area of water in the bath (see the example in the text) at different heights above the plug-hole is as follows:

Height (x cm)	10	20	30	40	50
Area (A cm³)	3·2.10³	4·8.10³	5·7.10³	6·3.10³	6·8.10³

Estimate the capacity of the bath.

2. The cross-section of a rugby football x cm from one end has area given by the formula $x(30-x)$ square cm. Calculate the volume of air inside the football.

3. The diameter of a tree trunk tapers uniformly from 1 m at its base to 0·6 m at a height of 20 m above the ground. Give a formula for the diameter at a height of x metres, and deduce the volume of wood in the tree trunk up to a height of 20 m.

4. A pyramid of perpendicular height h has a base of area A. What is the area of the cross-section parallel to the base at a depth x below the vertex? Use this to deduce the formula $\frac{1}{3}Ah$ for the volume of the pyramid.

5. The region bounded by the graph $y = 1/x$, the lines $x = 1$ and $x = N$ and the x-axis is rotated about the x-axis. Prove that as N increases indefinitely the volume of the solid of revolution remains bounded but that the area of the region is unbounded.

6. Find the volume of a solid spherical cap of height h cut from a sphere of radius r.

Hence find the volume which remains when a cylindrical hole having walls of length $2w$ is bored through a sphere of radius r.

7. The volume of a barrel is estimated by measuring its external circumference at the top, the bottom and half-way up. For a barrel of height 90 cm these measurements are found to be 150, 165 and 195 cm respectively. Allowing 0·25 cm for the thickness of the wood, give the internal capacity of the barrel.

8. A doughnut has a shape made by rotating a circle of radius r about a line distance d from its centre. Find a formula for the area of cross-section at a height x above its central horizontal section (supposing the doughnut to have been placed on a horizontal plate) and deduce a formula for the volume of the doughnut.

2. SUMMATION IN GENERAL

The replacement of the limit of a finite sum by an integral has many applications apart from the calculation of areas and volumes. In this section we shall illustrate this with some more examples, but it must be stressed that it is the general principle which is important rather than the formulae which are derived for specific situations.

2.1   Path of a moving body. We take our first illustration from kinematics. If at time t the position vector of a body in motion is $\mathbf{r}$, then its velocity $\mathbf{v}$ is given by the formula

$$\frac{d\mathbf{r}}{dt} = \mathbf{v}.$$

Assuming that $\mathbf{v}$ is known as a function of t, this differential equation can be integrated to give

$$\mathbf{r}_2 - \mathbf{r}_1 = \int_{T_1}^{T_2} \mathbf{v}\, dt,$$

where $\mathbf{r}_1$ and $\mathbf{r}_2$ are the position vectors at times T_1 and T_2.

We can look at this result from a different point of view. Imagine first a similar situation in which the body moves by jerks in a series of short time-intervals, having a constant velocity during each interval and changing speed and direction abruptly between one interval and the next. Its path will then consist of a number of straight line segments, as indicated in Figure 8.

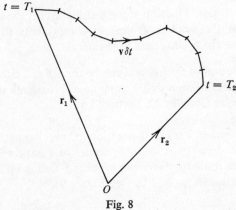

Fig. 8

Suppose that a typical one of these time-intervals is of duration δt, and that the velocity of the body over this interval is $\mathbf{v}$. Then the displacement during the interval is $\mathbf{v}\delta t$. The vector sum of all these displacements along line segments is equal to the change in position of the body over the complete interval $T_1 < t < T_2$. We therefore write

$$\mathbf{r}_2 - \mathbf{r}_1 = \mathop{\mathbf{S}}_{t=T_1}^{t=T_2} \mathbf{v}\delta t.$$

Now in practice bodies do not move in jerks like this, but by continuous change of speed and direction; and the finite sum on the right of this equation is then replaced by its limiting value, i.e. by an integral:

$$\mathbf{r}_2 - \mathbf{r}_1 = \int_{T_1}^{T_2} \mathbf{v}\, dt.$$

This is the same as the equation obtained previously from the differential equation approach.

2.2   The velocity-time graph. In particular, we may use this result in a one-dimensional form when the body moves along a straight line. In this case the displacement of the body along the line over the time-interval is

$$\int_{T_1}^{T_2} v\,dt,$$

where v is the velocity along the line.

Comparing this with the expression

$$\int_{X_1}^{X_2} y\,dx$$

for the area under the graph $y = f(x)$, we observe that:

> For one-dimensional motion along a straight line, the area under the graph of the velocity against time represents the distance travelled over the appropriate time-interval.

The actual calculation of the integral can be carried out either by reversing a formula for differentiation or by using an approximate method such as Simpson's Rule (see Chapter 22, Section 4.5).

2.3   Work. A rather harder illustration comes from the idea of the amount of work done by a variable force. In Chapter 13, Exercise F (p. 365), the work done by the constant force **F** acting on a body moving from A to B was shown to be **F**.**x** (see Figure 9).

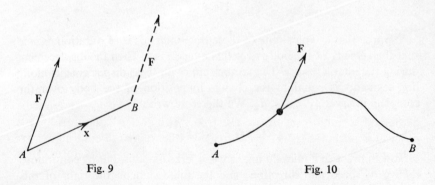

Fig. 9   Fig. 10

But how can we calculate the work done if **F** is variable, or if the body moves from A to B along a curve P (see Figure 10)?

Again, we imagine that the body moves in jerks, of which a typical one is $\delta \mathbf{s}$ (see Figures 11 and 12), and that the force remains constant throughout the jerk.

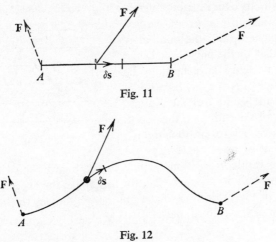

Fig. 11

Fig. 12

Then the work done in a typical one of these jerks is $\mathbf{F}.\delta \mathbf{s}$, and the total amount of work done is therefore

$$\mathbf{S}_P \, \mathbf{F}.\delta \mathbf{s}.$$

This is not, in general, precisely the same as the amount of work done in the original situation. It would be possible to find a value $\mathbf{F}^*$, which $\mathbf{F}$ actually takes at some point of the interval, such that $\mathbf{F}^*.\delta \mathbf{s}$ is precisely equal to the amount of work done in the part of the actual track which was replaced in imagination by the jerk. There is no need to find $\mathbf{F}^*$, however, because by allowing the magnitude of $\delta \mathbf{s}$ to tend to zero, we may write the sum as

$$\int_P \mathbf{F}.d\mathbf{s}.$$

In general, the path P chosen will affect the amount of work done in passing from A to B. But in the important special case when $\mathbf{F}$ is constant, the amount of work done always reduces to $\mathbf{F}.\mathbf{AB}$, independently of the path; and a number of other cases for which this is true are of great physical importance. This topic is treated rather more fully in Chapter 39.

In numerical cases, however, this is not the most useful form; it is generally better to derive it as

$$\int_{t_2}^{t_1} \mathbf{P}.\mathbf{v}\,dt,$$

in a manner very similar to Section 2.1.

1097

2.4 Buffon's needle. For a completely different example of the summation principle we turn to probability
theory. There is a famous experiment in
which a pin is thrown in a completely
random manner on a large board ruled
with parallel lines, and the number N
of lines crossed by the pin is noted each
time. The problem is to determine the
expected value of N for this experiment
in terms of the length l of the pin and
the width w of the ruling on the board.

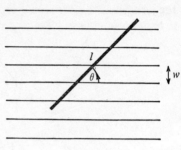

We begin by supposing that the pin
is dropped at a given angle θ to the

Fig. 13

lines, but in random position relative to the board. Then it is a simple
exercise in probability to show that, for this angle, the expected value of N
is the ratio of the projection of the pin at right-angles to the ruled lines,
to the width of the ruling; that is

$$\frac{l \sin \theta}{w}.$$

For if the projection $l \sin \theta$ is equal to $(n+f)w$, where n is a whole number
and f a fraction between 0 and 1, there is a probability $(1-f)$ that there
will be n intersections, and a probability f that there will be $(n+1)$ intersections. The expected value of the number of intersections is therefore

$$n(1-f)+(n+1)f$$

$$= n+f$$

$$= \frac{l \sin \theta}{w}.$$

We now consider the effect of varying the angle θ. All possible positions
of the pin are given by values of θ between 0 and π, and there is no reason
to think any one angle more likely than another. The probability that it
falls at an angle between θ and $\theta + \delta\theta$ is therefore $\delta\theta/\pi$. The formula

$$E[g(x)] = \Sigma g(x_i) \cdot p(x_i)$$

for the expected value of $g(x)$ (see Chapter 26, Section 4, p. 773) takes
the form for this experiment

$$E[N] = \overset{\theta=\pi}{\underset{\theta=0}{\mathbf{S}}} \frac{l \sin \theta}{w} \frac{\delta\theta}{\pi}.$$

There is in fact an approximation involved here, since the function
$(l \sin \theta)/w$ whose expected value we are finding does not remain constant

1098

for values of the angle between θ and $\theta + \delta\theta$. It would be more precise to replace the factor $\sin \theta$ in this formula by $\sin \theta'$, where θ' is an angle between θ and $\theta + \delta\theta$. However, since we intend to proceed to a limit this is unimportant; and by letting $\delta\theta$ tend to zero we obtain the exact result

$$
\begin{aligned}
\mathrm{E}[N] &= \int_0^\pi \frac{l \sin \theta}{w} \frac{d\theta}{\pi} \\
&= \left[-\frac{l}{w\pi} \cos \theta \right]_0^\pi \\
&= \frac{2l}{w\pi}.
\end{aligned}
$$

This experiment, known as 'Buffon's needle', has actually been carried out, and the mean value of N computed for a large number of trials. By equating this to the expected value $\mathrm{E}[N]$ given by the formula, an estimate was made of the numerical value of π. It has been suggested[†] that this could be regarded as an early example of a Monte Carlo technique.

2.5 Summary. The general pattern should now be clear. A continuous function $f(x)$ over an interval $a \leqslant x \leqslant b$ can be regarded as the limiting form of a function $g(x)$ which is constant over each of a set of subintervals. The length of a typical one of these subintervals is denoted by δx, and the value of $g(x)$ over this subinterval is equal to the value of $f(x)$ at some point of the subinterval (see Figure 14).

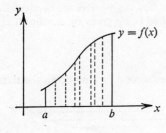

Fig. 14

Then a quantity defined for the discontinuous function $g(x)$ by the sum

$$
\mathop{\mathbf{S}}_{x=a}^{x=b} g(x)\,\delta x
$$

approaches the limiting value

$$
\int_a^b f(x)\,dx
$$

for the continuous function $f(x)$.

† See J. M. Hammersley and D. C. Handscomb, Monte Carlo Methods, Methuen, 1964.

Exercise B

1. For a body moving along a straight line, prove that the displacement, velocity and time are related by the formula

$$t = \int \frac{1}{v}\,dx,$$

and interpret this as a sum.

2. In many oscillating systems it can be proved that, as x increases from $-a$ to $+a$, the velocity is given by the formula

$$v = n\sqrt{(a^2 - x^2)}.$$

Find the time that it takes to cover this distance.

3. The acceleration of which a car is capable at various speeds is given in the following table:

Speed (m/s)	20	25	30	35	40
Acceleration (m/s²)	1·8	1·6	1·4	0·9	0·2

Estimate the time the car would take to increase speed from 20 m/s to 40 m/s.

4. For a particle of mass m acted upon by a constant force **P** the equation

$$\mathbf{P}t = m\mathbf{v} - m\mathbf{u}$$

has been obtained. Suggest a similar equation which would remain valid if the force **P** were a variable function of time, and interpret this equation in two ways as in the example of Section 2.1. (Compare Chapter 33, Section 2.)

5. Figure 15 shows the cross-section of a river, with the width of the river at intervals of 5 m in depth above the bed. Water flows in the river to a depth of 20 m, the average speed of flow at x m above the bed being given by the formula

$$\frac{40x - x^2}{50} \text{ m/s.}$$

Give an estimate of the quantity of water per second flowing down the river.

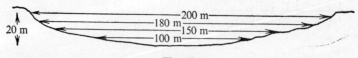

Fig. 15

6. A plane region is bounded by parts of the curve whose polar equation is $r = f(\theta)$ and by the radii $\theta = \alpha$ and $\theta = \beta$. By considering a region which approximates to this, establish the formula

$$\int_\alpha^\beta \tfrac{1}{2}\{f(\theta)\}^2\,d\theta$$

for the area.

What is the total area contained inside the cardioid whose equation is

$$r = a(1 + \cos\theta)?$$

7. A body is moved in a straight line by a force which varies in magnitude, but which always acts in the straight line. Suggest a definition of work which applies to such cases, and use it to find the work done in the following situations:

(*a*) The force required to stretch a spring is proportional to the amount by which the spring is stretched.

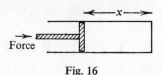

Fig. 16

(*b*) Air is compressed slowly in a cylinder by means of a force applied to a piston (see Figure 16). When the length of the column of gas in the cylinder is *l*, the pressure of the air inside is atmospheric, and the piston is in equilibrium.
In general position the pressure of the air inside the cylinder is inversely proportional to *x*.

8. A small body *A* moves in a horizontal circle of radius *a* with centre *O*, and a force of magnitude *F* acts upon it. Find the work done in one revolution by this force, if it always acts:

(*a*) along the radius *OA*;

(*b*) along the tangent *AT*, opposing the motion;

(*c*) along the bisector of $\angle OAT$.

9. A constant force $-g\mathbf{j}$ acts upon a body as it moves from $(1, 1)$ to $(0, 0)$ (*a*) along $y = x$, (*b*) along $x = 1$ and $y = 0$, (*c*) along $y = x^2$. Find the work done by it.

[Write ds in the integral as $dx\,\mathbf{i} + dy\,\mathbf{j}$.]

10. Answer Question 9 if the constant force is replaced

(*a*) by a force $-y\mathbf{j}$,   (*b*) by a force $-x\mathbf{j}$.

11. A certain spring has the property that, if it is placed horizontally, a force equal to its own weight will stretch it by 20 % of its unstretched length. If it is held by one end and allowed to hang vertically under its own weight, by what proportion will it stretch?

12. The density ρ of the atmosphere at height x above the ground depends on the pressure p. Explain why these quantities are connected by an equation of the form

$$x = \int \frac{1}{\rho g}\, dp.$$

(The pressure depends on the weight of the column of air above an area at the level in question.)

13. In a certain scientific experiment the probability of a reaction taking place between times t and $t + \delta t$ after the apparatus is switched on is

$$a e^{-at}\, \delta t.$$

What is the expected time when the reaction will take place?

14. Explain why the sum

$$\frac{1}{n+1} + \frac{1}{n+2} + \frac{1}{n+3} + \dots + \frac{1}{2n}$$

is approximately equal to $\displaystyle\int_1^2 \frac{1}{x}\, dx$

if *n* is a large integer.

1101

15. Find an approximate value of the sum

$$\frac{1}{n}\left(\sqrt{\frac{1}{n}} + \sqrt{\frac{2}{n}} + \dots + \sqrt{\frac{n}{n}}\right),$$

by a method like that of Question 14.

3. FIGURES WITH CIRCULAR SYMMETRY

3.1   An argument similar to that used in Section 1.2 can be used to explain the connection between the formulae

$$C = 2\pi r \quad \text{and} \quad A = \pi r^2$$

for the circumference and area of a circle of radius r, that

$$\frac{dA}{dr} = C.$$

Figure 17 shows two concentric circles. The inner one has radius r, circumference C and area A; and the corresponding values for the outer circle are $r + \delta r$, $C + \delta C$ and $A + \delta A$. Therefore δr is the width of the annular region between the two circles, and δA its area.

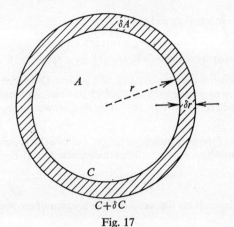

Fig. 17

It is possible to give bounds within which the value of δA must lie. For if we consider a rectangular strip (of slightly elastic material) of length C and width δr, as in the upper diagram in Figure 18, to be wrapped around the

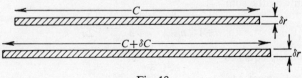

Fig. 18

inner circle, it is clear that it would have to be stretched along the outer edge to fit on the annulus. Similarly a strip of length $C+\delta C$ and width δr wrapped inside the outer circle would be compressed. It follows that

$$C\delta r < \delta A < (C+\delta C)\delta r,$$

so that
$$C < \frac{\delta A}{\delta r} < C+\delta C.$$

Now as δr tends to zero the value of $C+\delta C$ tends to C. Therefore

$$\frac{dA}{dr} = C.$$

3.2 This result is frequently useful in solving problems dealing with figures having circular symmetry. An example will help to make the method clear.

Example 1. A city is to be built in a circle of radius 2 km, having a density of population which falls uniformly from 20000 persons per square kilometre at the centre to 2000 per square kilometre at the outer fringe. Estimate the population of the city.

Inhabitants of a city form a set of discrete units, but the number is large enough for it to be reasonable to represent this by a continuous distribution over the area of the city. With this model the population density, ρ persons per square km, at points distant r km from the centre is given by the formula

$$\rho = 20000 - 9000r.$$

We ought to ask ourselves what can be meant by a 'variable density' expressed by a formula of this kind. Normally a population density is calculated by dividing the population by the number of units of area covered; since in this case the density is variable, this must be considered as a limiting value of the density over a small region. Let the population in an area of δA square km be δP; then the average density over this area is $\delta P/\delta A$, and ρ is the limiting value of this as δA tends to zero. That is,

$$\frac{dP}{dA} = \rho,$$

so that
$$P = \int \rho \, dA.$$

We may look at this equation as representing a summation, rather than approaching it through derivatives. Let Figure 17 be a diagram of the city, and let P stand for the population within the circle of radius r km. Then δP will represent the population within the annulus, and this will be equal to $\rho^* \delta A$, where ρ^* is the average population density over the annulus;

which is approximately $20000 - 9000r$ if δr is small. The total population will then be written as the limiting value of the sum

$$\underset{r=0}{\overset{r=2}{S}} \rho^* \, \delta A$$

as the width of each individual annulus tends to zero and their number is correspondingly increased; that is, as

$$\int_{r=0}^{r=2} \rho \, dA,$$

or, more familiarly, as
$$\int_0^2 \rho \, \frac{dA}{dr} \, dr.$$

To complete the calculation we note that
$$\rho = 20000 - 9000r$$

and
$$\frac{dA}{dr} = 2\pi r.$$

The population is therefore

$$\int_0^2 (20000 - 9000r) \cdot 2\pi r \, dr$$
$$= \left[\pi(20000r^2 - 6000r^3) \right]_0^2$$
$$= 32000\pi,$$

that is, about 100000 inhabitants.

Since the area of the city is 4π square km, we notice that the *average* density of population is 8000 persons per square kilometre.

Exercise C

1. If V and S are the volume and surface area of a sphere of radius r, explain why

$$S = \frac{dV}{dr}.$$

Is the same true of a cube of side x? Explain your answer.

2. Suppose that a sphere of gas comprising a star of radius a has a density at a distance r from the centre given by

$$\frac{k(a-r)}{r}.$$

Calculate the mass of the star.

3. The thickness of a discus at a distance r cm from the centre is given by the formula
$$t = \frac{20 - r^2}{20} \text{ cm}.$$

Find the volume of the discus.

1104

4. A solid of revolution is formed by rotating about the y-axis a region bounded by parts of the two axes, the graph $y = f(x)$ and the line $x = b$. By approximating to this solid by a set of hollow tubes, give an integral formula for the volume. For the solid of this kind generated by the graph

$$y = e^{-x^2}$$

prove that the volume approaches a finite limit as b tends to infinity. What proportion of the volume of this unbounded solid lies outside a cylinder of radius a centred on the y-axis?

5. Find the volume of the solid formed by rotating about the y-axis the region bounded by the axes and the graph $y = \cos x$ over the interval $0 < x < \frac{1}{2}\pi$.

6. Liquid flows in a circular pipe of radius r, the speed of flow at a distance x from the axis being given by the formula

$$v = k(r^2 - x^2).$$

Give a formula for the total rate of flow of the liquid in the pipe.

7. A certain quantity of illumination is spread uniformly over a disc of radius r. Compare its effect at a point on the perpendicular axis, distant s from the centre of the disc, with the effect of a point source of light of the same intensity placed at the centre of the disc.

(*Note*. The effect of a given source of illumination may be taken to vary inversely as the square of the distance from the source.)

8. Use the formula $A = \pi l^2 \sin \alpha$ for the surface area of a cone to find the area added when the slant height l is increased by δl and the semi-vertical angle α is kept constant.

Hence show that the surface area of the *zone* of a sphere of radius a between latitude α and latitude β is

$$\int_\alpha^\beta 2\pi a^2 \cos \theta \, d\theta;$$

and deduce Archimedes's result that the area of a zone of a sphere is equal to the area cut off by the bounding planes on the circumscribing cylinder.

4. AVERAGES

4.1 We have seen that integration is useful in resolving various problems involving the notion of summation. An important application is to the calculation of averages.

Example 2. AB is a line 3 cm long, and C is a point 4 cm from A on the line through A perpendicular to AB. What is the average distance from C of points on AB?

We must first decide what we are to mean by an average distance. If we imagine N points distributed uniformly along AB, then a typical interval of the line of length δx will contain $(\delta x/3)$. N of these points (taking N to be a large number, so that the distribution is not very different from a

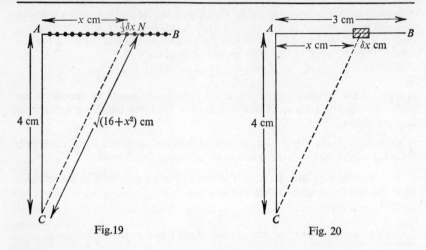

Fig.19   Fig. 20

continuous one). If then we replace this distribution of points by $(\delta x/3).N$ points at the left-hand end of each of the intervals (Figure 20), the average distance from C of the points of this new distribution will be

$$\frac{1}{N} \cdot \mathop{\mathbf{S}}_{x=0}^{x=3} \left(\frac{\delta x}{3}.N\right) \sqrt{(16+x^2)},$$

which can be simplified to

$$\mathop{\mathbf{S}}_{x=0}^{x=3} \tfrac{1}{3}\sqrt{(16+x^2)}\,\delta x.$$

If now we let the length δx of these intervals tend to zero, this distribution will approximate to the uniform continuous distribution with which we are concerned. The average distance is therefore calculated as

$$d = \frac{1}{3} \int_0^3 \sqrt{(16+x^2)}\,dx.$$

This is not an easy integral to compute, but a numerical value can be obtained using Simpson's rule. For this we require the values of the function to be integrated for $x = 0$, 1·5 and 3:

$$y_0 = \sqrt{(16+0^2)} = 4\cdot00,$$

$$y_1 = \sqrt{(16+1\cdot5^2)} = 4\cdot27,$$

$$y_2 = \sqrt{(16+3^2)} = 5\cdot00.$$

The x-interval is $h = 1\cdot5$. This gives the approximation

$$\int_0^3 \sqrt{(16+x^2)}\,dx \simeq \tfrac{1}{3} \times 1\cdot5 \times (4\cdot00+4\times4\cdot27+5\cdot00) = 13\cdot04,$$

whence $$d = \tfrac{1}{3} \times 13\cdot04 = 4\cdot35.$$

The average distance is therefore 4·35 cm.

1106

(An explicit form for the integral can be obtained as follows. An outline of the method is given, the details being left for the student to complete. Writing $x = 4 \sinh u$,

$$d = \frac{1}{3} \int_0^\alpha 16 \cosh^2 u \, du,$$

where

$$\alpha = \sinh^{-1} \tfrac{3}{4} = \log 2.$$

Therefore

$$d = \frac{4}{3} \int_0^{\log 2} (e^{2u} + e^{-2u} + 2) \, du$$

$$= \tfrac{5}{2} + \tfrac{8}{3} \log 2 = 4 \cdot 35.)$$

4.2 An especially important kind of average is that known as the *centre of mass* of a mechanical system. Where this system consists of a number of discrete elements of masses $m_1, m_2, m_3, ..., m_k$ located at points whose position vectors (referred to some origin) are $\mathbf{r}_1, \mathbf{r}_2, \mathbf{r}_3, ..., \mathbf{r}_k$, the position vector $\bar{\mathbf{r}}$ of the centre of mass is defined by the equation

$$M\bar{\mathbf{r}} = \sum_{i=1}^k m_i \mathbf{r}_i,$$

where

$$M = \sum_{i=1}^k m_i,$$

the total mass of the system. The centre of mass therefore defines a mean position for elements of the system, giving prominence to each proportional to its mass.

Amongst the properties of the centre of mass two deserve particular mention:

(i) If the system is moving under the action of various external forces, the equation
$$\Sigma \mathbf{F} = M\mathbf{a}$$
determines the acceleration $\mathbf{a}$ of the centre of mass.

(ii) If the system is in a uniform gravitational field (a close approximation to the actual situation for small systems near the surface of the earth), the centre of mass is the 'centre of gravity', the point at which the weight of the system may be supposed to act.

The concept of summation developed in this chapter makes it possible to extend the idea of centre of mass to continuous distributions of mass, e.g. to solid bodies. For bodies of regular shape whose mass is evenly distributed the centre of mass coincides with the geometrical centre; for a circle or a sphere, for example, it is at the centre, for a parallelogram at the intersection of the diagonals, and so on. The calculation for more complicated shapes usually involves integration. The mass-distribution is defined by the density, which may in some cases vary over the region occupied by the body.

In practice, the calculation is usually carried out by writing the vector in terms of its components in the directions of the coordinate axes. The defining equation then takes the form of the three equations

$$M\bar{x} = \sum_{i=1}^{k} m_i x_i, \quad M\bar{y} = \sum_{i=1}^{k} m_i y_i, \quad M\bar{z} = \sum_{i=1}^{k} m_i z_i.$$

Example 3. The block of metal shown in Figure 21 has a rectangular base 20 by 10 cm, and a rectangular top 16 by 2 cm, the rectangles having parallel sides and their centres in the same vertical line 4 cm apart. Locate the centre of mass of the block.

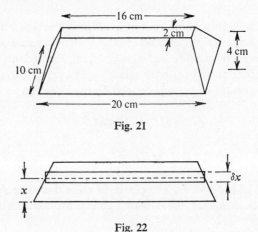

Fig. 21

Fig. 22

Figure 22 shows a side elevation of the block; at a height x cm above the base the cross-section is a rectangle having dimensions $(20-x)$ cm by $(10-2x)$ cm. We regard this as a limiting form of a solid composed of rectangular sheets with vertical sides of thickness δx cm laid one above another; a typical sheet is shown in the diagram. It is convenient in this example to make the dimensions of the sheet such that its *central* section coincides with a section of the block; the centre of mass of the sheet then lies in this section, and is a height x cm above the base of the block.

If the density of the metal is k g/cm³, the mass of this typical sheet is

$$k(20-x)(10-2x)\delta x \text{ g.}$$

For the 'stepped' solid, therefore, the expressions M and $\Sigma m_i x_i$ which appear in the formulae for $\bar{x}$ are

$$M = \mathop{\mathbf{S}}_{x=0}^{x=4} k(20-x)(10-2x)\delta x$$

and
$$\Sigma m_i x_i = \mathop{\mathbf{S}}_{x=0}^{x=4} k(20-x)(10-2x)\delta x . x.$$

1108

It follows that for the original block the corresponding expressions are

$$M = \int_0^4 k(20-x)(10-2x)\,dx$$

$$= \left[k(200x - 25x^2 + \tfrac{2}{3}x^3) \right]_0^4$$

$$= 442\tfrac{2}{3}k;$$

and

$$\Sigma m_i x_i = \int_0^4 kx(20-x)(10-2x)\,dx$$

$$= k \left[100x^2 - \tfrac{50}{3}x^3 + \tfrac{1}{2}x^4 \right]_0^4$$

$$= 661\tfrac{1}{3}k.$$

Therefore

$$\bar{x} = \frac{661\tfrac{1}{3}k}{442\tfrac{2}{3}k} = 1\cdot49.$$

The centre of mass, which is clearly on the line of symmetry joining the centres of the top and the base, is thus 1·49 cm above the base.

Example 4. The rudder shown in Figure 23, b units high and a units wide, is cut from a thin metal sheet in the shape of the parabola

$$\frac{y}{b} = 1 - \left(\frac{x}{a}\right)^2.$$

Find the position of its centre of mass.

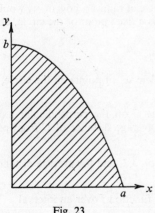

Fig. 23

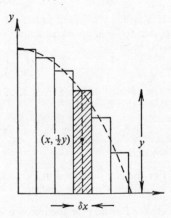

Fig. 24

Let the surface density of the metal sheet be s per unit area. We replace the rudder by a set of rectangular elements as shown in Figure 24, and again it is convenient to arrange for the central vertical of each

1109

rectangle to terminate at a point of the boundary. Then a typical rectangle has height y, width δx and its centre of mass at the point $(x, \frac{1}{2}y)$.

For the set of rectangles the expressions which occur in the centre of mass formulae are

$$M = \overset{x=a}{\underset{x=0}{\mathbf{S}}} sy\,\delta x, \quad \Sigma m_i x_i = \overset{x=a}{\underset{x=0}{\mathbf{S}}} sy\,\delta x.x, \quad \Sigma m_i y_i = \overset{x=a}{\underset{x=0}{\mathbf{S}}} sy\,\delta x.\tfrac{1}{2}y.$$

Therefore, for the rudder,

$$M = \int_0^a sy\,dx = \int_0^a \frac{sb}{a^2}(a^2-x^2)\,dx = \tfrac{2}{3}sab,$$

$$\Sigma m_i x_i = \int_0^a sxy\,dx = \int_0^a \frac{sb}{a^3}(a^2x - x^3)\,dx = \tfrac{1}{4}sa^2b,$$

$$\Sigma m_i y_i = \int_0^a \tfrac{1}{2}sy^2\,dx = \int_0^a \frac{sb^2}{2a^4}(a^2-x^2)^2\,dx = \tfrac{4}{15}sab^2;$$

so that
$$\bar{x} = \frac{\tfrac{1}{4}sa^2b}{\tfrac{2}{3}sab} = \tfrac{3}{8}a$$

and
$$\bar{y} = \frac{\tfrac{4}{15}sab^2}{\tfrac{2}{3}sab} = \tfrac{2}{5}b.$$

Would you have expected $\bar{x}$ to be independent of b? If so, why?

Exercise D

1. If N points are spaced equally around a circle of radius r, how many would be expected to lie in an arc of length $r\,\delta\theta$? If K is a fixed point of the circle, obtain the expression

$$\int_0^{2\pi} \left(2r \sin\frac{\theta}{2}\right).\frac{1}{2\pi}\,d\theta$$

for the average distance from K of the complete set of points on the circle, and evaluate this integral.

2. Given a disc of radius 3 cm and a point C on the perpendicular axis of symmetry 4 cm from the disc, calculate the average distance of C from points of the disc.

3. For the city described in Example 1, Section 3.2, find the average distance of an inhabitant from the centre.

4. Give a formula for the average value of a function f over an interval

$$\{x: a \leqslant x \leqslant b\}.$$

Suggest a geometrical interpretation in terms of the graph of $y = f(x)$.

5. A swarm of bees is clustered round the queen in a sphere of radius 10 cm. Estimate the average distance of a member of the swarm from the centre.

6. Use the method of Section 4.1 to express as an integral the average value of a variable velocity v over a time-interval $\{t: t_1 \leqslant t \leqslant t_2\}$, and deduce that this is equal to

$$\frac{\mathbf{r}_2 - \mathbf{r}_1}{t_2 - t_1},$$

where $\mathbf{r}_1, \mathbf{r}_2$ are the position vectors of the moving particle at the ends of the interval.

7. From the two mechanical properties of the centre of mass given in Section 4.2, prove that if a system is moving subject to the force of gravity alone in a uniform gravitational field, then the path described by the centre of mass is of a kind which could be described by a single particle moving under gravity. Can you think of any familiar illustrations of this?

8. Find the centre of mass of a piece of card in the shape of a quadrant of a circle.

9. Locate the centre of mass of a uniform solid circular cone of base radius r and height h.

10. Where is the centre of mass of the spherical cap described in Exercise A, Question 6?

11. How far up the y-axis is the centre of mass of the solid described in Exercise C, Question 5?

12. We have assumed the following facts about the centre of mass of a system:

(*a*) The position of the centre of mass does not depend on the origin from which position vectors are taken.

(*b*) If a system is split into subsystems of masses $M_1, M_2, \ldots$ having their centres of mass at points $\bar{\mathbf{r}}_1, \bar{\mathbf{r}}_2, \ldots$, the centre of mass of the complete system coincides with that of a system of single masses of these magnitudes at these points.

Justify these assumptions.

1111

PROBABILITY DENSITY FUNCTIONS

1. POPULATIONS DRAWN FROM A CONTINUUM

1.1 For all the probabilities which have been discussed so far, the possibility space has been a set of discrete elements. These might be, for example, card suits ♣, ♢, ♡, ♠, or scores on a die; or they might be the number of successes 0, 1, 2, ..., n when an experiment is performed n times. Occasionally we have met situations for which the possibility space is not finite: for example, in counting the number of times a die must be thrown before a six appears, where the possibilities are 0, 1, 2, ..., without any upper bound. But in every example the different possibilities have been clearly separated from each other.

There are, however, many occasions when this is not so. Imagine, for example, a machine which produces sausages to a specified length of 10 cm. It is certain that not every sausage produced by this machine will be exactly 10 cm long. Because of play in different parts of the mechanism and the pliability of sausage meat, it might be that the sausages vary in length between 9·4 and 10·5 cm; and we should wish to say that, for a trial in which it was proposed to record the lengths of sausages produced by the machine, the possibilities would be drawn from the interval

$$\{x: 9{\cdot}4 < x < 10{\cdot}5\}.$$

Again, an electronic device might produce a spot of light in random position on the screen of an oscilloscope; the possibilities are then all the points of the screen.

In this chapter the idea of probability will be extended to apply to situations of this kind. To guide us in this development, we recall two observations from earlier chapters:

(i) A population of measurements is conveniently studied with the aid of a histogram. This is constructed by grouping the data into classes and counting the frequency with which members of the population fall into each class. To combat the effect of unequal class-lengths, the height of each rectangle in the histogram is taken to be the *frequency density*, defined as the frequency per unit length of class-interval; the frequency itself is then represented by the area of the rectangle (see Chapter 12, Section 3.6).

(ii) Probability is closely associated with the *relative frequency* in a population of results of trials. If an event **A** is associated with a subset A

of the possibility space, and if the frequency with which this occurs in the sequence of trials is fr A, then for a large number fr $\mathscr{E}$ of trials we expect the relative frequency, fr A/fr $\mathscr{E}$, to be approximately equal to the probability $p(\mathbf{A})$ (see Chapter 20, Section 2.3).

1.2 In Chapter 12 (Section 3.6) we considered an example in which two telephone operators timed the calls handled by their switchboard. Both sets of figures referred to the same 100 calls, but the two girls used different methods of grouping the data into classes:

Ann		Zena	
Duration (min)	Number of calls	Duration (min)	Number of calls
0–1	18	0–1	18
1–2	14	1–2	14
2–3	26	2–3	26
3–4	12		
4–5	6	3–6	33
5–6	15		
6–7	2		
8–9	2	6–12	9
9–10	3		
11–12	2		

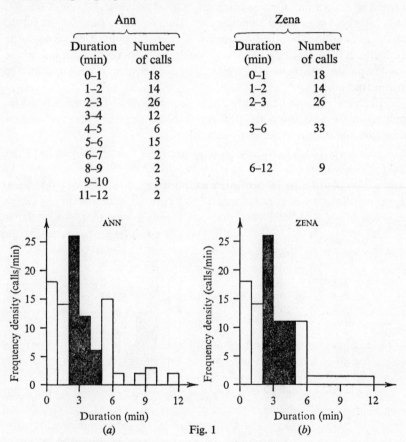

Fig. 1

The corresponding histograms are shown in Figure 1. If we wish to read off from these the number of calls lasting between, say, 2 minutes and 5 minutes, then we find the area of the relevant part of the histogram (indicated by shading). Notice that Figure 1(a) gives this exactly as

$$1 \times 26 + 1 \times 12 + 1 \times 6 = 44,$$

1113

since 2 minutes and 5 minutes appear as ends of class-intervals; but that Figure 1(*b*) gives it only approximately as

$$1 \times 26 + 2 \times 11 = 48.$$

This is because the frequency density of 11 used in this second calculation is averaged over the interval $3 < t < 6$, and this average value is not equal to the precise value over the interval $3 < t < 5$.

1.3   Now the aim of such an investigation might well be to make forecasts. From the known fact that, in this particular experiment, 44 out of the 100 calls lasted between 2 and 5 minutes, we could decide to plan for the future on the assumption that the probability of calls of this duration through the exchange is 0·44. For this purpose it would be more convenient if areas in the histogram indicated directly the relative frequency, rather than the actual frequency.

To achieve this, we need only divide the individual frequency densities plotted in the histogram by 100, the population size. This gives a new quantity, the *relative frequency density*:

$$\text{Relative frequency density} = \frac{\text{frequency density}}{\text{population size}}.$$

Ann's data could now be presented as follows:

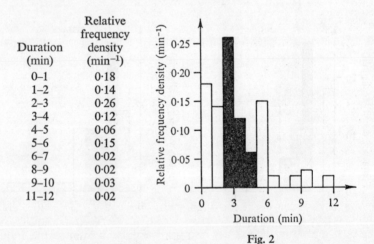

Duration (min)	Relative frequency density (min⁻¹)
0–1	0·18
1–2	0·14
2–3	0·26
3–4	0·12
4–5	0·06
5–6	0·15
6–7	0·02
8–9	0·02
9–10	0·03
11–12	0·02

Fig. 2

The corresponding histogram is drawn in Figure 2; it differs from Figure 1*a* merely in a change of vertical scale. The area of the shaded region between 2 minutes and 5 minutes is now

$$1 \times 0.26 + 1 \times 0.12 + 1 \times 0.06 = 0.44,$$

indicating that 0·44 of the calls recorded lasted this long.

Since all the calls lasted less than 12 minutes, we should expect to find that the relative frequency of calls between 0 and 12 minutes is 1. This is measured by the area of the complete histogram, and it is easily verified that this area is

$$0{\cdot}18+0{\cdot}14+0{\cdot}26+0{\cdot}12+0{\cdot}06+0{\cdot}15+0{\cdot}02+0{\cdot}02+0{\cdot}03+0{\cdot}02 = 1.$$

1.4 One hundred calls would not provide much evidence on which to base future planning. Let us suppose, then, that a larger sequence of trials is carried out, in which 5000 calls are timed. It would now become practicable to group the data into more class-intervals, each with a shorter class-length, say of $\frac{1}{4}$ minute. Figure 3 shows the histogram of relative frequency densities that might arise from this experiment. Although there are fifty times as many calls, this histogram can be compared directly with Figure 2 because of the scaling down; the area of the complete histogram is still 1, and the shaded area again gives the proportion of calls lasting between 2 and 5 minutes.

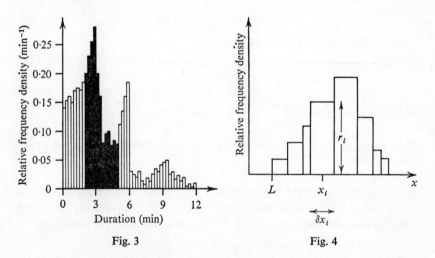

Fig. 3   Fig. 4

1.5 It will now be useful to introduce some fresh notation. Figure 4 shows a typical histogram of relative frequency densities. As in Chapter 12, the class-mark for the ith class-interval is denoted by x_i, and the frequency for this interval by $f(x_i)$, so that the population size N is given by

$$N = \sum_{i=1}^{n} f(x_i).$$

Let us denote the length of the class-interval by δx_i, and the relative frequency density over this interval by r_i. Then the various quantities which we have defined are displayed in the following scheme:

1115

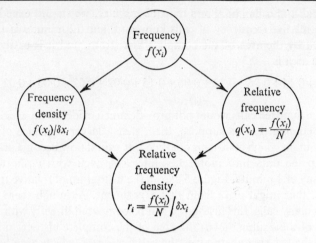

This final relation can be put into the form

$$r_i \delta x_i = \frac{f(x_i)}{N} = q(x_i).$$

It was proved in Chapter 26 that

$$\sum_{i=1}^{n} q(x_i) = 1.$$

This can now be written $\quad \sum_{i=1}^{n} r_i \delta x_i = 1.$

That is, the total area of the histogram is 1, a result already noticed in our example.

1.6 It is now a simple matter to find expressions for the mean, m, and the standard deviation, s, in terms of relative frequency density. Adapting the formulae obtained in Chapter 26, Sections 1.1 and 3.1, we obtain

$$m = \Sigma x_i q(x_i) = \Sigma x_i r_i \delta x_i$$

and $\quad\quad s^2 = \Sigma(x_i - m)^2 q(x_i) = \Sigma(x_i - m)^2 r_i \delta x_i.$

As usual, the formula for s can be put into an alternative form,

$$s^2 = \Sigma x_i^2 r_i \delta x_i - m^2.$$

These formulae are in fact less convenient for calculation than those given previously; their importance lies in the analogies which they suggest for probability density later in the chapter.

1.7 Another useful way of looking at the data on telephone calls would be to ask the question 'What proportion of the calls last for less than

1116

X minutes?'. This can be found by adding the relative frequencies over all the intervals to the left of X; this sum is called the *cumulative relative frequency*. For Ann's observations of 100 calls, the values can be set out in a table as follows:

Interval	Relative frequency	X	Cumulative relative frequency up to X
		0	0
0–1	0·18	1	0·18
1–2	0·14	2	0·32
2–3	0·26	3	0·58
3–4	0·12	4	0·70
4–5	0·06	5	0·76
5–6	0·15	6	0·91
6–7	0·02	7	0·93
7–8	—	8	0·93
8–9	0·02	9	0·95
9–10	0·03	10	0·98
10–11	—	11	0·98
11–12	0·02	12	1

The layout of the table is important: whereas each relative frequency is associated with an interval of values of x, the cumulative relative frequency goes with a single particular value of X. It therefore defines a function, which we will denote by F.

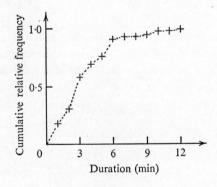

Fig. 5

Figure 5 shows the graph of the cumulative relative frequency $F(X)$ for this example. The points have been joined by a broken line because the values within the class-intervals are indicated only approximately by the graph. This may be compared with the remark made earlier, that the relative frequencies are averaged over the class-interval.

In the general case, typified by Figure 4, the cumulative relative frequency at the end of any class-interval is given by

$$F(X) = \sum_{x=L}^{x=X} q(x_i)$$

$$= \sum_{x=L}^{x=X} r_i \delta x_i,$$

where L is the left end of the first class-interval. This is represented by the area of the histogram of relative frequencies from L to X (see Figure 6).

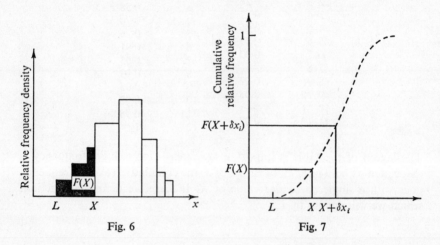

Fig. 6   Fig. 7

There is another important way of looking at the relationship between relative frequency density and the cumulative function. If the ith class-interval runs from X to $X+\delta x_i$, then over this interval the cumulative relative frequency increases by

$$F(X+\delta x_i) - F(X);$$

and this is equal to $q(x_i)$, or $r_i \delta x_i$. Therefore

$$\frac{F(X+\delta x_i) - F(X)}{\delta x_i} = r_i.$$

The expression on the left is the gradient of the graph of the cumulative function, and we have shown that this is equal to the relative frequency density (see Figure 7).

The reader will recognize here an example of the relationship between a function and its primitive, summed up in the 'fundamental theorem of analysis' (see Chapter 22, Section 5.2).

Exercise A

1. Draw graphs of relative frequency density and of cumulative relative frequency from Zena's records of 100 telephone calls (Section 1.2). Use these to find approximately the median duration of call and the mean absolute deviation from the median.

2. Is the precise shape of the cumulative relative frequency graph a smooth curve? If not, describe it.

3. In the Barsetshire Constabulary no man is under 170 cm in height. 10 % of the force is under 175 cm, 55 % under 185 cm; 5 % is over 190 cm, and 1 % over 200 cm. Represent this information on (*a*) a cumulative graph, (*b*) a histogram. Find approximately the mean height and the standard deviation.

2. PROBABILITY DENSITY

2.1   We return now to the question: how can the concept of probability be extended to situations where the possible outcomes of a trial may be, for example, numbers of an interval $L \leqslant x \leqslant R$ rather than elements of a set of discrete objects?

Figure 6 gives us a clue. We are used to thinking of probabilities as numbers to which relative frequencies approximate if a large number of trials is carried out. Now it would seem that a curve such as Figure 8 cuts off a region above the *x*-axis to which the histogram in Figure 6 might be described as a fair approximation; and we would expect that such a curve might enable us to predict with reasonable accuracy the pattern of results in any subsequent run of trials under similar conditions. Thus the function represented by this curve plays a part similar to the probabilities which we have discussed previously.

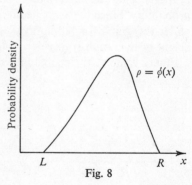

Fig. 8

There is, however, one important difference. The histogram is a diagram not of relative frequencies, but of relative frequency densities. This leads us to suggest that the graph we have drawn should be one of *probability density* rather than probability. We shall denote probability density by the letter ρ; and the graph displays this as a function of *x*, so that

$$\rho = \phi(x).$$

How, then, can actual probabilities be obtained from this graph? The analogy with the histogram again helps us. We saw in Section 1.3 that the relative frequency of telephone calls lasting between 2 and 5 minutes was

1119

measured by the area of the histogram lying within this interval. This suggests that probabilities might be found similarly as the areas under the probability density graph; that is,

$$p(\mathbf{a} < \mathbf{x} \leqslant \mathbf{b}) = \int_a^b \rho\, dx.$$

Example 1. Lines are measured with a ruler graduated in centimetres and tenths, and the lengths given to the nearest tenth of a centimetre. Find a probability density function for the error involved in making such measurements.

The error x cm, defined as

actual length – measured length,

clearly lies between $-0\cdot05$ and $+0\cdot05$ cm. If the lines are drawn at random, there is no reason to expect any one error to be more likely than any other; this means that the probability density is constant over the interval $\{x: -0\cdot05 < x \leqslant +0\cdot05\}$.

It remains to find the value of the constant, and for this we use the property that the area under the probability density graph gives the probability. Since the error has to lie between $-0\cdot05$ and $+0\cdot05$, the area under the graph for the interval $-0\cdot05 < x \leqslant +0\cdot05$ is equal to 1. The height of the graph is therefore $1/0\cdot1$, or 10.

Figure 9 shows the probability density graph.

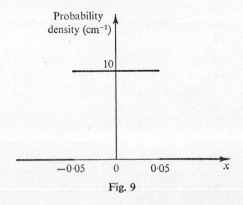

Fig. 9

2.2 It is important to stress that probability density is in no sense a 'limit' of relative frequency density. Indeed, any actual experiment from which frequencies are obtained must be restricted to a finite number of trials; we cannot look into a crystal ball and assert categorically that, if the number of trials were increased indefinitely, the histogram would tend to such-and-such a form.

1120

What we are doing in inventing a probability density function is to construct a probability model,† just as was described for the discrete case in Chapter 26. Our model is now a function defined over an interval, chosen so as to fit well to the observations we have been able to make, and which we believe intuitively would be an even better approximation for a larger population of observations.

We may therefore ask what properties we shall wish to assign to a probability density function defined over an interval $\{x: L \leqslant x \leqslant R\}$. These properties will be determined by the intention that areas under the graph are to represent probabilities. Three which come immediately to mind are:

(i) The function must not be so discontinuous that its integral cannot be defined.

(ii) Since probabilities cannot be negative, we want

$$\phi(x) \geqslant 0$$

throughout the interval.

(iii) Since, at every trial, x must fall within the interval $L \leqslant x \leqslant R$,

$$\int_L^R \phi(x)\,dx = 1.$$

Furthermore, probabilities obtained from the density function must obey the laws which have been established for probabilities in earlier chapters. The four fundamental laws (given in Chapter 20, Sections 3.3 and 4.2) were:

Law 1. $p(\mathbf{S}) + p(\sim \mathbf{S}) = 1.$

Law 2. $p(\mathbf{S} \wedge \mathbf{T}) + p(\sim \mathbf{S} \wedge \mathbf{T}) = p(\mathbf{T}).$

Law 3. $p(\mathbf{S} \vee \mathbf{T}) = p(\mathbf{S}) + p(\mathbf{T}) - p(\mathbf{S} \wedge \mathbf{T}).$

Law 4. $p(\mathbf{S}|\mathbf{T}) = p(\mathbf{S} \wedge \mathbf{T})/p(\mathbf{T}).$

We have seen, however, that Law 1 can be regarded as a special case of Law 2 by writing $\mathbf{T} = \mathbf{E}$, the event which 'always occurs'; and that Law 3 can be deduced from Laws 1 and 2 and de Morgan's laws (see Chapter 20, Section 3.4). Moreover, Law 4 may now be treated as the definition of conditional probability. It will therefore suffice to verify that the probabilities defined by the density function ϕ meet the requirements of Law 2.

Here we shall verify this in just one particular case, taking $\mathbf{S}$ to be the event $\mathbf{a} < \mathbf{x} \leqslant \mathbf{b}$ and $\mathbf{T}$ the event $\mathbf{c} < \mathbf{x} \leqslant \mathbf{d}$, where the numbers a, b, c, d fall within the interval (L, R) in the order shown in Figure 10. Then $\mathbf{S} \wedge \mathbf{T}$ is the event $\mathbf{c} < \mathbf{x} \leqslant \mathbf{b}$, and $\sim \mathbf{S} \wedge \mathbf{T}$ is the event $\mathbf{b} < \mathbf{x} \leqslant \mathbf{d}$. Since the

---

† 'Every model is an abstraction designed to analyse a slice of life with the object of understanding it better and, if it is at all controllable, adapting it better to our wishes.' Professor R. Stone, *Operational Research Quarterly*, vol. 14, 1963.

probability of an event is to equal the integral of the density function over the corresponding interval, it follows that

$$p(\mathbf{S} \wedge \mathbf{T}) + p(\sim \mathbf{S} \wedge \mathbf{T}) = \int_c^b \phi + \int_b^d \phi$$

$$= \int_c^d \phi \quad \text{(using a standard property of integrals)}$$

$$= p(\mathbf{T}).$$

The proof for other events $\mathbf{S}$, $\mathbf{T}$ is similar. We restrict ourselves to events of the form 'x lies within a certain interval, or a finite set of intervals', so that there is no difficulty in defining the integrals.

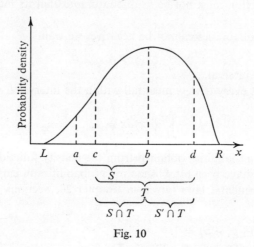

Fig. 10

The results of this section can be summarized as follows:

A *density function* ϕ is an integrable non-negative function defined over an interval (L, R) with the property that

$$\int_L^R \phi = 1.$$

For a particular situation in which a quantity x may assume values within an interval (L, R) we may define the *probability density* ρ by an equation of the form

$$\rho = \phi(x),$$

where ϕ is a density function; such that, if the interval (a, b) is contained in (L, R),

$$p(\mathbf{a} < \mathbf{x} \leqslant \mathbf{b}) = \int_a^b \rho \, dx.$$

Probabilities determined in this way satisfy the usual laws.

2.3   An apparent paradox. In our machine producing sausages of lengths between 9·4 and 10·5 cm, what is the probability of turning out a sausage of length 'exactly' 10 cm? Obviously it is not impossible; but since 10 is just one number of the infinite set of numbers in the interval (9·4, 10·5), we shall run into difficulty if we assign any positive probability, however small, to the event. For example, if we were to take the probability to be 0·001, then we could also find more than a thousand other 'equally likely' lengths to which the same probability should be attached; and since the events are exclusive, the probability of one or other of them occurring would be greater than 1, which is impossible. The only choice that makes sense logically is to define

$$p(\mathbf{x}=10) = 0.$$

This seems paradoxical, since the definition of probability given in Chapter 20 leads immediately to the conclusion:

$$\text{Event } \mathbf{A} \text{ cannot occur} \Leftrightarrow p(\mathbf{A}) = 0.$$

This definition, however, specifically excluded situations with an infinite universal set of possibilities; and in the more general situations with which we are concerned in this chapter, all that we can assert is the more restricted statement:

$$\text{Event } \mathbf{A} \text{ cannot occur} \Rightarrow p(\mathbf{A}) = 0.$$

The converse is, in general, false.

In fact all practical difficulties vanish when we realize that, however precise our instruments, we can only in reality measure lengths within limits of accuracy. The concept of a sausage of length exactly 10 cm is a purely theoretical one; and as soon as we quote bounds (for example, that the length lies between 9·995 cm and 10·005 cm) the definition from a density function gives a positive probability to the event. The narrower the interval, the smaller the probability—as we would expect.

A consequence of this reasoning is that, for probabilities defined from a density function, the addition of a single point to an interval does not change the probability. For example,

$$p(\mathbf{a} \leqslant \mathbf{x} \leqslant \mathbf{b}) = p(\mathbf{x}=\mathbf{a}) + p(\mathbf{a} < \mathbf{x} \leqslant \mathbf{b}) \quad \text{(from the law for}$$
$$\text{exclusive events)}$$
$$= p(\mathbf{a} < \mathbf{x} \leqslant \mathbf{b}).$$

Similarly
$$p(\mathbf{a} < \mathbf{x} < \mathbf{b}) = p(\mathbf{a} < \mathbf{x} \leqslant \mathbf{b}).$$

It is not, therefore, important to specify when assigning probabilities whether or not an interval includes its end-points; either way the probability is given by the same definite integral.

(Strictly speaking, this is not quite the whole story. We might imagine that Zeus made half his thunderbolts of mass exactly 5 tonnes, and that the other half had masses between 5 and 10 tonnes with constant probability density. The statement we have just made would not then apply, because the situation cannot be described completely in terms of a density function. But such examples are rare, and can be ignored in a general discussion.)

2.4 Sometimes it is possible that a quantity may vary randomly over all the real numbers, rather than over a finite interval (L, R). We can provide for this within the framework of the general theory by writing L as $-\infty$, and/or R as $+\infty$, in the appropriate intervals. For example, the probability that x is greater than a would be given by

$$\int_a^\infty \rho \, dx.$$

It may be convenient anyway to suppose that the domain of a density function is the set of all real numbers, and to define the probability density to be zero for any value which cannot in fact occur. Thus in Example 1 the probability density might be defined by the equations

$$\rho = \begin{cases} 0 & \text{if } x \leqslant -0.05, \\ 10 & \text{if } -0.05 < x \leqslant 0.05, \\ 0 & \text{if } x > 0.05. \end{cases}$$

The condition to be satisfied by the density function would then be

$$\int_{-\infty}^\infty \phi = 1.$$

Exercise B

1. Verify that, if x can vary over the interval $(0, 2)$,

$$\phi(x) = \tfrac{1}{2}x$$

is a density function for x. Find:

(a) $p(\mathbf{x} < 1)$;   (b) $p(\tfrac{1}{2} < \mathbf{x} < 1)$;
(c) the probability that $x > 1\tfrac{1}{2}$ given that $x > 1$.

In case (b) sketch the graph of $\phi(x)$ and shade the relevant area.

2. The quarantine period for a certain disease lasts for 100 hours. The probability of showing the first symptoms at various times during the quarantine period is described by the density function

$$\phi(t) = 6t(100-t) \times 10^{-6}.$$

Find the probability that the symptoms will appear within the first 20 hours of the period.

1124

3. Elementary particles are fired into a cylinder containing gas. The probability density function describing the distance x travelled by a particle before it collides with a nucleus is of the form

$$\phi(x) = k e^{-ax} \quad (x > 0).$$

Express k in terms of a, and find the distance down the cylinder beyond which only half the particles will penetrate.

4. A mathematical model for the age to which a new-born infant will live assigns to this a probability density function proportional to $x^3(90-x)$. On this basis, calculate:

    (a) the proportion of the population who would live to be over 80;

    (b) the commonest age at which people would die.

5. Verify that $$\phi(z) = \frac{2}{(1+4|z|)^2},$$

for all z, is a density function for z. Sketch the graph and answer the following questions, marking on your graph the relevant areas:

    (a) Find $a > 0$ such that $p(\mathbf{z} \geqslant a) = 5\%$.

    (b) Find $b > 0$ such that $p(|\mathbf{z}| \geqslant b) = 5\%$.

(The first is called a one-tail criterion, the second a two-tail criterion).

6. Verify that events **S** and **T** defined by inequalities $a < x \leqslant b$ and $c < x \leqslant d$, with probabilities defined by a density function, satisfy Law 2 of probability for the cases:

    (a) $a < c < d < b,$ (b) $a < b < c < d.$

7. Draw a sketch to show the relation between some simple function $f(t)$ and the function $f(t/k)$. If $f(t)$ is a density function for t, and $\lambda f(t/k)$ is another density function for t, find λ.

    Hence show that, if $\rho = \phi(t)$ is the probability density function for t, then $\rho = (1/k).\phi(u/k)$ is the probability density function for $u = kt$.

8. By considering the relation

$$\int \phi(x)\,dx = \int \phi(x)\frac{dx}{du}\,du,$$

show that if $\rho = \phi(x)$ is the probability density function for x, and if $x = g(u)$, then $\rho_1 = \phi\{g(u)\}.g'(u)$ is the probability density function for u.

3. PROBABILITY PARAMETERS

3.1 In Chapter 26 it was shown how, with a given probability model, we could associate various parameters, corresponding to the statistics which we calculate from a population. For example, we defined the expected value of x, denoted by $E[x]$ or μ, by means of the formula

$$\mu = \sum_{i=1}^{n} x_i p(x_i).$$

1125

This was devised by analogy with the mean of a population,

$$m = \sum_{i=1}^{n} x_i q(x_i),$$

where $q(x_i)$ is the relative frequency of x_i in the population. We shall now seek definitions for these parameters appropriate to models described by probability density functions.

Now in Section 1.6 above the formula just quoted for m was applied to situations for which the set of possible values of x is an interval of the real numbers; we saw that, in terms of relative frequency density r_i, it takes the form

$$m = \sum x_i r_i \delta x_i.$$

This suggests immediately how the definition of expected value might be extended to apply to the 'continuous' case. It is natural to replace relative frequency density by the probability density ρ; and since a graph with a finite number of steps is being replaced by a continuous graph, the finite sum becomes an integral. We therefore define

$$\mu = \int_{L}^{R} x\rho\,dx.$$

If we adopt the convention suggested in Section 2.4 that ρ is defined to be zero outside the interval (L, R) this may be written,

$$\mu = \int_{-\infty}^{\infty} x\rho\,dx.$$

3.2 A mechanical analogy. It is interesting to compare this formula for μ with one which arises in mechanics for the position of the centre of mass of a straight rod.

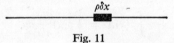

Fig. 11

Consider a rod of unit mass and of variable line density ρ. Then if the coordinate of a general point of the rod is x, the mass of a short portion, length δx, is $\rho\,\delta x$ (see Figure 11). Since the total mass is 1, we know that

$$\int \rho\,dx = 1.$$

The coordinate of the centre of mass of the rod is therefore given by the equation

$$1 . \bar{x} = \int x\rho\,dx,$$

the integral being taken over the interval of values of x occupied by the rod. Thus the expected value of x for a given probability density function is the same as the x-coordinate of the centre of mass of a rod with this as its density function.

This can also be regarded as the x-coordinate of the centre of area of the region under the probability density graph (Figure 12)—that is, the centre of mass of a uniform thin sheet occupying the region.

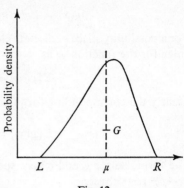

Fig. 12

3.3 Again, by analogy with the formula $s^2 = \Sigma(x_i - m)^2 r_i \delta x_i$ of Section 1.6, we define the variance $E[(x - \mu)^2]$, or σ^2, by

$$\sigma^2 = \int_L^R (x - \mu)^2 \rho \, dx.$$

The reader who has met the idea of moment of inertia in mechanics will recognize the integral for σ^2 as the formula for the moment of inertia about the centre of mass of a rod with line density ρ. If the rod has unit mass, the moment of inertia has the same numerical value as k^2, the square of the radius of gyration; so that the standard deviation σ for the given probability density function is analogous to the radius of gyration of the rod about a perpendicular axis through its centre of mass. Alternatively, it is the radius of gyration of the region in Figure 12 about the line through the centre of area parallel to the ρ-axis.

As usual, there is an alternative form of the formula for variance:

$$\sigma^2 = \int_L^R x^2 \rho \, dx - \mu^2.$$

(This may be compared with the 'parallel axes' theorem for radius of gyration in mechanics.)

Example 2. Find the mean and standard deviation of the errors in Example 1 (Section 2.1).

The formulae for μ and σ^2 give

$$\mu = \int_{-0.05}^{0.05} x \cdot 10 \, dx = \left[5x^2 \right]_{-0.05}^{0.05} = 0,$$

and $\qquad \sigma^2 = \int_{-0.05}^{0.05} x^2 \cdot 10 \, dx = \left[\frac{10}{3} x^3 \right]_{-0.05}^{0.05} = 0.000833;$

the mean error is therefore zero, and the standard deviation 0·029 cm.

*3.4   Expected value in general. The formula for the mean value of a function g defined over the domain of a frequency function is

$$\overline{g(x)} = \Sigma g(x_i)q(x_i) = \Sigma g(x_i)r_i\delta x_i.$$

For a possibility space of discrete elements we defined similarly the expected value for the function g, as

$$E[g(x)] = \Sigma g(x_i)p(x_i).$$

Clearly the corresponding formula in terms of probability density is

$$E[g(x)] = \int_L^R g(x)\rho\, dx.$$

The formulae for μ and σ^2 are special cases of this, taking $g(x)$ as x and $(x-\mu)^2$ respectively.

Exercise C

1. Find μ and σ for the probability density function $\phi(x) = \frac{1}{2}x$ defined over the interval $(0, 2)$.

2. Continue Exercise B, Question 3, by finding the mean distance travelled by particles down the cylinder.

3. Continue Exercise B, Question 4, by finding the mean length of life on the basis of this model.

4. A positive variable x has probability density

$$\rho = xe^{-x}.$$

Verify that this satisfies the conditions for a density function, and find the expected value of x and the standard deviation. What are the probabilities: (a) that $x > \mu$, (b) that $x > \mu + 2\sigma$?

5. Prove the equivalence of the two formulae for variance given in Section 3.3 directly from the integral expressions.

6. The following three equations define probability density functions over the interval $(-a, a)$:

   (a) $\rho = k(a^2 - x^2)$;   (b) $\rho = k(a^2 - x^2)^2$;   (c) $\rho = k(a - |x|)$.

For each equation draw the graph and find k in terms of a. Calculate the standard deviation, and find the probability that x lies within two standard deviations of the mean. Suggest also a definition for the mean absolute deviation, and express it as a multiple for σ for each of the three functions.

7. An angle θ has constant probability density over the interval $(0, \frac{1}{2}\pi)$. Calculate the expected value of $\sin \theta$.

8. Interpret the idea of the 'average value of a function f over an interval (a, b)', as described in Chapter 36, in the light of the definitions of Section 3.

4. CUMULATIVE PROBABILITY FUNCTIONS

In Section 1.7 we introduced the cumulative relative frequency $F(X)$, the proportion of the population for which $x < X$. By analogy we now define the *cumulative probability*, the probability that $x < X$:

$$\Phi(X) = \int_L^X \rho \, dx,$$

or
$$\Phi(X) = \int_L^X \phi.$$

Clearly $\Phi(L) = 0$ and $\Phi(R) = 1$; and if the domain of Φ is extended beyond the interval (L, R) as described in Section 2.4, then $\Phi(X) = 0$ for $X < L$ and $\Phi(X) = 1$ for $X > R$.

Figure 13 shows the relationship between the functions ϕ and Φ. It is one which we met previously in Chapter 22, Section 5; Φ is described as an integral function of ϕ, and it will be recalled that we deduced (if ϕ is continuous) that $\quad \Phi' = \phi \quad$ (see Figure 14).

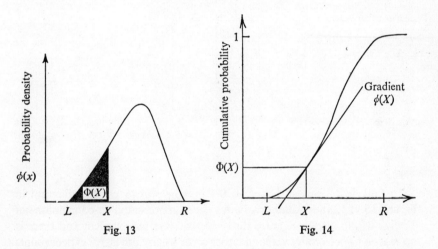

Fig. 13   Fig. 14

This was the 'fundamental theorem of analysis'. The relationship has two aspects:

The cumulative probability is measured by the AREA under a suitable portion of the probability density graph.

The probability density is measured by the GRADIENT of the cumulative probability graph.

It is important to notice that $\Phi(X)$ is a probability, not a probability density.

1129

Since ϕ is a non-negative function, the gradient of the cumulative probability graph is always positive or zero; thus the cumulative probability function is everywhere either increasing or stationary.

Example 3. Pairs of lines are measured and their lengths added. All measurements are subject to errors between $-0{\cdot}05$ and $+0{\cdot}05$ cm, as in Example 1. Find a cumulative probability function for the combined error in the sum, and deduce the form of the probability density function for the error in the sum.

Let the two errors be x_1 and x_2. Then we want to find

$$\Phi(X) = p(\mathbf{x}_1 + \mathbf{x}_2 \leqslant \mathbf{X})$$

for a general X. Since neither error can be greater in absolute value than $0{\cdot}05$, the combined error cannot exceed $0{\cdot}1$. That is,

$$\Phi(X) = 0 \quad \text{for} \quad X \leqslant -0{\cdot}1 \quad \text{and} \quad \Phi(X) = 1 \quad \text{for} \quad X > 0{\cdot}1.$$

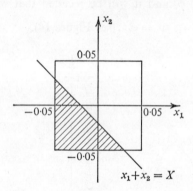

Fig. 15

To find $\Phi(X)$ for $-0{\cdot}1 < X \leqslant 0{\cdot}1$ it is helpful to use the diagram in Figure 15. The individual errors x_1, x_2 are represented as coordinates of a point within a square. Since the two errors are independent and there is no reason to prefer any value of either error to any other, we expect points representing the errors to be spread uniformly over the square. It would therefore seem that the probability $p(\mathbf{x}_1 + \mathbf{x}_2 \leqslant \mathbf{X})$ is equal to the fraction of the area of the square which lies in the region defined by this inequality, shown shaded in the figure. It is easily calculated that

$$\Phi(X) = \frac{\frac{1}{2}(X + 0{\cdot}1)^2}{0{\cdot}01} = 50(X + 0{\cdot}1)^2 \quad \text{for} \quad -0{\cdot}1 < X \leqslant 0,$$

and

$$\Phi(X) = 1 - \frac{\frac{1}{2}(0{\cdot}1 - X)^2}{0{\cdot}01} = 1 - 50(0{\cdot}1 - X)^2 \quad \text{for} \quad 0 < X \leqslant 0{\cdot}1.$$

1130

The graph of the cumulative probability therefore comprises parts of two parabolas, extended outside the interval of possibility by a pair of horizontal lines (see Figure 16).

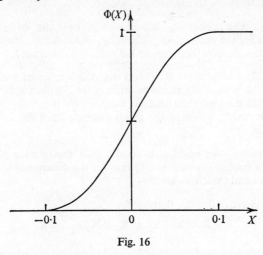

Fig. 16

The probability density function can now be found by differentiating, using the relation $\Phi' = \phi$. This gives

$$\phi(x) = \begin{cases} 100(x+0\cdot1) & \text{for} \quad -0\cdot1 < x \leqslant 0, \\ 100(0\cdot1-x) & \text{for} \quad 0 < x \leqslant 0\cdot1, \end{cases}$$

a 'triangular' probability density function (see Figure 17).

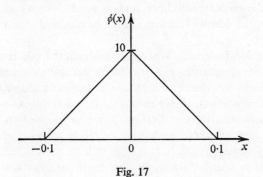

Fig. 17

Exercise D

1. Sketch the graph of the cumulative probability function for the errors of measurement in Example 1 (Section 2.1).

2. Give a formula for the cumulative probability function corresponding to the mathematical model for the age to which an infant will live in Exercise B, Question 4. State in words what $\Phi(X)$ means in this example. Use it to estimate the median length of life to the nearest year.

3. A variable x has probability density $\cos 2x$ over the interval $(-\tfrac{1}{4}\pi, \tfrac{1}{4}\pi)$. Find a formula for the cumulative probability, and sketch its graph. What is the ratio of the semi-interquartile range to the standard deviation?

4. Points are taken with equal likelihood over the interior of a circle of radius 2 cm. What is the probability that a random point is within a distance x cm of the centre? Deduce a probability density function for the distance of a random point from the centre, and find the mean distance from the centre of points within the circle.

5. Points are taken with equal likelihood within the interior of a sphere of radius a. Find a probability density function for the distance of a random point from the centre, and sketch its graph.

6. In Example 3 prove directly that

$$p(\mathbf{X} < \mathbf{x_1} + \mathbf{x_2} < \mathbf{X} + \delta\mathbf{X}) \simeq \frac{l}{\sqrt{2}}\,\delta X$$

where l is the length of the 'chord' in Figure 15; and hence deduce the nature of the probability density function.

5. CONSTRUCTING PROBABILITY DENSITY FUNCTIONS

5.1 How does one construct a density function appropriate to a particular problem? So far we have met two methods:

(i) *The a priori method.* In Example 1 we found no reason to prefer any one value of the error to any other, and so decided from considerations of symmetry that the density function should be constant over the interval of possible errors.

(ii) *The empirical method.* Where no theoretical basis is available, we may proceed by constructing a frequency density diagram for a large population of observations and then invent a smooth graph to which this is a good approximation. If, for example, the observations of our switchboard operators described in Section 1 are to be used to assist in the planning of a new telephone exchange, we might want a theoretical probability density function which would fit well to the histogram of observations actually timed. Obviously the more observations the better; Figure 3 would be more useful than Figure 1 for choosing a suitable function. Even so, we may have to make a compromise between a simple graph and a well-fitting one.

We shall now describe a third method which is sometimes fruitful, and which combines some features of the previous two. In this we take a known probability function for a discrete possibility space, and then derive a probability density function by some kind of limiting process in which the number of elements in the space increases indefinitely. This method will be illustrated by two simple examples.

*5.2 A rectangular density function. Imagine a rather unusual roulette wheel with $2n+1$ equal divisions, marked $-n$, $-(n-1)$, ..., -2, $-1, 0, 1, 2, ..., n$. The probability of any of these scores on a single spin is $1/(2n+1)$, and these probabilities are shown on a histogram in Figure 18 (a). Adopting the usual practice of making each rectangle of width 1 (so that it may be read as indicating either probability or probability density), the histogram extends over the interval $(-n-\frac{1}{2}, n+\frac{1}{2})$. Clearly the area of the complete histogram is 1.

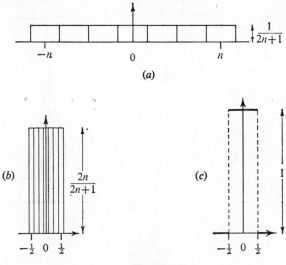

Fig. 18

Now if we make n tend to infinity, this diagram just becomes wider and less tall until it flattens down on the axis; this is no use for our purpose. We therefore make a change of scale to keep the height and width of the histogram finite in the limit. This could be done, for example, by dividing the horizontal lengths by $2n$ and multiplying heights by $2n$, as in Figure 18 (b). Since in a density graph probabilities are represented by areas, this change of scale does not alter the actual probabilities, though the elements of the possibility space are now closer together.

We now let n tend to infinity, and obtain Figure 18 (c), in which the region occupied by the histogram becomes a rectangle of height 1 stretching horizontally over the interval $(-\frac{1}{2}, \frac{1}{2})$.

*5.3   **A triangular density function.** Suppose now that the roulette wheel is spun twice, and the two scores added. The space of equally likely possibilities now consists of $(2n+1)^2$ ordered pairs of scores, which can give $4n+1$ different sums from $-2n$ to $2n$. The probabilities associated with these sums are:

Sum	$\pm 2n$	$\pm(2n-1)$	...	± 1	0
Probability	$\dfrac{1}{(2n+1)^2}$	$\dfrac{2}{(2n+1)^2}$	$\cdots$	$\dfrac{2n}{(2n+1)^2}$	$\dfrac{2n+1}{(2n+1)^2}$.

These are displayed in the histogram in Figure 19(*a*), whose area is again 1.

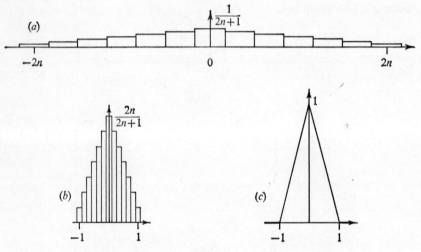

Fig. 19

If we make the same change of scale as before, dividing the widths and multiplying the heights by $2n$, we obtain Figure 19(*b*). The extremes of this diagram are

$$-1-\frac{1}{4n} \quad \text{and} \quad 1+\frac{1}{4n},$$

and its maximum height is $2n/(2n+1)$. Letting n tend to infinity, the result is the triangular graph in Figure 19*c*, which stretches over the interval $(-1, 1)$ and has maximum height 1.

This may also be shown algebraically. In Figure 19(*a*) the rectangle with class-mark $+i$ has height $(2n+1-i)/(2n+1)^2$. After the change of scale this is a rectangle with class-mark $\pm i/(2n)$ and height

$$2n(2n+1-i)/(2n+1)^2.$$

Writing x for $\pm i/(2n)$, this height is $2n(2n+1\mp 2nx)/(2n+1)^2$, which tends to $1\mp x$ as n tends to infinity. The probability density function is therefore

$$\phi(x) = \begin{cases} 1-x & \text{for} \quad 0 \leqslant x < 1, \\ 1+x & \text{for} \quad -1 < x < 0. \end{cases}$$

5.4 The decision in these examples to change the scale by a factor of $2n$ was to some extent an arbitrary one; any other multiple of n would have done as well. For example, had the factor been $20n$, we would have obtained probability density graphs of one-tenth the width and ten times as high—in fact, the rectangular and triangular density functions of Examples 1 and 3.

We must stress again that these probability density functions have been obtained as limiting forms of other probability models, and are in no sense limits of histograms depicting the results of statistical observations. Whether or not they are good models with which to describe a particular situation is a matter for personal judgement.

6. LIMITING FORM OF THE BINOMIAL FUNCTION

6.1 An important application of the method described in Section 5 is to the binomial probability function (see Chapter 25). It will be recalled that this relates to the probability of obtaining various numbers of 'successes' in a sequence of trials: if the probabilities of success and failure in a single trial are denoted by a, b respectively, the probability of i successes in a sequence is

$$\binom{n}{i} b^{n-i} a^i,$$

the possibility space being, of course, the set $\{0, 1, 2, \ldots, n\}$.

We shall consider the effect of letting n increase indefinitely. As a guide to what might happen, Figure 20 shows the histogram for a sequence of 20 trials with 0·4 probability of success. It was proved in Chapter 26, Section 5.4 that the expected value for the number of successes is na; in our example this is equal to 8, which is also the modal value. (In general, the mode of the binomial probability function is an integer within one unit distance of the expected value na: see Chapter 25, Exercise G, Question 8.) The standard deviation is $\sqrt{(nab)}$, which in this example comes to 2·2. The ordinates at μ, $\mu \pm \sigma$, $\mu \pm 2\sigma$ have been marked on the diagram; it can be calculated that 95·5 % of the area of the histogram lies within the interval $(\mu-2\sigma, \mu+2\sigma)$, which is a typical value for hump-shaped probability functions of this kind.

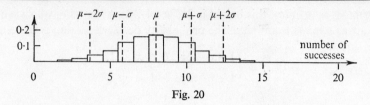

Fig. 20

What is specially remarkable about this histogram is that around the mean its shape is almost symmetrical; for example,

$$p(\textbf{4 successes}) = 0\cdot0351, \quad p(\textbf{12 successes}) = 0\cdot0356.$$

Of course, the mean itself is not symmetrically situated within the possibility space; but over the part of the possibility space within which almost the whole of the area lies, the effect of having a large value of n is to wipe out the skewness of the histogram. We shall find that in fact the limiting form of the density function is completely symmetrical about the mean.

*6.2   We proceed to obtain an algebraic expression for this limiting form. Figure 21(a) shows a typical histogram for the binomial probability function, with mean na and standard deviation $\sqrt{(nab)}$. It will be necessary, as before, to make certain adjustments to this before letting n tend to infinity, for two reasons:

(i)   the mean itself tends to infinity;
(ii) the spread of the histogram, measured by the standard deviation, is proportional to $\sqrt{n}$ and therefore tends to infinity.

To overcome this we shall:

(i)   move the origin to the mean, so that the class-marks vary from $-na$ to $n-na = nb$ rather than from 0 to n;
(ii) divide the horizontal lengths by $\sqrt{n}$ and (to preserve intact areas, which represent the actual probabilities) multiply heights by $\sqrt{n}$.

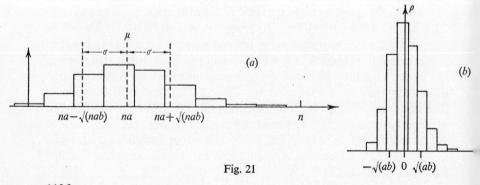

Fig. 21

1136

The effect of these changes is shown in Figure 21 (*b*). If the displacement from the origin of a typical class-mark is denoted by x, these two transformations can be effected algebraically by the equation

$$x = \frac{i - na}{\sqrt{n}},$$

and the corresponding probability density is

$$\rho = \sqrt{n} \cdot \binom{n}{i} b^{n-i} a^i.$$

The mean for this transformed histogram is 0, and its standard deviation is $\sigma = \sqrt{(ab)}$.

The problem is to express ρ in terms of x and to find its limit as n tends to infinity. Now it is possible to do this directly, but the analysis calls for certain results with which the reader will not yet be familiar. We can, however, overcome this difficulty by an indirect argument in which we find a differential equation satisfied by the limiting function.

Consider two consecutive rectangles in Figure 21 (*b*). Because of the horizontal scale reduction, their class-marks differ by an amount

$$\delta x = \frac{1}{\sqrt{n}}.$$

Their heights are respectively

$$\sqrt{n} \cdot \binom{n}{i} b^{n-i} a^i \quad \text{and} \quad \sqrt{n} \cdot \binom{n}{i+1} b^{n-i-1} a^{i+1},$$

so that we may write

$$\delta\rho = \sqrt{n} \cdot \left\{ \binom{n}{i+1} b^{n-i-1} a^{i+1} - \binom{n}{i} b^{n-i} a^i \right\}.$$

It is simpler to give the proportional change in ρ:

$$\frac{\delta\rho}{\rho} = \frac{\binom{n}{i+1}}{\binom{n}{i}} \frac{a}{b} - 1$$

$$= \frac{n-i}{i+1} \frac{a}{b} - 1 \quad \text{(see Chapter 25, Section 8)}$$

$$= \frac{na - ia - ib - b}{(i+1)b}$$

$$= \frac{na - i - b}{(i+1)b} \quad \text{(since } a + b = 1\text{)}.$$

Substituting $x\sqrt{n}+na$ for i, and dividing by δx, we obtain

$$\frac{1}{\rho}\frac{\delta\rho}{\delta x} = \frac{-x\sqrt{n}-b}{(x\sqrt{n}+na+1)b}\bigg/\frac{1}{\sqrt{n}}$$

$$= \frac{-xn-b\sqrt{n}}{(x\sqrt{n}+na+1)b}.$$

This is now in a form from which we can proceed to the limit. Since δx, or $1/\sqrt{n}$, tends to zero, $\delta\rho/\delta x$ may be replaced by $d\rho/dx$. On the right side the dominant terms in numerator and denominator are $-xn$ and nab respectively, so that this expression tends to $-x/ab$. We obtain therefore the differential equation

$$\frac{1}{\rho}\frac{d\rho}{dx} = -\frac{x}{ab};$$

or, since for the transformed graph $\sqrt{(ab)} = \sigma$,

$$\frac{1}{\rho}\frac{d\rho}{dx} = -\frac{x}{\sigma^2}.$$

This can be integrated directly to give

$$\log\rho = -\frac{x^2}{2\sigma^2}+A,$$

or

$$\rho = \exp\left(-\frac{x^2}{2\sigma^2}+A\right)$$

$$= B\exp\left(-\frac{x^2}{2\sigma^2}\right), \quad \text{say,}$$

where B is constant.

Figure 21 (c) shows the form of this graph. We notice at once that, since the formula involves x^2, the density is an even function, so that the graph is symmetrical about $x = 0$. Various other properties of the graph are investigated in Exercise E.

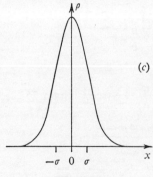

(c)

Fig. 21 (c)

The problem is still not quite solved, since the formula we have found involves an unknown number B. One way of finding this is to use the fact that the integral of a density function over the interval of possible values (here the whole set of real numbers) must be 1, so that

$$\int_{-\infty}^{\infty} B \exp\left(-\frac{x^2}{2\sigma^2}\right) dx = 1.$$

Now it can be proved† (though the calculation involves ideas which have not been discussed in this course, and here we merely quote the result) that

$$\int_{-\infty}^{\infty} \exp\left(-\frac{x^2}{2\sigma^2}\right) dx = \sigma\sqrt{(2\pi)},$$

from which it follows that

$$B\sigma\sqrt{(2\pi)} = 1,$$

$$B = \frac{1}{\sigma\sqrt{(2\pi)}}.$$

The final result is therefore:

The binomial probability function generated by $(b+at)^n$ has as a limiting form the probability density function

$$\phi(x) = \frac{1}{\sigma\sqrt{(2\pi)}} \exp\left(-\frac{x^2}{2\sigma^2}\right),$$

where σ is the standard deviation.

6.3 The calculation in Section 6.2 involved a horizontal shift which transferred the mean to the origin. This gives the equation in its simplest form; but since our concern was merely to keep the mean finite as n tends to infinity, we could equally well have transferred it to any other value μ. This would be effected by writing

$$x = \frac{i-na}{\sqrt{n}} + \mu,$$

and the graph in Figure 21c would then have undergone a translation $\binom{\mu}{0}$. This would lead to the density function

$$\phi(x) = \frac{1}{\sigma\sqrt{(2\pi)}} \exp\left(-\frac{(x-\mu)^2}{2\sigma^2}\right).$$

This is the most general form of the *Normal probability density function.*

† See p. 1350, Question 15.

4-2

Exercise E

1. Verify the values given for the probabilities of 4 and 12 successes in Section 6.1.

2. Using tables of the exponential function, draw the graph of the Normal probability density function with $\mu = 0$ and $\sigma = 1$. Then, on the same axes and without further calculation, draw the graphs of the function with (i) $\mu = 0, \sigma = 2$; (ii) $\mu = 1, \sigma = 2$.

Questions 3–6 refer to the Normal density function with $\mu = 0$, i.e. to the form given at the end of Section 6.2.

3. Locate the points of inflexion on the graph.

4. Use tables of the exponential function and Simpson's rule to find the areas under the graph over the intervals $((k-\frac{1}{2})\sigma, (k+\frac{1}{2})\sigma)$ for $k = -2, -1, 0, 1, 2$. Use your results to draw the graph of the cumulative probability function.

5. Calculate the mean absolute deviation from the mean.

6. From a suitable polynomial approximation for e^{α}, deduce a polynomial approximation of the fourteenth degree for $\phi(x)$. Use this to find approximately the probability that x lies in the interval $(-2\sigma, 2\sigma)$.

7. Assuming the result

$$\int_{-\infty}^{\infty} \exp(-\tfrac{1}{2}x^2)\,dx = \sqrt{(2\pi)},$$

deduce the more general result

$$\int_{-\infty}^{\infty} \exp\left(-\frac{x^2}{2\sigma^2}\right) dx = \sigma\sqrt{(2\pi)}.$$

8. Evaluate

$$(a) \int_{-\infty}^{\infty} x.\exp\left(-\frac{x^2}{2\sigma^2}\right) dx; \quad (b) \int_{-\infty}^{\infty} x^2.\exp\left(-\frac{x^2}{2\sigma^2}\right) dx.$$

Explain why your answers were already known.

9. A roulette wheel has n equal divisions, labelled $1, 2, ..., n$. Find the probability that it is spun i times with a score other than 'one' before the first 'one' appears, and prove that the generator for this probability is

$$\frac{1}{n-(n-1)t}.$$

Deduce that the mean is $n-1$. Now make a change of scale so as to produce a probability density function with mean $1-(1/n)$, and find an expression for the limiting form of the probability density function as n tends to infinity.

(*Hint.* Note that the limit of $\{1+r/n)\}^n$ is e^r. See Chapter 29, Exercise D, Question 11.)

1140

7. NORMAL PROBABILITY DENSITY

7.1 Tables. The Normal probability density function is one of the standard functions of statistics, and we frequently make use of tables of this function and its associated cumulative probability. (See, for example, *S.M.P. Advanced Tables*.) It is not, however, necessary to tabulate the function in the general form given in Section 7.3 for different values of μ and σ, any more than we need separate tables of sin x, sin $2x$, sin $3x$ and so on; instead we choose a 'standardized form' of the function, and then apply suitable transformations to this to obtain the general function.

The standardized form used is the one with mean 0 and standard deviation 1, having equation

$$\phi(x) = \frac{1}{\sqrt{(2\pi)}} \exp\left(-\tfrac{1}{2}x^2\right)$$

(see Figure 22). For this we tabulate both ϕ itself and the cumulative probability function

$$\Phi(X) = \int_{-\infty}^{X} \phi.$$

The tables usually cover just positive values of the argument, since the entries for corresponding negative values are easily found from these. The density itself is an even function, so that $\phi(-x) = \phi(x)$.

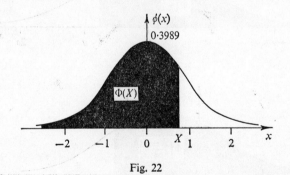

Fig. 22

Also from symmetry

$$\Phi(-X) = \int_{-\infty}^{-X} \phi$$

$$= \int_{X}^{\infty} \phi$$

$$= 1 - \Phi(X),$$

since the area under the entire graph is 1.

7.2 When the standard deviation is σ rather than 1, the graph is stretched horizontally in the ratio $\sigma:1$, and squashed vertically in the ratio $1/\sigma:1$ in order that the total area should remain 1. That is, we apply the transformation $\begin{pmatrix} \sigma & 0 \\ 0 & 1/\sigma \end{pmatrix}$, giving the density function

$$\rho = \frac{1}{\sigma\sqrt{(2\pi)}} \exp\left(-\frac{x^2}{2\sigma^2}\right) \quad \text{(see Figure 23)}$$

$$= \frac{1}{\sigma}\phi\left(\frac{x}{\sigma}\right).$$

For this function we must therefore look up in the standardized tables the entry x/σ, the 'number of standard deviations', rather than x. We then proceed as follows:

(i) If the actual ordinate of the density graph is required, the value of ϕ given in the tables must be divided by σ.

(ii) If we are using the tables to find a probability, represented by a certain area under the graph, this is given directly by the table of values for Φ, since the transformation leaves areas invariant.

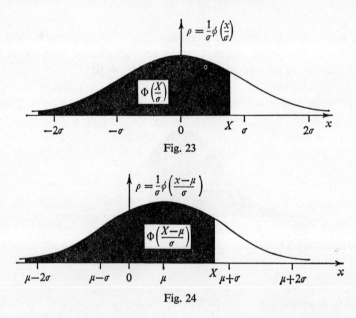

Fig. 23

Fig. 24

Furthermore, in the general case when the mean is μ rather than 0, the graph is translated by a vector $\begin{pmatrix} \mu \\ 0 \end{pmatrix}$, giving the density function

$$\rho = \frac{1}{\sigma}\phi\left(\frac{x-\mu}{\sigma}\right) \quad \text{(see Figure 24)}.$$

We then have to look up in the standardized tables the entry $(x-\mu)/\sigma$, the 'number of standard deviations from the mean', after which the tables are used as in (i) or (ii) above.

Example 4. Observations suggest that the heights of adult males in Ruritania fit a Normal density function with mean 175 cm and standard deviation 7 cm. What proportion of the population has a height between 160 and 180 cm?

The probability is measured by the area under the graph for the interval $\{x: 160 < x < 180\}$. This is not tabulated directly, but can be found as the difference between values of Φ corresponding to the two ends of the interval. Now 180 is five-sevenths, or 0·714, standard deviations above the mean; and 160 is fifteen-sevenths, or 2·143, standard deviations below. The required probability is therefore

$$\Phi(0\cdot714) - \Phi(-2\cdot143).$$

To find $\Phi(0\cdot714)$. The tables give $\Phi(0\cdot7) = 0\cdot7580$ and $\Phi(0\cdot8) = 0\cdot7881$, an increase of 0·0301. Using linear interpolation,

$$\Phi(0\cdot714) \simeq 0\cdot7580 + \tfrac{14}{100} \times 0\cdot0301 \simeq 0\cdot7622.$$

To find $\Phi(-2\cdot143)$. We have recourse to the fact that

$$\Phi(-X) = 1 - \Phi(X).$$

Using linear interpolation again,

$$\Phi(2\cdot143) \simeq 0\cdot9821 + \tfrac{43}{100} \times 0\cdot0040 \simeq 0\cdot9838,$$

so that $\qquad \Phi(-2\cdot143) \simeq 1 - 0\cdot9838 = 0\cdot0162.$

The probability of a Ruritanian man having a height between 160 and 180 cm is therefore approximately

$$0\cdot7622 - 0\cdot0162$$

$$= 0\cdot746,$$

and we expect that this is almost equal to the relative frequency of men of this height in the population.

7.3 Besides the tables of $\phi(x)$ and $\Phi(X)$, the *S.M.P. Advanced Tables* also give $2(1-\Phi(X))$, which is the area under the standardized graph shaded in Figure 25. For the general Normal density function, this measures the probability that a random variable will differ from the mean by more than X standard deviations.

The unshaded area between the two ordinates in Figure 25 is

$$1 - 2(1 - \Phi(X)).$$

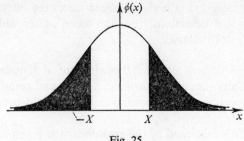

Fig. 25

This gives the probability that a random variable lies within X standard deviations of the mean. Some useful approximate values to remember are:

X	$1-2(1-\Phi(X))$
1	0·6826, or just over two-thirds
2	0·9544, or just over 95%
3	0·9973, or virtually all.

This shows the basis of the 'two standard deviation' check referred to in Chapter 12, Section 5. The proportions are illustrated in Figure 26.

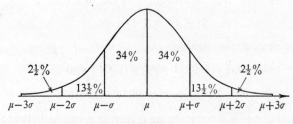

Fig. 26

Since the regular tables give $1-\Phi(X)$ to only two or fewer significant figures beyond $X = 3\cdot2$, the *S.M.P. Advanced Tables* also include additional tables with greater accuracy where $\Phi(X)$ is nearly equal to 1. The use of these is explained where they occur.

Exercise F

1. At a weather station the mean annual rainfall is 850 mm with standard deviation 100 mm. Assuming a Normal probability density, what is the probability that in a particular year the rainfall will not exceed 1000 mm?

2. With the data of Example 4 (Section 7.2), calculate the height which the Ruritanians should build their door lintels if 99% of men should be able to pass through without stooping.

3. An author averages 200 words to a page. If in a book of 300 pages twenty have more than 215 words, estimate the standard deviation, and the number of pages with more than 220 words.

4. Steel rods are required to be of length 10 cm, and a machine cuts them with a mean length of 10·02 cm and a standard deviation of 0·015 cm. Assuming a Normal probability density, what proportion of the rods will be rejected for being too short?

If the spread of the measurements is unaltered by adjusting the position of the cut, how large should the mean be made if only a 1 % rejection rate can be tolerated?

Alternatively, to what would the standard deviation have to be reduced if the mean length was to be unaltered but the 1 % rejection rate achieved?

5. A certain make of car battery has a mean life of 26 months, and the makers guarantee to pay compensation to anyone whose battery does not last two years. The firm in fact pays compensation for $\frac{1}{2}$ % of the batteries sold. Assuming that battery life has Normal probability density, find the standard deviation of the battery life. How many batteries per thousand will last longer than 27 months?

6. The I.Q. for students in a fixed age-group is reputed to have a mean of 100 and a standard deviation of 15, with a Normal probability density.

(*a*) What is the probability that a random child will have an I.Q. between 80 and 110?

(*b*) What is the lowest I.Q. of the top 3 %?

(*c*) What is the probability that, of three children selected at random, none will have an I.Q. below 120?

7. On a desert crossing a man takes a car with five new tyres (four fitted and one spare). The journey is 1000 km, and the tyres have a mean life of 1500 km each with standard deviation 500 km in these conditions. Before he starts, what is the probability that

(*a*) a given fitted tyre will not puncture in the first 500 km;

(*b*) exactly one of the fitted tyres will puncture in the first 500 km?

In fact, the first puncture occurs after 500 km. What is now the probability that

(*c*) a given tyre of the other three fitted originally will not puncture in the next 500 km, given that this is independent of its performance so far;

(*d*) exactly one more tyre (possibly the spare) will puncture before the journey is finished?

8. The weights in kilograms of the babies born in one hospital during a given month are as follows:

Weight (kg)	Frequency	Weight (kg)	Frequency
1·0–1·5	1	3·0–3·5	31
1·5–2·0	8	3·5–4·0	16
2·0–2·5	23	4·0–4·5	4
2·5–3·0	37		

Show this information on a histogram, and calculate the mean and standard deviation.

It is desired to make a probability model for this situation using a Normal density function. What values of μ and σ would you select for this purpose? Use your tables to draw this graph, superimposing it on the histogram.

Calculate the probabilities for this density function over each of the seven intervals specificed in the data; and, identifying these with relative frequencies, find the actual frequencies over these intervals which would be predicted by the Normal function. By comparing these with the given frequencies, comment on the suitability of using this probability model.

9. Carry out an analysis similar to Question 8 for the following data, representing the ages of marriage of girls in a certain town:

Age	Frequency	Age	Frequency
17	2	21	18
18	7	22	11
19	16	23	4
20	21	24	1

10. A firm decides to enter the export market to sell shoes in the Happy Isles. They find 26 islanders living in London and measure their feet, with the following result:

Shoe size	7	8	9	10	11
Frequency	4	5	8	6	3

They decide to fit these figures to a Normal curve, and to base the proportions of different sizes in their first consignment of 5000 shoes on this. How many size 9 and how many size 12 should they include?

11. Calculate the probabilities of various numbers of successes for a binomial probability function with $a = b = \frac{1}{2}$, $n = 10$, and draw the histogram. Approximate to this by a Normal density function with the same mean and standard deviation, and find what probabilities this gives.

12. Repeat Question 11 for the case $a = 0\cdot4$, $b = 0\cdot6$, $n = 10$.

13. A coin is tossed 100 times. Use the Normal approximation to the binomial probability function to find the probability of getting more than 55 heads. Repeat the calculation to find the probabilities of: (*a*) more than 550 heads in 1000 tosses; (*b*) more than 5500 heads in 10000 tosses.

14. Use the Normal approximation to the binomial probability function to calculate, for repeated tossing of a coin, the probabilities of:
  (*a*) exactly 55 heads in 100 tosses,
  (*b*) exactly 550 heads in 1000 tosses,
  (*c*) exactly 5500 heads in 10000 tosses.

15. A die is rolled 600 times. Calculate the probability of getting between 95 and 105 sixes (inclusive).

1146

16. Fat men are being divided into classes to do exercises at a slimming centre, and we want to have men of about the same build training together. To use the apparatus efficiently, however, all the classes are to have equal numbers of members. The mean girth of the men is 115 cm, with standard deviation 10 cm, and we shall suppose that the Normal curve gives a suitable approximation. If we require 6 classes, what should be the girth limits for each class to the nearest quarter of an inch?

Owing to excessive strain, one set of apparatus collapses and the men are reorganized into 5 equal classes. Reset the limits. If the classes are numbered consecutively, with the slimmest as class 1, what proportion of the men can truthfully report to their wives after the apparatus collapses that they are now in a lower class?

Summary. When the set of probabilities is an interval of the real numbers:

(Finite) statistical population	Probability model
Relative frequency density r_i	Probability density ρ
Relative frequency in an interval $\Sigma r_i \delta x_i$	Probability in an interval $\int \rho \, dx$

Statistics	*Parameters*
Mean $\quad m = \Sigma x_i r_i \delta x_i$	Mean $\quad \mu = \int x\rho \, dx$
Variance $s^2 = \Sigma(x_i - m)^2 r_i \delta x_i$	Variance $\sigma^2 = \int(x-\mu)^2 \rho \, dx$
$\quad = \Sigma x_i^2 r_i \delta x_i - m^2$	$\quad = \int x^2 \rho \, dx - \mu^2$

Normal probability density

$$\rho = \frac{1}{\sigma \sqrt{(2\pi)}} \exp\left(-\frac{(x-\mu)^2}{2\sigma^2}\right).$$

38

SAMPLING AND ESTIMATION

Our background of probability theory is now sufficient for us to investigate one of the central problems of statistics: to discover what we can of the nature of a population by examining a sample drawn from it.

The plan of this chapter is first to review the problem in its entirety for one simple case, that in which we wish to estimate what proportion of a set possesses a certain attribute. This will suggest ways of tackling the more complicated situation in which there is a population of numerical measures (as distinct from just yes/no answers to a specific question) and we wish to estimate a numerical parameter such as mean or variance.

1. SAMPLING OF ATTRIBUTES

Suppose that in a certain constituency 25000 people propose to vote Labour and 15000 Conservative in a straight fight between two candidates. On the eve of the poll a canvass is made of 200 constituents. What will this reveal?

It is possible, of course, that it will show solid support for the Conservative; but this is most unlikely if the voters are selected at random, rather than in the lounge of the local Conservative club. More probably the numbers of supporters of the two parties in the canvass will be roughly proportional to the numbers in the constituency as a whole; that is, about 125 people will say that they propose to vote labour, and 75 that they will vote conservative. But clearly there is no precise answer to the question.

This is a problem of 'sampling'. We have at our disposal a 'parent population', comprising the voting intentions of 40000 people. From this is selected a sample of 200 of these intentions; and it would be of interest to know how closely this resembles the parent population from which it is drawn.

Now this is a situation with which we are familiar. The canvass consists of a sequence of 200 separate trials, and in each of these the probability that the person asked will be a Labour supporter is $\frac{5}{8}$. The probabilities of the various possible results are therefore described by a binomial probability function. Thus for the sample to contain i Labour voters and $200-i$ Conservative the probability is the coefficient of t^i in

$$(\tfrac{3}{8}+\tfrac{5}{8}t)^{200}.$$

1148

(Strictly this is true only if we allow each voter to be included in the sample more than once. Otherwise, once his views have been ascertained, the probabilities for the rest of the population are very slightly changed. This is described as sampling 'with replacement'—each individual is replaced in the pool after being questioned. With a very large parent population, the differences between the probabilities for sampling with and without replacement are very small.)

A table of values for these probabilities would run as follows:

Number of Labour voters	Probability
0	$(\frac{3}{8})^{200} = 6\cdot3 \times 10^{-86}$
1	$200\ (\frac{3}{8})^{199}\ (\frac{5}{8})\ \ = 2\cdot1 \times 10^{-83}$
...	...
124	$\binom{200}{124} (\frac{3}{8})^{76} (\frac{5}{8})^{124} = 5\cdot6 \times 10^{-2}$
125	$\binom{200}{125} (\frac{3}{8})^{75} (\frac{5}{8})^{125} = 5\cdot7 \times 10^{-2}$
126	$\binom{200}{126} (\frac{3}{8})^{74} (\frac{5}{8})^{126} = 5\cdot6 \times 10^{-2}$
...	...
200	$(\frac{5}{8})^{200} = 1\cdot5 \times 10^{-41}$

It is plainly very laborious and unrewarding to calculate all the probabilities in this sequence. Fortunately there is a short cut for finding those we are likely to want. This relies on the fact that the histogram of the binomial function for a large number of trials differs very little from the graph of the Normal density function having the same mean and standard deviation. In our example these parameters are

$$\mu = 200 \times \tfrac{5}{8} = 125$$

and $$\sigma = \sqrt{(200 \times \tfrac{5}{8} \times \tfrac{3}{8})} = 6\cdot85;$$

so that Figure 1, based on the Normal curve, gives a good idea of the various probabilities.

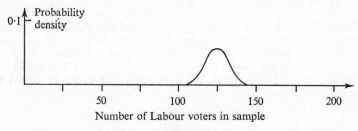

Fig. 1

From this we can answer questions such as:

(i) What is the probability of canvassing a sample which indicates a Conservative victory?

For this there must be not more than 99 Labour voters, so we find the area under the graph to the left of 99·5. (Why not 99; or 100?) This is 25·5 below the mean; that is, 25·5/6·85, or 3·72, standard deviations. From the tables of the Normal function,

$$\Phi(-3\cdot72) = 1 - \Phi(3\cdot72) = 1 - 0\cdot99990 = 0\cdot00010.$$

The probability of such an unrepresentative sample is therefore of the order of 1 in 10000.

(ii) Within what interval is there a 95% chance that the number of Labour supporters in the sample will lie?

This is a band of just under two standard deviations either side of the mean (see Chapter 37, Section 7.3). This gives the interval (111·3, 138·7), so that we could say that there is about a 95% probability that the sample will show between 112 and 138 Labour supporters.

Exercise A

1. Repeat the calculations of the preceding section for samples of sizes 40 and 1000. Also, for all three sample sizes, for a constituency in which 21000 people propose to vote Labour and 19000 Conservative. Comment on your results.

Is the size of the constituency at all relevant in the calculations?

2. Sixty per cent of the population prefer plain chocolate to milk chocolate. A person organizing a party for 100 guests, each of which is to be given a box of chocolates as a present, lays in a stock of 70 boxes of plain and 45 boxes of milk. What is the probability that every guest will be able to have the kind he prefers?

3. Two strains, *A* and *B*, of a certain species of plant occur in the population in proportions 80%, 20% respectively; they are indistinguishable at sight. It is desired to select a sample of specimens of this plant which contains these two strains in proportions which differ by less than 1% from those in the population as a whole. If a sample of a thousand were taken, what would be the probability of achieving this? How large a sample would you need to take to be virtually certain that it would meet the requirement? (Say what you mean by 'virtually certain' in this context.)

4. 'We conducted our own independent survey and found that 85% of housewives prefer Bubblo to any other detergent.' On what points would you want to satisfy yourself before accepting this advertiser's claim at its face value? Suggest the minimum acceptable size for a sample on which such a claim might be based, and state in more precise terms the conclusion that could be drawn from examining such a sample.

2. THE PROBLEM OF ESTIMATION

2.1 The trouble with the analysis in the last section is that it is concerned with a situation which is the exact reverse of those that usually arise in practice. We have seen that, if we know the composition of the parent population, we can find out what kind of sample we may reasonably expect to draw from it. But very often the point of taking a sample is to find out something of the composition of the parent population. We make a survey of political affiliations of 200 people in the constituency so that we may hazard a guess about the constituency as a whole. That is, the real problem is not 'what samples might I reasonably expect to draw from a given parent population?', but 'what parent populations might a given sample reasonably have been drawn from?'. Not surprisingly, the two questions are not entirely independent of each other; but it is important to appreciate that they are essentially different, and demand a different kind of analysis.

Suppose that there are two million television sets in the range of a certain transmitter, and that an advertiser wishes to know how many of these were tuned in to ITV at 8 o'clock on a Tuesday evening. He therefore conducts a survey of listeners, choosing a sample in as random a fashion as he can—avoiding methods likely to give an unrepresentative sample— and hopes to make suitable deductions from an analysis of the results.

The first question is, 'how large a sample must he choose?'. Clearly he will not learn much by asking only ten people; and it will be uneconomical to ask ten thousand. The larger the sample, the more precise will be the conclusion he can reach; but there comes a stage when the returns to be gained from this extra precision are offset by the extra cost of conducting the survey. There is no straightforward answer to this question; but we could examine the quality of the information he could get from samples of different sizes, and this would furnish a basis for the choice.

We will imagine that a sample size of 1000 has been selected, and that of these it is found that 30 % were tuned in to ITV at the time in question. What conclusion can be drawn from this? The facile answer would be to guess that, in the whole region, 30 % of two million (600000) were listening at the time. But such an answer is of little value unless some measure of reliability can be attached to it, and it is therefore worth while to examine the situation more thoroughly.

2.2 Could it be that in fact only 560000, or 28 %, were listening at the time? Obviously it is possible; so we must ask 'how likely is it?'. To answer this, we turn the problem round: if we begin with the assumption, or hypothesis, that 28 % of the sets in the region were tuned in, what would be the probability of drawing a sample of 1000 in which 300 people answered 'yes'?

This brings us back to the situation discussed in Section 1. The probabilities of various possible samples on this hypothesis are given by a binomial probability function generated by

$$(0.72 + 0.28t)^{1000},$$

to which we may approximate by a Normal density function with

$$\mu = 1000 \times 0.28 = 280 \quad \text{and} \quad \sigma = \sqrt{(1000 \times 0.28 \times 0.72)} = 14.2$$

(see Figure 2).

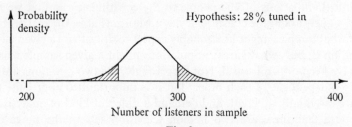

Fig. 2

This puts us in a position to answer various questions on the basis of the 28 % hypothesis. Perhaps the most obvious is: 'what is the probability of getting 300 "yes" answers in a sample of 1000?'. It is easily calculated that this is about 0·028, but the meaning to be attached to this figure is not very clear. One reason for the smallness of the figure is not that samples of around this size are all that unlikely, but simply that there are 1001 different possibilities for the number of 'yes' answers.

What might surprise us about drawing a sample of 300 in 1000 from a parent population with a 28 % probability is that 300 is some way from the 'expected value' of 280. A better question to ask is therefore: 'what is the probability of getting a sample value which differs from the expected number by 20 or more?'. This is the probability

$$p(|x-280| > 19.5),$$

represented in Figure 2 by the shaded area. Since 19·5 is 1·37σ, the probability is calculated as $2(1 - \Phi(1.37)) = 0.17$.

To sum up, what we have shown is that if there had been only 560000 sets tuned in to ITV, then there is a 0·17 probability that we should have drawn a sample whose composition differed from that which we might have expected by as much as the sample actually observed.†

† It might be thought that a better question to ask would be: 'what is the probability of getting a sample which exceeds the expected value by 20 or more?', represented by the right-hand shaded area; this is $p(x - 280 > 1.95)$, with value 0·09. There are in fact no rights and wrongs about this; but if a different question is asked, then a different answer will be given. In problems of statistical inference the important thing is to state with precision what the question is. The two questions compared here refer to 'two-tailed' and 'one-tailed' criteria respectively.

2.3 In Section 2.2. we began with an arbitrary assumption that there might have been 28 % of the population tuned in, and followed up the consequences of this in terms of the sample actually drawn. Other proportions might, of course, be investigated similarly, and we could find how

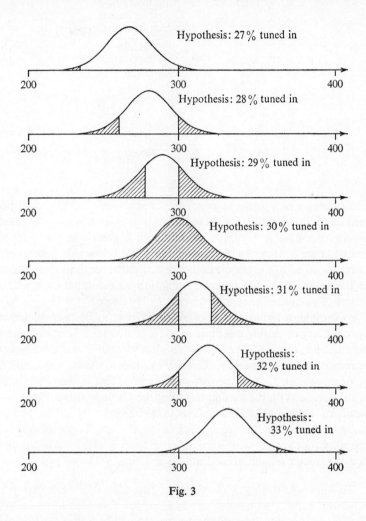

Fig. 3

likely it would be for the sample to have come from these. Figure 3 shows a sequence of graphs similar to Figure 2 for different assumptions about the parent population, in which the number of people tuned in varies from 540 000 (27 %) of the number of sets) to 660 000 (33 %).

For each such assumption we calculate the difference between the expected number of listeners in a sample of 1000 and the number actually observed (300); and we then find the probability of obtaining a sample which differs from the expected value by as much as or more than this.

Proportion tuned in (%)	Probability of a discrepancy not less than that observed
25	0·0003
26	0·0044
27	0·036
28	0·17
29	0·51
30	1
31	0·52
32	0·19
33	0·048
34	0·0080
35	0·0010

The time has now come to consider the question: 'what parent populations might reasonably have led to the sample which was actually drawn?' This question does not, of course, admit of a precise answer unless we define what we consider to be 'reasonable'; and this would depend on the importance to us of the conclusion. We can, however, find from the table how the estimate of the parent population might square up with any criterion of reasonableness that we care to lay down.

For example, a hypothesis is often considered to be 'unreasonable' if the probability of getting a sample in as bad or worse agreement than that observed is less than 0·05. With this criterion we could reject the thesis that the proportion tuned in on the Tuesday evening in question was less than 27 % or more than 33 % of the sets within range; that is, the advertiser will base his decisions on the assumption that the number of sets tuned in was somewhere between 540000 and 660000. These are called the 95 % *confidence limits* for the composition of the parent population; the probability that such a sample might have been drawn from a population with a parameter outside these limits is less than 0·05.

2.4 To sum up, the method of proceeding from the observation of a sample to a conclusion about the parent population is as follows:

(1) Set up various hypotheses about the composition of the parent population.

(2) For each hypothesis, consider the set of all possible samples which might be drawn from this population and calculate a probability function for a suitable statistic.

(3) Ask a suitable question about the probability of obtaining a statistic-value such as the one observed.

(4) Using some suitable criterion, find whether the observed sample could 'reasonably' have been drawn from the parent population.

(5) Reject any hypotheses about the parent population which are considered unreasonable.

Exercise B

1. Are the graphs in Figure 3 congruent to each other? If not, explain how they differ.

2. Investigate the hypothesis that 28 % of the sets in the region were tuned in: (a) if a sample of 250 produces 75 listeners, (b) if a sample of 4000 produces 1200.

3. Establish 95 % confidence limits for the number of sets in the region tuned in for the two cases described in Question 2.

4. At a General Election an eve-of-poll canvass in one constituency produces the following result:

Conservative, 520; Labour, 480.

What conclusions would you draw about the result of the election in that constituency?

5. A ship carries a cargo of ten thousand pineapples. A dealer examines a random sample of one hundred, and finds twenty bad. What is the largest number of bad fruit that one could reasonably estimate the cargo to contain, using a 1 % probability criterion?

3. THE CENTRAL LIMIT THEOREM

As a bridge to the problem of sampling from a population of numerical measures we shall now summarize the analysis of Section 1 and re-cast it in a form which suggests generalization.

The population with which we were concerned could be represented in the form
$$(L, C, L, L, C, ..., C, L),$$
in which the letter L (for Labour) appears 25000 times and the letter C (for Conservative) 15000 times. The probability of obtaining the letter L at a single draw is equal to the proportion of occurrences of this letter in the population, that is $\frac{5}{8}$.

Now we have seen that it is often useful to 'code' the elements of a population of attributes by using the mark 1 to denote success (which we shall, for this example, regard from the standpoint of the Labour party) and 0 to denote failure. The population would then be written
$$(1, 0, 1, 1, 0, ..., 0, 1).$$

Let the proportion of successes in the population be a, and the proportion of failures b; so that, if the population has N members in all, the number of ones is Na, and the number of zeros Nb. Clearly a and b are the probabilities of success and failure at a single draw. The population can therefore be represented graphically as in Figure 4(a).

The point of this coding is that it enables us to carry out numerical calculations on the members of the population. For example, if x stands for a typical member, we may write, using the notation of expected values,

$$\mu = E[x] = 0.b + 1.a = a;$$

so that the population mean is just the proportion of successes. Furthermore

$$\sigma^2 = E[(x-\mu)^2] = a^2.b + (1-a)^2.a$$
$$= a^2 b + b^2 a$$
$$= ab(a+b)$$
$$= ab,$$

so that $\qquad \sigma = \sqrt{(ab)}.$

(a) Parent population

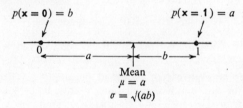

(b) Population of sample totals (not to scale)

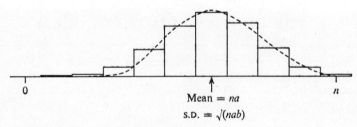

(c) Population of sample means

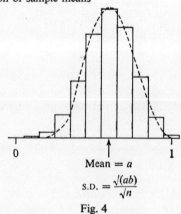

Fig. 4

1156

From this parent population samples are drawn, and the number of successes in the sample counted. Now with the 0, 1 coding the number of successes is simply the sample total. For example, a sample of size ten,

$$(0, 1, 1, 1, 0, 0, 1, 1, 0, 1),$$

with six successes, has a total of

$$0+1+1+1+0+0+1+1+0+1 = 6.$$

If therefore the size of the sample in general is n, the probability of a sample total of i is given by the coefficient of t^i in $(b+at)^n$. The probability function for sample totals is binomial, with a histogram such as Figure 4(b), which for large n approximates closely to the region under a Normal density curve. We know that the mean of this population of sample totals is na, and the standard deviation $\sqrt{(nab)}$.

Suppose now that each sample total is divided by n, to give a 'sample mean'. This is, in fact, the proportion of successes in the sample. Clearly the sample means themselves constitute a population, and the histogram for this is shown in Figure 4(c). Since each sample mean is $1/n$ times the corresponding sample total, the mean and standard deviation for this population are $1/n$ times those for the population of sample totals; that is, the mean is

$$\frac{na}{n} = a,$$

and the standard deviation

$$\frac{\sqrt{(nab)}}{n} = \frac{\sqrt{(ab)}}{\sqrt{n}}.$$

Remembering that the mean μ and the standard deviation σ of the parent population are a and $\sqrt{(ab)}$ respectively, we can state the result as follows:

> *The central limit theorem.* If samples of size n are drawn at random from a parent population with mean μ and standard deviation σ, the sample means constitute a population with mean μ and standard deviation $\sigma/\sqrt{n}$; and for large n the probability density function for this population approximates to Normal form.

So far this has been demonstrated only for a very special parent population. It is a remarkable fact that it can be proved to be true for any parent population whatever, provided only that the variance is finite.

4. SAMPLING FROM A RECTANGULAR POPULATION

4.1 Before going on with the theoretical discussion it would be useful to get some experience of the way in which the central limit theorem works out in practice. This can easily be done with a simple dice-rolling experiment, which could be carried out either individually or as a class.

First take a single die and roll it a large number of times (a hundred or two would do). After each roll record the score and build up a histogram from the results, as in Figure 5(a). What we are in effect doing is to take samples of size 1 from the parent population (1, 2, 3, 4, 5, 6).

Now take a pair of dice, and after each roll record the mean of the two scores. Build up a histogram as before, as in Figure 5(b), taking care to keep the horizontal scale the same so that the histograms can be compared. In this experiment we are taking the means of samples of size 2 from the same parent population as before.

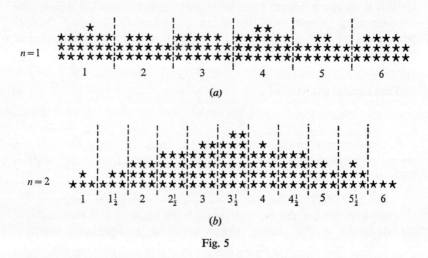

Fig. 5

Continue by repeating the experiment with 3, 4, 5 dice at a time.

Since the histograms record frequency densities from an experiment rather than theoretical probability densities, the central limit theorem will not of course be demonstrated accurately. But since, for a large number of repeated trials, we expect relative frequencies to be approximately equal to probabilities, its main features should show up. That is, every one of the histograms should cluster round the mean of the parent population, which is $3\frac{1}{2}$; but as n, the size of each sample, increases from 1 to 5, the sample means will be spread less widely about this value. More precisely, the standard deviations for the various histograms will be roughly proportional to $1/\sqrt{n}$.

4.2 It is quite a simple matter to find the probability functions corresponding to the experiment just described. For a single die all six possible scores are, of course, equally likely *a priori*, and the probability of any one of them is $\frac{1}{6}$. For two dice the possible sample totals are 2, 3, 4, ..., 12, giving sample means of 1, $1\frac{1}{2}$, 2, ..., 6; from a diagram of the possibility space it is easily seen that the probabilities of these are $\frac{1}{36}, \frac{2}{36}, \frac{3}{36}, ..., \frac{1}{36}$ respectively.

For larger numbers of dice the calculations are much simplified by imagining that, after each roll, the dice are examined successively. If r dice are rolled and a total of t is obtained, then the first $r-1$ dice examined must have shown totals of $t-1, t-2, ..., t-5$ or $t-6$; and the probability of a total of t with r dice, given any one of these totals with the first $r-1$ dice, is $\frac{1}{6}$. If therefore the probability of a total of t with r dice is written as $\phi(t, r)$, the laws of probability give the equation

$$\phi(t, r) = \tfrac{1}{6}\phi(t-1, r-1) + \tfrac{1}{6}\phi(t-2, r-1) + ... + \tfrac{1}{6}\phi(t-6, r-1).$$

In this way the table of probabilities for r dice can be built up from that for $r-1$ dice. The results for $r = 1, 2, 3, 4$ are as follows:

Sample total	Number of dice			
	1	2	3	4
1	1/6	—	—	—
2	1/6	$1/6^2$	—	—
3	1/6	$2/6^2$	$1/6^3$	—
4	1/6	$3/6^2$	$3/6^3$	$1/6^4$
5	1/6	$4/6^2$	$6/6^3$	$4/6^4$
6	1/6	$5/6^2$	$10/6^3$	$10/6^4$
7	—	$6/6^2$	$15/6^3$	$20/6^4$
8	—	$5/6^2$	$21/6^3$	$35/6^4$
9	—	$4/6^2$	$25/6^3$	$56/6^4$
10	—	$3/6^2$	$27/6^3$	$80/6^4$
11	—	$2/6^2$	$27/6^3$	$104/6^4$
12	—	$1/6^2$	$25/6^3$	$125/6^4$
13	—	—	$21/6^3$	$140/6^4$
14	—	—	$15/6^3$	$146/6^4$
15	—	—	$10/6^3$	$140/6^4$
...			...	...
...			...	...

From this we derive a table of probabilities of different sample means by dividing the sample totals by the number of dice rolled:

Sample mean	Number of dice			
	1	2	3	4
1	1/6	$1/6^2$	$1/6^3$	$1/6^4$
			$3/6^3$	$4/6^4$
		$2/6^2$	$6/6^3$	$10/6^4$
				$20/6^4$
2	1/6	$3/6^2$	$10/6^3$	$35/6^4$
			$15/6^3$	$56/6^4$
		$4/6^2$	$21/6^3$	$80/6^4$
				$104/6^4$
3	1/6	$5/6^2$	$25/6^3$	$125/6^4$
			$27/6^3$	$140/6^4$
		$6/6^2$	$27/6^3$	$146/6^4$
				$140/6^4$
4	1/6	$5/6^2$	$25/6^3$	$125/6^4$
...	...	...	...	...

(Only the upper part of the tables are shown, since there is obviously symmetry about the sample mean $3\frac{1}{2}$.)

The corresponding histograms are drawn in Figure 6. These of course show probability densities, which are respectively 1, 2, 3, 4 times the probabilities given in the table, since the widths of the class-intervals are $1, \frac{1}{2}, \frac{1}{3}, \frac{1}{4}$.

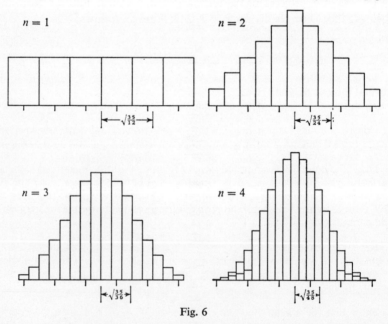

Fig. 6

It is immediately clear that, by taking a larger sample, one is more likely to draw one whose mean is close to the mean of the parent population. This can be shown numerically by calculating standard deviations. The detailed computations will be left to the reader (see Exercise C, Question 4) but the results are as follows:

	Parent population	Population of sample means			
		1 die	2 dice	3 dice	4 dice
Mean	$\mu = 3\frac{1}{2}$	$3\frac{1}{2}$	$3\frac{1}{2}$	$3\frac{1}{2}$	$3\frac{1}{2}$
Standard deviation	$\sigma = \sqrt{\frac{35}{12}}$	$\sqrt{\frac{35}{12}}$	$\sqrt{\frac{35}{24}}$	$\sqrt{\frac{35}{36}}$	$\sqrt{\frac{35}{48}}$

Thus each population of sample means has μ for its mean, and the variances are respectively σ, $\sigma/\sqrt{2}$, $\sigma/\sqrt{3}$ and $\sigma/\sqrt{4}$. We have therefore verified part of the central limit theorem for this particular parent population.

Exercise C

1. Reproduce Figure 1 and re-label the axes so that it refers to a population of sample means (i.e. proportions of Labour voters in samples). What is the mean and the standard deviation of this population?

2. Re-state the central limit theorem so that it refers to a population of sample totals rather than sample means.

3. Carry out (as a class project) experiments with 4, 5, 6 dice, as in Section 4.1. Obtain frequency tables for sample totals, and derive tables showing the *relative frequencies* of possible *sample means*. Draw histograms.

4. Verify the calculations of standard deviation for 1, 2, 3, 4 dice given in the table at the end of Section 4.2.
   (*Hint*: use $\sigma^2 = \Sigma(x_i - \mu)^2 f(x_i)$ rather than the alternative form.)

5. Construct a table of probabilities for a population of sample means when five dice are rolled and draw a histogram. Calculate the mean and standard deviation.

6. Draw the graph of the Normal density function with the mean and standard deviation you have calculated in Question 5. For this function calculate the probabilities that the variable lies within the intervals $(0.9, 1.1)$, $(1.1, 1.3)$, ..., $(5.9, 6.1)$. Compare these with the probabilities given in your table in Question 5, and comment on the result.

7. Repeat the experiments of Question 3, except that wherever a die shows a 2, count it as a 5. Calculate the means and standard deviations of the populations of sample totals and deduce the values of these statistics for the populations of sample means.

8. Show that for a single fair die with faces 1, 3, 4, 5, 5, 6 as in Question 7, $\mu = 4$ and $\sigma^2 = \frac{8}{3}$. Use the Central Limit Theorem to write down the parameters for the means of samples of 2, 3, 4, 5 such dice. Compare your answers with those obtained for Question 7.

9. A bag contains five tickets numbered 1, 3, 9, 11, 15. Calculate the mean and standard deviation of these numbers. Samples of two tickets are taken from this bag with replacement. (That is, one ticket is drawn and its number recorded; it is then replaced in the bag before a second ticket is withdrawn and recorded.) Draw up a table with one box for each possible sample, and record in each box the corresponding sample mean. Hence make up a table of probabilities of the different possible sample means, and calculate the mean and standard deviation for this population of sample means.

10. In a table of random numbers replace every even digit by a zero. Calculate the theoretical mean and variance of all the digits in the table. From the table take a large number of samples of ten digits each, and find the mean of each sample. Calculate the mean and variance of your population of sample means, and comment on the result.

5. SAMPLING FROM MORE GENERAL POPULATIONS

5.1 The situation illustrated in the foregoing examples can be summarized as follows:

(i) We begin with a parent population P of values of x. With this is associated a probability function, which may take any form whatever provided only that the variance of x in the population is finite. The mean of the parent population will be denoted by μ, and its variance by σ^2.

(ii) Random samples of fixed size n are drawn from the parent population. (If the population is finite, the sampling must be 'with replacement'.)

(iii) The mean values of x in the samples are calculated; these will be denoted by m. They are members of a population M of sample means, and there is a corresponding probability function for this population.

(iv) The expected value of m in M is equal to μ, and the variance of m in M is σ^2/n.

The proofs of the results in (iv) for a completely general parent population are rather difficult. Three different approaches are discussed in Sections 5, 6 and 7. If the reader chooses to omit these sections, he can still apply the results to the problems of Exercise D, Questions 15–18.

In any case, no proof is attempted here of the other part of the Central Limit Theorem, that for large n the population M is approximately Normal. We have demonstrated this for a rectangular parent population (which is symmetrical), and for a binomial one (whether symmetrical or not). In Exercise C, Questions 7 and 10, the values of n chosen were too small, though the tendency towards Normality may have been suggested.

*__5.2__ In this section, we approach the results in (iv) directly, starting with a parent population P having only three members a, b, c each with probability $\frac{1}{3}$. We shall suppose the elements of a sample to be taken one at a time, so that if samples of size 2 are taken then there are 3^2 equally likely possible samples:

$$a, a; \quad b, a; \quad c, a; \quad a, b; \quad b, b; \quad c, b; \quad a, c; \quad b, c; \quad c, c.$$

M consists of the numbers

$$\frac{a+a}{2}, \quad \frac{b+a}{2}, \quad \frac{c+a}{2}, \quad \frac{a+b}{2}, \quad \frac{b+b}{2}, \quad \frac{c+b}{2}, \quad \frac{a+c}{2}, \quad \frac{b+c}{2}, \quad \frac{c+c}{2},$$

with associated probabilities all equal to $\frac{1}{9}$.

The mean of this population is denoted by $E[m]$, and

$$\begin{aligned}
E[m] &= \left(\frac{a+a}{2} + \frac{b+a}{2} + \frac{c+a}{2} + \frac{a+b}{2} + \ldots\right) \times \frac{1}{9} \\
&= \frac{6(a+b+c)}{2} \times \frac{1}{9} \\
&= \tfrac{1}{3}(a+b+c) \\
&= \mu.
\end{aligned}$$

In the extended form of $E[m]$, we notice that each letter occurs first in each of three samples and also second in each of three samples. If samples of size n had been taken, each letter would occur 3^{n-1} times in each of the n positions in a sample—$n.3^{n-1}$ times in all. But there are now 3^n equally likely samples, so we have

$$\begin{aligned}
E[m] &= \left(\frac{a+a+\ldots a}{n} + \frac{b+a+a+\ldots a}{n} + \ldots\right) \times \frac{1}{3^n} \\
&= \frac{n.3^{n-1}(a+b+c)}{n} \times \frac{1}{3^n} \\
&= \mu.
\end{aligned}$$

It is easy now to make a further generalization to the case where samples of size n are drawn from a parent population with a finite number N of members each with equal probabilities $1/N$.

*5.3 Finding the variance of m in M is greatly simplified if we assume that the origin has been chosen at the mean of the parent population.

Then with the simple parent population (a, b, c) again, $a+b+c = 0$ and $\sigma^2 = \tfrac{1}{3}(a^2+b^2+c^2)$.

The variance of m in M is

$$\left(\left(\frac{a+a}{2}\right)^2 + \left(\frac{b+a}{2}\right)^2 + \left(\frac{c+a}{2}\right)^2 + \left(\frac{a+b}{2}\right)^2 + \left(\frac{b+b}{2}\right)^2 + \left(\frac{c+b}{2}\right)^2 \right.$$
$$\left. + \left(\frac{a+c}{2}\right)^2 + \left(\frac{b+c}{2}\right)^2 + \left(\frac{c+c}{2}\right)^2\right) \times \frac{1}{9}$$
$$= \left(\frac{a^2+2a^2+a^2}{4} + \frac{b^2+2ba+a^2}{4} + \frac{c^2+2ca+a^2}{4} + \ldots\right) \times \frac{1}{9}.$$

1163

This simplifies to $\qquad \dfrac{6(a^2+b^2+c^2)}{4}\times\dfrac{1}{9} = \dfrac{\sigma^2}{2}.$

The middle terms in the contribution from each sample give

$$\left(\frac{2a^2+2ba+2ca+2ab+2b^2+2cb+2ac+2bc+2c^2}{4}\right)\times\frac{1}{9}$$

$$= \frac{(a+b+c)(a+b+c)}{2}\times\frac{1}{9} = 0.$$

a^2, b^2, c^2 each appear a further 6 times.

Again, this proof can be extended (see Exercise D, Question 1), and the expression σ^2/n obtained for samples of size n from a parent population of any finite size N.

This method is based on fundamental ideas, but is difficult to formulate precisely. For this reason, among others, the alternative proofs given in Sections 6 and 7 are preferable.

*6. EXPECTATION ALGEBRA

6.1 We have introduced the notation $E[g(x)]$ in discussing probability parameters, and have used the definition

$$E[g(x)] = \sum_{i=1}^{i=n} g(x_i)p(x_i),$$

where the possibility space consists of discrete values $x_1, x_2, \ldots, x_n$. The definition

$$E[g(x)] = \int_{L}^{R} g(x)\phi(x)\,dx$$

is used when populations are drawn from a continuum.

In both cases we made the definitions $\mu = E[x]$ and $\sigma^2 = E[(x-\mu)^2]$.

This section develops the algebra associated with the expected value notation, and uses it to derive the results of Section 5. Most of the intermediate working has been suggested in the exercises of Chapter 26.

There are three basic results:

(1) **E[k] = k, where k is a constant,**

(2) **E[g(x)+h(x)] = E[g(x)]+E[h(x)],**

(3) **E[c.g(x)] = c.E[g(x)], where c is a constant.**

These are reminiscent of the basic properties of the Σ-notation:

$(1')\ \displaystyle\sum_{i=1}^{i=n} k = kn,$

$(2')\ \displaystyle\sum_{i=1}^{i=n} (g(x_i)+h(x_i)) = \sum_{i=1}^{i=n} g(x_i)+\sum_{i=1}^{i=n} h(x_i),$

$(3')\ \displaystyle\sum_{i=1}^{i=n} c.g(x_i) = c\sum_{i=1}^{i=n} g(x_i).$

Indeed, in the discrete case (1), (2) and (3) follow directly from the definition of expected values and (1'), (2'), (3'). The proofs are similar in the 'continuous' case using the properties of integrals.

The alternative expression for variance may now be derived as follows:

$$\begin{aligned}
\sigma^2 &= E[(x-\mu)^2] \\
&= E[x^2 - 2\mu x + \mu^2] \\
&= E[x^2] + E[-2\mu x] + E[\mu^2], \quad \text{using (2)} \\
&= E[x^2] - 2\mu E[x] + E[\mu^2], \quad \text{using (3)} \\
&= E[x^2] - 2\mu . \mu + \mu^2, \quad \text{using (1)} \\
&= E[x^2] - \mu^2.
\end{aligned}$$

This proof is equally applicable for the two types of probability model. With statistical populations we have often used the linear change of variable $x = k + ct$. The proof that $E[x] = k + cE[t]$ is straightforward; this corresponds, of course, to $\bar{x} = k + c\bar{t}$. It is now useful to introduce the notation $V[g(x)]$ to stand for $E[(g(x)-\gamma)^2]$ where $\gamma = E[g(x)]$. This may look rather forbidding, but it enables us to write $V[x]$ for the variance σ^2, and show that $V[k+ct] = c^2 V[t]$, a result which also has its counterpart in statistics and might have been used in Chapter 26 to simplify the calculation of probability parameters.

6.2 Combinations of two populations.

Suppose we have two populations with possibility spaces $\{x_1, x_2, ..., x_n\}$ and $\{y_1, y_2, ..., y_{n'}\}$ which may be the same or different. Then we can ascribe a meaning to $E[x+y]$ and $E[xy]$. The probability that x_i from the first population is paired with y_j from the second is denoted by the symbol p_{ij}. Now when we write

$$E[x] = \Sigma x_i p(x_i),$$

$p(x_i)$ is the total probability of x_i being chosen, irrespective of its pair from the y-population, so

$$p(x_i) = p_{i1} + p_{i2} + ... + p_{in'} = \sum_{j=1}^{j=n'} p_{ij}.$$

Similarly, if $p'(y_j)$ is the probability associated with y_j,

$$p'(y_j) = \sum_{i=1}^{i=n} p_{ij}.$$

To find the expected value of $x+y$ or xy, a summation must be carried out for all possible pairs, in other words for all i and all j.

$$\begin{aligned}
E[x+y] &= \sum_{i=1}^{i=n} \sum_{j=1}^{j=n'} (x_i + y_j)p_{ij} = \sum_i \sum_j x_i p_{ij} + \sum_i \sum_j y_j p_{ij} \\
&= \sum_i x_i p(x_i) + \sum_j y_j p'(y_j) \\
&= E[x] + E[y].
\end{aligned}$$

1165

The second step is justified since it does not matter in which order the ij elements are summed.

Again
$$E[xy] = \sum_i \sum_j x_i y_j p_{ij},$$

but this expression can only be simplified if we assume that the x's and y's are paired independently. Then $p_{ij} = p(x_i).p'(y_j)$, and

$$E[xy] = \sum_i \sum_j x_i y_j p(x_i) p'(y_j)$$

$$= \sum_i x_i p(x_i).E[y]$$

$$= E[x].E[y].$$

These proofs are most easily understood by considering simple specific examples (see Exercise D, Questions 6 and 7).

We now have all the basic results required for further developments; the two discussed in this section also apply to populations drawn from a continuum, though the proofs are omitted.

(4) **E[x+y] = E[x]+E[y] whether x and y are independent or not,**

(5) **E[xy] = E[x].E[y] if x and y are independent.**

We now deduce a result of great importance. If

$$E[x] = \mu \quad \text{and} \quad E[y] = \nu,$$

we can write
$$E[x+y] = \mu+\nu, \quad \text{using (4).}$$
Then

$$V[x+y] = E[((x+y)-(\mu+\nu))^2]$$

$$= E[(x-\mu)^2+2(x-\mu)(y-\nu)+(y-\nu)^2]$$

$$= E[(x-\mu)^2]+E[2(x-\mu)(y-\nu)]+E[(y-\nu)^2], \text{ using (4) again,}$$

$$= V[x]+2E[(x-\mu)(y-\nu)]+V[y].$$

$E[(x-\mu)(y-\nu)]$ is called the *covariance* of x and y, and its size indicates the extent of the *correlation* between x and y. If x and y are independent, so are $(x-\mu)$ and $(y-\nu)$, and (using (5))

$$E[(x-\mu)(y-\nu)] = E[x-\mu].E[y-\nu] = 0.$$

Then
$$V[x+y] = V[x]+V[y].$$
It can be deduced that

$$V[x+y+z] = V[x]+V[y]+V[z]$$

if x, y, z are independent, and the result can be extended by induction to apply to any number of independent variables.

1166

6.3 Applications to sampling. Suppose a sample $(e_1, e_2, ..., e_n)$ is drawn from a parent population with parameters μ and σ. Then if random sampling *with replacement* is employed, the e_i's are independent and

$$E[e_i] = \mu, \quad V[e_i] = \sigma^2 \quad \text{for} \quad i = 1, 2, ..., n.$$

The mean of the sample is given by

$$m = \frac{e_1 + e_2 + ... + e_n}{n},$$

and

$$E[m] = E\left[\frac{e_i + e_2 + ... + e_n}{n}\right]$$

$$= \frac{1}{n}(E[e_1] + E[e_2] + ... + E[e_n])$$

$$= \frac{1}{n} . n\mu$$

$$= \mu.$$

Also

$$V[m] = V\left[\frac{e_1 + e_2 + ... + e_n}{n}\right]$$

$$= \frac{1}{n^2} V[e_1 + e_2 + ... + e_n]$$

$$= \frac{1}{n^2}(V[e_1] + V[e_2] + ... + V[e_n])$$

$$= \frac{1}{n^2} . n\sigma^2$$

$$= \frac{\sigma^2}{n}.$$

These are the results of Section 5.1.

*7. USE OF GENERATORS

7.1 The results of the preceding section can also be obtained with the help of generators. Indeed, the special case of the sampling of attributes, which led up to the statement of the central limit theorem at the end of Section 3, has already been discussed using this technique; for the values na and $\sqrt{(nab)}$ for the mean and standard deviation of the population of sample totals, on which the argument rested, were obtained in Chapter 26, Section 5.4, from the binomial generator $(b+at)^n$. What follows is a generalization of the method used there.

We begin with a result about the generator for the combined scores from two separate experiments (see p. 780, Question 6):

Theorem. If the functions

$$G(t) = p_0 + p_1 t + p_2 t^2 + p_3 t^3 + \dots$$

and
$$H(t) = q_0 + q_1 t + q_2 t^2 + q_3 t^3 + \dots$$

generate the probabilities of scores 0, 1, 2, 3, ... in two independent experiments, then the function $G(t)H(t)$ generates the probabilities of total scores 0, 1, 2, 3, ... from the two experiments together.

To see this, consider, for example, the coefficients of t^3 in the product. This is
$$p_0 q_3 + p_1 q_2 + p_2 q_1 + p_3 q_0.$$

Now since the experiments are independent, $p_0 q_3$ is the probability of obtaining a score of 0 in the first and a score of 3 in the second; $p_1 q_2$ is the probability of a score of 1 in the first and a score of 2 in the second; and so on. These are exclusive events which together make up all the ways of getting a total score of 3 from the two experiments together; and the sum of the probabilities therefore gives the probability of obtaining a total score of 3.

A similar argument holds for all the coefficients in the product, and it follows that $G(t)H(t)$ is the generator for the probabilities of the total scores from the two experiments.

7.2 Sampling (with replacement) from a given parent population may be regarded as a sequence of n independent experiments, each consisting of the selection of one member from the parent population. If $G(t)$ denotes the generator for the probabilities of the various members of the parent population, then this is also the generator for the probabilities of scores in each individual experiment. A simple inductive argument based on the theorem of the preceding section therefore gives the following result:

Theorem. If $G(t)$ is the generator for the probabilities of various scores in a parent population, and $F(t)$ is the generator for the probabilities of total scores in the population of samples of size n, then

$$F(t) = \{G(t)\}^n.$$

The binomial probability function, based on the generator

$$G(t) = b + at$$

(see Figure 4(*a*), Section 3), is a special case of this result.

7.3 It is now a simple matter to derive the formulae for the mean and standard deviation for the population of sample totals. We recall the

1168

results established in Chapter 26, Section 5, that for a population whose probabilities are generated by the function $G(t)$,

$$\text{population mean} = G'(1)$$

and $\qquad\qquad \text{population variance} = G''(1)+G'(1)-\{G'(1)\}^2.$

We shall also need the fact that, for any probability generator,

$$G(1) = p_0+p_1+p_2+p_3+\dots$$
$$= 1.$$

Now if $G(t)$ is the generator for the parent population, we know that

$$\mu = G'(1)$$

and $\qquad\qquad \sigma^2 = G''(1)+G'(1)-\{G'(1)\}^2;$

and the problem is to evaluate the corresponding parameters for the population of sample totals with generator $F(t)$.

This is a simple exercise in differentiation. Since

$$F(t) = \{G(t)\}^n,$$

it follows that $\quad F'(t) = n\{G(t)\}^{n-1}G'(t)$

and $\qquad\qquad F''(t) = n(n-1)\{G(t)\}^{n-2}\{G'(t)\}^2+n\{G(t)\}^{n-1}G''(t).$

Therefore $\qquad\qquad F'(1) = n.1^{n-1}.G'(1)$

$$= n\mu,$$

and $\qquad\qquad F''(1) = n(n-1).1^{n-2}.\{G'(1)\}^2+n.1^{n-1}.G''(1)$

$$= n(n-1)\{G'(1)\}^2+nG''(1);$$

so that

$$F''(1)+F'(1)-\{F'(1)\}^2 = n(n-1)\{G'(1)\}^2+nG''(1)+nG'(1)-\{nG'(1)\}^2$$
$$= nG''(1)+nG'(1)-n\{G'(1)\}^2$$
$$= n\sigma^2.$$

This proves that the population of sample totals has mean $n\mu$ and variance $n\sigma^2$ (that is, standard deviation $\sigma\sqrt{n}$).

To find the parameters for the population M of sample means, it is merely necessary to divide the mean and standard deviation for the sample totals by n. This gives, for the population of sample means,

$$\text{mean} = \mu$$

and $\qquad\qquad \text{standard deviation} = \sigma/\sqrt{n}.$

This therefore establishes the results quoted in Section 5.1 for any parent population of integral scores.

Exercise D

1. (a) Extend the working of Section 5.3 to the case where samples of size 2 are taken from the parent population $\{a, b, c, d\}$ with equal probabilities $\frac{1}{4}$.

(b) Repeat for samples of size 3 taken from the parent population $\{a, b, c\}$ with equal probabilities $\frac{1}{3}$.

(c) Repeat for samples of size n taken from a parent population with N members each with probability $1/N$.

2. Show that $E[x - \mu] = 0$ if $E[x] = \mu$.

3. (a) Write out the proof of result (1) of Section 6.1 for both types of probability model.

(b) Write out in full the proofs that

$$E[k + ct] = k + cE[t] \quad \text{and} \quad V[k + ct] = c^2 V[t],$$

where k and c are constants.

4. A grocer sells raisins in packets which have mean net mass 320 g and standard deviation 12 g, and candied peel in cartons which have mean mass 160 g and standard deviation 7 g. Housewives who shop at this grocer's each use one packet of raisins and one carton of peel in making a Christmas cake. Find the expected value and variance of the total mass of fruit used in a cake.

5. A man goes to work by driving to the outskirts of a town and then catching a bus. He always starts his return journey at 5.30 p.m.; the time taken by the bus has mean 16 min and standard deviation 3 min, while the drive by car takes a mean 24 min with standard deviation 2 min. Assuming that these times are independent, find the mean and standard deviation of the total time for the journey. In what way, if at all, would your answers be changed if you think this assumption incorrect?

Make a further assumption (which should be stated) and find the probability that he will arrive home after 6.15 p.m.

6.

$y_3 = 6$	0·03	0·05	0·2	0·2
$y_2 = 2$	0·04	0·1	0·05	0·08
$y_1 = 1$	0·1	0·03	0·05	0·07
	$x_1 = 3$	$x_2 = 7$	$x_3 = 8$	$x_4 = 10$

The table gives the probabilities of each member of the x-population being paired with each member of the y-population. Thus, using the notation of Section 6.2, $p_{42} = 0·08$, for example, and in the population of values of $x + y$ the number 12 occurs with probability 0·08.

Find $E[x]$, $E[y]$, and $E[x + y]$, and show in detail how the first proof of Section 6.2 applies in this case.

Find also $E[xy]$, and comment on your answer.

7. With the same possibility spaces as in Question 6, but with all the probabilities equal to $\frac{1}{12}$, find $E[x]$, $E[y]$, $E[x + y]$, $E[xy]$, $V[x]$, $V[y]$, $V[x + y]$. Do your answers satisfy the relations of Section 6.2?

1170

8. (a) Prove that $E[x-y] = E[x] - E[y]$ and that $V[x-y] = V[x] + V[y]$ if x and y are independent.

(b) Lengths of firehose are joined by fitting the 'arm' end of one into the 'sleeve' end of the other. The arms have mean external diameter 7 cm, and the sleeves have mean internal diameter 7·4 cm. If the variances are both 0·04 cm², find the probability that the difference in diameter of a pair chosen at random will be less than 0·2 cm or greater than 0·6 cm.

9. Make up a table similar to that in Question 6, but with x and y independent; the probabilities should not all be equal.

Verify that
$$V[x+y] = V[x-y] = V[x] + V[y].$$

10. Show that the covariance of x and y can be written $E[xy] - E[x]E[y]$. Find its value for the population of Question 6. Under what circumstances will the covariance be negative? Make up a simple example to show that the covariance can be zero without x and y being independent.

11. (a) Use the relation $F(t) = G(t).H(t)$, where F, G, and H are the probability generators for $x+y$, x, y, to prove

$$E[x+y] = E[x] + E[y] \quad \text{and} \quad V[x+y] = V[x] + V[y]$$

for independent x and y.

(b) Explain why $F(t) = G(t).H(1/t)$ gives the probability generator for $x-y$ and hence prove that
$$V[x-y] = V[x] + V[y].$$

(c) Is it possible to prove $E[xy] = E[x].E[y]$ using probability generators?

12. Prove that the generator for the probabilities of scores on a throw of a single die can be written in the form

$$\tfrac{1}{6}t(1-t^6)(1-t)^{-1}.$$

Deduce the generator for the probabilities of total scores on three dice; and, using the expansion for $(1-t)^{-3}$, deduce the third column of the table of probabilities of various sample totals given in Section 4.2.

13. A die is rolled repeatedly until ten sixes have appeared. Find a generator for the probabilities that various numbers of rolls will be needed. If you wanted to bet that you would get ten sixes in a total of not more than N rolls, what value would you choose for N to have a 99·9 % certainty of winning?

14. On average 2 % of the transistors produced by a machine are faulty. A sample batch of 100 transistors is examined. Write down the generator giving the probabilities that 0, 1, 2, 3, ... of the transistors in the sample are faulty. Using the fact that (see Chapter 29, Exercise D, Question 11) for large values of n $\{1 + (r/n)\}^n$ is approximately equal to e^r, show that this generator is approximately $e^{2(t-1)}$, and deduce the probabilities of 0, 1, 2, ..., 6 faulty transistors in the batch. Calculate also the mean and standard deviation for the number of faulty specimens in a sample. (This is an example of a *Poisson probability function*.)

15. Samples of size 50 are taken from a population with mean 17 and standard deviation 4. Draw a graph showing the approximate probability density function for the means of the samples, and calculate the probability of obtaining a sample whose mean is less than 16.

16. Packets of butter, of nominal mass 240 g, are turned out by machine with mean mass 241·5 g and standard deviation 3 g. Give approximately the probability of being sold an underweight packet. If the butter is packed in boxes of 36 packets, what is the probability of getting a box for which the mean mass is less than 240 g per packet?

17. A map shows the distances between the centres of towns to the nearest mile. In planning a long journey I add up 25 such distances in order to find the total mileage. What is the probability that this gives the total distance to the nearest mile?

18. In a game of ludo a player is within reach of home in one throw when he has scored a total of 64 on his die. Find the probability that he will achieve this within sixteen throws.

(*Hint*. Find the probability of getting 64 or more in exactly 16 throws.)

8. POPULATIONS OF OTHER SAMPLE STATISTICS

8.1 So far we have concentrated our attention entirely on the population M of sample means and its relation to the parent population P; but it would, of course, be possible to investigate the probability functions for sample statistics other than the mean. For example, we might take samples of given size n from a parent population and calculate for each the median, or the range, or the largest element. These would all give new populations, whose probability functions could be found.

8.2 A particularly important statistic to examine from this point of view is the variance v, or s^2. We shall begin by studying one or two examples in some detail.

One very simple case is when samples of size 1 are drawn from the parent population. The variance of such a sample is, of course, zero; so that the probability function for the variance takes the value 1 for $v = 0$, and 0 otherwise.

For samples of size 2, comprising two numbers e_1 and e_2, the variance is

$$\frac{1}{2}\left\{\left(\frac{e_1-e_2}{2}\right)^2 + \left(\frac{e_2-e_1}{2}\right)^2\right\} = \tfrac{1}{4}(e_1-e_2)^2.$$

Let us investigate the variances of the samples of size 2 taken from the parent population (1, 2, 3, 4, 5, 6), which we may obtain by rolling a pair of dice. The variances of the 36 possible samples can be shown in a table as follows:

1172

Sample variance

Score on red die	1	2	3	4	5	6
6	$\frac{25}{4}$	$\frac{16}{4}$	$\frac{9}{4}$	$\frac{4}{4}$	$\frac{1}{4}$	0
5	$\frac{16}{4}$	$\frac{9}{4}$	$\frac{4}{4}$	$\frac{1}{4}$	0	$\frac{1}{4}$
4	$\frac{9}{4}$	$\frac{4}{4}$	$\frac{1}{4}$	0	$\frac{1}{4}$	$\frac{4}{4}$
3	$\frac{4}{4}$	$\frac{1}{4}$	0	$\frac{1}{4}$	$\frac{4}{4}$	$\frac{9}{4}$
2	$\frac{1}{4}$	0	$\frac{1}{4}$	$\frac{4}{4}$	$\frac{9}{4}$	$\frac{16}{4}$
1	0	$\frac{1}{4}$	$\frac{4}{4}$	$\frac{9}{4}$	$\frac{16}{4}$	$\frac{25}{4}$

Score on green die

By counting the numbers of entries for each possible variance the following probabilities are obtained:

Variance (v)	Probability	
0	6/36	0
$\frac{1}{4}$	10/36	10/144
1	8/36	32/144
$2\frac{1}{4}$	6/36	54/144
4	4/36	64/144
$6\frac{1}{4}$	2/36	50/144
		210/144

The final column is the product of the variance and the respective probability, so that the sum gives the expected value of the variance. This is

$$E[v] = \tfrac{210}{144} = \tfrac{35}{24}.$$

The probability function is illustrated in Figure 7; but it is more striking to convert probabilities into probability densities over suitable intervals, and to show these in a histogram such as Figure 8.

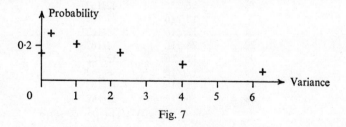

Fig. 7

It is interesting to note that the variance of the parent population (1, 2, 3, 4, 5, 6) has been calculated as $\tfrac{35}{12}$ (see Section 4.2). Thus the expected value of the sample variance is just half the population variance. These two parameters are shown in Figure 8; and it will be noticed that the great majority of samples have a variance which is less than that of the population from which the samples are drawn. We might expect this, since each sample has its variance calculated from its own mean (not the mean of the parent population), so that even if the sample is concentrated far from the mean of P the variance is not necessarily large.

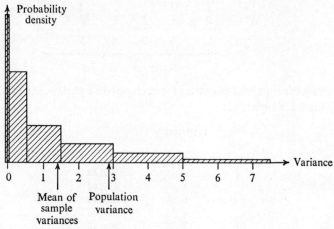

Fig. 8

For samples of size 3 drawn from the same population, it can be shown that the table of probabilities is as follows:

Variance (v)	Probability	
0	6/216	0
$\frac{2}{9}$	30/216	5/162
$\frac{2}{3}$	24/216	12/162
$\frac{8}{9}$	24/216	16/162
$1\frac{5}{9}$	36/216	42/162
2	18/216	27/162
$2\frac{2}{3}$	12/216	24/162
$2\frac{8}{9}$	24/216	52/162
$3\frac{5}{9}$	12/216	32/162
$4\frac{2}{9}$	12/216	38/162
$4\frac{2}{3}$	12/216	42/162
$5\frac{5}{9}$	6/216	25/162

$$E[v] = 315/162 = 35/18$$

A histogram (suitably smoothed) for these probabilities is shown in Figure 9. We now calculate $$E[v] = \tfrac{35}{18},$$

so that the expected value of the sample variance is two-thirds of the population variance. Again most of the samples have a variance less than

1174

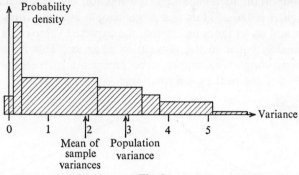

Fig. 9

that of the population, although with the larger sample the proportion of these is not quite so great.

We therefore have, for this particular parent population, the following set of results:

Size of sample	1	2	3
$E[s^2]$	0	$\frac{1}{2}\sigma^2$	$\frac{2}{3}\sigma^2$

These are special cases of a general theorem, which holds for any parent population whatsoever with finite variance:

> If samples of size n are drawn at random from a parent population with variance σ^2, the sample variances constitute a population with mean $\{(n-1)/n\}\sigma^2$.

8.3   The methods used in Section 6 are now applied to give a proof of the theorem just quoted.

With the notation of Section 6.3

$$s^2 = \frac{1}{n} \sum_{i=1}^{i=n} (e_i - m)^2 = \frac{1}{n} \Sigma e_i^2 - m^2 = \frac{1}{n} \Sigma (e_i - \mu)^2 - (m - \mu)^2.$$

Of these three forms for the variance of a typical sample, the last turns out to be the most convenient.

For
$$\begin{aligned}
E[s^2] &= E[(1/n) \ \Sigma(e_i - \mu)^2 - (m - \mu)^2] \\
&= E[(1/n) \ \Sigma(e_i - \mu)^2] - E[(m - \mu)^2] \\
&= (1/n) \ E[\Sigma(e_i - \mu)^2] - V[m] \\
&= (1/n) \ \Sigma(E[(e_i - \mu)^2]) - V[m] \\
&= (1/n) \ \Sigma(V[e_i]) - V[m] \\
&= (1/n).n\sigma^2 - (\sigma^2/n) \\
&= (n-1)/n.\sigma^2.
\end{aligned}$$

1175

8.4 It is important to remark that the fraction $(n-1)/n$ is very nearly equal to 1 if n is large. Thus if a large sample is taken from a parent population and its variance calculated, the expected value of its variance is approximately equal to the population variance. This is hardly surprising; a large sample is more likely to be 'representative' of the population from which it is drawn than is a small one.

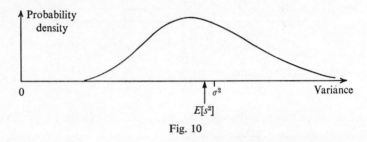

Fig. 10

Nevertheless, even for quite large samples it is possible that the variance may be considerably different from the population variance. It could be very misleading to interpret the expected value as 'the value we expect to get'. As an illustration of this, Figure 10 shows the graph of the probability density for the population of variances of samples of size 25 drawn from a Normal parent population. The spread of this graph is remarkably wide; for example, less than one-third of all the samples have a variance within 10 % of the population variance. This presents serious difficulties when we come to estimate the spread of a parent population from observation of a sample.

Exercise E

1. Take a large number of samples of size 5 from a table of two-digit random numbers, and calculate for each: (*a*) the median, (*b*) the range, (*c*) the largest member. Draw histograms for each of these three sample statistics, and mark on your diagrams the corresponding parameter for the parent population. Comment on your observations.

2. Repeat Question 1 for samples of size 15. What is the effect in each case of increasing the sample size?

3. Find the variance of all the samples of size (*a*) 2, (*b*) 3, which can be drawn from the parent population (1, 2, 3, 4). Calculate in each case the expected value of the variance, and verify the result stated at the end of Section 8.2.

4. Repeat Question 3 for the unsymmetrical parent population (0, 3, 9).

5. If samples of size n are drawn from a Normal parent population, the population of variances (v) of the samples can be shown to have a probability density function proportional to $x^{\frac{1}{2}(n-3)}e^{-x}$, where $x = nv/2\sigma^2$. Draw the graph of this function for $n = 203$, proving that it has a maximum at $x = 100$; and compare its spread with that of Figure 10 (drawn for $n = 25$). Mark the values $E[v]$ and σ^2 on your diagram.

9. ESTIMATION OF POPULATION PARAMETERS

9.1 We are now in a position to discuss further the question first raised in Section 2: how to estimate the characteristics of a parent population from a sample. Previously we concerned ourselves merely with estimating the proportion of the population which possessed a certain attribute; now we shall look at a more complicated situation, in which the sample is drawn from a population of numerical measures. Obviously we cannot determine in this way detailed information about all the individuals; but we shall try to find out what we can about statistical parameters which describe the population, such as its mean and variance.

Suppose, for example, that we wish to discover the effective life of a signal amplifier which is to be used in a space capsule. Since testing takes a long time and involves destroying the article, there is a practical limit to the number of amplifiers that can be examined; on the other hand, since the successful operation of the equipment may be a life-or-death matter, the information is of great importance. The manufacturer decides to test a batch of ten, and obtains the following figures for the effective life in days:

$$192 \cdot 3, \quad 185 \cdot 8, \quad 207 \cdot 3, \quad 263 \cdot 1, \quad 196 \cdot 4,$$
$$232 \cdot 6, \quad 202 \cdot 3, \quad 194 \cdot 0, \quad 224 \cdot 6, \quad 210 \cdot 7.$$

Now this population of ten numbers can be regarded as a sample from a parent population, which consists of the effective lives of all the amplifiers that might be produced to this specification.

We know very little about this parent population. We are unaware, for example, whether its probability function is of rectangular form, or Normal, or negative exponential, etc. But the practical issue is to try to estimate the smallest member of the population, and to know how reliable our estimate is. We know that it is not greater than $185 \cdot 8$ (the smallest member of the sample) and not less than zero; but can we assert, for example, that there is no amplifier whose effective life is less than 150 days with such certainty that we are prepared to risk a man's life on the conclusion? How can we bring our experience of sampling to bear on this problem?

9.2 The problem posed above may be stated in more general form as follows. We have a parent population of numerical measures which can be described with the help of a number of parameters such as the mean μ, the variance σ^2, the range ρ, and so on; our particular concern for the present is with the least member λ. It is conventional to denote the population parameters by Greek letters; and usually all these parameters are unknown. (The comparative simplicity of the situation discussed in

1177

Section 2 rested on the fact that there was essentially only one population parameter involved, the proportion of sets tuned in.)

To obtain information about the population, a sample is taken, and from this various statistics are calculated. These are usually denoted by the corresponding italic letters: the mean m, variance s^2, range r, least member l, etc.

On the basis of these sample statistics we make estimates of the population parameters. These estimates are denoted by Greek letters with circumflex accents: the estimated mean $\hat{\mu}$, estimated variance $\hat{\sigma^2}$, estimated least member $\hat{\lambda}$, and so on. They will be expressed as functions of the sample statistics; the determination of suitable functions constitutes the problem of *point estimation*.

It is important to emphasize that, in the determination of estimators, mathematics will take us only a certain way. We are no longer in the realm of 'right' and 'wrong' answers, but of 'informed guesswork'. On one occasion we may decide that one estimator for, say, the population variance is most appropriate; on another a different estimator may be thought more suitable. Various criteria have been proposed for what might be considered a good estimator, but these criteria are not always consistent with each other.

It should also be pointed out that the estimator for some population parameter may involve sample statistics other than the obvious corresponding one. This is well illustrated by the example discussed in Section 9.1. For the sample the least member is $l = 185{\cdot}8$; but in estimating the least member of the population, it would seem obvious that the other members of the sample are also relevant. For example, if the sample values were

$$186{\cdot}2, \quad 185{\cdot}8, \quad 186{\cdot}0, \quad 185{\cdot}9, \quad 186{\cdot}3,$$
$$185{\cdot}9, \quad 186{\cdot}7, \quad 186{\cdot}3, \quad 186{\cdot}5, \quad 185{\cdot}9,$$

then we might be so impressed by the consistency that we would confidently assert that the least member of the population is greater than $185{\cdot}0$. But the situation would be very different if the sample values were

$$517{\cdot}3, \quad 185{\cdot}8, \quad 732{\cdot}4, \quad 263{\cdot}0, \quad 526{\cdot}8,$$
$$357{\cdot}1, \quad 442{\cdot}9, \quad 410{\cdot}3, \quad 197{\cdot}4, \quad 625{\cdot}6,$$

even though the value of l for this sample is the same as for the other one. Thus the estimator $\hat{\lambda}$ will not be expressed solely in terms of l: indeed, it might be given as a function of, say, m and s not involving l at all. The simple rule for estimating a population parameter, 'take a sample and measure the corresponding sample statistic', would be a bad one to use in this instance.

9.3 How, then, do we go about finding an estimator for a particular population parameter? The short answer to this question is that we make use of the experience which we have built up of the results of sampling from given parent populations. We shall illustrate the point by discussing the estimation of the two most important population parameters: the mean and the variance.

(i) *Point estimation of the mean.* We have seen that, if samples are taken from a parent population with mean μ, then the means of samples form a population which clusters round the value μ. More precisely, the expected value of the sample mean is μ, and the standard deviation is $\sigma/\sqrt{n}$. Figure 11 shows a typical probability density graph for a population of sample means.

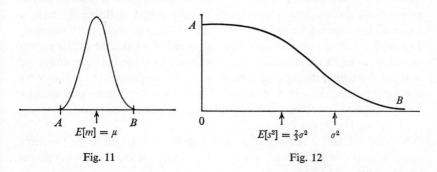

Fig. 11   Fig. 12

Now the mean, m, of the sample which we actually observe might reasonably fall anywhere between the values at the points A and B on the diagram. Therefore, even if m is known, we cannot state the value of μ with any certainty; but it is clear that the best estimate we are likely to be able to give for it is

$$\hat{\mu} = m.$$

(ii) *Estimation of the variance.* A similar approach to the problem of estimating the variance reveals a somewhat different situation. This is best illustrated by supposing that the sample used to estimate σ^2 is a very small one—say of size 3. Figure 12 shows a typical probability density graph for the population of variances of such samples from a given parent population.

Now it was proved in Section 8.3 that the variances of samples of size 3 have expected value $\frac{2}{3}\sigma^2$. The sample actually selected might reasonably have variance represented by any point between A and B on the diagram; but if it is a 'typical sample' we would be more inclined to take its variance as $\frac{2}{3}\sigma^2$ than as σ^2. Therefore, if we are proposing to estimate the value of σ^2 from a *known* value of s^2, we would probably prefer to take $\hat{\sigma^2}$ as $\frac{3}{2}s^2$ rather than s^2.

Similarly, for a sample of size n, we know that

$$E(s^2) = \frac{n-1}{n} \sigma^2,$$

and so the estimator for population variance is often taken as

$$\widehat{\sigma^2} = \frac{n}{n-1} s^2.$$

A warning should be given, however, against reading too much significance into the factor $n/(n-1)$. One of the difficulties of estimating variance is that, even for quite large samples, the spread of variances obtainable from a given parent population is very wide. Reference to Figure 10, which refers to samples of size 25 drawn from a Normal parent population, shows that a particular sample might quite easily have a variance between about $\frac{1}{2}\sigma^2$ and $\frac{3}{2}\sigma^2$ without being thought at all unusual; so that if a sample with variance s is observed, the variance of the parent population might quite reasonably have had any value between about $\frac{2}{3}s^2$ and $2s^2$. So whilst it might be best to estimate the population variance by the formula above as $\frac{25}{24}s^2$, it would be a mistake to imagine that thereby a high degree of precision is being introduced into the estimate.

9.4 The estimators for μ and σ^2 given in Section 9.3 have the property that their expected values are equal to the respective corresponding population parameters. Thus

$$E[\hat{\mu}] = E[m] = \mu,$$

and $$E[\widehat{\sigma^2}] = E\left[\frac{n}{n-1} s^2\right] = \frac{n}{n-1} E[s^2] = \frac{n}{n-1} \cdot \frac{n-1}{n} \sigma^2 = \sigma^2.$$

Estimators with this property are said to be *unbiassed*. In general, an estimator $\hat{\theta}$ for a population parameter θ is unbiassed if

$$E[\hat{\theta}] = \theta.$$

In this context it must be remembered that the 'expected values' are mean values taken over all possible samples of size n.

10. INTERVAL ESTIMATION

10.1 A single number estimating a population parameter is by itself of little value. It would be far more useful to know a set of values for the parameter which, on the evidence available from the sample, might be regarded as 'not unreasonable'.

This was the procedure adopted in Section 2 to find confidence limits for the proportion of a population possessing a certain attribute. The principles outlined in Section 2.4 remain valid for the more complicated problem of estimating parameters for a population of numerical measures.

We shall illustrate the method by applying it to the estimation of a population mean from sample statistics. The analysis is simplest for large samples, which are more representative of the population from which they are drawn. What constitutes a 'large' sample is not precisely defined; but in general terms a sample whose size is reckoned in hundreds might be considered large enough in this context.

10.2 Estimation from a large sample. Suppose that 400 apples of a certain variety are selected at random and weighed; and that the mean weight of apples in the sample was 156 g, with standard deviation 28 g. What could one assert about the mean weight of apples of this variety?

Let us set up a specific hypothesis—for example, that the mean weight might be 150 g—and investigate whether this is reasonable. We remark first that, if samples of 400 apples are taken from a population with this mean weight, then the population of sample means will have approximately a Normal probability density with mean 150 g and standard deviation $\sigma/20$, where σ is the standard deviation of the population.

Here we run into a difficulty, since the value of σ is not known. The best that we can do is to estimate it. With a sample of size 400, the value of $n/(n-1)$ is almost 1, so that s^2 can be taken as an estimator for σ^2. If we take this to mean that s is used as an estimator for σ, this gives a standard deviation for the population of sample means of 28/20, or 1·4 g.

Could we, then, reasonably draw a sample with mean 156 g if the population of sample means is approximately Normal with mean 150 g and standard deviation 1·4 g? Tables of the Normal probability function show that the probability of a difference as big as 6 g, or 4·3 standard deviations, is of the order of 10^{-5}. This is so small that we certainly reject the hypothesis of a mean weight of 150 g.

It should be clear that if, for example, we decide to reject any hypothesis giving a probability of less than 0·05, then we should not accept any estimate for the population mean which differs from the sample mean by more than about two standard deviations. On this criterion the only values for the population mean which we should not discard are those in the interval (153·2, 158·8). Figure 13 shows the graphs for the parent population corresponding to various population means within this interval; the shaded areas represent the probability of obtaining a sample whose mean differs from the population mean by as much as the observed sample; we have specified that this area should be not less than 0·05 for the population mean to be acceptable.

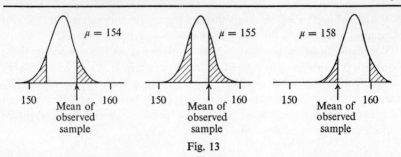

Fig. 13

*10.3   Estimation from a small sample. With a small sample the situation is more complicated. We have already seen that there is greater difficulty in estimating the variance σ^2. But another factor enters into the situation, which is well illustrated by the table at the beginning of Section 8.2; the samples with mean around the population mean of $3\frac{1}{2}$ may have either large or small variances, but those with unusually high or unusually low means all have very small variances. Thus in this case the estimate of σ^2 would depend on the mean of the sample selected. Normal populations form an important exception to this, since their means and variances of samples are independent.

Early this century Gosset—writing under the pseudonym 'Student'—showed that to take account of this a probability function (usually called the t-function) different from the Normal function should be used. This function is tabulated (see *S.M.P. Advanced Tables*) for different values of n and for a variety of criteria of 'unreasonableness', expressed in terms of a minimum acceptable probability. (The quantity ν appearing in the table is in fact $n-1$; it is known as the number of 'degrees of freedom' in the calculation.) The evaluation of the t-function is based on the assumption that the underlying parent population is Normal.

For example, suppose that a sample of ten numbers has mean 15·0 and standard deviation 1·8. We begin, as before, by estimating σ; but the factor $n/(n-1)$ is now important, and we take

$$\widehat{\sigma^2} = \tfrac{10}{9} \times 1\cdot8^2.$$

Then the variance of the population of sample means will be $\widehat{\sigma^2}/10$, or $1\cdot8^2/9$; so that the standard deviation of this population is estimated to be $1\cdot8/3$, or 0·6.

Let us decide to take 'unreasonable' to mean 'having a probability of less than 2%'. We look in the tables under the entry $\nu = 9$ and $P = 2$; this gives $t = 2\cdot82$. The implication is that we should be prepared to accept any value for the population mean which differs from the sample mean by less than $2\cdot82 \times 0\cdot6$, or 1·7. Thus we are prepared to assert that the population from which the given sample was drawn has a mean between 13·3 and 16·7.

1182

Exercise F

1. A sample of 1000 adult men has a mean height of 174·6 cm with standard deviation 5·8 cm. Estimate the interval within which the mean height of adult men in the population lies. State your conclusion clearly and precisely in non-technical language.

2. Two hundred experiments were carried out independently to determine the value of a physical constant. The values obtained had a mean of 9·8094 with standard deviation 0·0523. What could you confidently assert about the true value of the constant?

3. The following is a random sample from a Normal population:

$$30, 62, 16, 34, 46, 46, 43, 49, 27, 29,$$
$$36, 26, 34, 57, 29, 36, 51, 21, 39, 26.$$

Give a 95 % confidence interval for the mean of the population.

4. The annual rainfall in centimetres at Marlborough over the period 1960–65 was as follows:

| 1960 | 111·1 | 1961 | 73·67 | 1962 | 75·24 |
| 1963 | 79·30 | 1964 | 55·55 | 1965 | 79·91 |

Estimate the mean annual rainfall and the standard deviation. What rainfall would you say qualifies for the description 'an abnormally wet year'?

5. With the data of Question 4, establish 95 % confidence limits for the value of the mean annual rainfall at Marlborough. It is in fact known that the mean annual rainfall over the hundred year period 1865–1964 was 83·2 cm. Does this fall within the limits? What conclusion do you draw about long-term changes in the climate?

6. The following determinations of the melting points of pieces of a sample of quartz are made by a metallurgist:

$$1742, \quad 1730, \quad 1768, \quad 1753, \quad 1749, \quad 1761, \quad 1746 \, (°C).$$

Assuming Normality of the parent population of possible readings, give a value *above* which we may be 95 % confident that the melting point will lie. (Use a one-tail criterion; see footnote to Section 2.2.)

7. Samples are taken from a population of $\rho + 1$ consecutive integers with least member λ and range ρ; that is,

$$(\lambda, \lambda+1, \lambda+2, ..., \lambda+\rho).$$

If the samples are of size 2, find the expected values of (*a*) the range *r*, (*b*) the least member *l*, and show that if ρ is not too small these are approximately $\frac{1}{3}(\rho+1)$ and $\lambda+\frac{1}{3}\rho-\frac{1}{6}$.

If the only evidence about a population of this kind is that furnished by a sample of size 2 with least member *l* and range *r*, suggest suitable estimators for ρ and λ. Test the reliability of your estimators by applying the method to samples from a collection of random numbers.

8. If $e_1, e_2, ..., e_n$ is a sample taken from some parent population, prove that

$$k_1 e_1 + k_2 e_2 + ... + k_n e_n$$

is an unbiassed estimator for the mean if the k_i are any numbers such that $\Sigma k_i = 1$. What reason would you give for preferring the estimator with $k_i = 1/n$ to any of the other possibilities? Might there be occasions when you would prefer to use some other values of k_i?

REVISION EXERCISES

36. MORE APPLICATIONS OF INTEGRATION

1. A cylindrical water-trough is 2 m long, and its cross-section is of the same shape as the graph of $\sin x$ for $\frac{1}{2}\pi \leqslant x \leqslant \frac{3}{2}\pi$. When placed so as to hold as much water as possible, the greatest depth is 16 cm. Find how many litres of water it then holds.

2. A beaker is formed by rotating the curve $y^2 = \frac{1}{2}x + 1$ for $0 \leqslant x \leqslant 6$ about the x-axis, and removing the volume generated by rotating the curve $y^2 = \frac{1}{2}x + \frac{3}{4}$ for $\frac{1}{4} \leqslant x \leqslant 6$ about the x-axis. (Units are inches.) Find the volume of plastic needed to make 20 such beakers. To what depth must a beaker be filled in order to half fill it (by volume) with tea?

3. Find the volume and the position of the centre of mass of a frustum of a solid cone formed by rotating the line segment $5x + y = 10$, $0 \leqslant y \leqslant 4$, about the axis of y.

4. As a result of an atomic explosion at a height h above a flat desert, radioactive atoms are deposited on the ground. If the number of atoms deposited per unit area at a distance r from the explosive is ae^{-kr^2}, show that the total number deposited is ae^{-kh^2}/k. Find the area of the circle which contains just half the number of atoms.

5. A plantation of trees in the shape of a trapezium lies on a sloping mountain-side which can be thought of as a plane with gradient 1 in 3. The upper boundary of the plantation is a horizontal fence 300 m long at an elevation of 1750 m above sea-level. The lower boundary is also horizontal, 700 m long, at an elevation of 1550 m. Find the average elevation of the plantation.

The height to which a tree will grow can be taken to be directly proportional to the amount by which its elevation falls short of 2200 m. The trees at the bottom of the plantation are 13 m high. What is the average height of tree in the plantation?

Do the trees at the average elevation grow to average height?

6. From the fact that
$$\int_0^T [f(t) + \lambda g(t)]^2 \, dt$$
is positive for all values of λ, $f(t)$ and $g(t)$ being given functions of t, deduce that
$$\left\{ \int_0^T f(t)g(t) \, dt \right\}^2 \leqslant \int_0^T (f(t))^2 \, dt \cdot \int_0^T (g(t))^2 \, dt.$$

A particle, initially at rest at time $t = 0$, has acceleration $f(t)$ at time t. Prove that its displacement at time T is
$$\int_0^T (T - t) f(t) \, dt. \quad \left[\text{Integrate} \int_0^T v \, dt \text{ by parts.} \right]$$

Deduce that its average velocity does not exceed $RT/\sqrt{3}$, where R is the root-mean-square acceleration defined by the equation
$$R^2 = \frac{1}{T} \int_0^T (f(t))^2 \, dt. \tag{CS}$$

37. PROBABILITY DENSITY FUNCTIONS

1. A fair coin is tossed 400 times. Find, as accurately as your tables permit, the probability of throwing exactly 200 heads. (Use Stirling's approximation, $n! \simeq (n/e)^n \sqrt{(2\pi n)}$.) What does the Normal probability function give for this probability? What does it give for the probability of scoring less than 180 heads?

2. A population has a probability density function

$$\phi(x) = 2e^{-2x}, \quad x > 0.$$

Find:
        (a) the mean;
        (b) the lower and upper quartiles;
        (c) the standard deviation.   (M.A. Dip.).

3. A pond contains 300 fish. 60 fish are caught, marked, and released again. A week later, 60 fish are again taken from the pond. Find, approximately, the probabilities: (a) that more than 16 of the sample are marked, (b) that less than 10 are marked. State some of the assumptions on which your answers are based.

4. Find the mean and variance of a population with a probability density function

$$\phi(x) = \begin{cases} \frac{2}{3}x & \text{for } 0 \leqslant x \leqslant 1 \\ \dfrac{3-x}{3} & \text{for } 1 \leqslant x \leqslant 3 \\ 0 & \text{otherwise.} \end{cases}$$

Draw the graph of $\phi(x)$ and use it to find the probability of x deviating from its mean by more than twice the standard deviation.

5. Two points are selected at random, one on each long edge of a sheet of foolscap paper. They are then joined with a ruler, and the fraction

$$x = \frac{\text{area of lower portion}}{\text{area of whole sheet}}$$

is computed. Construct a probability density function for x. What is the probability of the smaller area being less than a quarter of the sheet?

6. A pointer with an arrow at each end can spin freely in a horizontal plane. It is placed with its centre 3 m from the centre O of a wall 8 m long and spun so that it comes to rest at random. The point P of the wall to which it points is marked; if there is no such point, the spin is ignored and the experiment is done again.
    Find the probability density function for the distance x of P from O.
    Find the mean absolute value of x, and its mean square value. What is the probability that P lies within 1 m of O?
    What difference would it make to your answers if the wall were indefinitely long and all spins were registered?

38. SAMPLING AND ESTIMATION

1. An investigator collects data on the expenditure in a given week of each of 300 households. He rounds off the figures to the nearest pound and takes the average. Assuming that for any one household the error he makes is equally likely to have any value between plus and minus ten shillings, find the standard deviation of the departure of his answer from the true average.

2. Define the expected value, $E[X]$, of a continuous random variable X with frequency function f.

Let $X_1, X_2, ..., X_n$ be a random sample for a population having frequency function f and mean μ. Let the sample mean

$$(X_1 + X_2 + ... + X_n)/n$$

be denoted by $\overline{X}$. Show that $E[\overline{X}] = \mu$.

How large a sample would you take in order to estimate the mean of a population, so that the probability is 0·95 that the sample mean will not differ from the true mean of the population by more than 0·2 of the standard deviation of the population? (OC)

3. Wire cables are formed from 10 separate wires, the strength of each wire being normally distributed with a mean of 2500 N, and a standard deviation of 98 N. Assuming that the strength of a cable is the sum of that of its separate wires, what proportion of cables will have a breaking strain of less than 24 600 N? If this proportion is to be reduced to 1 in 1000, and the variance of the strength of individual wires cannot be changed, what mean strength of wire must be demanded? (M.A. Dip.)

4. Tent-poles for a frame tent are in three sections, supposedly of length (from foot to shoulder in each case) 70 cm, 62 cm, 55 cm. A batch of 50 long sections shows a mean length of 70 cm and a standard deviation of 0·4 cm; a batch of 60 mid-sections also has the correct mean, with a standard deviation of 0·35 cm; but a sample of 50 short sections proves to have a mean of only 54·4 cm and a standard deviation of 0·6 cm. How likely is it that a complete pole as sent out by the manufacturers will be more than 2 cm too short?

5. A factory makes components in the form of a rectangle whose length is intended to be twice its breadth. There is, however, a random error with standard deviation 0·1 % in the lengths; similarly, the breadths are distributed independently about a certain value with standard deviation 0·1 %. Find the percentage standard deviations of the perimeters and of the areas of the components produced.

6. Twelve drawing pins are dropped from a fixed height onto a table and the numbers landing 'point up' are counted. The following table gives frequencies for r pins landing 'point up' in 300 trials:

r	0	1	2	3	4	5	6	7	8	9
f	2	14	37	64	70	59	34	15	4	1

Find the mean and variance of this sample, and from them estimate the probability of a pin landing point up. What would be the variance for a set of 12 trials with this probability? Compute the expected value of the frequency for $r = 2$,

    (a) using the binomial distribution with your estimated probability and 12 trials;

    (b) using the Normal distribution with your estimated mean and variance.

39

WORK AND ENERGY

1. INTRODUCTION

1.1 We have already met the work done by a force as an example of the use of scalar products; now we propose to develop this concept to form a theory complementary to that in the Impulse–Momentum chapter.

Consider a book resting on a horizontal table. If we push it, we can accelerate it from rest, and if we stop pushing it, it will come to rest at a different place on the table. Let us put some numbers to this situation and investigate what happens.

If the book is of mass 0·5 kg, the frictional force being 0·4 kgf, and we push it with a constant force of 1 kgf in a straight line over a metre of the table then the force and mass-acceleration diagrams are given in Figure 1.

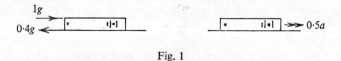

Fig. 1

Applying Newton's Law in the form $F = ma$, we obtain

$$1g - 0\cdot4g = 0\cdot5a, \quad \text{where} \quad g = 9\cdot8,$$

giving
$$a = 11\cdot76 \text{ m/s}^2.$$

If this constant acceleration continues over one metre then we can apply the kinematical relation

$$v^2 - u^2 = 2as$$

to give
$$v^2 = 2 \times 11\cdot76 \times 1 \text{ m}^2/\text{s}^2;$$

$$v = 4\cdot86 \text{ m/s}.$$

The fact that we use two equations containing the acceleration, which we are not really interested in, but have, nevertheless, calculated, suggests that we might eliminate the acceleration between $F = ma$ and $v^2 - u^2 = 2as$ and proceed from there.

Now
$$Fs = mas$$

$$\Rightarrow \quad m(v^2 - u^2) = 2Fs.$$

1188

This is usually written in the form

$$Fs = \tfrac{1}{2}mv^2 - \tfrac{1}{2}mu^2,$$

and you will remember that Fs is the work done by F when its point of application is displaced through s.

Now use this relation to consider the second part of the motion of the book. For this part $v = 0$, $u = 4\cdot86$ m/s and $F = -0\cdot4g$ N. Consequently if s is the displacement of the book then

$$-0\cdot4gs = -\tfrac{1}{2}\times0\cdot5\times4\cdot86^2 \text{ m},$$

giving $s = 1\cdot5$ m. That is, the book slides a further $1\cdot5$ metres before coming to rest.

Notice that the work done by the force acting on the book is negative in this part of the motion and that the book is slowing down. If you calculate the work done by the force acting on the book for the first part of the motion when the book is speeding up you will find that it is positive.

Furthermore, we can avoid calculating the intermediate speed if all we require is the total distance the book takes to come to rest. Applying the relation

$$Fs = \tfrac{1}{2}mv^2 - \tfrac{1}{2}mu^2$$

we have

$$1g\,.\,1 + (-0\cdot4g)(1+s) = 0$$

giving

$$s = 1\cdot5 \text{ m}.$$

1.2 Principle of energy.

The previous section introduced the relation

$$Fs = \tfrac{1}{2}mv^2 - \tfrac{1}{2}mu^2$$

and as it is our intention to broaden the scope of its application we must discuss the various terms.

As we have seen, Fs is the work done by F when its point of application is displaced through s. Consequently the units are those of the product of distance with force and are metre–newtons, usually called joules (J), in the m.k.s. system, or centimetre-dynes, usually called ergs, in the c.g.s. system.

The quantity $\tfrac{1}{2}mv^2$ is called the *kinetic energy* (K.E.) of the body of mass m when its velocity is v. Obviously the units are the same as those for work done and we can interpret the above relationship as expressing an identity between the work done by the force and the change in kinetic energy of the body to which the force is applied. This is the *principle of energy*.

Thus, in the example we have already discussed, we supply energy in the first place so that the resultant force on the book does positive work. This is converted into the kinetic energy of the book, which represents the amount of work done on the book to get it moving at that speed. Finally, as the book slides to rest, the resultant force does negative work and the kinetic energy is dissipated in one form or another.

Since the relation $Fs = \frac{1}{2}mv^2 - \frac{1}{2}mu^2$ reflects these changes in the form of energy, it is referred to as the *equation of energy*.

2. UNIFORM MOTION

In the example we have just considered, the motion took place in a straight line. However, the assumption underlying the elimination of the acceleration is that it is constant, and this allows a greater freedom for motion than is suggested by the example. We have already considered uniform motion in general terms and we know that

$$\mathbf{F} = m\mathbf{a}$$

and $$v^2 - u^2 = 2\mathbf{a.s}$$

are two relations referring to this situation and that the acceleration is constant in these circumstances. Consequently

$$\mathbf{F.s} = m\mathbf{a.s}$$

implies that $$m(v^2 - u^2) = 2\mathbf{F.s}.$$

As before, this is usually written in the form

$$\mathbf{F.s} = \frac{1}{2}mv^2 - \frac{1}{2}mu^2.$$

In this case the body will move along a plane curve, a parabola in fact, and the force acting on it will not bear a constant angle with the direction of motion. However, if the path of the body is the curve in Figure 2, then

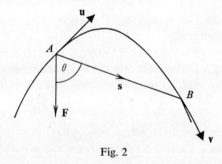

Fig. 2

the theory implies that the work done by $\mathbf{F}$ acting on the body during its displacement along the curve from A to B is given by

$$\mathbf{F.s} = Fs \cos \theta.$$

This can be interpreted as the product of the magnitude of the force with the projection on its line of action of the displacement of the body.

Two properties arise from the distributive property of the scalar product. First, if $\mathbf{P}$ and $\mathbf{Q}$ are constant forces such that

$$\mathbf{P}+\mathbf{Q} = \mathbf{F}$$

then
$$\mathbf{F}.\mathbf{s} = (\mathbf{P}+\mathbf{Q}).\mathbf{s}$$

$$\Rightarrow \quad \mathbf{F}.\mathbf{s} = \mathbf{P}.\mathbf{s}+\mathbf{Q}.\mathbf{s}.$$

This is to say that the work done by the resultant force $\mathbf{F}$ is equal to the sum of the works done by the constituent forces $\mathbf{P}$ and $\mathbf{Q}$. Secondly, if $\mathbf{s}_1$ and $\mathbf{s}_2$ are displacements from one point to another on the plane curve followed by the body, so that

$$\mathbf{s} = \mathbf{s}_1+\mathbf{s}_2,$$

then
$$\mathbf{F}.\mathbf{s} = \mathbf{F}.(\mathbf{s}_1+\mathbf{s}_2),$$

or
$$\mathbf{F}.\mathbf{s} = \mathbf{F}.\mathbf{s}_1+\mathbf{F}.\mathbf{s}_2.$$

This can be generalized to any number of displacements, and then says that the work done by $\mathbf{F}$ over the displacement $\mathbf{s}$ is equal to the sum of the works done by $\mathbf{F}$ over the component displacements from point to point on the curve. This is illustrated in Figure 3 for three displacements $\mathbf{s}_1$, $\mathbf{s}_2$ and $\mathbf{s}_3$ where $\mathbf{s} = \mathbf{s}_1+\mathbf{s}_2+\mathbf{s}_3$.

Notice that $\mathbf{F}.\mathbf{s}$ can take positive and negative values depending on the size of θ (see Figure 2); the interpretation of positive and negative work is similar to that given in the example of the book.

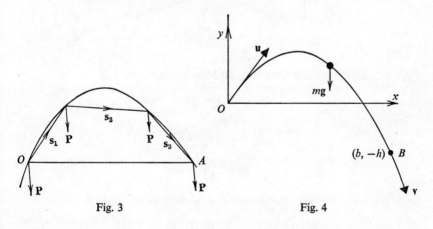

Fig. 3   Fig. 4

Example 1. A cannon ball is fired from a point A with speed u so that it passes through a point B whose coordinates are $(b, -h)$. Find its speed at B.

Figure 4 shows the path of the cannon ball from $(0, 0)$ to $(b, -h)$. Since the force acting on the projectile is $m\begin{pmatrix} 0 \\ -g \end{pmatrix}$ and the displacement from O

to B is $\begin{pmatrix} b \\ -h \end{pmatrix}$, the energy equation

$$\mathbf{F}.\mathbf{s} = \tfrac{1}{2}mv^2 - \tfrac{1}{2}mu^2$$

gives $$m\begin{pmatrix} 0 \\ -g \end{pmatrix}.\begin{pmatrix} b \\ -h \end{pmatrix} = \tfrac{1}{2}mv^2 - \tfrac{1}{2}mu^2.$$

That is, $$mgh = \tfrac{1}{2}mv^2 - \tfrac{1}{2}mu^2$$

or $$v^2 = u^2 + 2gh.$$

We can see from this that positive work leads to an increase in the speed of the cannon ball whereas negative work will lead to a decrease in speed.

Example 2. A child of mass m slides down a smooth slide AB such that the position vector of B relative to A is $\begin{pmatrix} b \\ -h \end{pmatrix}$.

If the child is pushed off from the top with a speed of u ft/s down the slide find its speed when passing B.

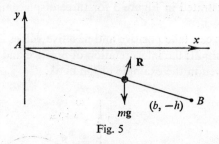

Fig. 5

Figure 5 illustrates the situation, and the energy equation

$$\mathbf{F}.\mathbf{s} = \tfrac{1}{2}mv^2 - \tfrac{1}{2}mu^2$$

gives $$(\mathbf{R}+mg).\begin{pmatrix} b \\ -h \end{pmatrix} = \tfrac{1}{2}mv^2 - \tfrac{1}{2}mu^2.$$

Now $$\mathbf{R}.\begin{pmatrix} b \\ -h \end{pmatrix} = 0$$

since the angle between these vectors is a right-angle, and

$$mg.\begin{pmatrix} b \\ -h \end{pmatrix} = m\begin{pmatrix} 0 \\ -g \end{pmatrix}.\begin{pmatrix} b \\ -h \end{pmatrix} = mgh.$$

Consequently, $$mgh = \tfrac{1}{2}mv^2 - \tfrac{1}{2}mu^2$$

giving $$v^2 = u^2 + 2gh.$$

1192

Notice that the final speeds given by the equation of energy in these two examples are identical, but that the corresponding velocities are different. This highlights the important fact that the equation of energy is a *scalar* relation, whereas the impulse–momentum equation is a relation between vectors.

Example 3. A body of mass 4 kg is moving east at 10 m/s. 3 seconds later it is moving north at 12 m/s. Find (a) the impulse and (b) the work done on the body during the interval.

Figure 6 illustrates the situation with the body moving from A to B during the interval. Choosing **i** and **j** as shown

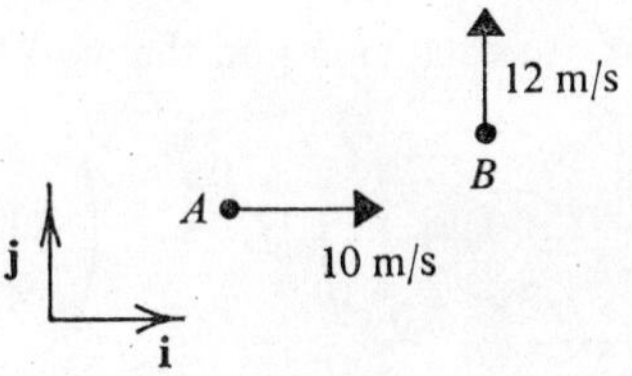

$$\mathbf{u} = \begin{pmatrix} 10 \\ 0 \end{pmatrix} \text{ m/s} \quad \text{and} \quad \mathbf{v} = \begin{pmatrix} 0 \\ 12 \end{pmatrix} \text{ m/s}.$$

Fig. 6

(a) $m\mathbf{v} - m\mathbf{u} = 4\begin{pmatrix} 0 \\ 12 \end{pmatrix} - 4\begin{pmatrix} 10 \\ 0 \end{pmatrix}$

$$= 4\begin{pmatrix} -10 \\ 12 \end{pmatrix} \text{ s N.}$$

(b) $\frac{1}{2}mv^2 - \frac{1}{2}mu^2 = \frac{1}{2}.4\begin{pmatrix} 0 \\ 12 \end{pmatrix}.\begin{pmatrix} 0 \\ 12 \end{pmatrix} - \frac{1}{2}.4.\begin{pmatrix} 10 \\ 0 \end{pmatrix}.\begin{pmatrix} 10 \\ 0 \end{pmatrix}$

$$= 2(144 - 100)$$

$$= 88 \text{ J.}$$

Notice the vector form of the impulse compared with the scalar form of the work done.

Example 4. A particle of mass 5 kg is acted upon by a force of

$$\begin{pmatrix} 12 \\ -5 \\ 5 \end{pmatrix} \text{ N}$$

whilst it is displaced through

$$\begin{pmatrix} 5 \\ 4 \\ 2 \end{pmatrix} \text{ m.}$$

If its final speed is 6 m/s, calculate its initial speed.

The equation of energy gives

$$\begin{pmatrix} 12 \\ -5 \\ 5 \end{pmatrix}.\begin{pmatrix} 5 \\ 4 \\ 2 \end{pmatrix} = \frac{1}{2}.5.6^2 - \frac{1}{2}.5.u^2.$$

That is $$50-90 = -\tfrac{5}{2}u^2,$$

giving $$16 = u^2.$$

Since speed is a magnitude, the positive solution of this equation is the one required. That is, the initial speed is 4 m/s.

Exercise A

1. In each case find the work done by the force **F** in the displacement **s**.

(a) $\mathbf{F} = \begin{pmatrix} 1 \\ 2 \\ 3 \end{pmatrix}$ N, $\quad \mathbf{s} = \begin{pmatrix} 3 \\ -1 \\ 4 \end{pmatrix}$ m;

(b) $\mathbf{F} = \begin{pmatrix} -3 \\ 2 \\ 5 \end{pmatrix}$ dyne, $\quad \mathbf{s} = \begin{pmatrix} 1 \\ -2 \\ 4 \end{pmatrix}$ cm;

(c)

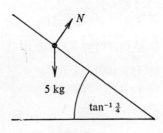

Fig. 7

The particle of mass 5 kg is moved 12 m down a slope making $\tan^{-1}\tfrac{3}{4}$ with the horizontal.

2. In each case find the K.E. of the body with the given velocity.

(a) A satellite of mass 2 tonnes with velocity

$$\begin{pmatrix} 720 \\ 1080 \\ 54 \end{pmatrix} \text{ km/h.}$$

(b) A Big Wheel carriage of mass 60 kg and velocity

$$\begin{pmatrix} 10 \\ 10\sqrt{3} \end{pmatrix} \text{ m/s.}$$

(c) A bullet of mass 30 g travelling at 600 m/s.

1194

(*d*) A ship's passenger of mass 80 kg whose velocity is

$$\begin{pmatrix} 54 \\ 9 \end{pmatrix} \text{ km/h.}$$

3. A toy rocket is fired with velocity $\begin{pmatrix} 3{\cdot}5 \\ 14 \end{pmatrix}$ m/s from (0, 0). Assuming that the only force on the rocket is that due to gravity, find the speed of the rocket at the following points on its trajectory: (1·5, 5·1), (6·0, 9·6), (7·5, 7·5), (10·5, −2·1). The *x*-axis is taken to be horizontal, the *y*-axis vertically upwards.

4. With the initial data from Question 3 write down the velocity of the rocket at its highest point. Hence use the energy equation to find its greatest height.

In what circumstances will the energy equation give a component of the displacement when the force and the terminal velocities are known?

5. Given that $\mathbf{F.s} = \frac{1}{2}mv^2 - \frac{1}{2}mu^2$, in what circumstances are the initial and final speeds equal?

6. Find the unknown speed in the following cases:

(*a*) $\mathbf{F} = \begin{pmatrix} -5 \\ 10 \\ 4 \end{pmatrix}$ N, $\mathbf{s} = \begin{pmatrix} 16 \\ -4 \\ -4 \end{pmatrix}$ m, $\mathbf{u} = \begin{pmatrix} 10 \\ 20 \\ 30 \end{pmatrix}$ m/s, $m = 200$ g;

(*b*) $\mathbf{F} = \begin{pmatrix} 4 \\ -8 \\ 10 \end{pmatrix}$ dyne, $\mathbf{s} = \begin{pmatrix} -50 \\ 20 \\ -8 \end{pmatrix}$ cm, $\mathbf{v} = \begin{pmatrix} -3 \\ 2 \\ 5 \end{pmatrix}$ cm/s, $m = 200$ g.

7. A ball of mass 4 kg is moving with velocity $\begin{pmatrix} 4 \\ 3 \end{pmatrix}$ m/s. Some time later it is moving with a velocity of $\begin{pmatrix} 0 \\ 7 \end{pmatrix}$ m/s. Find (*a*) the impulse, (*b*) the work done during the interval.

8. A ball of mass 5 g is moving north with a velocity of 6 cm/s. Some time later it is moving south-west at 8 cm/s. Find (*a*) the impulse, (*b*) the work done during the interval. (in Newtons)

9. If the time interval in Question 7 is 2 seconds, find the constant force acting on the body. Hence find its acceleration and displacement during the interval.

10. If the displacement in Question 8 is $\begin{pmatrix} -3 \\ -6 \end{pmatrix}$ cm, find the length of the time interval and hence the constant force acting on the body.

11. (*a*) The efficiency of the brakes of a car is defined as the percentage of the weight of the car which they can supply as a resistance to motion. Find how far it takes to stop a car travelling at 80 km/h with brakes that are 75 % efficient.

(*b*) With brakes that are only 60 % efficient how far does it take to stop a 4000 kg car travelling at 50 km/h?

12. A cricket ball is travelling at 13 m/s when it is struck by a batsman. If its mass is 150 g find the impulse and the work done when:

(*a*) it is struck back to the bowler at 13 cm/s;

(*b*) it is deflected 20° to go through the slips at 13 m/s.

Comment on your answers.

13. A railway truck weighing 5 tonnes runs freely from rest down an incline of 1 in 100, 100 metres in length. Find an expression for the work done by the forces and calculate the final velocity.

14. A man pulls a 25 kg block along a rough road by a chain. He exerts a tension of 200 N in the chain. The resistance due to the ground is half the normal reaction between the road and block.

Find the final speed of the block after it has been moved 4 m along the road from rest in each of the cases where the chain makes an angle of: (i) 0°, (ii) $\theta°$, (iii) $(90 - \theta)°$ with the ground ($\tan\theta° = 0.75$).

15. A toboggan of mass 5 kg runs from rest down an incline of 1 in 5. After travelling 80 m it has reached a speed of 10 m/s. Find the resistance, assumed constant.

16. By plunging through a deep puddle 3 m wide, a 750 kg car increases the resistance from 500 N to 3000 N. The front and back wheels are 3 m apart so that one and only one pair of wheels is in the puddle at a time. The speed on emerging from the puddle is 20 m/s. Find the speed on entering the puddle.

17. A car starts to climb a hill of 1 in 10 (along the road) at a speed of 100 km/h. After 0.8 km, against the incline, and with the engine giving a constant force to the wheels, the speed has dropped to 50 km/h. If the car and contents weigh 750 kg and the resistance to motion (except that due to gravity) amount to a constant 600 N, find the force exerted by the wheels.

18. A ball weighing 120 gm is dropped from a height of 2 m. Find the velocity on hitting the ground. It rebounds and reaches a height of 1.5 m. Find the impulse of the reaction from the ground on the ball. What force is exerted if the ball is of steel and contact lasts for 1/5000 s, and if it is of rubber and contact lasts 1/100 s? What are the forces if both the heights are multiplied by 4?

19. A golf ball is dropped from a height *h* onto a horizontal marble surface. Find the velocity of impact if the ball, of mass *m*, is dropped from rest.

1196

If the coefficient of restitution between the ball and the surface is e, write down the velocity of the ball immediately after impact and hence find the height to which the ball will rebound in terms of e and h.

If the ball continues to bounce write down the sum of a series that will represent the total distance travelled after n bounces. Hence, when the ball has stopped bouncing, what total distance has it travelled?

20. A climber of mass M is tied to one end of a rope l long and is h ($h < l$) vertically above his 'second' who has the rest of the rope by his side and passes it out round his body to the upper climber, keeping the rope just slack. The upper climber comes off and falls freely until the rope becomes taut between them. Find his K.E. at this instant.

The 'second' allows x ($x < l-h$) of rope to slide round his body and through his hands at a constant tension while bringing the falling man to rest. Assuming that the rope does not stretch (though, fortunately, nylon does) find the work done by the climber's weight and by the tension at the point of attachment during the final x of fall. Hence find the tension T at the point of attachment and sketch the graph of T against x.

The breaking strain of the rope is B and the knot at the climber's waist reduced this by 50 %; find the minimum value of x/h for the rope *not* to break, and the minimum value of the tension at the climber's waist if less than l of the rope is used.

3. FORCES WHICH DO NO WORK

So far we have used the equation of energy more or less as a short cut to avoid intermediate calculation. However, we can do better than this and a good starting point is to return to Example 2.

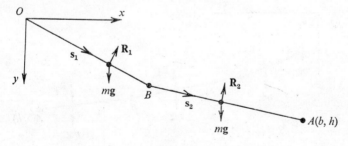

Fig. 9*

Children's slides are not usually this shape and we will propose a few modifications and see how the theory works out. Suppose that the slide has two distinct grades as in Figure 9. We have already seen from Exercise A, Question 12, that it is possible to deflect a body by applying an impulse without changing its speed. Consequently, although there is a bend in the slide at B, we can suppose that it is rounded so that the speed of the

* Fig. 8 was excluded when producing the metric reprint.

child is unaltered by it. If we apply the principle of energy to the motions down OB and BA we have

$$(R_1 + mg) . s_1 = \tfrac{1}{2}mv_B^2 - \tfrac{1}{2}mu^2,$$

$$(R_2 + mg) . s_2 = \tfrac{1}{2}mv^2 - \tfrac{1}{2}mv_B^2.$$

As before $R_1 . s_1 = 0$ and $R_2 . s_2 = 0.$

Adding, $mg . (s_1 + s_2) = \tfrac{1}{2}mv^2 - \tfrac{1}{2}mu^2,$

and since $s_1 + s_2 = s$ it follows that

$$mgh = \tfrac{1}{2}mv^2 - \tfrac{1}{2}mu^2$$

as before. In other words, despite the bend in the slide the speed of the child on passing A is still given by

$$v^2 = u^2 + 2gh.$$

If we increase the number of different grades as shown in Figure 10 and repeat the argument, we know that the normal reaction will never do any work and that the speed is continuous at the bends. Consequently,

$$mg . (s_1 + s_2 + s_3 + s_4) = \tfrac{1}{2}mv^2 - \tfrac{1}{2}mu^2$$

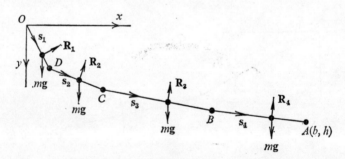

Fig. 10

and since $s_1 + s_2 + s_3 + s_4 = s$

it follows that $mgh = \tfrac{1}{2}mv^2 - \tfrac{1}{2}mu^2.$

This is to say that the speed of the child as it passes A is still given by $v^2 = u^2 + 2gh.$

1198

From this stage it is straightforward to imagine that the number of distinct grades can be increased without limit until the usual continuous curve of a child's slide is reached. At any point in this process the normal reaction will do no work and we are left with the conclusion that the equation of energy can be written in the form

$$\Sigma \mathbf{F}.\mathbf{s} = \tfrac{1}{2}mv^2 - \tfrac{1}{2}mu^2;$$

also that when the point of application of a force is displaced perpendicular to its line of action, the work done is zero whether or not the force is constant. This is a substantial extension of the principle of energy and two examples are given to illustrate its use.

Example 5. A ball-bearing of mass m is travelling in a horizontal tube at A with a speed u when the tube gently alters direction so that at B, with coordinates (b, h) referred to A, the tube is vertical. Calculate the speed of the ball-bearing at B assuming that friction is negligible.

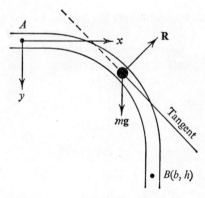

Fig. 11

Figure 11 illustrates the situation where $\mathbf{R}$ is always perpendicular to the line of motion of the ball-bearing. Consequently the work done by $\mathbf{R} + m\mathbf{g}$, the force acting on the ball-bearing, between A and B reduces to that done by the constant force $m\mathbf{g}$. Hence the equation of energy gives

$$m\mathbf{g}.\binom{b}{h} = \tfrac{1}{2}mv^2 - \tfrac{1}{2}mu^2$$

from which $v^2 = u^2 + 2gh.$

In this case **R** is a force always normal to the direction of motion and, as in the example of the slide, does no work.

Example 6. A man of mass 70 kg swings on a rope of length 8 m. If he lets himself go with the rope taut from a platform 1 m below the level of the point of suspension of the rope, what will be his speed at the lowest point of the swing?

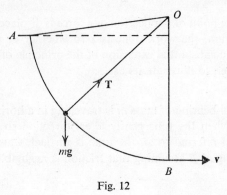

Fig. 12

Figure 12 illustrates the situation. As before, **T** is a force which is always perpendicular to the direction of the displacement of its point of application. Consequently **T** does no work during the swing and the work done by the force **T**+*m*g between *A* and *B* reduces to the work done by the constant force *m*g only. Consequently

$$\Sigma\mathbf{F}.\mathbf{s} = \tfrac{1}{2}mv^2 - \tfrac{1}{2}mu^2$$

gives

$$mg \times 7 = \tfrac{1}{2}mv^2.$$

That is

$$v^2 = 2 \times 9.8 \times 7,$$

or

$$v = 11.7.$$

The speed of the man as he passes *B* is 11·7 m/s.

However, this is not the only use for the principle of energy in connection with motion in a vertical circle, of which this is an example. We can use the principle to enable us to calculate the tension in the rope at any point, which we will now do for the instant when the man has descended 5·4 m. For convenience the force and mass-acceleration diagrams are given side by side in Figure 13. For a drop through 5·4 m, *ON* = 6·4 m and triangle *OMN* is a '3, 4, 5' triangle. Applying Newton's Second Law in the direction of the radius *MO* gives

$$T - mg \cos \theta = \frac{mv^2}{r},$$

$T - 650 \mathrm{N} = 65 \times \dfrac{6 \cdot 74^2}{5}$

$T - 650 = 590 \cdot 5580$

$T = 1240 \cdot 56$

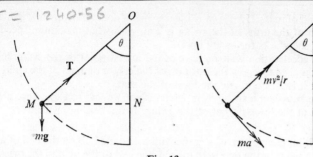

Fig. 13

or
$$T = 70 \times 9{\cdot}8 \times \frac{4}{5} + \frac{70{\cdot}v^2}{8}.$$

Now v^2 is given by using the equation of energy. That is,

$$70 \times 9{\cdot}8 \times 5{\cdot}4 = \tfrac{1}{2} \times 70 \times v^2,$$

so that
$$T = 70 \times 9{\cdot}8 \times \frac{4}{5} + \frac{70 \times 9{\cdot}8 \times 5{\cdot}4}{4},$$

giving $T = 1500$ to 2 significant figures.

Thus the tension in the rope is 1500 N at this point in the swing.

Exercise B

1. A child sitting on a mat slides down a helter-skelter. If the friction is negligible and the helter-skelter is 8 m high what will the child's speed be at the bottom?

2. A boy swings on the end of a 5 m rope in a gymnasium. If he jumps off a horse at 2·5 m/s on a level 3 m below the point of suspension of the rope, which is taut, find

(a) his maximum speed;

(b) his maximum height above the ground;

(c) the tension in the rope in the vertical position if he is of mass 65 kg.

3. A scout travels along an aerial runway starting from 10 m up a tree. If the lowest point he reaches is 3 m off the ground and the friction of the system can be neglected, at what speed will he pass that point?

If you take into account the sag in the rope what effect on the answer will this have?

If the end of the aerial runway is 4 m off the ground, with what speed will he reach it and what effect will the sag on the rope have on this answer?

4. A steam-boat at a fair consists of a cabin suspended from a pivot at the top of a pole. If the mass of the cabin is 1000 kg and its centre of mass is 5 m from the pivot, calculate the speed at the lowest point of its swing if the cabin is at rest when its centre of mass is level with the pivot.

8   SAM 4

5. (a) A child of mass 25 kg is working a swing of comparatively negligible mass. If the length of the arms of the swing is 2 m, with what maximum speed is she travelling if she works the swing up 1·25 m?

(b) What acceleration will she have at the lowest point of the swing?

(c) Do you need to know the position of the centre of mass of the child? If so, assume that it is 20 cm above the level of the seat.

If you 'lie back' on a swing as it descends you appear to experience a greater acceleration at the lowest point of the swing. Is this feeling justified?

6. A demolition gang operates a crane with a 1 tonne bob on the end of a cable. The centre of mass of the bob is 10 m from the end of the jib and the mass of the cable can be neglected. Assuming that the bob travels along the arc of a vertical circle, centre the stationary extremity of the jib, starting 2 m above the lowest point, find v^2, the square of the speed of the bob, after it has descended 0·5 m, 1 m, 1·5 m, 2 m. At each of these points find the value of the tension in the cable. If θ is the acute angle the cable makes with the vertical, find an expression for v^2 and hence for the tension in the cable for this general position.

7. A marble is placed on the top of a smooth up-turned hemispherical bowl and gently pushed off. If the radius of the outside of the bowl is 20 cm and the marble is of mass 2 g, find its speed after descending through a vertical distance of 4 cm, 8 cm, 12 cm, 16 cm and 20 cm. If R is the normal reaction between the bowl and the marble find R for each of the speeds found above. Comment on your results.

If the question was about a bead threaded onto a smooth semicircular wire standing in a vertical plane, what modifications would you make to your answers?

8. An eskimo sits on the highest point of a smooth hemispherical igloo of radius 3 m. He eases himself gently from the top and slides down the outside of the igloo. Obtain an expression for the speed of the eskimo whilst he remains in contact with the igloo. Give your answer in terms of θ, the angle the position vector of the eskimo relative to the centre of the igloo makes with the vertical. Write down the acceleration of the eskimo in the direction of this position vector and hence obtain an expression giving the reaction between the eskimo and the igloo in terms of θ. At what point will the eskimo leave the surface of the igloo?

9. A conker of mass 25 gm is held on the end of a piece of string 22·5 cm long. Find its speed and the tension in the string after rising through 10 cm, 20 cm, 22·5 cm, 25 cm, 35 cm, 45 cm for the following initial speeds from the lowest point:

(a) 1·4 m/s; (b) 2·1 m/s; (c) 2·5 m/s; (d) 4 m/s. Take $g = 9\cdot8$ m/s².

Comment on your results.

If the question was about a bead threaded onto a smooth circular wire standing in a vertical plane, what modifications would you make to your answers?

10. A bob of mass m is attached to one end A of an inextensible string of length l, the other end of which is attached to a fixed point O. The particle is projected horizontally with a velocity u when OA is vertical with A below O. Find the velocity of the particle when AO makes an angle of θ with the downward vertical through O and the string is still taut; i.e. show that $v^2 = u^2 - 2gl(1 - \cos\theta)$.

Apply Newton's Second Law radially at this point to find the tension T in the string in terms of m, g, θ, v and l. Hence show that

$$T = mg(3\cos\theta - 2) + \frac{mu^2}{l}.$$

Now investigate the following situations:

(a) $u^2 < 2gl$; (b) $u^2 = 2gl$; (c) $2gl < u^2 < 5gl$;

(d) $u^2 = 5gl$; (e) $u^2 > 5gl$.

11. A bead of mass m is threaded on a smooth circular wire of radius l situated in a vertical plane. By applying the methods suggested in Question 10 to the situation when the bead is projected from the lowest point with a horizontal velocity of u, establish corresponding equations for the velocity and reaction between the bead and the wire when the radius to the bead makes an angle θ with the downward vertical through the centre of the circle.

Find:

(a) when the reaction becomes zero;

(b) the velocity, u, necessary for the bead to make a complete revolution. (N.B. it is *not* $u^2 \geqslant 5gl$.) Explain what happens in physical terms.

12. Using the relations for v^2 and T obtained in Question 10 show that, when $\pi \geqslant \theta > \frac{1}{2}\pi$, T will always become zero before v.

4. VARIABLE FORCES WHICH DO WORK

4.1 As you have probably realized, the previous section avoided the calculation of the work done by a variable force by confining attention to cases where its point of application was displaced perpendicular to its line of action. This is not always possible nor in fact desirable, and we turn now to the work done by a variable force for the special case when its point of application is displaced along the line of action of the force.

One example of a variable force is that due to the gravitational attraction of the earth along straight lines passing through its centre. Suppose that Figures 14(a) and (b) illustrate the circumstances at two instants for a ball of mass m acted on by a variable force F and moving along the line of action of F. The work done by F during the displacement δs, which we will denote by δW, must satisfy the inequality $F\delta s < \delta W < (F + \delta F)\delta s$. At this stage we have a choice of procedure, and as the result of each is useful we will follow first one, then the other.

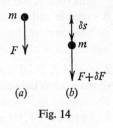

Fig. 14

(a) Since $\delta s > 0$,

$$F < \frac{\delta W}{\delta s} < F + \delta F$$

and if we proceed to the limit as $\delta s \to 0$ it follows that

$$\frac{dW}{ds} = F.$$

This is to say that the rate of doing work per unit of displacement is the value of the force. Consequently, to find the work done in a displacement from A to B it follows that

$$W = \int_A^B F\,ds.$$

(b) Since $\delta t > 0$, $\quad F\dfrac{\delta s}{\delta t} < \dfrac{\delta W}{\delta t} < (F+\delta F)\dfrac{ds}{\delta t}$

and if we proceed to the limit as $\delta t \to 0$ it follows that

$$\frac{dW}{dt} = Fv.$$

This is to say that the rate of doing work per unit of time is the product of the force with the velocity of its point of application. This is an important property and we shall return to it in the last section of this chapter.

For the present, to find the work done during a time interval $(0, t)$, it follows that

$$W = \int_0^t Fv\,dt.$$

In these circumstances $F = m(dv/dt)$ is variable, so that

$$W = \int_0^t Fv\,dt = \int_0^t mv\,\frac{dv}{dt}\,dt$$

$$= m\left[\frac{v^2}{2}\right]_0^t.$$

That is, $\qquad \displaystyle\int_A^B F\,ds = \int_0^t Fv\,dt = \tfrac{1}{2}mv^2 - \tfrac{1}{2}mu^2,$

where u and v are the initial and final speeds of the ball.

This then is the modified form of the equation of energy when the force is variable and the displacement is along the line of the force. The principle is, however, unchanged: the work done, however it is calculated, remains equal to the change in kinetic energy.

Example 7. Find the work done on a satellite of mass 1000 kg when it is lifted up to 4000 km above the earth's surface. Take the radius of the earth to be $6\cdot4 . 10^6$ m.

Figure 15 illustrates the situation where F is the force on the satellite, defined by Newton's Law of Gravitational Attraction as

$$F = Gmm_1/r^2$$

where G is the universal gravitational constant, m the mass of the earth, m_1 the mass of the satellite and r the distance between their centres.

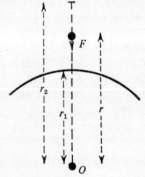

Fig. 15

Consequently the work done by this force is given by

$$\int_A^B -F\,ds = \int_{r_1}^{r_2} -F\,ds.$$

The negative sign indicates that the point of application of F is being moved in the opposite direction to F.

That is,   the work done $= \int_{r_1}^{r_2} -\dfrac{Gmm_1}{r^2}\,dr$

$$= Gmm_1\left[\frac{1}{r}\right]_{r_1}^{r_2} = Gmm_1\left(\frac{1}{r_2}-\frac{1}{r_1}\right).$$

Now $r_1 = 6{\cdot}4.10^6$ m and $r_2 = 10{\cdot}4.10^6$ m; further, when the satellite is on the earth's surface, we know that

$$\frac{Gm.1000}{(6{\cdot}4.10^6)^2} = 1000.9{\cdot}8.$$

Consequently,

the work done $= 9{\cdot}8.(6{\cdot}4.10^6)^2.1000\left[\dfrac{1}{10{\cdot}4.10^6}-\dfrac{1}{6{\cdot}4.10^6}\right]$

$$= \frac{-9{\cdot}8(6{\cdot}4.10^6)^2.10^9.4}{10{\cdot}4.6{\cdot}4.10^{12}}$$

$$= -2{\cdot}41.10^{10}\ \text{J}.$$

The negative sign means that energy is being absorbed by the gravitational field, and external energy of this amount will have to be supplied to raise the satellite.

4.2 Elastic strings. One other common variable force that we shall discuss is that which arises when an elastic string or spring is compressed or stretched. A suitable mathematical model to describe an elastic string or spring is formulated in Hooke's Law which states that the tension in an elastic string is proportional to the extension of the string. That is,

$$T \propto x$$

where x is the extension. Springs can be represented by admitting positive and negative values of x and T. If we denote by λ the tension in the elastic string when it has been stretched to twice its natural length l, then

$$\frac{T}{\lambda} = \frac{x}{l},$$

leading to $T = \dfrac{\lambda x}{l}.$

λ is called the *elastic constant* (sometimes, though wrongly, the *modulus of elasticity*) of the string and has the same units as T. Consequently, if one end of an elastic string of length l is attached to a fixed point and the other

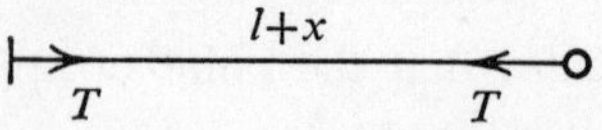

Forces exerted by the string

Fig. 16

end pulled so that the string is stretched to a total length of $l+x$, then the work done by the force (tension) opposing the pulling force is given by

$$\int_A^B F\,ds = \int_0^x -\frac{\lambda x}{l}\,dx$$

$$= -\frac{\lambda x^2}{2l}.$$

The work done is negative because the tension on the pulling agent is acting in the opposite sense to the direction of the displacement of its point of application. This is to say that energy has to be supplied to the string in order to stretch it. In this way a stretched elastic string can be regarded as a *store* of energy.

Example 8. A mass of 2 kg is attached to one end of an elastic string, of elastic constant 8 g N and natural length 1 m, the other end of which is attached to a fixed point O. The mass is released from rest when at O. Find the distance below O at which the mass first comes instantaneously to rest.

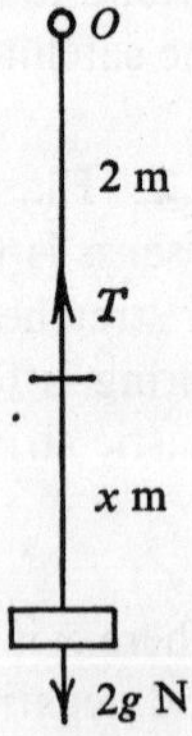

Let x m be the extension of the string beyond its natural length. Then

work done = change in K.E.

In this case the change in K.E. is zero and the work done is that due to the weight and the tension. These give

$$mg(1+x)-\frac{\lambda x^2}{2l} = 0.$$

Consequently $2.9(1+x)-\dfrac{8.9.x^2}{2.1} = 0$

$$\Rightarrow 1+x-2x^2 = 0$$

$$\Rightarrow (1+2x)(1-x) = 0$$

$$\Rightarrow x = 1 \quad \text{or} \quad -0.5.$$

Fig. 17

From the conditions of the problem $x \geqslant 0$, so that $x = 1$. The mass first comes instantaneously to rest 2 m below O.

1206

Exercise C

1. A particle of mass m kg moves along the x-axis and when it is x m from O it is acted on by a variable force PN in the direction of x increasing, and by a force QN in the direction opposite to that of the velocity. The particle starts at $x = a$ with a velocity of u m/s in the direction of x increasing and travels to the point $x = b$, where it has velocity v m/s, in the same direction.

    (a) $m = 90, P = 5x, Q = \frac{5}{3}, a = 0, u = 1, b = 6$, find v;
    (b) $m = 90, P = -5x, Q = \frac{5}{3}, a = 0, u = \frac{5}{2}, b = 6$, find v;
    (c) $m = 32, P = -5x, Q = \frac{5}{3}, a = 0, b = 6, v = 6$, find u;
    (d) $m = 12, P = 3(10-x), Q = 0, a = 0, b = 2, v = 3$, find u and the velocity when the particle is at $x = 4$;
    (e) $m = 8, P = -120/x^2, Q = 3, a = 2, u = 4, b = 8$, find v and (harder) the point where the particle comes instantaneously to rest.

2.

Distance (m)	0	1	2	3	4	5	6	7	8
Force (kgf)	40	30	24	21	19	16	13	8	0

A body of mass 10 kg is projected by a machine with the above force–distance relationship. Find the velocity of the body at intervals of one metre during the thrust.

3. A light spring of natural length 25 cm and elastic constant 20 N is attached to a fixed point at one end and hangs freely. A 1 kg mass is hung from the lower end and is released from rest with the spring unstretched. How long is the string when the mass comes instantaneously to rest?

4. The elastic constant of a spring of natural length 1·5 m is 50 kgf. Find the work done in stretching the spring and the energy stored in the spring at the end of the stretching for an increase of total length from:

    (a) 1·5 m to 2·5 m;   (b) 1·5 m to 2·0 m;   (c) 2·0 m to 2·5 m;
    (d) 2·5 m to 3·5 m;   (e) 3 m to 4 m.

5. Show that the work done in stretching an elastic string from a to b where $b > a > l$, the natural length of the string, is given by $\frac{1}{2}(T_a + T_b)(b - a)$ where T_a and T_b are the tensions when the string is of length a and b respectively.

6. (a) Two springs of lengths a_1, a_2 and each of elastic constant λ are attached end to end. Show that the combined spring has elastic constant λ.

    (b) Two springs of elastic constants λ_1, λ_2 and each of length a are attached side by side. Show that the combined spring has elastic constant $(\lambda_1 + \lambda_2)$.

7. A 10 kg mass lies on a rough table (the coefficient of friction being $\frac{1}{2}$). It is attached to a point A, 3 m away, by a string of natural length 1 m. (N.B. It is *not* a spring; it becomes slack at less than 1 m.) The mass is projected towards A with velocity 3 m/s. It reaches A with velocity 1 m/s. What was the elastic constant of the string?

8. Two masses are connected by a spring of elastic constant 1 dyne and natural length 20 cm. The masses are released from rest when they are 50 cm apart on a smooth horizontal table. Find the sum of their kinetic energies when the spring has contracted to its natural length.

9. If a particle of mass m is distant r from a particle of mass M then, by Newton's Law of Gravitation, there is a force GMm/r^2 between them. (It can be shown that for extended bodies that are spherical the same law holds if r is the distance between their centres.)

Calculate the work done by a force P which moves the body of mass m radially at constant speed from $r = a$ to $r = x$ while the mass M remains fixed. (N.B. m does *not* accelerate.) Put $x = a(1+k)$ in the result and show that for k small, so that $(1/x) \simeq (1/a)(1-k)$, the work done by moving a mass m a small distance h radially, near the earth's surface, is given by mgh.

10. Two climbers have 50 m of rope between them when the higher one falls off. If he is 48 m vertically above the second who is firmly belayed to the rock face, find where the falling climber of mass 85 kg will come to rest first of all if the elastic constant of the rope is 1000 kgf.

11. A spring, whose natural length is 0·5 m and whose elastic constant is 20 kgf has one end attached to a fixed support and the other end attached to a mass of 10 kg. The mass is released when it is 0·5 m below the support. Calculate the speed of the mass when it has fallen 0·2 m and find where it comes instantaneously to rest. (Two places.)

12. A car of mass 1000 kg starts from rest on a level road. The propulsive force on it is initially 400 kgf, but this falls in proportion to the distance travelled so that after 200 m its value is 70 kgf. There is a constant frictional resistance of 70 kgf. Find the speed of the car after every 25 m and sketch a graph to show the relation between the speed and the distance travelled.

*5. VARIABLE FORCES

5.1 We are now in a position to deduce the principle of energy when the force varies in direction as well as magnitude.

Consider a body moving in a plane under the action of a variable force **F**. Suppose that at time t the body is at A, whose position vector relative to O is **s**, and that at time $t + \delta t$ the body is at B, whose position is $\mathbf{s} + \delta\mathbf{s}$. If **F** is the value of the force at A then an approximation to the work done in the displacement is given by $\mathbf{F}.\delta\mathbf{s}$. This is illustrated in Figure 18(a).

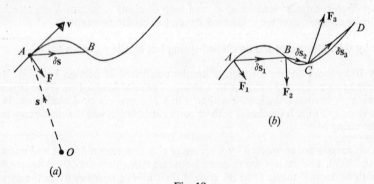

(a)

(b)

Fig. 18

Consequently, if **F** is evaluated at a sequence of points along the path of the body as the body passes through them, and the displacements from point to point are known, then an approximation to the work done by **F** as the body moves along the curve is given by $\Sigma\mathbf{F}.\delta\mathbf{s}$. This is illustrated for three displacements in Figure 18(b). If the sum tends to a limit as $\delta\mathbf{s}$ tends to zero, we denote the limit by $\int\mathbf{F}.d\mathbf{s}$, where the integral is evaluated along the path of the body. (Compare Section 2.3 of Chapter 36.)

An alternative procedure, similar to that in Section 4.1, is to denote the work done by **F** in the displacement $\delta\mathbf{s}$ by δW and to write $\delta W = \mathbf{F}^{*}.\delta\mathbf{s}$ where $\mathbf{F}^{*}$ is the *average* force acting on the body in this displacement. If the corresponding time interval is δt then

$$\frac{\delta W}{\delta t} = \mathbf{F}^{*}.\frac{\delta\mathbf{s}}{\delta t}.$$

Assuming that the limits of
$$\frac{\delta W}{\delta t} \quad \text{and} \quad \frac{\delta\mathbf{s}}{\delta t}$$

exist and that $\mathbf{F}^{*}$ tends to **F** as δt tends to zero, it follows that taking the limits gives

$$\frac{dW}{dt} = \mathbf{F}.\mathbf{v}.$$

Notice the similarity with the result obtained in Section 4.1. Consequently

$$W = \int_{0}^{T}\mathbf{F}.\mathbf{v}\,dt$$

is the work done by **F** in the time interval T of the displacement.

Now
$$\mathbf{F} = m\frac{d\mathbf{v}}{dt}$$

$$\Rightarrow \int_{0}^{T}\mathbf{F}.\mathbf{v}\,dt = \int_{0}^{T}m\mathbf{v}.\frac{d\mathbf{v}}{dt}\,dt.$$

$$\Rightarrow W = m\left[\frac{v^{2}}{2}\right]_{0}^{T}.$$

$$\Rightarrow \int_{A}^{D}\mathbf{F}.d\mathbf{s} = \int_{0}^{T}\mathbf{F}.\mathbf{v}\,dt = \tfrac{1}{2}mv^{2} - \tfrac{1}{2}mu^{2},$$

where u and v are the initial and final velocities as before. This is the equation of energy for a generally variable force, and we notice that it still expresses the principle that the work done by the force is equal to the change in kinetic energy of the body.

Example 9. A bob of mass m swings on the end of a light pendulum of length l in a medium whose resistance is R (constant). The pendulum is

1209

released from a horizontal position. Find the position of the bob when it next comes instantaneously to rest.

The velocity of the bob is $l\dot\theta$ along the tangent at A.

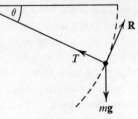

The force system on the bob is

$$(\mathbf{T}+\mathbf{R}+m\mathbf{g}),$$

where $\mathbf{R}$ is constant in magnitude but variable in direction.

The equation of energy in the form

Fig. 19

$$\int_0^T \mathbf{P}\cdot\mathbf{v}\,dt = \tfrac{1}{2}mv^2 - \tfrac{1}{2}mu^2$$

gives

$$\int_0^T (\mathbf{T}+\mathbf{R}+m\mathbf{g})\cdot\mathbf{v}\,dt = 0 \qquad (1)$$

where T is the time from release to rest.

Now

$$\mathbf{R}\cdot\mathbf{v} = -Rl\dot\theta;$$

$$\mathbf{T}\cdot\mathbf{v} = 0;$$

$$m\mathbf{g}\cdot\mathbf{v} = mgl\dot\theta\cos\theta;$$

so that (1) gives

$$\int_0^T \left(mgl\cos\theta\,\frac{d\theta}{dt} - Rl\frac{d\theta}{dt}\right)dt = 0$$

$$\Rightarrow \Big[\,mgl\sin\theta - Rl\theta\,\Big]_0^\alpha = 0$$

if $\theta = 0$, when $t = 0$, and $\theta = \alpha$, when $t = T$;

$$\Rightarrow mgl\sin\alpha - Rl\alpha = 0.$$

A solution to this equation in the form $\sin\alpha = (R/mg)\alpha$ can be found graphically if $y = \sin\alpha$ and $y = (R/mg)\alpha$ are plotted with the same axes, as in Figure 20.

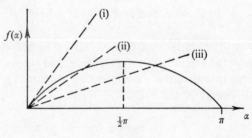

Fig. 20

The following situations arise:

(i) $R/mg \geqslant 1$; then the meeting points of the graphs reduce to $(0, 0)$ only, i.e. the only solution is $\alpha = 0$ and the bob does not fall at all.

(ii) $1 > (R/mg) > (2/\pi)$; then $0 < \alpha < \frac{1}{2}\pi$ and the bob does not reach the lowest point.

(iii) $(2/\pi) > (R/mg) > 0$; then $\frac{1}{2}\pi < \alpha < \pi$ and the bob swings beyond the lowest point.

(iv) $R = 0$; then $\alpha = \pi$ and the bob swings back to the same level. Note that the quantity R/mg is dimensionless since R and mg are both forces, and its numerical value which appears in the equation of the straight line

$$y = \frac{R}{mg}\alpha$$

alone determines the type of motion.

5.2 Component form. If the velocity of the body and the components of the force $\mathbf{F}$ are known, two alternative forms of

$$\int_0^T \mathbf{F} . \mathbf{v}\, dt$$

are useful. If in the Cartesian frame of Figure 21 (a),

$$\mathbf{v} = \begin{pmatrix} \dot{x} \\ \dot{y} \end{pmatrix} \quad \text{and} \quad \mathbf{F} = \begin{pmatrix} X \\ Y \end{pmatrix}$$

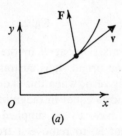

(a)	(b)

Fig. 21

then $\qquad \displaystyle\int_0^T \mathbf{F} . \mathbf{v}\, dt = \int_0^T \begin{pmatrix} X \\ Y \end{pmatrix} . \begin{pmatrix} \dot{x} \\ \dot{y} \end{pmatrix} dt = \int_0^T (X\dot{x} + Y\dot{y})\, dt.$

Similarly, in a polar frame, see Figure 21 (b), if

$$\mathbf{v} = \dot{r}\mathbf{e} + r\dot{\theta}\mathbf{n} \quad \text{and} \quad \mathbf{F} = R\mathbf{e} + T\mathbf{n},$$

where $\mathbf{e}$ and $\mathbf{n}$ are unit radial and transverse vectors, then

$$\int_0^T \mathbf{F} . \mathbf{v}\, dt = \int_0^T (R\mathbf{e} + T\mathbf{n}) . (\dot{r}\mathbf{e} + r\dot{\theta}\mathbf{n})\, dt = \int_0^T (R\dot{r} + Tr\dot{\theta})\, dt.$$

Example 10. A particularly important application of the polar form is to a gravitational field. We know from Newton's Law of Gravitation that the force exerted by one mass on another is given by $F = G.(m_1 m_2/r^2)$ (Example 7). Thus the work done is

$$\int_0^T (R\dot{r} + Tr\dot{\theta})\,dt = \int_0^T -G\frac{m_1 m_2}{r^2}\dot{r}\,dt.$$

$$= -Gm_1 m_2 \int_0^T \frac{\dot{r}}{r^2}\,dt$$

$$= -Gm_1 m_2 \int_{r_1}^{r_2} \frac{1}{r^2}\,dr$$

$$= +Gm_1 m_2 \left(\frac{1}{r_2} - \frac{1}{r_1}\right).$$

This is a particularly significant result because whatever the path from A to B the work done is the same. It follows directly that in these circumstances the work done when a body moves round *any* closed curve in this field of force is zero. In other words, when $r_2 > r_1$ the energy needed to move the body from A to B will become available again as the body returns to A. In such cases the field of force is said to be *conservative*.

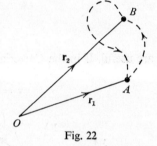

Fig. 22

If r_1 is taken to be a fixed distance, then the work done in moving the body from A to B is called the *potential energy* of the mass m_2 at B in the gravitational field due to the presence of m_1 at the origin. It is customary to take A so far away that $Gm_1 m_2/r_1$ is effectively zero; when this is done the potential energy is negative $(-Gm_1 m_1/r_2)$ and is equal in magnitude but opposite in sign to the work which would have to be supplied by an external agent to move m_2 'to infinity'—that is, to remove it from the gravitational field altogether.

Exercise D

1. A switchback car is constrained to move on a rough track in the form shown in Figure 23. This consists of two arcs of equal circles AB and CD and a straight piece BC. The radius of the circles is r, the angle θ as shown and h is the total height of A above D. The frictional resistance to the motion of the car is constant in magnitude and equal to R.

The car passes A with a speed along the track of u. Find the speed of the car as it passes D and deduce the limitation on R that ensures that the car actually reaches D.

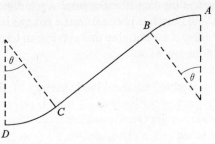

Fig. 23

2. An aeroplane of mass 10^4 kg lands on an aircraft carrier with a relative velocity of 45 m/s along the flight deck. It catches the mid-point of a cable 70 m long which is at right-angles to the line of flight. The cable is unstretched, but not slack, and the force in it is given by $F = kx$ where x is the extension of the cable. If, on catching the cable, the aeroplane's engines have their thrust reversed, thus producing a constant retarding force of 10^3 kgf, find the value of k so that the aeroplane is brought to rest in 40 m.

3. The force towards the earth on a rocket of mass m is mgd^2/r^2 where d is the radius of the earth, r the distance of the rocket from the centre of the earth and g the acceleration due to gravity on the earth's surface. Calculate the initial velocity required to lift the rocket to a height of x above the earth's surface.

Hence find the initial velocity necessary if the rocket is to escape from the earth's gravitational field.

4. Prove for a body moving in a gravitational field of force that the sum of the kinetic energy and potential energy is constant. Extend your theorem to any conservative field of force.

6. SYSTEMS OF PARTICLES

6.1 So far we have treated a body as though it were a particle. However, this is not always justified and we need to know the circumstances which decide the question. As before we will suppose that a body is composed of a number of particles fixed relative to each other. This is to say that the distances between particles are invariant under all circumstances.

Suppose that $\mathbf{P}_i$ is the resultant force acting on one of these particles whose mass is $\mathbf{m}_i$. If, during a displacement $\mathbf{s}_i$ the velocity of m_i changes from $\mathbf{u}_i$ to $\mathbf{v}_i$ then the principle of energy states that

$$\mathbf{P}_i.\mathbf{s}_i = \tfrac{1}{2}mv_i^2 - \tfrac{1}{2}mu_i^2.$$

For a system of n particles this is a typical relation; summing for all the particles we obtain
$$\Sigma\mathbf{P}_i.\mathbf{s}_i = \Sigma\tfrac{1}{2}mv_i^2 - \Sigma\tfrac{1}{2}mu_i^2.$$

This relation expresses the fact that the total work done by the system of forces acting on the n particles is equal to the change in kinetic energy of the system of particles. If we examine this expression term by term we shall obtain the restrictions we want.

6.2 Since $\frac{1}{2}m_i v_i^2$ is defined as the kinetic energy of the particle m_i we define the kinetic energy of the body as $\Sigma \frac{1}{2}m_i v_i^2$. If m_i has position vector $\mathbf{r}_i$ referred to an arbitrary origin O and position vector $\mathbf{r}_{Gi}$ referred to an origin at the centre of mass, G, of the system of particles, then if $\bar{\mathbf{r}}$ is the position vector of G referred to O, it follows that

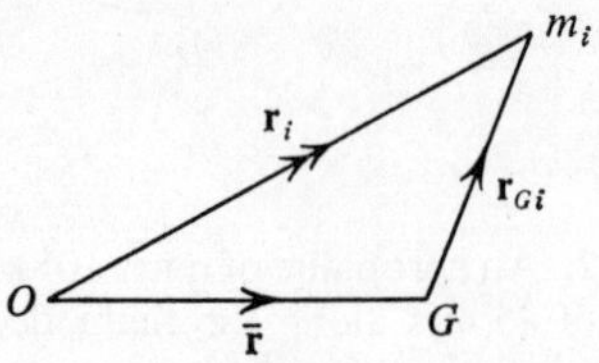

$$\mathbf{r}_i = \bar{\mathbf{r}} + \mathbf{r}_{Gi}.$$

Fig. 24

Differentiating with respect to time gives
$\mathbf{v}_i = \bar{\mathbf{v}} + \mathbf{v}_{Gi}$ where $\mathbf{v}_{Gi}$ is the velocity of m_i relative to G. Consequently

$$\Sigma \tfrac{1}{2} m_i v_i^2 = \tfrac{1}{2}\Sigma m_i(\bar{\mathbf{v}} + \mathbf{v}_{Gi})^2$$

$$= \tfrac{1}{2}\Sigma m_i(\bar{v}^2 + 2\bar{\mathbf{v}}\cdot\mathbf{v}_{Gi} + v_{Gi}^2)$$

giving $\Sigma \tfrac{1}{2} m_i v_i^2 = \tfrac{1}{2}\Sigma m_i \bar{v}^2 + \Sigma m_i \bar{\mathbf{v}}\cdot\mathbf{v}_{Gi} + \tfrac{1}{2}\Sigma m_i v_{Gi}^2.$

Now $\bar{\mathbf{v}}$ is constant over the summation, so that

(a) $\tfrac{1}{2}\Sigma m_i \bar{v}^2 = \tfrac{1}{2}\bar{v}^2 \Sigma m_i$

$$= \tfrac{1}{2}\bar{v}^2 M,$$

where $M = \Sigma m_i$, the total mass of the body.

(b) $\Sigma m_i \bar{\mathbf{v}}\cdot\mathbf{v}_{Gi} = \bar{\mathbf{v}}\cdot\Sigma m_i \mathbf{v}_{Gi}$

$$= \bar{\mathbf{v}}\cdot\Sigma m_i \frac{d}{dt}(\mathbf{r}_{Gi})$$

$$= \bar{\mathbf{v}}\cdot\frac{d}{dt}\Sigma m_i \mathbf{r}_{Gi}$$

$$= 0$$

since $\Sigma m_i \mathbf{r}_{Gi} = 0$ by definition.

(c) No simplification is convenient at present with $\frac{1}{2}\Sigma m_i v_{Gi}^2$.

Hence $\Sigma \tfrac{1}{2} m_i v_i^2 = \tfrac{1}{2} M \bar{v}^2 + \tfrac{1}{2}\Sigma m_i v_{Gi}^2,$

which states an important theorem: the kinetic energy of a system of particles is equal to the sum of the kinetic energy of the total mass M moving with the velocity of the centre of mass of the system and the kinetic energy of the system of particles when their motion is referred to their centre of mass.

1214

This is a significant theorem which is true for a system of particles whether or not they form a rigid body. When the particles do form a rigid body the term $\frac{1}{2}\Sigma m_i v_{Gi}^2$ can be simplified to incorporate a factor called the *moment of inertia* of the body about an axis through its centre of mass.

If $v_{Gi} = 0$ for all i, it follows that the body is not moving relative to its centre of mass. That is, the motion of the body is one of translation only, and the kinetic energy reduces to $\frac{1}{2}M\bar{v}^2$.

6.3 Now let us consider the term $\Sigma \mathbf{F}_i . \mathbf{s}_i$, where $\mathbf{F}_i$ is the resultant force acting on the ith particle. It is the vector sum of the internal and external forces acting on the particle. Obviously not all the particles have external forces applied to them, but they all experience internal forces of one form or another.

Consider two typical particles of mass m_1 and m_2 at A and B; represent the internal forces on each due to the presence of the other as $\mathbf{P}$ and $\mathbf{Q}$. If the body, which is rigid, is displaced, then AB will be displaced to $A'B'$, say, as shown in Figure 25. In this case both masses undergo different displacements and in the light of this we must examine the work done by $\mathbf{P}$ and $\mathbf{Q}$.

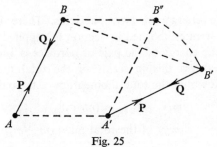

Fig. 25

Since the body is rigid any displacement can be expressed as a translation followed by a rotation. As $\mathbf{P}$ and $\mathbf{Q}$ are internal forces, $\mathbf{P}+\mathbf{Q} = 0$ regardless of whether they vary during the displacement. This being the case, the work done during the translation $\mathbf{s}$ is given by $(\mathbf{P}+\mathbf{Q}).\mathbf{s}$ and this is zero since $\mathbf{P}+\mathbf{Q} = 0$.

For the rotation of $A'B''$ about A', $\mathbf{P}$ does no work because its point of application is stationary; and $\mathbf{Q}$ does no work because the rigidity of the body ensures that its point of application is always moving in a direction perpendicular to its line of action.

Consequently the internal forces $\mathbf{P}$ and $\mathbf{Q}$ do no work in the displacement when considered as a pair. Since this pair is typical of all pairs of internal forces, it follows that the sum of the works done by all internal forces in a rigid body is zero for all displacements which do not deform the body.

Because the external forces are not predictable the work done by them cannot in general be simplified. However, if we restrict the displacement of the body to one of translation only it follows that the point of application of each of the external forces is translated through the same displacement $\mathbf{s}$, say. Consequently

$$\Sigma \mathbf{F}_i . \mathbf{s}_i = (\Sigma \mathbf{F}_i) . \mathbf{s} = \mathbf{F} . \mathbf{s},$$

where $\mathbf{F}$ is the resultant force acting on the body.

6.4 Collecting the results from these sections it follows that for a rigid *non-rotating* body the principle of energy again yields the simple equation

$$\mathbf{F} . \mathbf{s} = \tfrac{1}{2}mv^2 - \tfrac{1}{2}mu^2.$$

This is equivalent to saying that a rigid non-rotating body behaves like a particle of the same mass situated at its centre of mass.

It follows quite readily that for a system of such bodies the principle of energy yields the equation

$$\Sigma \mathbf{F} . \mathbf{s} = \Sigma \tfrac{1}{2}mv^2 - \Sigma \tfrac{1}{2}mu^2,$$

as might have been expected.

6.5 The kinetic energy of two particles. There is an important variant of the theorem established in Section 6.2 applied to two particles. Basically the kinetic energy of the pair of particles is $\tfrac{1}{2}m_1 v_1^2 + \tfrac{1}{2}m_2 v_2^2$. It is often useful to express this in terms of the total momentum. From Chapter 33 we know that the total momentum of the pair is

$$m_1 \mathbf{v}_1 + m_2 \mathbf{v}_2 = (m_1 + m_2)\bar{\mathbf{v}}.$$

Therefore the kinetic energy of the total mass $(m_1 + m_2)$ moving with the mass-centre is

$$\tfrac{1}{2}(m_1 + m_2)\bar{\mathbf{v}}^2 = \frac{(m_1 \mathbf{v}_1 + m_2 \mathbf{v}_2)^2}{2(m_1 + m_2)}.$$

Now it is a matter of simple algebra to verify that

$$\tfrac{1}{2}m_1 v_1^2 + \tfrac{1}{2}m_2 v_2^2 = \frac{(m_1 \mathbf{v}_1 + m_2 \mathbf{v}_2)^2}{2(m_1 + m_2)} + \frac{m_1 m_2 (\mathbf{v}_1 - \mathbf{v}_2)^2}{2(m_1 + m_2)}.$$

The first term on the right-hand side is the kinetic energy of the total mass moving with the mass-centre; the second term depends only on the relative velocity of the two masses.

Now when any internal explosion or impulse takes place $m_1 \mathbf{v}_1 + m_2 \mathbf{v}_2$ is constant, since this is the total momentum of the system which is conserved under these conditions; hence any change in the kinetic energy of the system depends only on a change in $\mathbf{v}_1 - \mathbf{v}_2 = \mathbf{u}$, the velocity of A relative to B. In any collision, $\mathbf{u}$ is reduced and kinetic energy is lost; in any explosion, $\mathbf{u}$ is increased and the system gains kinetic energy.

1216

Example 11. Two equal particles of mass m are joined by a light rod of length $2l$. The centre of the rod moves with velocity $\mathbf{v}$ and the rod rotates with angular velocity ω. Find the kinetic energy of the system and show that it is independent of the angle between the rod and the direction of $\mathbf{v}$.

Figure 26 shows the situation when the rod makes an angle θ with the direction of $\mathbf{v}$. The mid-point of AB is also the centre of mass of the system. O is an arbitrary origin and for convenience $\mathbf{i}$ and $\mathbf{j}$ are taken parallel and perpendicular to $\mathbf{v}$ respectively.

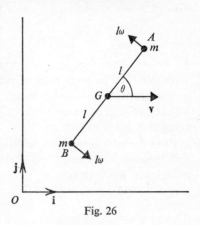

Fig. 26

It follows that the velocity of A relative to G is $l\omega$ perpendicular to the rod as shown in Figure 26. Similarly, for the velocity of B relative to G.

Consequently the theorem of Section 6.2 can be written as

$$\text{kinetic energy} = \tfrac{1}{2}(m+m)v^2 + \tfrac{1}{2}[m(l\omega)^2 + m(l\omega)^2]$$

$$= m(v^2 + l^2\omega^2).$$

An alternative method is to evaluate $\Sigma \tfrac{1}{2} m_i v_i^2$ from first principles. The velocities of A and B relative to 0 may be written in the form

$$\mathbf{v} + l\omega \begin{pmatrix} -\sin\theta \\ \cos\theta \end{pmatrix} \quad \text{and} \quad \mathbf{v} - l\omega \begin{pmatrix} -\sin\theta \\ \cos\theta \end{pmatrix}$$

respectively, from which the above result is easily obtained.

Example 12. Calculate the change in K.E. of the particles in Example 14 of Chapter 33.

From the solution to the problem the initial and final velocities of the particles A and B in m/s are respectively

$$\text{for } A, \quad \begin{pmatrix} 4 \\ 3 \end{pmatrix} \quad \text{and} \quad \begin{pmatrix} -2 \\ 3 \end{pmatrix}; \quad \text{and for } B, \quad \begin{pmatrix} -5 \\ 12 \end{pmatrix} \quad \text{and} \quad \begin{pmatrix} 4 \\ 12 \end{pmatrix}.$$

Consequently the initial K.E. of the system is

$$\tfrac{1}{2}.3 \begin{pmatrix} 4 \\ 3 \end{pmatrix} . \begin{pmatrix} 4 \\ 3 \end{pmatrix} + \tfrac{1}{2}.2 \begin{pmatrix} -5 \\ 12 \end{pmatrix} . \begin{pmatrix} -5 \\ 12 \end{pmatrix}$$

giving $\tfrac{3}{2}.25 + 169 = \tfrac{413}{2}$ J.

The final K.E. of the system is

$$\tfrac{1}{2}.3.\begin{pmatrix}-2\\3\end{pmatrix}.\begin{pmatrix}-2\\3\end{pmatrix}+\tfrac{1}{2}.2\begin{pmatrix}4\\12\end{pmatrix}.\begin{pmatrix}4\\12\end{pmatrix}$$

giving $\qquad\qquad\qquad \tfrac{3}{2}.13+160 = \tfrac{359}{2}$ J.

Hence $\qquad$ the K.E. lost $= \dfrac{413-359}{2} = 27$ J.

Example 13. The nose cone of mass $\tfrac{1}{4}$ tonne is ejected from the front of a space capsule of mass $\tfrac{1}{2}$ tonne when travelling at 750 m/s with a relative velocity of 30 m/s at an angle of 60° to the initial line of motion of the combined mass.

Find the new directions, relative to the initial direction, of the capsule and the nose cone and the difference between the initial and final kinetic energies of the system.

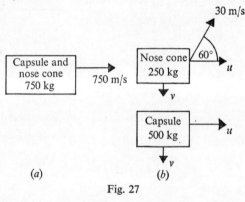

(a) $\qquad\qquad\qquad\qquad$ (b)

Fig. 27

Figures 27(a) and (b) give the initial and final velocities of the system and its components. Notice that all that is known of the final velocities is the relative velocity of the nose cone to the capsule. Hence the relative velocity of the capsule to earth in component form $\begin{pmatrix}u\\v\end{pmatrix}$ must be considered.

The unknown velocity $\begin{pmatrix}u\\v\end{pmatrix}$ can only be obtained by appealing to the impulse–momentum equation. Considering nose cone and capsule to make up the system and taking unit vectors **i** and **j** across and down the page, momentum is conserved since there is no external impulse on the system giving

$$750\begin{pmatrix}750\\0\end{pmatrix} = 500\begin{pmatrix}u\\v\end{pmatrix}+250\begin{pmatrix}u+15\\v-15\sqrt3\end{pmatrix}$$

where the velocities are in m/s.

1218

This gives

$$\begin{pmatrix} u \\ v \end{pmatrix} = \begin{pmatrix} 745 \\ 5\sqrt{3} \end{pmatrix}$$

as the final velocity of the capsule and $\begin{pmatrix} 760 \\ -10\sqrt{3} \end{pmatrix}$ as the final velocity of the nose cone.

Hence the final direction of the capsule is at θ to the initial line of flight, where

$$\tan \theta = \frac{v}{u} = \frac{5\sqrt{3}}{745}$$

$$= \frac{\sqrt{3}}{149}.$$

Also the final direction of the nose cone makes an angle ϕ with the initial line of flight where

$$\tan \phi = \frac{\sqrt{3}}{76}.$$

Initial K.E. of system $= \frac{1}{2} \times 750 \times 750^2$ J

    $= 210\,937\,500$ J.

Final K.E. of capsule $= \frac{1}{2} \times 500 . (v^2 + u^2)$ J

    $= 138\,775\,000$ J.

Final K.E. of nose cone $= \frac{1}{2} \times 250[(u+15)^2 + (15\sqrt{3}-v)^2]$ J

    $= 72\,237\,500$ J.

Final K.E. of system $= 211\,012\,500$ J, and the gain in K.E. of the system is $75\,000$ J.

The points to notice in this solution are:
(i) the form of the final K.E. of the capsule;
(ii) the form of the final, more complicated, K.E. of the nose cone;
(iii) the fact that the K.E. increased during the propulsion of the nose cone, due to the conversion to kinetic energy (among other forms of energy) of the fuel used to give the nose cone its required separation velocity; whereas, for the system as a whole, the momentum was conserved, there being no externally applied force during the activity.

Example 14. Design an experiment to find the velocity of a pellet from an air gun and produce the necessary theory.

The experiment could consist of firing a pellet into a lump of clay suspended by a light thread from a fixed support. If we ensure that the pellet comes to rest in the clay we can measure the height h above the initial position at which the clay and pellet come momentarily to rest.

The theory requires us to express the unknown speed v of the pellet in terms of the masses of the clay and the pellet and the height h.

To find the combined horizontal velocity u of the pellet and clay we apply the principle of conservation of momentum to the impact in a horizontal direction. This gives

$$mv = (m+M)u.$$

To find the height of the clay and pellet when they come to rest, we recollect from a previous section that the tension does no work, and the equation of energy gives

$$\tfrac{1}{2}(m+M)u^2 = (m+M)gh.$$

Hence
$$u = \sqrt{(2gh)}$$

and
$$v = \left(\frac{m+M}{m}\right)\sqrt{(2gh)}.$$

This is a straightforward theory, but two points arise from our restrictions to particle motion and our use of conservation of momentum:

(*a*) the clay and pellet must not rotate;

(*b*) the velocity of the pellet on impact must be horizontal—otherwise there will be an impulse in the string and the subsequent momentum will not be equal to the total momentum of the pellet before impact.

Exercise E

1. Find the change in K.E. of the trucks in Example 12 of Chapter 33.

2. A truck of mass 6 tonnes moving at 2 m/s catches up and collides with one of 4 tonnes moving at 1·5 m/s, the two trucks remaining together after the collision. With what speed may they be expected to move off, and what is the corresponding loss of energy in Joules?

3. A truck of mass 2 tonnes moving with speed u m/s collides and couples with a truck of mass 5 tonnes moving in the same straight line with speed v m/s. Prove that, for any values of u and v for which collision is possible, there is necessarily a loss of kinetic energy.

State briefly how this result is reconciled with the law of conservation of energy.

4. A body is composed of four particles of equal mass fastened to the end of two light rods of length $2a$. The rods are rigidly attached at their mid-points and are mutually perpendicular. If the centre of the rods is moving with velocity v and the system is rotating with angular velocity ω in the plane of the rods, calculate the total K.E. and show that it is independent of the angle made by the rods with the direction of v.

5. Use the results of Question 4 to find the K.E. of a thin circular hoop of radius a and mass M rotating at an angular rate of ω and having its centre moving at a rate u. Does your result depend on whether the centre moves in a straight line or not?

What is the K.E. of the circular hoop if it rolls along (without slipping) at a speed u?

6. A dart of mass m travelling horizontally with speed u strikes a block of mass M which is freely suspended from a long string and sticks in it so that they move off together without rotation. Calculate the total K.E. of the bodies before and immediately after impact and find the loss of K.E. If the block had been thrown with velocity u at a suspended stationary dart and had stuck on it and they had moved off without rotation, what would have been the energy loss?

7. A frog of mass 125 g is standing on a brick of mass 500 g, which is free to move on the smooth ice of a frozen pond. The frog leaps with a horizontal velocity of 0·24 m/s onto a second brick of mass 250 g, also free to move on the smooth ice of the same pond. Discuss the subsequent motion of the two bricks giving their separate kinetic energies. If the total energy supplied by the frog for the leap is 3.10^{-3} J, explain possible sources of the loss of energy.

8. A boy of mass m gently mounts a sledge of mass M which is being pulled by a horizontal force P to give a constant velocity u. The boy slips on the sledge, the coefficient of friction being μ, but there is no friction between the sledge and the ground. Calculate:
  (a) the distance moved by the boy relative to the sledge;
  (b) the distance moved by the sledge relative to the ground;
  (c) the work done by the internal forces in the system;
  (d) the work done by P;
  (e) the gain in K.E. of the system.
Explain the discrepancy between (a) and (e), the calculations relating to the interval of the boy's motion relative to the sledge.

9. A cricket ball of mass m is batted along a platform with a speed u. What is the work done by the batsman on the ball? What is the gain in kinetic energy of the ball?

The same cricket ball is then batted by the same batsman at a relative speed u forwards along the corridor of a train travelling at speed v. What is the work done by the batsman on the ball and what is the gain in kinetic energy of the ball? Comment on your results.

10. A child and a bicycle together are of mass 50 kg. The bicycle is accelerated from rest to 3 m/s in 4 s. Find the work done by the frictional force acting on the bicycle and the kinetic energy of the bicycle and rider.

If that part of the earth is travelling at v m/s find the work done by the frictional force producing the acceleration of the bicycle and the change in kinetic energy of the bicycle and rider. Calculate the work done by the friction on the earth, and the quantities of energy supplied by the rider and the earth. Comment on your results.

11. Two conkers are of equal mass. One is tightly held on a piece of string of length 25 cm. The other is wielded so that it strikes the stationary conker with a velocity of 6 m/s along a line making 30° with the string. If the striking conker is brought momentarily to rest by the impact, describe the subsequent motion of the other conker.

If the support remains stationary, will the conker describe a complete circle? If not, where will it leave the circular path?

How much energy is lost through the impact? Give some explanation of why it is lost.

12. A satellite weighing 1000 kg moving at 1200 m/s breaks up into two equal parts so that one part then moves at 1202 m/s in a direction which makes an angle of 0·03° with the original direction. Give, correct to four significant figures, the new speed of the other part.

13. An airborne firework of mass $2m$ kg explodes into two equal parts. Before the explosion the velocity was

$$\mathbf{u} = \begin{pmatrix} 5u \\ 0 \end{pmatrix}.$$

After the explosion the velocity of one part was $\mathbf{v} = \begin{pmatrix} u \\ 3u \end{pmatrix}$. Find the velocity of the other part
(a) if $\mathbf{v}$ is relative to the same frame of reference as $\mathbf{u}$,
(b) if $\mathbf{v}$ is relative to the new velocity of the other part.
In each case calculate the increase in kinetic energy of the system.

14. A body of mass 6 kg moving with velocity

$$\begin{pmatrix} 3 \\ 6 \\ 11 \end{pmatrix} \text{ m/s}$$

collides with and sticks to a body of mass 10 kg moving with velocity

$$\begin{pmatrix} 3 \\ -2 \\ 3 \end{pmatrix} \text{ m/s.}$$

Find the change in kinetic energy due to the impact and verify the conclusion of Section 6.5.

15. Find the change in kinetic energy of the systems in Questions 6–11 of Exercise D in Chapter 33.

16. A man stands on a motionless trolley which can run on rails with negligible resistance. He walks briskly towards the front of the trolley. What happens? When he reaches the front of the trolley he stays there. Is the trolley again at rest? If so, where? And if not, what has happened? Does it matter qualitatively whether the man is heavier or lighter than the trolley? Does it matter quantitatively?

2.

before

→ 2m/s

| 6,000 kg |

→ 1·5 m/s.

| 4,000 kg |

after

| 10,000 kg |

← v

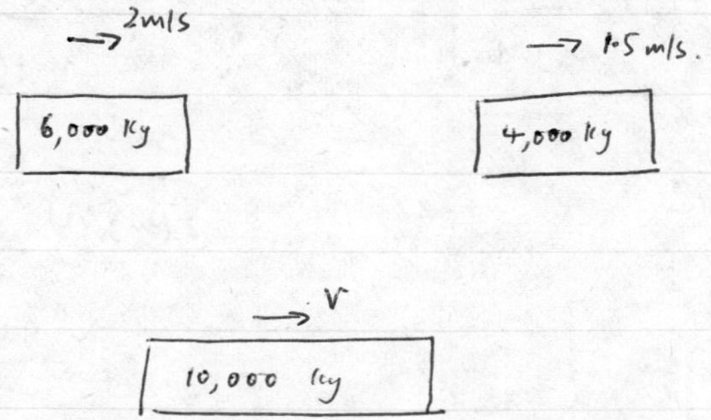

conservation of momentum

$6,000 \times 2 + 1·5 \times 4,000 = 10,000 v$

$12 + 6 = 10 v$

$18 = 10 v$

$v = 1·8$ m/s

loss in k.t. $= \dfrac{1}{2}mu^2\left[1 - \dfrac{m}{M+m}\right] = \dfrac{1}{2}mu^2\left(\dfrac{M}{M+m}\right)$

$= \dfrac{Mm}{2(M+m)}u^2$

C.o.f.m

$Mu = (M+m)v$

$v = \dfrac{M}{M+m}u$

$\dfrac{1}{2}(M+m)v^2 = \dfrac{1}{2}\dfrac{M^2u^2}{(M+m)}$

(7).

$$2 \qquad \boxed{\frac{1}{M+m}}$$

$$= \frac{1}{2} M u^2 \frac{m}{M+m} = \frac{M m u^2}{2(m+m)} \qquad \text{the same!}$$

before →0   125g stay

after

$.125(.2+) - .5 v = 0$

$v = .06 \text{ m/s}$

• 2+ m/s

mom π

$\underline{\text{k.e. after}} \;=\; \dfrac{1}{2}\,(10{,}000)(1.8) \cdot \;=\; 9000 \ J$

6.

$\text{loss of k. energy} \;=\; 7500 \ J$

$\underline{\text{C. of M.}}$

$$mu \;=\; (M+m)\,V$$

$$V \;=\; \frac{m}{m+M}\,u.$$

$\underline{\text{k.e. before}} \qquad \dfrac{1}{2} m u^{2} \qquad\qquad \underline{\text{k.e. after}} \qquad \dfrac{1}{2}\,\dfrac{(m+M)\,V^{2}}{\rule{1cm}{0.4pt}} \;=\; \dfrac{1}{2}\,\dfrac{(m+M)\,m^{2}}{(m+M)^{2}}\,u^{2}$

$$=\; \dfrac{1}{2}\,\dfrac{m^{2}}{m+M}\,u^{2}$$

17. A plank *AB* of length *l* and mass *M* is at rest on a smooth horizontal floor. A 'man' of mass *m* is originally at rest on the plank at the end *A*. He 'walks' along the plank from *A* to *B*, without slipping, at constant speed *V* relative to plank, stopping just as he reaches *B*. Find:

    (*a*) the time of the motion;

    (*b*) the distance moved by the plank;

    (*c*) the kinetic energy (man plus plank) at any instant during the motion.

18. (*a*) A pile driver of mass 100 kg is dropped through 1·6 m onto a pile of mass 1 tonne. The driver does not bounce. If the pile is driven 15 cm into the earth what resistance does the earth offer, if it is assumed to be constant?

    (*b*) Find the height from which a pile driver of mass 200 kg must be dropped onto a pile of mass 1·4 tonnes if the combined pile and driver drive the pile 10 cm into the earth. The earth offers a constant resistance of $1·8 \times 10^4$ N.

19. A pile driver consists of a block of mass 800 kg which strikes a pile of mass 100 kg. The block falls from a height of 1·8 m above the pile top onto the pile and does not rebound. The pile encounters a resistance of $2·5 \times 10^4$ N in the soil. Find the depth of penetration of the pile.

20. Find the velocity at height *h* m above the nozzle of a water jet issuing *m* kg of water per second vertically upwards at *v* m/s. If this water impinges on a surface at this height and does not rebound from the surface (i.e. falls from the surface starting from rest), find the force exerted by it and hence find the height at which the jet will support a ball of mass *M* kg.

7. POWER

7.1 Two cars are driven up a hill. One does the journey in one minute, the other takes three minutes. Assuming that the external conditions for the two cars are more or less the same, they do comparable amounts of work. But the work is done in different intervals of time and we acknowledge that the first car is more powerful than the second.

In fact *power* is defined as the rate of doing work per unit time. We have already met expressions for the rate of doing work in Sections 4.1 and 5.1, and you will remember that we obtained the expression

$$\frac{dW}{dt} = \mathbf{F}.\mathbf{v},$$

where *W* denotes the work done by a variable force **F** whose point of application is being displaced with a velocity **v**. Since **F** is variable the expression is applicable in all circumstances; and further, since

$$\mathbf{F} = m\mathbf{a}$$

it follows that $\qquad \dfrac{dW}{dt} = \mathbf{F}.\mathbf{v} = m\mathbf{a}.\mathbf{v},$

an alternative form which is sometimes useful.

7.2 Units of power. Since we frequently wish to compare different powers, the conventional time interval used is the second. Consequently, the unit of power in the m.k.s. system is 1 joule/second, which is usually called 1 *watt* (W). The unit in the c.g.s. system is 1 erg/s; 1 W = 10⁷ erg/s. Even so, a watt is a small unit of power and the kilowatt (kW) is often used for convenience.

Example 15. A pump takes water from rest in a tank and delivers it at the same level with a speed of 15 m/s at a flow rate of 100 kg/s. Find the power of the pump assuming that there is no turbulence in the water giving large relative motions.

In t seconds the mass of water shifted is $100t$ kg and the kinetic energy imparted is

$$\tfrac{1}{2} \times 100t \times (15)^2 \text{ J.}$$

The rate of change of kinetic energy is thus $\dfrac{100 \times 225}{2}$ J/s and the power of the pump is 11·25 kW.

Example 16. A pump takes water at a certain speed and delivers it at the same speed 15 m higher at a flow rate of 100 kg/s. Find the power of the pump.

Since the water does not accelerate, the resultant force acting on each particle all the time is equal to the weight of the particle. In t seconds a total mass of $100t$ kg is raised 15 m; the work done is therefore

$$100t \times 9\cdot8 \times 15 \text{ J.}$$

The power of the pump is thus 980×15 W or 14·6 kW.

Example 17. At what steady speed can an engine whose pulling force can work at a rate of 400 kW pull a train of 250 tonnes: (*a*) along the level, (*b*) up a slope of 1 in 125, if the resistance to motion of the train is 60 N per tonne of train in each case? (*c*) If the slope levels off when the train is travelling at its steady uphill speed what will be the initial acceleration?

(*a*) On the level.

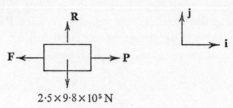

Fig. 28

At a steady speed
$$\mathbf{P}+\mathbf{R}+\mathbf{F}-2{\cdot}5\times9{\cdot}8\times10^5\mathbf{j} = 0,$$

so that
$$\mathbf{P}.\mathbf{v}+\mathbf{F}.\mathbf{v} = 0,$$

the other scalar products being zero. Now $\mathbf{P}.\mathbf{v}$ is the power of the engine, given as 4.10^5 W; hence

$$4.10^5\text{ W} = 60\times250\text{ N}\times v.$$

Hence
$$v = \tfrac{80}{3}\text{ m/s} = 96\text{ km/h}.$$

Note that both $\mathbf{P}.\mathbf{v}$ and $\mathbf{F}$ are given in 'Engineers' units'.
(b) Up an incline.

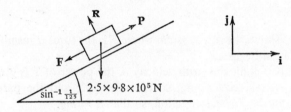

Fig. 29

Arguing as before when the speed is steady, we have

$$\mathbf{P}+\mathbf{R}+\mathbf{F}-2{\cdot}5\times9{\cdot}8\times10^5\mathbf{j}\text{ N} = 0$$

whence
$$\mathbf{P}.\mathbf{v}+\mathbf{F}.\mathbf{v}-2{\cdot}5\times9{\cdot}8\times10^5(\mathbf{j}.\mathbf{v})\text{ N} = 0$$
giving
$$4\times10^5\text{ W}-250\times60\text{ N}\times v-2{\cdot}5\times9{\cdot}8\times10^5\text{ N}\times\tfrac{1}{125}\times v = 0$$

that is
$$4000\text{ W} = 346\,v.$$

Finally
$$v = 11{\cdot}6\text{ m/s} = 41{\cdot}6\text{ km/h}.$$

(c) When the train levels out we have, from Figure 28(a),

$$\mathbf{P}+\mathbf{R}+\mathbf{F}-2{\cdot}5\times9{\cdot}8\times10^5\mathbf{j}\text{ N} = (2{\cdot}5\times10^5\text{ kg})\,\mathbf{a}$$

whence
$$\mathbf{P}.\mathbf{v}+\mathbf{F}.\mathbf{v} = (2{\cdot}5\times10^5\text{ kg})\,\mathbf{a}.\mathbf{v}$$

giving
$$4\times10^5-250\times60\times11{\cdot}6 = 2{\cdot}5\times10^5\times11{\cdot}6\times a$$

from which
$$a = 7{\cdot}79\times10^{-2}\text{ m/s}^2.$$

Example 18. A parcel of mass m is placed on a conveyor belt moving at a constant speed of u such that on contact with the belt the parcel has negligible velocity. The parcel initially slips on the conveyor belt, the coefficient of friction being μ. Investigate the situation and find the power required to maintain the speed of u whilst the parcel is coming to rest.

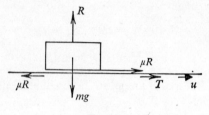

Fig. 30

The figure shows the force system where T is the force transmitted to the belt to maintain its speed.

Since the belt is moving with velocity u, the power of T is given by Tu.

The belt is not accelerating, so that $T = \mu R$; and the parcel is not accelerating in the vertical direction, so that $R = mg$.

Consequently, the required power is μmgu.

However, before we leave this example, it is worth making one or two other observations.

The time taken for the parcel to come to rest relative to the belt is given by the impulse–momentum equation applied to the parcel. This gives $\mu mgt = mu$, from which we obtain $t = u/\mu g$. Since the acceleration of the parcel is μg, the distance it moves in this time is given by

$$\tfrac{1}{2} \times \mu g \times \left(\frac{u}{\mu g}\right)^2 = \frac{u^2}{2\mu g}.$$

Consequently the work done by the frictional force μR on the parcel is given by

$$\mu mg \times \frac{u^2}{2\mu g} = \tfrac{1}{2}mu^2,$$

and this is the gain in kinetic energy of the parcel. However, the work done by T whilst the parcel is coming to rest is given by

$$Tut = \mu mgu + \frac{u}{\mu g} = mu^2.$$

In other words the energy supplied to the system is twice the energy gained by the system. The difference must be dissipated in other forms such as

1226

heat due to friction. In fact, the relative distance which the parcel slips back on the belt is $u^2/\mu g - u^2/2\mu g = u^2/2\mu g$, so that

$$-\mu mg \times \left(\frac{u^2}{2\mu g}\right) = -\tfrac{1}{2}mu^2$$

is the work done by friction in the relative slipping, and this is the energy dissipated by the friction.

Exercise F

1. A man steadily winds up the 2 kg 'weight' of a grandfather clock through 1·5 m in ¼ min. Find the power of the tension in this chain over the 'weight'. Is the power of the force between the man's finger and the key likely to be larger than this?

2. (*a*) A crane steadily raises a 7½ tonnes ingot at a rate of 2 m/s. What is the power of the force at the attachment? Is the power of the force on the chain at the drum likely to be larger than this?

(*b*) If the power of the force at the axle of the chain drum is increased to 250 kW, and the power at the point of attachment is 70 % of this, what will the acceleration of the ingot be when the velocity is 2 m/s?

(*c*) If the crane continues to produce this power at the point of attachment, what will be the final steady speed achieved by the ingot?

3. Find the power of the projector machine at intervals of 1 m during the thrust in Question 2 of Exercise C.

4. A pump takes water from rest in a hole in the road and delivers it 2 m higher on the road surface at 3 m/s at a flow rate of 25 kg/s. If the pump is 80 % efficient find the power of the pump in kW.

5. The following specification of modern British Rail passenger haulage equipment is for a train of mass 475 tonnes. A steady speed of 140 km/h on the level; a steady speed of 90 km/h up a gradient of 1 in 70.

Find the resistance to motion, assumed constant, in N/tonne of the train's mass, and the power required to deliver these performances.

6. Repeat Question 5, but for modern British Rail freight haulage equipment. The mass of the train is 950 tonnes, 110 km/h is required on the level and 70 km/h is required up a gradient of 1 in 70.

7. The Pacific steam locomotive 'Mallard' had a tractive effort rating of $1·4 \times 10^5$ N. At what horsepower would she have been working when making her record breaking run of 202 km/h?

8. A Diesel Multiple unit is expected to accelerate at 0·5 m/s² per second on the level. If the mass of the train is 180 tonnes and the track resistance amounts to 320 N/tonne of the train, calculate the power output of the diesel unit when travelling at 50 km/h.

9. A diesel-electric locomotive has an output of 3000 kW when maintaining a steady 160 km/h. Calculate the resistance to motion if this is on a level track.

With the same resistance, find the acceleration of a train of mass 475 tonne when travelling at 60 km/h on the level.

10. On a level road a car can develop 30 kW when travelling at a maximum speed of 90 km/h. Find the resistance to motion.

Assuming the resistance to be constant, at what maximum speed in the same gear can the car climb a gradient of 1 in 20? Assume the mass of the car to be 1000 kg.

11. A motor bus can develop 75 kW. If the total resistance to motion when the bus is fully loaded and of mass 14000 kg, is 350 kgf, calculate the maximum speed of the bus (*a*) on the level, (*b*) up an incline of 1 in 80.

12. The speed of a train of mass 100 tonnes varies with time in accordance with the following table:

Speed (km/h)	0	30	45	60	65	70	72
Time (s)	0	10	20	30	40	50	60

The train is running down an incline of 1 in 500. Find the power being exerted at the ends of the first 20 s, and the first 40 s, if the frictional and air resistance to motion amount to 40 N and 80 N per tonne at each instant respectively.

13. 60 kg of anthracite grains are deposited on a conveyor belt moving with a constant speed of 5 m/s horizontally. If the centre of mass of the load moves 2 m relative to the belt before coming to rest on the belt, calculate the power required to maintain the speed of 5 m/s whilst the load is being deposited. (Assume that the load will move bodily along the belt, although in practice this will not be the case.)

14. For how long is the calculated output of power in Question 13 required? Consequently, at what rate can anthracite grains be deposited on the conveyor belt if this power rating is maintained indefinitely?

What power is required if the loading is 5 tonne/minute?

15. A frigate is driven at a speed of 50 km/h by means of engines delivering an effective $2·5 \times 10^4$ kW. Calculate the resistance to motion of the ship and, assuming that the resistance varies as the square of the speed, what effective power would be required for a speed of 60 km/h?

16. The power of the wind resistance on a car at 55 km/h is -3 kW. The force of the resistance varies as the square of the speed; find the power of the resistance at 110 km/h.

The power of the forces flexing the tyres rises approximately linearly with speed, being zero at rest and $-3·5$ kW at 55 km/h. Find the total power of these two forces at 110 km/h. The total power of the driving force at 55 km/h is 19·7 kW and at 110 km/h is 33 kW. Find the acceleration of the car at each speed if its mass is 720 kg.

17. A boat has to steam a given distance upstream. If it does so at constant speed, and if the power varies as the cube of the velocity relative to the water, write down the total time taken for the journey, and the total work done during the journey. Hence show that the most economical speed is half that of the stream relative to the bank.

1228

18. A man of mass 70 kg walking at 1·5 m/s walks onto a moving pavement travelling at 2 m/s. If the man eventually stands still on the pavement, find the power required to maintain the speed of the pavement. Do you need to know how long the man takes to come to rest on the pavement? If so take the time to be 5 s.

Discuss the situation that arises if the man starts to walk at 1·5 m/s relative to the moving pavement in the same direction.

19. If on an escalator the man in Question 18 comes to rest before it begins to ascend a slope of 1 in 1, find the power required to maintain the speed of the escalator while the man is being carried up the incline.

Discuss the situation that arises if the man starts to walk up the escalator at 1·5 m/s relative to it whilst it is ascending the incline.

40

DIMENSIONAL ANALYSIS

1. DIMENSIONAL CONSISTENCY

In Chapter 18 we discussed the group of dimensions generated by combination on the set $\{\mathbf{L}, \mathbf{T}\}$. The idea of dimension was developed further in Chapter 24 by the addition of $\mathbf{M}$, the dimension of mass. We found that all mechanical quantities could be expressed in terms of these three dimensions; but the choice of these three as fundamental is based on experience and convenience.

It is important to recognize that dimensional systems can be based on fundamental dimensions other than $\mathbf{M}$, $\mathbf{L}$ and $\mathbf{T}$. For example, the fact that the speed of light is a universal constant might encourage us to use the dimensions of speed $\mathbf{V}$, time $\mathbf{T}$, and (say) force $\mathbf{F}$ as the fundamental dimensions. On such a basis, what would be the dimensions of mass and length?

When we attempt to set up a mathematical model of a physical system it is necessary that the model is *dimensionally consistent*. This means that all the terms in any equation we write down must refer to objects of the same physical kind; only Bears of Very Little Brain can be allowed such whimsical statements as

'Whatever his weight in pounds, shillings, and ounces,
He always seems bigger because of his bounces.'

as an expression of the connection between momentum and impulse. In other words, all the terms must have the same dimensions; if they do not, a change in the unit of measurement of any fundamental quantity will destroy the validity of the equation. This is the basic principle of dimensional analysis.

Dimensions of the most useful mechanical and electrical quantities, with the equations that define them, are given in Table 1 at the end of the chapter. You are advised to cover up the column of dimensions and to see if you can derive them yourself from the defining equations. Note that the units of work and power are identical in both electrical and mechanical systems.

Exercise A

1. Check the dimensional consistency of the following equations:

(a) $F = mv$; (b) $Fvx = \frac{1}{2}mv^3$;
(c) $t = RC = L/R = \sqrt{(LC)}$; (d) $VI = Fv = P$.

1230

2. State which of the following quantities are dimensionless:

$$(a)\ \rho v l / \eta; \quad (b)\ v^2/(gl); \quad (c)\ v^2 l \rho / \sigma; \quad (d)\ RI/(\Phi f).$$

3. m kilograms of water per second fall through a height of h metres and drive a turbine of 50 % efficiency. The turbine drives an electrical generator of 80 % efficiency. How many kilowatts of energy are produced?

4. If c is a velocity and h has the dimensions of energy × time, what is the nature of the following physical quantities:

(a) mc^2;   (b) hf;   (c) $4\pi m v/h$;

(d) $\dfrac{c^2}{IV} \dfrac{dQ}{dx} \dfrac{d\Phi}{dy}$;   (e) $cRCf$?

2. MECHANICAL AND OTHER SYSTEMS

Some of the physical quantities listed in Table 1 at the end of the chapter are readily understandable in the context of the physical phenomena with which we are all in contact in our everyday lives. Measurement of areas, volumes and weights, movements of cars and bicycles, the power of aeroplanes and trains, the orbiting of satellites—all these involve properties which are tolerably familiar. The same is also true of some properties of *elastic* media—of fluids and gases. Thus the motion of the oceans, the movement of the wind, the flow of water in pipes, are often comprehended within a system whose fundamental dimensions are **M, L, T** and whose basic dynamical law is Newton's second law. Such systems are sometimes called mechanical systems, or occasionally Newtonian systems.

But there are many physical phenomena which go far beyond the capabilities of this second law and we mention a few of them. First, come those which involve heat and temperature. The heating of a kettle, the explosion of petrol vapour in a car cylinder, the solar processes of energy conversion, are all examples of systems which require physical laws in addition to the mechanical ones. Even some of the systems mentioned in the last paragraph sometimes exhibit features which require these additional laws. For example, the wind, if now regarded on a meteorological scale, carries with it thermal properties which can seldom be ignored. The connection between speed and temperature of a moving gas becomes significant at the high speeds of supersonic flight, while a factory hot-water system could not be efficiently designed, even from a dynamical viewpoint, without taking proper account of temperature effects.

Electric and magnetic effects add to our list. The forces induced by electrostatic charges, the currents produced by movement in magnetic fields, the heating of wires by the passage of currents, the magnetohydrodynamic effects of conducting fluids flowing in magnetic fields all represent situations in which, again, more is required than Newton's second law.

Finally, the phenomena of atomic physics require a combination of many of the laws we have implicitly mentioned in the fields of heat and thermo-dynamics, and of magnetism and electricity; and the basic dimensions are correspondingly more numerous. In fact, convention has it that thermo-dynamics has four fundamental dimensions; electromagnetism also has four, but different ones; and atomic physics has five.

3. DIMENSIONS IN ELECTRICITY

3.1 The fourth fundamental dimension in electromagnetism can of course be any electromagnetic quantity, and a number of different ones have from time to time been proposed. Nowadays when electric currents can be produced very easily and can be measured accurately with a current balance, current is often taken to be the fundamental electrical quantity. From a theoretical point of view charge, the time-integral of current, is a little simpler to work with, and we shall adopt this as our fundamental dimension **Q**; this has in fact been done in Table 1, p. 1245. This enables us to consider the dimensions of a number of electrical quantities which occur in the equations concerned with electric circuits which we have studied. First of all, let us compare an electrical and a mechanical situation.

Example 1. (*a*) An alternating e.m.f. $V \sin \omega t$ is applied as shown to a circuit containing capacitance and resistance. Derive a mathematical model to represent the situation.

A circuit diagram is shown in Figure 1; the mathematical model is a very precise representation of the physical situation in this case. If the current flowing is I (which equals dQ/dt), then

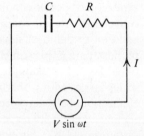

$$V \sin \omega t = IR + Q/C.$$

Differentiating this and dividing by R, we obtain

$$\frac{dI}{dt} + \frac{I}{RC} = \frac{\omega V}{R} \cos \omega t.$$

Fig. 1

We note that the dimensions of each term in this equation are $\mathbf{QT^{-2}}$.

(*b*) A horizontal oscillating force $F \cos \omega t$ is applied to a sphere that is floating submerged in a fluid of the same density, such that the motion is resisted by a force proportional to the velocity of the sphere. Derive a mathematical model to describe the displacement of the sphere.

1232

The forces and acceleration are shown in the diagram (Figure 2). Equating the force and mass-acceleration vectors, we obtain

$$F \cos \omega t - kv = m(dv/dt),$$

that is, $\dfrac{dv}{dt} + \dfrac{kv}{m} = \dfrac{F}{m} \cos \omega t.$

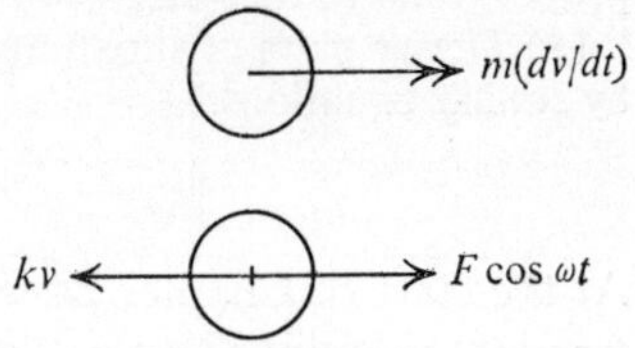

We note that the dimensions of each term in this equation are LT^{-2}.

Fig. 2

3.2 Electrical analogues.

The close analogy between equations found in (a) and (b) suggests that the behaviour of the mechanical system might be investigated by using the analogous electrical system, which is more flexible, and from which it is easier to record results. This is the basis of the idea of *simulation* as used in an analogue computer. Here a problem in some branch of applied science is replaced by a mathematical model, which is translated in its turn into electrical terms and set up in appropriate circuitry. Currents, voltages and so on derived from this are then translated back into results related to the original problem.

In this particular problem we should, if possible, choose $1/RC$ to be equal to k/m, and $\omega V/R$ so that it is equal to F/m. Then the current I represents the velocity v. Since it is easy to vary the magnitudes of R and C, and possible, though perhaps less convenient, to vary the frequency ω, a wide variety of situations can be investigated. The initial conditions are the starting values of t and I; these are first fed in, and the results are then read off as a series of values of I and t, or they can be displayed as a graph on a plotter or an oscilloscope.

Exercise B

1. Suggest suitable values for V, R and C in the above example, given that the unit of time in (a) is 1 millisecond, in (b) 1 s; $m = 2$ kg, $k = 1$ N s/m, $F = 5$ N, ω (in (b)) $= \frac{1}{3}\pi$.

2. Obtain and compare mathematical models of each of the following situations. In each case, check your equations for dimensional consistency.

(a) A stone is dropped into the sea from a height; once in the water its motion is resisted by a force proportional to its velocity.

(b) A battery of e.m.f. E is suddenly connected across a resistance R in series with an inductance L.

(c) The rate of decay of a fungus varies as the sum of a constant term and a term proportional to the amount of fungus present.

(d) A potential difference increasing from zero uniformly with time is applied to a capacitance C and resistance R in series.

(e) When the accelerator pedal of a car is held steady, the acceleration has a constant value (depending on how far the pedal is depressed) minus a term proportional to the velocity of the car.

(f) Devise pairs of situations which, while physically unlike, can be modelled by similar equations.

4. SCALE

At the start of Chapter 24 we considered the problem of determining the terminal velocity of a free-falling parachutist. We realized that there were numerous factors involved, too many to achieve an exact theoretical solution. But is it possible to simplify the situation, and construct a mathematical model which will give a good representation and predict the answer with reasonable accuracy?

Consider the following falling objects: a small spider, a particle of mist, a raindrop from a thunder-cloud, a stone down an old mine-shaft, a bomb, ... What are the factors which have most effect on the terminal velocity of these objects? Is not size the major factor? For a start, then, let us isolate this factor by considering similar bodies.

Since, at least to begin with, it is sensible to try to solve the very simplest problem before going on to more complicated ones, we will choose to investigate the class of bodies with the simplest three-dimensional characteristics, namely, spheres. And, so that attention is directed only on their size, we will take a number of spheres of different sizes, but otherwise identical—that is, they will be as smooth as possible and made of exactly the same uniform material.

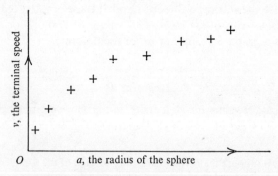

Fig. 3 The terminal speed of a falling sphere.

So our experiment is quite simple. An apparatus is set up to measure the final, constant, speed v of a sphere dropping through air, and the results, when plotted on a graph, would look something like Figure 3.

You should now think hard about these results. Why should a bigger sphere fall faster than a smaller one?

1234

We shall assume that the problem of determining the terminal velocity of a sphere of given size is:

(a) capable of being modelled by the equations of mechanics;

(b) sensibly posed, with a unique solution.

Any equations obtained must be dimensionally consistent. Now our experiment suggests that $v = f(a)$, but clearly this will not do. Why not? Would our experimental results have been different on the moon, or in a spaceship? Clearly gravity must be involved; no gravity, no acceleration. Let us try $v = f(a, g)$. This implies that

$$[f(a, g)] = [v], \tag{4.1}$$

where the square brackets are a shorthand for 'the dimensions of', as usual. We can split up the function f into two parts: a simple product of powers of a and g with the dimensions of v, multiplied by a function of any dimensionless combinations of a and g which we may be able to construct. In this particular case, as we shall soon see, there are none, and this second part of f reduces to a numerical constant. In general, however, such combinations can occur, and when they do the nature of this second function can be determined only by experiment; there is no reason to suppose that it will be given by any simple mathematical formula.

Now if
$$[a^{\alpha}.g^{\beta}] = [v]$$

then
$$L^{\alpha}(LT^{-2})^{\beta} = LT^{-1};$$

from which we obtain in turn, by equating the indices of L and T,

$$\left.\begin{array}{l} \alpha+\beta = 1, \\ -2\beta = -1. \end{array}\right\} \tag{4.2}$$

and

It is at once apparent that $\alpha = \beta = \frac{1}{2}$, and that no dimensionless combinations of a and g can be found. Hence

$$v = k(ag)^{\frac{1}{2}} \tag{4.3}$$

where k is a numerical constant. Because the equation (4.2) has a unique solution, $(ag)^{\frac{1}{2}}$ is the only combination of a and g which can have the dimensions of a speed.

The numerical constant k would no doubt be a very complicated expression if a full solution of the equations of motion had been successfully made, but the important thing is that k is a *number* which cannot in any way depend on a or g. This also means that the value of k is the same for all the spheres in the experiment; there is no scope for k to vary from sphere to sphere: the mechanical theory is the same for each sphere, and the difference between one sphere and the next is described wholly by the value of a.

We can now answer the original question. Do large spheres fall faster or slower than small ones?

Equation (4.3) gives the answer at once: $v \propto a^{\frac{1}{2}}$, so the larger the sphere, the greater its terminal speed.

The final comment on this section refers back to the title—'Scale'. The *size*, or *scale*, of a sphere has an effect on its terminal speed. In general, scale is a very important characteristic of any physical system. A change in the value of any one characteristic feature of a system is bound to cause changes in the values of other characteristics of the system. But these resulting changes can sometimes be calculated by the process of 'dimensional analysis' which we have exemplified in this section. Thus we now know that if the radius of one of our falling spheres is quadrupled, its terminal velocity will be doubled. The fact that this result is obtainable without any solutions of the equations being obtained, indicates the power of dimensional analysis. Further applications are described in the remaining sections of this chapter.

Exercise C

1. A string-and-bob pendulum of length a is released from a horizontal position. If v is the bob's speed at the lowest point, find the variation of v with a. (You are not required to find the constant of variation.)

2. The pendulum of Question 1 is now taken to the moon. What information about the moon and earth situations would you require to enable you to calculate the value of v on the moon from a knowledge of the value of v on the earth?

3. Repeat Questions 1 and 2 for a pendulum consisting of a uniform bar freely pivoted at one end.

4. Explain why you felt justified in neglecting air resistance in these questions.

5. REFINEMENT AND EXTENSION

By now you may have decided that in Section 4 we were very lucky to obtain an apparently reasonable answer. As soon as we substitute oil or water for air, or the moon for the earth, or a balloon or lead for the wooden sphere, our predicted answers may be very inaccurate. Clearly we then have other factors to take into account. These will certainly include ρ, the density of the sphere, and ρ', the density of the fluid through which it falls. Let us first see what forms are obtained by the inclusion of these two densities. As in equation (4.1), we write

$$v = f(a, g, \rho, \rho') \tag{5.1}$$

and look for indices α, β, γ, δ which will give

$$[a^{\alpha} . g^{\beta} . \rho^{\gamma} . \rho'^{\delta}] = [v].$$

This implies $\quad L^{\alpha} . (LT^{-2})^{\beta} . (ML^{-3})^{\gamma} . (ML^{-3})^{\delta} = LT^{-1}.$

Equating indices of

$$\mathbf{L}: \alpha + \beta - 3\gamma - 3\delta = 1,$$

$$\mathbf{T}: \qquad -2\beta = -1,$$

$$\mathbf{M}: \qquad \gamma + \delta = 0.$$

Once again we have $\alpha = \beta = \frac{1}{2}$, and also $\gamma + \delta = 0$. $(ag)^{\frac{1}{2}}$ is still the only combination yielding the dimensions of velocity, but in addition we now have a dimensionless form $(\rho/\rho')^\gamma$, where γ is arbitrary. In fact, we may write

$$v = (ag)^{\frac{1}{2}} f(\rho/\rho'), \tag{5.2}$$

where f is an arbitrary function of whose form we know nothing. Nevertheless, despite the fact that we only have three equations with four unknowns, we have unravelled a meaningful result. We can also see why the factor $f(\rho/\rho')$ escaped us in Section 4, for so long as we kept to the same material for the spheres and the same air, it simply reduces to the constant k. To predict successfully, we must reason in the light of experience, yet avoid preconceptions, and experiment carefully.

Logically we should now experiment with spheres and fluids of different densities, to see whether or not the value of $v/\sqrt{(ag)}$ depends only on their ratio, as predicted. But we probably realize that it will be difficult to do this without taking another factor into account. Let us therefore take the plunge into viscosity—after all, treacle has approximately the same density as water!

Viscosity η has dimensions $\mathbf{ML^{-1}T^{-1}}$. In place of equation (5.1) we must write

$$v = f(a, g, \rho, \rho', \eta)$$

$$\Rightarrow [v] = [a^\alpha . g^\beta . \rho^\gamma . \rho'^\delta . \eta^\epsilon]$$

$$\Rightarrow \mathbf{LT^{-1}} = \mathbf{L}^\alpha (\mathbf{LT^{-2}})^\beta . (\mathbf{ML^{-3}})^\gamma . (\mathbf{ML^{-3}})^\delta . (\mathbf{ML^{-1}T^{-1}})^\epsilon$$

$$\Rightarrow \begin{cases} 1 = \alpha + \beta - 3\gamma - 3\delta - \epsilon, & \textbf{(L)} \\ -1 = -2\beta - \epsilon, & \textbf{(T)} \\ 0 = \gamma + \delta + \epsilon. & \textbf{(M).} \end{cases}$$

Two of the variables in these equations are now arbitrary and it is a matter of experience and experiment which two to choose. Because the viscosity of the fluid and the density of the sphere are totally unrelated, let us choose these, and express everything in terms of γ and ϵ.

Then

$$\beta = \frac{1}{2}(1 - \epsilon),$$

$$\delta = -\epsilon - \gamma,$$

$$\alpha = \frac{1}{2} - 3\epsilon/2.$$

Once again, $(ag)^{\frac{1}{2}}$ appears, of dimension $[v]$, but there are now two dimensionless quantities, (ρ/ρ'), and $(\eta.a^{-\frac{3}{2}}.g^{-\frac{1}{2}}.\rho'^{-1})$. Taking the square of the second, as more convenient, we can write

$$\frac{v}{\sqrt{(ag)}} = f\left(\left(\frac{\rho}{\rho'}\right),\ \left(\frac{\eta^2}{a^3g\rho'^2}\right)\right). \tag{5.3}$$

where the three quantities on both sides of the equation are now all dimensionless. By keeping each of these constant in turn, we can investigate experimentally the inter-relation of the other two.

In our first approach we did in fact keep ρ/ρ' constant, and we might have usefully conducted experiments in which we varied $(\eta^2/a^3g\rho'^2)$, while maintaining this constant density ratio; for example, we could have used mixtures of glycerine and water in different proportions, in which the density does not change appreciably, but the viscosity changes enormously. We could then have plotted $v/\sqrt{(ag)}$ against $(\eta^2/a^3g\rho'^2)$ and we might have got some such graph as that in Figure 4.

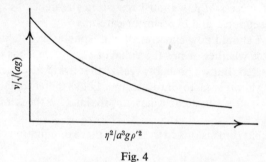

Fig. 4

Suppose, however, that the viscosity had no effect at all; what would the resulting graph have looked like?

6. SIMILARITY

In 1940 the Tacoma Narrows suspension bridge in Washington State collapsed, simply because of a steady 40 m.p.h. wind which caused resonant vibrations of immense magnitude. (It had already earned the nickname of 'galloping Gertie'.) Since then most large suspension bridges have been investigated in advance by testing models of them in wind tunnels. In fact, models of many structures are tested in this way in an attempt to predict full-scale performance; for example, sky-scrapers, cooling towers, and aircraft are tested in wind-tunnels; boats, submarines, piers and dams are tested in water tunnels. How does this work?

If we revert to the equation (5.3) for $v/\sqrt{(ag)}$, it should be clear that, for a whole variety of bodies and fluids, and indeed for different gravitational situations, provided only that the numbers (ρ/ρ') and $(a^3g\rho'/\eta^2)$ are the

same, the behaviour of the falling spheres will be entirely characterized by
the equation
$$v/\sqrt{(ag)} = k,$$

where k takes the same value for all cases. This presumably means that in
all such cases the pattern of flow of the fluid around the sphere is the same.
If, however, we were to vary η by itself then the constant k would be
altered because the pattern would be changed. Only by varying, say η
and ρ' together in such a way that $(a^3 g \rho'^2 / \eta^2)$ is unchanged can we leave k
unaltered; in this case we should say that the situations were *similar*. Such
similar circumstances are characterized by the value of the constant, and
such a constant is often called a *scale factor*. Thus the whole class of falling
spheres of different sizes and in different gravitational situations is typified
by this scale factor.

The word 'scale' therefore may be used to indicate more than just the
relative sizes of, for example, two diameters a_1 and a_2; it may refer to the
class or classes of situations for which some non-dimensional combination takes constant values.

Exercise D

1. If, for the falling spheres, $v/\sqrt{ag} = k$, and we estimate k by choosing an
integer n, positive or negative, such that
$$10^n < k < 10^{n+1},$$
suggest a reasonable value of n for each of the following cases:
  (a) spheres of lead dropped from the Eiffel Tower;
  (b) spheres of cork released from the bottom of the sea;
  (c) balloons filled with air dropped from the gallery in St Paul's;
  (d) droplets of mercury rolling off the bench.

2. Which of the four cases in Question 1 have roughly the same scale factor?

3. What is the scale factor of the system described by an acceleration of
a ft s^{-2} being produced by a force of P pdl acting on a mass m lb? Is it possible
for this scale factor to take different values?

4. A jet of fluid of density ρ and speed U impinges on a wall and creates a local
pressure maximum of p. How does p vary if (a) ρ is doubled; or (b) U is trebled?

5. The speed v at which a sailing boat begins to plane depends primarily on its
length l and the gravitational acceleration. If you wish to increase your planing
speed by 50 %, by what percentage must the length of your new boat exceed (or
otherwise) that of your old one?

6. The air resistance R of a motorcar is found to depend mainly on its frontal
area A, its speed U and the air density ρ. Determine the appropriate
non-dimensional quantity.

7. A hammer of mass m hits, with an impact speed v, a nail into a plank through
a distance s against a resistance R. Estimate the value of the appropriate scale
factor. Does this value depend on the units in which m, v, s, R are measured?

7. DESIGN OF EXPERIMENTS: SIMILARITY; EXTRAPOLATION

We return to our falling spheres once again, this time by assuming that we wish to predict how fast our biggest and best (spherical) bomb will be falling when it reaches the ground. For various good reasons, we are unable to do a full-scale test and so we must resort to a small-scale laboratory experiment. The question therefore reduces to this: if a small model bomb is dropped in the laboratory and its terminal speed measured, is it possible to deduce the terminal speed of the full-scale bomb?

The answer is (with a few qualifications described below) YES and the reasoning follows at once from earlier results: if $v/\sqrt{(ag)}$ takes the same value for both the laboratory experiment and the full-scale drop, we can write

$$\left(\frac{v}{\sqrt{(ag)}}\right)_{\text{full scale}} = \left(\frac{v}{\sqrt{(ag)}}\right)_{\text{experiment}}.$$

Assuming that we are conducting the experiment on earth where g may be taken as constant, we may then write

$$v_{\text{full scale}} = \left(\sqrt{\frac{a_{\text{full scale}}}{a_{\text{experiment}}}}\right) v_{\text{experiment}}.$$

Such a formula is sometimes described as an extrapolation formula, since it deduces the value of a quantity in a set of circumstances which are placed (extrapolated) outside those in which direct observations can be made.

The qualifications, referred to above, arise as follows. It is unlikely that the formulation of a problem involving, say, a speed v, a length a, and an acceleration g will involve no other quantities at all. For example, the problem of the falling spheres, when formulated, would probably involve the mass of the spheres, or equivalently, their *density*; this is indicated by our intuition that a sphere of lead will, other things being equal, fall faster than a sphere of foam rubber. It is therefore essential for the validity of the extrapolation process that all quantities other than those involved in the non-dimensional combination remain strictly constant; any variation of these other quantities will immediately introduce errors of unknown magnitude.

Similarity therefore refers not only to constant values of all non-dimensional combinations, but also to the constancy of all other physical characteristics involved.

The complete satisfaction of the requirement of similarity is usually of great practical difficulty and it is one of the hall-marks of a fine experimentalist that he can, by chance or by design, attain in his experiments such a high degree of similarity that his results are accepted as reliable for the purposes of extrapolation.

To illustrate this, we mention some of the quantities which should be kept constant between the full-scale and laboratory situations for the falling spheres: the density of the spheres, their surface properties of smoothness or roughness, their rigidity, their angular velocity (if it is not zero), the density of the air through which they are falling, the air temperature, the viscosity of the air, its degree of turbulence—and this by no means exhausts the list.

Exercise E

1. Make a list of as many properties as you can which should be kept constant for strict similarity, for each question in Exercise D.

2. Water of density ρ flows along a pipe of length l under a pressure difference Δp between the two ends. What is the effect on the average speed due to the doubling of the density and halving the pressure difference? What conditions of similarity need to be satisfied to render your answer reliable?

3. A flywheel mounted on a horizontal axle has wrapped round its rim a string at the loose end of which a weight hangs freely. The system is initially at rest and is released so that after the weight has fallen a distance s the angular speed of the flywheel is Ω. It is suspected that $\Omega \propto s^n$, where n is some fixed number. Suggest a value for n. Does n depend on
  (a) the ratio of the masses of the flywheel and the hanging weight;
  (b) frictional forces of various kinds;
  (c) the shape of the flywheel?

8. PREDICTIONS FROM DIMENSIONAL ANALYSIS

8.1   We are now in a better position to tackle the problem posed at the start: what is the terminal velocity of a parachutist?

The factor $a^3 g \rho'^2 / \eta^2$ is the difficult one. g and η are not easily altered, and it may be simpler to alter ρ than ρ'. So let us combine this factor with $(\rho/\rho')^2$ and consider $a^3 g \rho^2 / \eta^2$. It was, in fact, entirely arbitrary whether we included ρ or ρ' in this factor originally. Now let us make a model of the parachutist on a scale of, say, one-tenth. Then if we ensure that

$$a_m^3 \rho_m^2 = a_p^3 \rho_p^2,$$

where the suffix m denotes the model, and suffix p the parachutist, no matter what function of $a^3 g \rho^2 / \eta^2$ is involved, it will have the same value for both parachutist and model, assuming g and η are the same for both. If therefore we have shown from our sphere-dropping experiments that

$$v / \sqrt{(ag)} = (\rho/\rho') . f(a^3 g \rho^2 / \eta^2),$$

we can immediately conclude that

$$\frac{v_p / \sqrt{(a_p g)}}{v_m / \sqrt{(a_m g)}} = \frac{(\rho_p / \rho')}{(\rho_m / \rho')} = \frac{\rho_p}{\rho_m}.$$

1241

If now we drop our model in the same air and the same gravity field and measure its terminal velocity, we can predict the terminal velocity of the parachutist. We should have better control of the experiment if alternatively we directed the outlet of an air tunnel vertically and measured the velocity of flow of the air needed just to support the model of the parachutist.

Of course there are still assumptions that we have made in comparing the model with the reality; for example, what is the effect of variation of density and temperature of the air with height, and can we allow for it?

8.2 To illustrate the method further, let us see how to estimate the force required to propel a nuclear submarine. There are two separate situations, one on, and one under the surface. In the latter case, gravity can play no part; since this simplifies the working, we will consider this first.

What factors are involved? We must obviously take into account the speed v of the submarine, some measure of its size, l, and the density ρ and viscosity η of the water. For comparison with a model any measurement l will do, so long as we use the same measurement for both. Let us therefore try

$$F = f(v, l, \rho, \eta)$$

and look for indices which will give

$$[v^\alpha . l^\beta . \rho^\gamma . \eta^\delta] = [F].$$

This implies $\quad L^\alpha T^{-\alpha} L^\beta M^\gamma L^{-3\gamma} M^\delta L^{-\delta} T^{-\delta} = MLT^{-2}.$

Equating indices of $\quad$ **L:** $\alpha + \beta - 3\gamma - \delta = 1,$

$\qquad\qquad$ **T:** $\qquad \alpha + \delta = 2,$

$\qquad\qquad$ **M:** $\qquad \gamma + \delta = 1.$

Solving these equations in terms of δ, we have

$$\alpha = 2 - \delta, \quad \gamma = 1 - \delta, \quad \beta = 2 - \delta.$$

Hence $v^2 l^2 \rho$ has dimensions of force; in addition a dimensionless quantity $\rho v l / \eta$ appears. We can therefore write

$$\frac{F}{\rho v^2 l^2} = f\left(\frac{\rho v l}{\eta}\right).$$

The dimensionless quantity $\rho v l / \eta$ crops up repeatedly in problems of fluid flow, and is called the *Reynolds Number*, abbreviated to *Re*.

It is sometimes difficult to achieve similarity by giving the model the same Reynolds number as that demanded by the actual situation. Fortunately over wide ranges of values of *Re* there is little change in the flow patterns, and so the ratio $F/\rho v^2 l^2$ is little affected. Figure 5 shows the variation of $F/\rho v^2 l^2$ with Reynolds number for flow past a circular cylinder, and, beneath the graph, the corresponding flow patterns.

1242

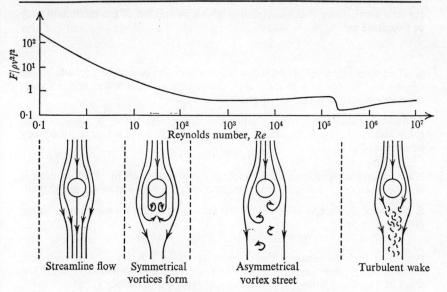

Fig. 5. (Note the logarithmic scale on both axes.)

If in this case we made a scale model of the submarine on the scale of $1:100$, we should have $l_m/l_s = 1/100$, where the suffix m refers to the model, and s to the submarine. To find F_s, the force required for the full-scale submarine, testing in water, and maintaining the same value of Re, we should then need to make $v_m = 100v_c$, which is quite impracticable. But provided we are in a region where variations in Re are not very significant—and this can be checked by experiment, plotting $F/v^2l^2\rho$ against Re—then we can treat $F/v^2l^2\rho$ as constant, and obtain

$$\frac{F_s}{F_m} = \left(\frac{v_s}{v_m}\right)^2 \left(\frac{l_s}{l_m}\right)^2 \left(\frac{\rho_s}{\rho_m}\right)^2.$$

The corresponding solution for the surface situation is outlined in Exercise F, Question 6.

Exercise F

1. The force in the main cables of a suspension bridge due to wind loading depends on the velocity v and density ρ of the air together with the span l of the bridge. Determine an equation for the force in each cable.

Compare the force in a $1/100$ scale model at half the predicted maximum air speed in the full-scale situation with the force on the bridge.

2. The period of torsional oscillation of a mass suspended from a quartz thread depends on the moment of inertia of the mass, I, the radius of the thread, r, the length of the thread, l, and its modulus of rigidity n (with dimensions of force

1243

per unit area). Show that the equation giving the period of the oscillation may be expressed as

$$T = \sqrt{\left(\frac{I}{nr^3}\right) \cdot f\left(\frac{r}{l}\right)}.$$

3. The power extracted per metre width of a sea barrage scheme depends on the speed v and the height h of the waves, the density ρ of the water, and g. Determine an equation for the power available per foot.

4. Assuming that the factors affecting the power required by a hovercraft are v, l, g and ρ, where ρ is the density of the air, show that the power required may be expressed as

$$P = \rho v^3 l^2 . f(gl/v^2).$$

If a 3 m hovercraft built to a scale of 1:25 requires a power of 15 kW to drive it at $\frac{1}{5}$ the speed of the full-scale craft, estimate the power needed by the actual craft.

5. What are the factors affecting (a) the maximum speed, (b) the corresponding power, for a fish?

Prove that $\qquad v = k\eta/\rho l \quad \text{and} \quad P = \rho l^2 v^3 . f(\rho v l/\eta).$

Assuming that the effect of the different Reynolds number can be neglected, compare the power required by a 5 m shark at 8 m/s with that of an 0·5 m trout at 4 m/s, assuming they have the same shape and surface skin.

6. What are the factors affecting the power required to drive a submarine, of given shape, on the surface? Derive a relationship involving the terms $P/v^3 l^2 \rho$, $\rho v l/\eta$ and v^2/gl. This last is known as *Froude's number*. If a 1:40 scale model is made, and Re is not important, at what speed should the model be tested to estimate the power needed by the submarine to be capable of travelling at 30 knots?

7. Derive an expression for the frictional torque due to the surrounding gas in an electrical alternator running at constant speed, on the assumption that it depends on the diameter D, the speed v, the clearance c, the viscosity η and the density ρ. Compare the ratio of the torques in air and in hydrogen, if hydrogen has 1/44 of the density of air, and half its viscosity.

Table 1

Quantity	S.I. symbol	Defining equation	Dimensions	Unit — m.k.s.	Unit — Abbreviation	Unit — c.g.s.
Length	s‡		L	metre	m	cm
Time	t		T	second	s	s
Speed	v	$v = ds/dt$	LT^{-1}	m s^{-1}	—	cm s^{-1}
Acceleration	a	$a = dv/dt$	LT^{-2}	m s^{-2}	—	cm s^{-2}
Mass	m	$F = ma$	M	kilogram	kg	g (gm)
Force	F	$F = ma$	MLT^{-2}	newton	N	dyn
Work	W	$\left. W = \int F.ds \right\}$	ML^2T^{-2}	joule	J	erg
Kinetic energy	T	$\left. \int F.ds = \tfrac{1}{2}mv^2 \right\}$		*newton second*		
Momentum	p	$p = mv = \int F\,dt$	MLT^{-1}	second-newton	sNS *(or kg m s⁻¹)*	s dyn
Power	P	$P = dW/dt$	ML^2T^{-3}	watt	W	erg s^{-1}
Frequency	n, f		T^{-1}	hertz (c/s)	Hz	c/s
Density	ρ	Mass/volume	ML^{-3}	kg m^{-3}	—	g cm^{-3}
Pressure (stress)	p	Force/area	$ML^{-1}T^{-2}$	N m^{-2} *Pa*	—	dyn cm^{-2}
Viscosity	η	Pressure/velocity gradient	$ML^{-1}T^{-1}$	N m^{-2} *N S m⁻² Pas*	—	poise
Surface tension	σ	Energy/area	MT^{-2}	N m^{-1}	—	dyn cm^{-1}
Charge	Q		Q	coulomb	C	
Current	I	$I = dQ/dt$	QT^{-1}	ampere	A	= coulomb/second
Potential difference	V	$\left. V = W/Q \right\}$	$ML^2Q^{-1}T^{-2}$	volt	V	= joule/coulomb
Electromotive force	E	As above				
Power	P		ML^2T^{-3}	watt	W	= joule/second
Resistance	R	$R = V/I$	$ML^2Q^{-2}T^{-1}$	ohm	Ω	= volt/ampere
Capacitance	C	$C = Q/V$	$M^{-1}L^{-2}Q^2T^2$	farad	F	= coulomb/volt
Magnetic flux	Φ	$E = -d\Phi/dt$	$ML^2Q^{-1}T^{-1}$	weber	Wb	= volt-second
Inductance	L	$\Phi = LI$	ML^2Q^{-2}	henry	H	= ohm-second

‡ Displacement.

REVISION EXERCISES

39. WORK AND ENERGY

1. A gun fires a shell of mass 10 kg with a muzzle velocity of 600 m/s. The part of the gun which is free to recoil has a mass of 1200 kg. Find
   (a) the energy created by the burning of the charge;
   (b) the constant force required to absorb the recoil in 0·60 m.

2. A skier descends a slope 150 m long on a gradient (sine) of 1 in 3. His course then levels out smoothly and finally takes the form of a sine curve $y = 5 \sin x/a$, the y-axis being vertical, which he enters at the lowest point. Find the minimum wavelength of the sine curve if he does not leave the ground at the crests of the humps. (The radius of the circle which just fits the crests is $a^2/5$.) Assume 36 % loss of energy due to resistances.

3. Find the power needed to raise 16 cm³ of water per second and deliver it through a nozzle of cross-section 6·4 cm² at a height of 10 m. Find also the force exerted by the jet on a wall which it strikes horizontally, without rebounding, 2 m above the level of the nozzle.

4. A locomotive of mass m is working at constant power P against a resistance mkV, proportional to its velocity. What is its maximum velocity? If this is u, write down a differential equation for the velocity as a function of time in terms of k and u. What are the dimensions of k?
   Find, in terms of k, the time taken to accelerate from $\frac{1}{3}u$ to $\frac{1}{2}u$, and explain why the maximum speed will never be attained.

5. A particle is moved in the (x, y)-plane in a field of force with components $(2x, y)$. If the particle is moved from $(0, 0)$ to (a, b) along a straight line, then from (a, b) to $(0, b)$ along the line $y = b$, and finally from $(0, b)$ back to $(0, 0)$ along the y-axis, find the work done.
   Assuming that the work done during a movement from $(0, 0)$ to (x, y) is a function $W(x, y)$ of x, y, independent of the particular path taken, find an expression for $W(x, y)$. Illustrate by sketching some curves on which W takes a constant value.   (OC)

6. An escalator lifts a passenger who remains stationary on it through a total height of 20 m in 50 s. People, whose average mass is 70 kg, step onto the escalator smoothly at a rate of one every 2 s, stand still while on it, and step off smoothly at the top. Find the power produced by the escalator.
   At a rush hour, the people enter the escalator at a rate of 1 per second and walk up it, reaching the top in 35 s. At what rate is it working now? How many watts does each person develop while walking up? (Consider how many people there are on the escalator at any moment.)

40. DIMENSIONAL ANALYSIS

1. Early experimenters on the flow of fluids through capillary tubes proposed a formula of the form

$$Q \propto \frac{1}{\eta} \left(\frac{dp}{dx}\right) r^n,$$

where Q is the volume flow per unit time,

η is the coefficient of viscosity (of dimensions $\mathbf{M^{-1}T^{-1}}$),
dp/dx is the pressure gradient along the tube,
r is the radius of the tube, and
n is a numerical index to be found.

Suggest a suitable value for n. (OC)

2. A boy is bowling a bicycle wheel of external radius r directly at a step of height h and he wants to estimate the bowling speed v at which the wheel will just surmount the step.

Describe briefly the mathematical model you would make to determine the speed v.

Give an argument to show that the final result of a detailed calculation of v will probably be expressible in the form

$$\frac{v^2}{gr} = f\left(\frac{h}{r}\right),$$

f being a function of (h/r). Use your common sense to sketch, without doing any calculations, a graph of v^2/gr versus h/r. (OC)

3. We propose a new quantity of force, a grav, defined as follows:

'P, the gravitational force of attraction measured in gravs between two masses m_1 and m_2 measured in kilograms, at a distance r measured in metres is given by the formula $P = m_1 m_2/r^2$.' Explain why this definition is not sufficiently precise to define 1 grav uniquely, and suggest an improvement.

Newton's second law is retained in the form $P = ma$ in which the force P is expressed in gravs. Regarding mass $[\mathbf{M}]$ and distance $[\mathbf{L}]$ as the fundamental dimensions in this system, show that the dimensions of time are

$$[\mathbf{M^{-\frac{1}{2}}L^{\frac{3}{2}}}].$$

Give an argument to suggest whether the unit of time in this system is greater or less than 1 second. (OC)

4. The electrostatic unit of charge was defined by means of the equation $F = Q_1 Q_2/r^2$, where F dynes is the force of repulsion between two point charges *in vacuo*, r cm apart. What are the dimensions of charge on this system, in terms of $\mathbf{M}$, $\mathbf{L}$ and $\mathbf{T}$? In the m.k.s. system, this force is given by

$$F = \frac{Q_1 Q_2}{\epsilon_0 4\pi r^2},$$

where F is now measured in Newtons, r in metres, and Q in coulombs. What are the dimensions of ϵ_0 in terms of $\mathbf{M}$, $\mathbf{L}$, $\mathbf{T}$ and $\mathbf{Q}$?

If ϵ_0 has numerical value $(1/36\pi) \times 10^{-9}$ farad/metre, find the number of e.s.u. of charge in 1 coulomb.

5. The force between two straight parallel wires l m long d m apart, carrying I_1 and I_2 amperes of electric current, is given by $F = \mu_0 l I_1 I_2 / 2d$, in m.k.s. units. Find the dimensions of μ_0.

What are the dimensions of $1/\sqrt{(\mu_0 \epsilon_0)}$?

What is the value of this constant, if $\mu_0 = 4\pi \times 10^{-7}$ henry/metre? Do you recognize this quantity?

6. Suppose we took velocity [**v**], momentum [**p**], frequency [**f**], and charge [**Q**] as fundamental quantities. Express in terms of these the dimensions of mass, length, time, energy, potential difference, resistance, inductance. If the unit of v is the velocity of light (3×10^8 m/s), the unit of p is the momentum of the electron in a hydrogen atom, (2×10^{-24} sN), the unit of f is the ionization frequency for a hydrogen atom ($3 \cdot 3 \times 10^{15}$ s^{-1}), and the unit of charge that of the electron ($1 \cdot 6 \times 10^{-19}$ C), find the units of mass, length and time. For what purpose would this in fact be quite a sensible selection of units?

41

RATIONAL FORMS

1. RESEMBLANCES TO THE RATIONAL NUMBERS

1.1 Equality. In Chapter 3 we showed that rational numbers are rightly thought of as equivalence classes of ordered pairs of integers which we call fractions. When we write, for example,

$$\tfrac{3}{4} = \tfrac{6}{8}$$

we should really say that these two fractions (which are the ordered pairs (3, 4) and (6, 8) conventionally written in this way) are *equivalent* and thus qualify as members of the same class $\{\tfrac{3}{4}, \tfrac{6}{8}, \tfrac{9}{12}, \ldots\}$ which is the rational number $\tfrac{3}{4}$. The equivalence relation is defined in terms of integers only, as follows:

'a/b is equivalent to c/d' means that $ad = bc$, $b, d \neq 0$.

This in its turn simply means that ad and bc are two names for the same integer. These classes, the rational numbers, form what is called a quotient field of the integers, induced by this equivalence relation.

In exactly the same way we showed that rational forms are equivalence classes of ordered pairs of polynomials, called 'algebraic fractions'. When we write.

$$\frac{(x-1).(x+2)}{(x-1).(x+3)} = \frac{x+2}{x+3}$$

we are again stating that these fractions are equivalent, and qualify as members of the class of fractions

$$\{[(x+2).P]/[(x+3).P], \quad P \text{ any polynomial}\},$$

which is the rational form $(x+2)/(x+3)$. It is very important to realize that this equivalence relation is once again defined in terms of polynomials only, as follows:

'$\dfrac{P}{Q}$ is equivalent to $\dfrac{R}{S}$' means that $P.S = Q.R$, $Q, S \neq O$,

where O is the zero polynomial. Thus the two algebraic fractions above are *formally equivalent*, that is, they name the same rational form. Again, we say that rational forms are elements of a quotient field of the polynomials, induced by this equivalence relation.

Now if x is a real number, a polynomial P defines a function $x \rightarrow P(x)$. In the equation defining the equivalence relation above, $P.S$ and $Q.R$ are the same polynomial, and therefore the functions

$$x \rightarrow P(x).S(x) \quad \text{and} \quad x \rightarrow Q(x).R(x)$$

are one and the same function. Put another way, this means that

$$P(x).S(x) \quad \text{and} \quad Q(x).R(x)$$

take the same value for all values of x. It so happens that the converse of this is also true; that is, if two polynomials take the same value for all real values of x, they are in fact the same polynomial. (Actually 'for all real values' in this statement can be replaced by 'for more than n values', where n is the degree of the polynomials concerned.) Accordingly we can say that

$$\frac{P}{Q} \text{ is equivalent to } \frac{R}{S} \Leftrightarrow P(x).S(x) = Q(x).R(x)$$

for all real x, provided neither Q nor S is the zero polynomial.

In contrast to polynomials, however, two rational algebraic fractions which are formally equivalent need not define the same function; thus the functions

$$x \rightarrow \frac{(x-1).(x+2)}{(x-1).(x+3)} \quad \text{and} \quad x \rightarrow \frac{x+2}{x+3}$$

are different (the first being undefined when $x = 1$), although the forms are equivalent. Note also that the equation expressing this equivalence

$$(x-1).(x+2).(x+3) = (x-1).(x+3).(x+2)$$

is still true, even when $x = 1$.

1.2 Order. Just as the integers can be ordered by the relation 'greater than', so the polynomials can be partially ordered by degree. The most useful consequence of this for rational forms is the distinction between proper and improper forms, corresponding to the distinction between proper and improper fractions. A rational form is proper if the degree of its numerator is less than the degree of its denominator; otherwise it is improper. It is easy to show that the sum of two (and therefore of any number of) proper forms is proper. Just as we can always, by means of the division algorithm, express an improper fraction as the sum of a rational integer and a proper rational number, so we can express an improper rational form as the sum of a polynomial and a proper rational form. From the fact that $14 = 2 \times 5 + 4$ we deduce that $\frac{14}{5} = 2 + \frac{4}{5}$, where we write (as usual) the integer 2 for the rational number $\frac{2}{1}$; in the same way we deduce from the identity

$$2x^3 - 3x^2 + 4x - 5 = (2x+1).(x^2-2x-3)+12x-2$$

1250

the equivalence of the two forms

$$\frac{2x^3-3x^2+4x-5}{x^2-2x-3} = 2x+1+\frac{12x-2}{x^2-2x-3},$$

where the polynomial $2x+1$ has been written for the rational form $(2x+1)/1$.

Exercise A

1. Express, as the sum of a polynomial and a proper rational form, each of the following improper rational forms.

(a) $\dfrac{x^2}{x-1}$;

(b) $\dfrac{x^3+2x^2-x+1}{x^2+x-2}$;

(c) $\dfrac{x^2}{x^2-1}$;

(d) $\dfrac{x^6}{x-1}$ (put $x-1 = u$);

(e) $\dfrac{x^2+1}{x^2+x-2}$;

(f) $\dfrac{(x+1)(x+2)}{x(x-3)}$.

2. Find a so that $\dfrac{x^2+2x-1}{x+1} - \dfrac{a}{x+1}$ is equivalent to a polynomial.

3. Find b, c so that $\dfrac{x^3}{x^2-1} - \dfrac{bx+c}{x^2-1}$ is equivalent to a polynomial.

2. PARTIAL FRACTIONS

2.1 The problem of integration. In Chapters 23 and 27 we have learnt how to integrate some simple rational forms; for example,

$$\int \frac{dx}{x-1} = \log|x-1|, \quad \int \frac{dx}{(x-1)^2} = -\frac{1}{x-1}, \quad \int \frac{dx}{x^2+1} = \tan^{-1} x.$$

But even so simple a form as $1/(x^2-1)$ is not at first sight integrable, and more complicated rational forms appear quite intractable. We shall, however, outline a method which, in theory at least, is capable of casting any rational form whatever into an equivalent form which can be integrated immediately. This is the method of *partial fractions*.

We recall that the clue to the integration of $1/(x^2-1)$ is to express it in the equivalent form

$$\frac{1}{2}\left(\frac{1}{x-1} - \frac{1}{x+1}\right).$$

The question arises whether this can always be done, and whether the result is unique. With rational numbers we have such equivalences as

$$\tfrac{19}{30} = \tfrac{1}{2}-\tfrac{2}{3}+\tfrac{4}{5} = \tfrac{1}{3}-\tfrac{1}{2}+\tfrac{4}{5} = \tfrac{1}{2}+\tfrac{1}{3}-\tfrac{1}{5},$$

and we might suppose that a similar variety of choices was available for rational forms. Before reading further, you might like to try the problem for the forms

$$\frac{5x+1}{(x-1)(x+2)} \quad \text{and} \quad \frac{6x-1}{(x-3)(x+1)}.$$

2.2 Form and function. When integrating, we are concerned with functions of x. We have seen that equivalent forms may not always represent the same function, but the difference can only arise at points where the denominator of the form takes the value zero. Since we do not propose to consider integrals over ranges including such points, there will be no harm in replacing the form giving the function to be integrated by any equivalent form. In point of fact all the equivalent forms we shall consider will represent equivalent functions as well, since they will be undefined at precisely those points where the original functions are undefined. But the method of partial fractions is concerned with formal equivalence, and this is all we need.

2.3 The cover-up rule. Consider the problem of expressing the form

$$\frac{6x-1}{(x-3)(x+1)}$$

as the sum of two forms, with denominators $x-3$ and $x+1$. It is clear that the basic problem is to subtract from the form given a fraction $A/(x-3)$, where A is a number, so as to leave a fraction whose denominator is $(x+1)$. Now

$$\frac{6x-1}{(x-3)(x+1)} - \frac{A}{x-3} = \frac{6x-1-A(x+1)}{(x-3)(x+1)},$$

which can only be equivalent to a form with denominator $(x+1)$ if the numerator contains $x-3$ as a factor. But, by the factor theorem, this will be so if and only if the numerator, regarded as a function of x, is zero when $x = 3$. The only possible value of A which achieves this is therefore given by

$$6.3-1-A(3+1) = 0, \quad \text{from which} \quad A = \tfrac{17}{4}.$$

At the risk of appearing unduly fussy, we stress again that the form

$$\frac{6x-1-A(x+1)}{(x-3)(x+1)}$$

does not define a function when $x = 3$, but this fact is irrelevant, since we are concerned only with formal equivalence, and this is defined in terms of identity of polynomials and not of rational forms. Unlike the rational forms, the polynomials do define functions when $x = 3$.

1252

Having now found the value of A, we observe that it is precisely equal to the value of the form with the bracket $(x-3)$ deleted, that is,

$$\frac{6x-1}{(\quad)(x+1)},$$

when x is put equal to 3. In colloquial terms we may say 'cover up the bracket with the factor $(x-3)$, and A is equal to the value of the rest of the fraction when x is put equal to 3'. For this reason the result is usually known as the '*cover-up rule*'.

If the term so obtained is now subtracted from the form, what is left is

$$\frac{4(6x-1)-17(x+1)}{4(x-3)(x+1)}$$

which reduces to $\qquad \dfrac{7}{4(x+1)}.$

Finally $\qquad \dfrac{6x-1}{(x-3)(x+1)} = \dfrac{17}{4(x-3)}+\dfrac{7}{4(x+1)},$

and this expression is unique.

Example 1. Express

$$\frac{12x}{(x-1)(x^2+1)} \quad \text{in the form} \quad \frac{A}{x-1}+\frac{q(x)}{x^2+1}.$$

Cover up $x-1$ and put $x = 1$ in the rest. We get $12.1/(1+1)$ which is equal to 6. Hence

$$\frac{12x}{(x-1)(x^2+1)} - \frac{6}{x-1} = \frac{12x-6x^2-6}{(x-1)(x^2+1)}$$

$$= \frac{6-6x}{x^2+1}, \quad \text{dividing,}$$

so that $\qquad \dfrac{12x}{(x-1)(x^2+1)} = \dfrac{6}{x-1}+\dfrac{6-6x}{x^2+1}.$

Exercise B

Use the method of Example 1 to find A, B, ... and $q(x)$ in the following expressions:

1. $\dfrac{3x+1}{(x-2)(x+5)} = \dfrac{A}{x-2}+\dfrac{B}{x+5}.$

2. $\dfrac{x+4}{x(x^2+2)} = \dfrac{A}{x}+\dfrac{q(x)}{x^2+2}.$

3. $\dfrac{4x+2}{x(x-1)(x+2)} = \dfrac{A}{x}+\dfrac{q(x)}{(x-1)(x+2)}.$

4. $\dfrac{4x+2}{x(x-1)(x+2)} = \dfrac{A}{x}+\dfrac{B}{x-1}+\dfrac{C}{x+2}.$

5. $\dfrac{10x}{(x-1)(x^2+4)} = \dfrac{A}{x-1} + \dfrac{q(x)}{x^2+4}.$

6. $\dfrac{2x-8}{x^2+4} = \dfrac{A}{x-2j} + \dfrac{B}{x+2j}.$

7. $\dfrac{4}{x^2-3} = \dfrac{A}{x-\sqrt{3}} + \dfrac{B}{x+\sqrt{3}}.$

8. $\dfrac{3x+1}{(x+1)(x-1)^2} = \dfrac{A}{x+1} + \dfrac{q(x)}{(x-1)^2}.$

2.4   The complete set of partial fractions. If we apply the cover-up rule to the rational form

$$\frac{x^2+5}{x(x+1)(x-2)}$$

we can obtain three alternative forms:

$$\frac{x^2+5}{x(x+1)(x-2)} = -\frac{5}{2x} + \frac{q(x)}{(x+1)(x-2)}$$

$$= \frac{1}{x+1} + \frac{r(x)}{x(x-2)}$$

$$= \frac{3}{2(x-2)} + \frac{s(x)}{x(x+1)}.$$

This strongly suggests that in fact

$$\frac{x^2+5}{x(x+1)(x-2)} = -\frac{5}{2x} + \frac{1}{x+1} + \frac{3}{2(x-2)},$$

and this is easily verified by expressing the forms on the right with a common denominator. We shall prove later that this is generally true; the cover-up rule applied to each factor in turn gives the complete set of partial fractions for a proper rational form with linear non-repeated factors in its denominator. It is clearly necessary for the original form to be proper, since the sum of any number of proper forms is proper. With an improper form, the first step is to divide and replace it by a polynomial together with a proper form.

Example 2. Express in partial fractions the rational form

$$\frac{5x+4}{x(x-1)(x+2)}.$$

Method I. By the cover-up rule,

$$\frac{5x+4}{x(x-1)(x+2)} = \frac{4}{x(-1)(2)} + \frac{9}{(1)(3)(x-1)} + \frac{-6}{(-2)(-3)(x+2)}$$

$$= \frac{-2}{x} + \frac{3}{x-1} - \frac{1}{x+2}.$$

This assumes the result which we have not yet proved. Alternatively, we may use

1254

Method II.

$$\frac{5x+4}{x(x-1)(x+2)} = \frac{-2}{x} + \frac{f(x)}{(x-1)(x+2)} \quad \text{by cover-up rule}$$

$$\Leftrightarrow \frac{5x+4+2(x^2+x-2)}{x(x-1)(x+2)} = \frac{f(x)}{(x-1)(x+2)}$$

$$\Leftrightarrow f(x) = 2x+7, \quad \text{on dividing the numerator by } x.$$

Again
$$\frac{2x+7}{(x-1)(x+2)} = \frac{3}{x-1} + \frac{g(x)}{x+2} \quad \text{by cover-up rule}$$

$$\Leftrightarrow \frac{2x+7-3(x+2)}{(x-1)(x+2)} = \frac{g(x)}{x+2}$$

$$\Leftrightarrow g(x) = -1, \quad \text{on dividing the numerator by } (x-1).$$

Hence finally,
$$\frac{5x+4}{x(x-1)(x+2)} = \frac{-2}{x} + \frac{3}{x-1} - \frac{1}{x+2}.$$

Method II assumes no theory and is self-checking. If Method I is used, it is recommended that the result is checked.

Example 3. Express in partial fractions

$$\frac{x^3+x^2+3x+4}{x(x-1)(x+2)}.$$

Here the form is improper. If Method I is used, we begin by dividing:

$$\frac{x^3+x^2+3x+4}{x^3+x^2-2x} = 1 + \frac{5x+4}{x(x-1)(x+2)}$$

$$= 1 - \frac{2}{x} + \frac{3}{x-1} - \frac{1}{x+2}, \quad \text{as before.}$$

Method II can be used directly:

$$\frac{x^3+x^2+3x+4}{x(x-1)(x+2)} = \frac{-2}{x} + \frac{x^3+x^2+3x+4+2(x^2+x-2)}{x(x-1)(x+2)} \quad \text{by cover-up rule}$$

$$= \frac{-2}{x} + \frac{x^2+3x+5}{(x-1)(x+2)} \quad \text{dividing by } x$$

$$= \frac{-2}{x} + \frac{3}{x-1} + \frac{x^2+3x+5-3(x+2)}{(x-1)(x+2)} \quad \text{by cover-up rule}$$

$$= \frac{-2}{x} + \frac{3}{x-1} + \frac{x+1}{x+2}, \quad \text{dividing by } (x-1)$$

$$= \frac{-2}{x} + \frac{3}{x-1} - \frac{1}{x+2} + 1.$$

Exercise C

Express in partial fractions:

1. $\dfrac{2x-1}{(x+1)(2x+1)}$.

2. $\dfrac{10}{x(3x+2)(x-1)}$.

3. $\dfrac{3x}{(x-1)(x+2)(2x-1)}$.

4. $\dfrac{1}{x^2-1}$.

5. $\dfrac{2x+1}{x^3-x}$.

6. $\dfrac{x+1}{x(x-1)(x-2)}$.

7. $\dfrac{2x^3}{x^2-1}$.

8. $\dfrac{3x}{(x+2)(x^2-1)}$.

9. $\dfrac{35}{(4x^2-1)(x+3)}$.

10. Express in partial fractions (a) in the rational field, (b) in the real field:
$$\frac{24x}{(x-1)(x+2)(x^2-3)}.$$

11. Express $\dfrac{1}{(x^2-3)(x^2+4)}$ in the form $\dfrac{A}{x^2-3}+\dfrac{B}{x^2+4}$.

12. Express $\dfrac{1}{(x+b)(x^2-a^2)}$ in partial fractions.

3. INTEGRATION OF RATIONAL FUNCTIONS

We can now express any rational form with linear unrepeated factors in its denominator in a form suitable for immediate integration. The methods available can best be shown by a few examples.

Example 4. Since
$$\frac{1}{2x^2-7x+3} = \frac{1}{(2x-1)(x-3)} = \frac{1}{5(x-3)} - \frac{2}{5(2x-1)},$$
we have
$$\int \frac{dx}{2x^2-7x+3} = \frac{1}{5}\int \frac{dx}{x-3} - \frac{2}{5}\int \frac{dx}{2x-1} = \frac{1}{5}\log|x-3| - \frac{1}{5}\log|2x-1|$$
$$= \frac{1}{5}\log\left|\frac{x-3}{2x-1}\right|.$$

Where there is a repeated factor, the remaining factors can be 'peeled off' by the cover-up rule, and the integral completed by substitution.

Example 5. Evaluate $\displaystyle\int_0^1 \frac{dx}{(2-x)(x+1)^3}$.

Putting $x+1 = u$, the integral becomes
$$\int_1^2 \frac{du}{u^3(3-u)}.$$

1256

Now

$$\frac{1}{u^3(3-u)} = \frac{1}{27(3-u)} + \frac{27-u^3}{27u^3(3-u)}$$

$$= \frac{1}{27(3-u)} + \frac{9+3u+u^2}{27u^3} = \frac{1}{27(3-u)} + \frac{1}{3u^3} + \frac{1}{9u^2} + \frac{1}{27u}.$$

Hence

$$\int_1^2 \frac{du}{u^3(3-u)} = \left[\frac{-1}{27}\log|3-u| - \frac{1}{6u^2} - \frac{1}{9u} + \frac{1}{27}\log|u|\right]_1^2$$

$$= \tfrac{1}{27}\log 2 - \tfrac{1}{6}(\tfrac{1}{4}-1) - \tfrac{1}{9}(\tfrac{1}{2}-1) + \tfrac{1}{27}\log 2$$

$$= \tfrac{2}{27}\log 2 + \tfrac{13}{72}.$$

Example 6. Evaluate $\displaystyle\int \frac{x\,dx}{(x^2-1)(x^2+2)}$.

Putting $x^2 = u$, we see that the integral becomes

$$\int \frac{\tfrac{1}{2}du}{(u-1)(u+2)},$$

so that we have at once

$$\int \frac{du}{2(u-1)(u+2)} = \int \left[\frac{1}{6}\frac{1}{u-1} - \frac{1}{6}\frac{1}{u+2}\right] du = \frac{1}{6}\log\left|\frac{x^2-1}{x^2+2}\right|.$$

Example 7. The acceleration of a car (moving under constant power against resistances) is given in m/s² by the formula

$$a = \frac{(30-v)(50+v)}{40v} \text{ m/s}^2,$$

where v m/s is the speed after t s. Find how long it takes to accelerate from 15 m/s to 25 m/s.

We have

$$\frac{dt}{dv} = \frac{1}{a} = \frac{40v}{(30-v)(50+v)} = \frac{15}{30-v} - \frac{25}{50+v}$$

so that

$$t = \int_{15}^{25} \left\{\frac{15}{30-v} - \frac{25}{50+v}\right\} dv$$

$$= \left[-15\ln(30-v) - 25\ln(50+v)\right]_{15}^{25}$$

$$= 15\ln 3 - 25\ln 1{\cdot}154$$

$$= 13 \text{ seconds, approximately.}$$

Exercise D

Evaluate the following:

1. $\int \dfrac{dx}{x^2-1} \quad (x>1)$.

2. $\int \dfrac{dx}{1-x^2} \quad (-1<x<1)$.

3. $\int \dfrac{dx}{x^2-a^2}$.

4. $\int \dfrac{x\,dx}{x^2-4}$.

5. $\int \dfrac{2x+3}{(x-1)(x+4)}\,dx$.

6. $\int \dfrac{x+1}{x^2-3x+2}\,dx$.

7. $\int \dfrac{x^2\,dx}{x^2-9}$.

8. $\int \dfrac{x^2\,dx}{(x^2+1)(x^2+4)}$.

9. $\int \dfrac{2x-1}{x(x+1)^4}\,dx$.

10. $\int \dfrac{x^4\,dx}{x^2-1}$.

11. $\int \dfrac{x^5\,dx}{x^2-1}$.

12. $\int \dfrac{5x-6}{(3-x)(x-2)^5}\,dx$.

13. Find the area between the curve

$$y = \frac{10}{(x+2)(3-x)},$$

the lines $x=1$ and $x=2$, and the x-axis.

14. Find the distance travelled while the velocity is increasing from 15 m/s to 25 m/s for the car in Example 7.

15. What is the car's maximum speed? Give a reason why the formula cannot be expected to hold for small velocities. If it did, how long would the car take to reach 15 m/s from rest?

16. Find the solution of the differential equation

$$2x\frac{dy}{dx}-3 = y(2-y)$$

for which $x=1$ when $y=2$.

4. NON-LINEAR FACTORS

There are two main methods of finding partial fractions for a rational form which has non-linear irreducible factors in its denominator.

Method I. Since all polynomials over the complex field are reducible, we can always (in theory) find linear complex factors and use the cover-up rule to find partial fractions corresponding to them. These can then be recombined to give real partial fractions.

Example 8.
$$\frac{x^2+2x+7}{(x-1)(x^2+4)} = \frac{x^2+2x+7}{(x-1)(x-2j)(x+2j)}$$

$$= \frac{2}{x-1} + \frac{3+4j}{(2j-1)4j(x-2j)} + \frac{3-4j}{(2j+1)4j(x+2j)}$$

$$= \frac{2}{x-1} + \frac{(3+4j)(2-j)}{-4(5)(x-2j)} + \frac{(3-4j)(2+j)}{-4(5)(x-2j)}$$

$$= \frac{2}{x-1} - \frac{2+j}{4(x-2j)} - \frac{2-j}{4(x+2j)}$$

$$= \frac{2}{x-1} - \frac{x-1}{x^2+4}.$$

Method II. If there is not more than one irreducible quadratic factor we can peel off the partial fractions for the linear factors and the remaining core will be the partial fraction we need. In this case we have

$$\frac{x^2+2x+7}{(x-1)(x^2+4)} = \frac{2}{x-1} + \frac{Q(x)}{x^2+4}, \quad \text{by the cover-up rule}$$

$$\Rightarrow Q(x) = \frac{x^2+2x+7-2(x^2+4)}{x-1} = \frac{-x^2+2x-1}{x-1}$$

$$= 1-x$$

$$\Rightarrow \frac{x^2+2x+7}{(x-1)(x^2+4)} = \frac{2}{x-1} + \frac{1-x}{x^2+4}.$$

Exercise E

1. Use both methods to find partial fractions for

$$\frac{4x+7}{(2x-3)(x^2+1)}.$$

2. Find, by either method, partial fractions for

$$\frac{6}{(x-2)(x^2+2)}.$$

3. Find complex and real partial fractions for

    (a) $\dfrac{1}{x(x^2+1)}$;   (b) $\dfrac{1}{x^3-1} = \dfrac{1}{(x-1)(x-\omega)(x-\omega^2)}$,

where $\omega^3 = 1$, and $1+\omega+\omega^2 = 0$.

4. Use Method II to express in real partial fractions

$$\frac{3(2x-5)}{(x+2)(x^3-1)}.$$

5. Experience of Method II enables us to deduce that it is possible to express

$$\frac{x-4}{(x+2)(x^2+x+2)} \quad \text{in the form} \quad \frac{A}{x+2} + \frac{Bx+C}{x^2+x+2}.$$

Assuming this, obtain A by the cover-up rule, C by putting $x = 0$, and B by considering the coefficient of x^2 in the equation connecting polynomials which expresses the equivalence. Check that your result is in fact correct.

(This method can be used when the desired form is known on theoretical grounds, but it should always be checked.)

6. Express in partial fractions

$$\frac{15}{(x-1)(x+2)(x^2+2x+2)}.$$

5. REPEATED FACTORS

5.1 Simple repeated factors. The ancient Egyptians preferred to think of $\frac{7}{8}$ as $\frac{1}{2}+\frac{1}{4}+\frac{1}{8}$, and on some occasions we might agree with them that this is a simpler form, for example, in dividing seven round pies among eight people. Certainly we are not likely to regard a form such as

$$\frac{x^2-x+1}{(x-1)^3}$$

with any great enthusiasm, especially if we are required to integrate it, and we should consider the equivalent form

$$\frac{1}{(x-1)^3} + \frac{1}{(x-1)^2} + \frac{1}{(x-1)}$$

as much more tractable. In point of fact, were we faced with evaluating

$$\int \frac{x^2-x+1}{(x-1)^3}\,dx,$$

the obvious line of attack is to use the substitution $u = x-1$, which reduces the integral to the form

$$\int \frac{u^2+u+1}{u^3}\,du = \int \left\{\frac{1}{u^3}+\frac{1}{u^2}+\frac{1}{u}\right\}\,du.$$

Alternatively, we might realize that the problem is the same as that of expressing x^2-x+1 in the form $A(x-1)^2+B(x-1)+C$, and this can be effected by successive division by $(x-1)$. This lends itself more readily to mechanical computation, using the method of *synthetic division* explained in Chapter 3, Miscellaneous Exercise, Questions 11–13.

Contrary to what might be imagined, the cover-up rule can still be used, provided that the fractions are 'peeled off' one at a time. In this example, the cover-up rule gives, putting $x = 1$,

$$\frac{1-1+1}{(x-1)^3};$$

removing this, we get

$$\frac{x^2-x+1-1}{(x-1)^3} = \frac{x}{(x-1)^2},$$

and the process may now be repeated. This is, however, of more theoretical than practical use, since substitution is usually quicker.

5.2 Repeated factors with others. The simplest procedure, when it is possible, is to find the fractions corresponding to the other factors first, peel them off, and then continue as in the last paragraph. Alternatively, now the form of the partial fractions is known, we may use a variety of methods to obtain them, as outlined in Exercise F, Question 5.

Example 9. (Use of cover-up rule.)

$$\frac{1}{x(x-1)^3} = \frac{-1}{x}+\frac{(x-1)^3+1}{x(x-1)^3}, \quad \text{by the cover-up rule}$$

$$= \frac{-1}{x}+\frac{x^2-3x+3}{(x-1)^3}, \quad \text{dividing by } x$$

$$= \frac{-1}{x}+\frac{1}{(x-1)^2}+\frac{x^2-3x+2}{(x-1)^3}, \quad \text{by the cover-up rule}$$

$$= \frac{-1}{x}+\frac{1}{(x-1)^3}+\frac{x-2}{(x-1)^2}, \quad \text{dividing by } x-1$$

$$= -\frac{1}{x}+\frac{1}{(x-1)^3}-\frac{1}{(x-1)^2}+\frac{1}{x-1}, \quad \text{finally.}$$

Example 10. (Cover-up rule, followed by substitution.)

$$\frac{9x+2}{(x+3)(x-2)^3} = \frac{1}{5(x+3)}+\frac{Q(x)}{(x-2)^3}, \quad \text{by the cover-up rule,}$$

$$\Rightarrow Q(x) = \frac{5(9x+2)-(x-2)^3}{5(x+3)}.$$

Now put $x-2 = u$, giving

$$Q(x) = P(u) = \frac{5(9u+20)-u^3}{5(u+5)} = \frac{-u^2+5u+20}{5};$$

so that, finally,

$$\frac{9x+2}{(x+3)(x-2)^3} = \frac{1}{5(x+3)}-\frac{1}{5(x-2)}+\frac{1}{(x-2)^2}+\frac{4}{(x-2)^3}.$$

Exercise F

1. Express in partial fractions:

(a) $\dfrac{1}{x^3(x-2)}$;

(b) $\dfrac{1}{x^4(2x-1)}$;

(c) $\dfrac{1}{(x+1)^4(2x+1)}$;

(d) $\dfrac{1-x}{x(x+1)^3}$.

2. Express in partial fractions:

(a) $\dfrac{2-x}{x^3(x-1)}$;

(b) $\dfrac{x^2+40}{(x+3)(x-4)^2}$;

(c) $\dfrac{8x-72}{(x+1)(x-3)^2}$;

(d) $\dfrac{5x^2-x-13}{(x-2)^2(x^2+1)}$.

3. Reduce
$$\frac{9x^2}{(x-1)^2(x+2)^2}$$
to partial fractions by first reducing
$$\frac{3x}{(x-1)(x+2)}$$
and squaring the result.

4. Assuming that
$$\frac{5x+7}{(x-5)(x+3)^2}$$
is expressible in the form
$$\frac{A}{x-5}+\frac{B}{(x+3)^2}+\frac{C}{x+3},$$
obtain A, B, C by multiplying up and substituting suitable values for x. Check that your answer is correct.

5. Evaluate:

(a) $\displaystyle\int\frac{dx}{(x+1)(x-1)^2}$;

(b) $\displaystyle\int\frac{x\,dx}{(x+1)(x-1)^2}$.

6. Evaluate:

(a) $\displaystyle\int_2^3\frac{x\,dx}{(x^2-1)^2}$;

(b) $\displaystyle\int_2^3\frac{x^2\,dx}{(x^2-1)^2}$.

7. Evaluate:
$$\int_0^1\frac{dx}{(2-x)(x+1)^3}.$$

6. FURTHER USES OF PARTIAL FRACTIONS

6.1 Turning values. It is often easier to find the turning values of a rational function by using the expanded partial fraction form to obtain the derived function than by differentiating the form as it stands using the quotient rule.

1262

Example 11. Find the turning values of the function

$$f: x \to \frac{x+2}{(x-2)(x+1)}.$$

We find that
$$f(x) = \frac{4}{3(x-2)} - \frac{1}{3(x+1)},$$

from which
$$f'(x) = -\frac{4}{3(x-2)^2} + \frac{1}{3(x+1)^2}.$$

$$f'(x) = 0 \Leftrightarrow 4(x+1)^2 = (x-2)^2$$

$$\Leftrightarrow 2(x+1) = \pm(x-2)$$

$$\Leftrightarrow x = 0 \quad \text{or} \quad -4.$$

Examination of the sign of $f'(x)$ shows that, as x passes through the value -4, $f'(x)$ changes from $-$ to $+$; as x passes through zero, $f'(x)$ changes from $+$ to $-$. Therefore $f(-4) = -\frac{1}{9}$ is a minimum value, and $f(0) = -1$ a maximum value. The graph of $f(x)$ should be sketched as a check on this.

The alternative method of finding the turning values of such a function using quadratic inequalities should be noted.

Suppose we seek to locate the values of x for which $f(x) = k$. Then

$$k(x^2 - x - 2) = x + 2.$$

If this quadratic equation for x is to have roots in the real field, we must have
$$(1+k)^2 + 4k(2k+2) \geqslant 0.$$

$$\Rightarrow (1+k)(1+9k) \geqslant 0.$$

There are therefore no roots for values of k between -1 and $-\frac{1}{9}$; from which we conclude that -1 is a maximum turning value of $f(x)$ and $-\frac{1}{9}$ a minimum turning value.

6.2 Polynomial approximations. To derive polynomial approximations for small values of x to rational functions it is again easier to use the partial fraction form. Suppose we wish to find an approximation of the third degree to the function defined in Example 11 when x is small. Using the binomial theorem, cubic expansions for $1/(x+1)$ and $1/(x-2)$ are given by

$$\frac{1}{x+1} = (1+x)^{-1} \simeq 1 - x + x^2 - x^3,$$

$$\frac{1}{x-2} = -\frac{1}{2}(1-\frac{1}{2}x)^{-1} \simeq -\frac{1}{2} - \frac{1}{4}x - \frac{1}{8}x^2 - \frac{1}{16}x^3.$$

Hence
$$f(x) = \frac{4}{3(x-2)} - \frac{1}{3(x+1)}$$

$$= \tfrac{1}{3}(-2-x-\tfrac{1}{2}x^2-\tfrac{1}{4}x^3-1+x-x^2+x^3)$$

$$= -1-\tfrac{1}{2}x^2+\tfrac{1}{4}x^3.$$

The form of this incidentally confirms that -1 is a maximum value.

Example 12. Find a quadratic approximation for

$$f: x \to \frac{12x-1}{(x-3)(x+2)} \quad \text{near } x = 2.$$

Put $x = 2+u$. Then

$$f(x) = \frac{23+12u}{(4+u)(u-1)} = \frac{7}{u-1}+\frac{5}{4+u}$$

$$= -7(1-u)^{-1}+\tfrac{5}{4}(1+\tfrac{1}{4}u)^{-1}$$

$$= -7-7u-7u^2+\tfrac{5}{4}-\tfrac{5}{16}u+\tfrac{5}{64}u^2$$

$$= -\tfrac{23}{4}-\tfrac{117}{16}u-\tfrac{443}{64}u^2.$$

Exercise G

1. Find turning values of the following, and sketch their graphs:

(a) $\dfrac{x}{(x-1)(x-4)}$;

(b) $\dfrac{(2x+1)(x-7)}{x(x-3)}$.

2. Use the second method of Example 11 to show that

$$-1 \leqslant \frac{x}{x^2+x+1} \leqslant \frac{1}{3}.$$

3. Find the range of:

$$f: x \to \frac{x^2-1}{5x^2+20x+24},$$

the domain being all real x.

4. Show that there is a 'gap' in the range of

$$f: x \to \frac{2x^2+x+2}{x(x+1)}$$

and find it.

5. Obtain quadratic polynomial approximations to the following (i) for small x, (ii) near $x = 6$:

(a) $\dfrac{1}{x-4}$;

(b) $\dfrac{1}{3x+2}$.

1264

6. Obtain quadratic approximations to the following (i) for small x, (ii) near $x = -4$:

(a) $\dfrac{7x-10}{x^2-3x+2}$; 　　(b) $\dfrac{x+4}{x^2+5x+6}$; 　　(c) $\dfrac{-2x}{(x+1)(x+2)(x+3)}$.

7. Find a cubic polynomial which approximates to

$$\frac{x-43}{(x-3)(x+2)}$$

in the neighbourhood of $x = 1$.

8. Find the equation of the parabola which approximates most closely to the shape of the graph of

$$y = \frac{x}{(x-1)^2(2x+1)^3}$$

at the origin.
　(Do not attempt to find partial fractions.)

*7. SOME FORMAL PROOFS

We conclude this chapter by establishing some of the general theory of partial fractions.

7.1　The cover-up rule. Suppose that we have a rational form

$$\frac{f(x)}{(x-\alpha)g(x)},$$

where $x-\alpha$ is a linear unrepeated factor of the denominator, so that $g(x)$ does not have $(x-\alpha)$ as a factor and therefore $g(\alpha) \neq 0$. We wish to express this as the sum of two forms,

$$\frac{A}{x-\alpha}+\frac{q(x)}{g(x)}, \quad \text{so that} \quad \frac{f(x)}{(x-\alpha)g(x)}-\frac{A}{x-\alpha}$$

is a form with $g(x)$ alone in the denominator. Now

$$\frac{f(x)}{(x-\alpha)g(x)}-\frac{A}{x-\alpha}=\frac{f(x)-Ag(x)}{(x-\alpha)g(x)},$$

and this will be a form with $g(x)$ alone in the denominator if and only if $f(x)-Ag(x)$ has $(x-\alpha)$ as a factor; i.e. by the factor theorem, if and only if $f(\alpha)-Ag(\alpha) = 0$. Since $g(\alpha) \neq 0$, the unique value of A which achieves this is $f(\alpha)/g(\alpha)$. We have thus proved that, if $g(\alpha) \neq 0$,

$$\frac{f(x)}{(x-\alpha)g(x)}=\frac{f(\alpha)/g(\alpha)}{x-\alpha}+\frac{q(x)}{g(x)},$$

which is the justification for the rule.

We must now show that, for a proper rational form with linear un-repeated factors in its denominator, the various partial fractions which the cover-up rule gives do in fact add up to the original form. We shall prove this for two factors; its truth for any number follows by repetition of the argument.

Consider
$$\frac{f(x)}{(x-\alpha)(x-\beta)g(x)},$$

where $\alpha \neq \beta$ and neither $g(\alpha)$ nor $g(\beta)$ is 0. By the cover-up rule

$$\frac{f(x)}{(x-\alpha)(x-\beta)g(x)} = \frac{f(\alpha)}{(x-\alpha)(\alpha-\beta)g(\alpha)} + \frac{q(x)}{(x-\beta)g(x)} \qquad \text{(A)}$$

$$= \frac{f(\alpha)}{(x-\alpha)(\alpha-\beta)g(\alpha)} + \frac{q(\beta)}{(x-\beta)g(\beta)} + \frac{r(x)}{g(x)}.$$

Does
$$\frac{q(\beta)}{g(\beta)} = \frac{f(\beta)}{(\beta-\alpha)g(\beta)},$$

so that the coefficient of $1/(x-\beta)$ could have been obtained directly from the use of the cover-up rule in the original form? From (A) we have

$$f(x)(\alpha-\beta)g(\alpha) = f(\alpha)(x-\beta)g(x) + q(x)(x-\alpha)(\alpha-\beta)g(\alpha).$$

This identity between polynomials must be true when $x = \beta$; it then gives

$$f(\beta)(\alpha-\beta)g(\alpha) = q(\beta)(\beta-\alpha)(\alpha-\beta)g(\alpha), \quad \text{i.e. } q(\beta) = \frac{f(\beta)}{\beta-\alpha},$$

which establishes the result. To complete the proof we must show that there is no polynomial 'core' left when all the partial fractions have been peeled off. This, however, follows immediately from the fact that the difference between the original proper rational form and the sum of any number of proper partial fractions must itself be proper, and cannot therefore be a polynomial.

7.2 Repeated factors. The proof in 7.1 does not apply when $g(\alpha) = 0$, i.e. when the denominator contains $(x-\alpha)^2$ as a factor. Obviously we cannot express
$$\frac{1}{(x-\alpha)^3} \quad \text{as} \quad \frac{A}{x-\alpha} + \frac{B}{x-\alpha} + \frac{C}{x-\alpha},$$

and in general it is not possible to express
$$\frac{f(x)}{(x-\alpha)^3 g(x)} \quad \text{as} \quad \frac{A}{(x-\alpha)^3} + \frac{q(x)}{g(x)}.$$

To see what is possible, we consider what the cover-up rule gives.

$$\frac{f(x)}{(x-\alpha)^3 g(x)} = \frac{f(\alpha)}{(x-\alpha)^3 g(\alpha)} + \frac{f(x)g(\alpha)-f(\alpha)g(x)}{(x-\alpha)^3 g(x)g(\alpha)},$$

the first term being given by the cover-up rule, the second being what is left.

By the factor theorem, the numerator of the second term is divisible by $(x-\alpha)$; suppose it is $(x-\alpha)q(x)$. Then

$$\frac{f(x)}{(x-\alpha)^3 g(x)} = \frac{f(\alpha)}{(x-\alpha)^3 g(\alpha)} + \frac{q(x)/g(\alpha)}{(x-\alpha)^2 g(x)},$$

and the process may now be repeated, leading ultimately to an expression of the form

$$\frac{f(x)}{(x-\alpha)^3 g(x)} = \frac{A}{(x-\alpha)^3} + \frac{B}{(x-\alpha)^2} + \frac{C}{x-\alpha} + \frac{d(x)}{g(x)},$$

A being given by the cover-up rule.

7.3   Quadratic factors. Any real quadratic form without real factors can be factorized into two conjugate complex linear factors:

$$px^2 + qx + r = p(x-a)(x-\bar{a}), \text{ say.}$$

Hence

$$\frac{f(x)}{(px^2+qx+r)g(x)} = \frac{f(a)}{p(a-\bar{a})g(a)} \cdot \frac{1}{x-a} + \frac{f(\bar{a})}{p(\bar{a}-a)g(\bar{a})} \cdot \frac{1}{x-\bar{a}} + \frac{q(x)}{g(x)},$$

by the cover-up rule

$$= \frac{A}{x-a} + \frac{\bar{A}}{x-\bar{a}} + \frac{q(x)}{g(x)},$$

where A and $\bar{A}$ are conjugate complex numbers. These two fractions may now be combined to give

$$\frac{pA(x-\bar{a}) + p\bar{A}(x-a)}{p(x-a)(x-\bar{a})} = \frac{Cx+D}{px^2+qx+r},$$

where C and D are real. For $p(A+\bar{A})$ and $p(A\bar{a}+\bar{A}a)$ both have zero imaginary parts. This is therefore the form of the partial fraction corresponding to an irreducible quadratic factor.

Finally, since by the Fundamental Theorem of Algebra every polynomial is reducible over the complex field, we can always factorize (in theory) any real polynomial into linear factors which will be real or will occur in conjugate complex pairs. It follows that the methods of these sections provide a categorical procedure for splitting any proper rational form over the real field into real partial fractions. It must, however, be realized that in practice it may be sufficiently laborious even to find the factors of the denominator, and when these are found the evaluation of the coefficients in the partial fractions may involve arduous computation. Once we know they exist, other quicker methods may often be used to obtain them; in particular it is not necessary in practice to find complex factors for real quadratic denominators. We may appeal directly to the equivalence condition and find coefficients by giving values to x or by equating coefficients of like powers.

Miscellaneous Exercise

1. Find the turning-points of the function

$$f: x \to \frac{x^2+2}{(x+1)(x-5)}.$$

2. For what value of x does $\dfrac{2x-9}{x(x-4)}$ have (a) a maximum, (b) a minimum value? Sketch the graph of this function.

3. Evaluate:

(a) $\displaystyle\int_1^2 \frac{dx}{9-x^2};$ $\qquad$ (b) $\displaystyle\int_1^2 \frac{x\,dx}{9-x^2};$ $\qquad$ (c) $\displaystyle\int_1^2 \frac{x^2\,dx}{9-x^2}.$

4. Find $\displaystyle\int_{\frac{1}{3}a}^{\frac{1}{2}a} \frac{dx}{a^2-x^2}$ and $\displaystyle\int_{\frac{1}{3}a}^{\frac{1}{2}a} \frac{dx}{(x+a)(a^2-x^2)}.$

Evaluate the following integrals, Questions 5–10.

5. $\displaystyle\int \frac{x\,dx}{(x^2+1)(x^2+4)}.$ $\qquad$ **6.** $\displaystyle\int_2^3 \frac{dx}{(x-1)x^3}.$ $\qquad$ **7.** $\displaystyle\int_1^2 \frac{dx}{x(x+1)^3}.$

8. $\displaystyle\int_{1\frac{1}{2}}^{2\frac{1}{2}} \frac{dx}{(2x+1)(2x-1)^3}.$ $\qquad$ **9.** $\displaystyle\int \frac{(x+1)\,dx}{x(x-1)}.$ $\qquad$ **10.** $\displaystyle\int \frac{dx}{x^4-1}.$

11. Show that $\displaystyle\int_0^1 \frac{x^3\,dx}{9-x^4} < \int_0^1 \frac{x^2\,dx}{9-x^4} < \int_0^1 \frac{x\,dx}{9-x^4}$

without evaluating these integrals. Evaluate them and state any conclusion you can draw from the inequalities.

12. Express

$$\frac{1}{x(x+1)(x+2)}$$

in partial fractions. Find the sum of the first 100 terms of the series

$$\frac{1}{1.2.3}+\frac{1}{2.3.4}+\frac{1}{3.4.5}+\dots.$$

Does the sum to n terms of this series have a limit as $n \to \infty$?

13. Find the sum of the first n terms of the series

$$\frac{1}{1.2}+\frac{1}{2.3}+\frac{1}{3.4}+\dots.$$

Hence show that the series $\quad \dfrac{1}{1^2}+\dfrac{1}{2^2}+\dfrac{1}{3^2}+\dfrac{1}{4^2}+\dots$

is convergent, and that its sum is less than 2. How could you make a better estimate of its limiting sum? (The sum is in fact equal to $\frac{1}{6}\pi^2$.)

1268

14. Express $\dfrac{x^5}{(x^2+1)^3}$ in the form

$$\frac{Ax+B}{(x^2+1)}+\frac{Cx+D}{(x^2+1)^2}+\frac{Ex+F}{(x^2+1)^3}.$$

15. Consider the following method of finding quadratic partial fractions:

$$\frac{2x}{(x^2-2x+2)(x^2+2x+2)} = \frac{1}{x^2-2x+2}\times\left[\frac{2x}{x^2+2x+2}\right]_{\text{where }x^2-2x+2=0}$$

$$+\frac{1}{x^2+2x+2}\times\left[\frac{2x}{x^2-2x+2}\right]_{\text{where }x^2+2x+2=0}$$

$$=\frac{1}{x^2-2x+2}\times\left[\frac{2x}{4x}\right]+\frac{1}{x^2+2x+2}\times\left[\frac{2x}{-4x}\right]$$

$$=\frac{\frac{1}{2}}{x^2-2x+2}-\frac{\frac{1}{2}}{x^2+2x+2}.$$

Justify this method, and, if you like, try some further experiments. To deal, for example, with

$$\frac{2x}{(x-1)(x+2)(x^2+1)},$$

we may proceed as follows:

$$\left[\frac{2x}{(x-1)(x+2)}\right]_{x^2+1=0} = \left[\frac{2x}{x-3}\right]_{x^2+1=0}$$

$$=\left[\frac{2x(x+3)}{x^2-9}\right]_{x^2+1=0} = \frac{-2+6x}{-10} = \frac{1-3x}{5}.$$

So that $\dfrac{2x}{(x-1)(x+2)(x^2+1)} = \dfrac{1}{3(x-1)}+\dfrac{4}{15(x+2)}+\dfrac{1-3x}{5(x^2+1)}.$

16. Express in partial fractions

$$\frac{17x^2-6x-3}{(x-1)^2(x^2+1)^2}.$$

42

LINEAR DEPENDENCE AND DETERMINANTS

1. DETERMINANTS AND THE SOLUTION OF EQUATIONS

When we considered linear equations in Chapter 21, we found that they sometimes had no solutions, sometimes an infinity of solutions, and sometimes a unique solution. The distinction between these cases hinged on the properties of the matrix of the coefficients of the equations. Our object now is to investigate this phenomenon more deeply. We shall find that the vanishing or not vanishing of a certain number associated with the matrix, its 'determinant', sometimes gives us a simple means of distinguishing the cases that can arise. Determinants are also important in other branches of mathematics.

1.1 Types of solution set. A look at a few examples of three linear equations in three unknowns (in brief: 3×3 equations) will serve to remind us of the different possible types of solution sets, and the characteristic ways in which they emerge in the process of solving the equations.

Example 1. Solve the set of equations:

$$\begin{cases} 2x+ y- z = 2, \\ 4x- y-3z = -2, \\ 2x+2y+ z = 9. \end{cases}$$

Row transformations to eliminate x from the last two equations reduce them to

$$\begin{cases} 2x+ y- z = 2, \\ -3y- z = -6, \\ y+2z = 7; \end{cases}$$

eliminating y between the last pair reduces them to the echelon form

$$\begin{cases} 2x+ y- z = 2, \\ -3y- z = -6, \\ 5z = 15. \end{cases}$$

These steps may be written in matrix form as

$$\begin{pmatrix} 2 & 1 & -1 \\ 4 & -1 & -3 \\ 2 & 2 & 1 \end{pmatrix} \begin{pmatrix} x \\ y \\ z \end{pmatrix} = \begin{pmatrix} 2 \\ -2 \\ 9 \end{pmatrix} \Rightarrow \begin{pmatrix} 2 & 1 & -1 \\ 0 & -3 & -1 \\ 0 & 1 & 2 \end{pmatrix} \begin{pmatrix} x \\ y \\ z \end{pmatrix} = \begin{pmatrix} 2 \\ -6 \\ 7 \end{pmatrix}$$

$$\Rightarrow \begin{pmatrix} 2 & 1 & -1 \\ 0 & -3 & -1 \\ 0 & 0 & 5 \end{pmatrix} \begin{pmatrix} x \\ y \\ z \end{pmatrix} = \begin{pmatrix} 2 \\ -6 \\ 15 \end{pmatrix}.$$

Here the solutions are $z = 3$, $y = 1$, $x = 2$; that is, $(x, y, z) = (2, 1, 3)$.

In this process there is a point of logic which we should observe. If the original set of equations is the statement P, the next set the statement Q, the next R and the final set $(x, y, z) = (2, 1, 3)$ the statement S, the argument has run: $P \Rightarrow Q \Rightarrow R \Rightarrow S$. From this we can deduce that S *contains* the solution set of P, but to show that S *is* the solution set of P involves either checking in the original equations or being sure that the steps taken are reversible. The step $S \Rightarrow R$ is beyond reproach considering the way S was derived from R, and the other steps are multiplication by non-zero numbers and the addition of equations, both of which are here reversible. Hence there is a proper process by which the equations P could be recovered from those of R. It is worth realizing that the theoretical solution of general equations is rendered more difficult than that of specific numerical ones because of the need to guard against such things as multiplying by a coefficient which might be zero, since this would vitiate the reverse implication; in numerical cases this just does not arise because the terms are not there.

Returning to Example 1, if we change the third equation to

$$2x + 2y - \tfrac{2}{3}z = 9$$

the same process gives:

$$\left. \begin{array}{r} 2x + y - z = 2, \\ 4x - y - 3z = -2, \\ 2x + 2y - \tfrac{2}{3}z = 9, \end{array} \right\} \qquad \left. \begin{array}{r} 2x + y - z = 2, \\ -3y - z = -6, \\ y + \tfrac{1}{3}z = 7, \end{array} \right\} \qquad \left. \begin{array}{r} 2x + y - z = 2, \\ -3y - z = -6, \\ 0z = 15. \end{array} \right\}$$

The last equation is now $0z = 15$, and as no value of z satisfies this, our new equations have no solutions.

If, however, we change the original third equation to $2x + 2y - \tfrac{2}{3}z = 4$ we shall have:

$$\left. \begin{array}{r} 2x + y - z = 2, \\ 4x - y - 3z = -2, \\ 2x + 2y - \tfrac{2}{3}z = 4, \end{array} \right\} \qquad \left. \begin{array}{r} 2x + y - z = 2, \\ -3y - z = -6, \\ y + \tfrac{1}{3}z = 2, \end{array} \right\} \qquad \left. \begin{array}{r} 2x + y - z = 2, \\ -3y - z = 6, \\ 0z = 0. \end{array} \right\}$$

Now we can choose any value for z, since this will satisfy $0z = 0$, and then determine y and x correspondingly; in this case, therefore, our new set of equations has an infinity of solutions. Notice in this case that the second equation is the difference between the first one multiplied through by 5 and the third one multiplied through by 3, so that one of the original equations was effectively redundant.

1.2 Linear dependence. An idea which is extremely valuable in the sequel is that of linear dependence, which was touched on briefly in Chapter 9. We showed there (p. 264) by a geometrical argument, that if **p**, **q**, **r** are coplanar vectors, then there is an equation of the form

$$a\mathbf{p} + b\mathbf{q} + c\mathbf{r} = \mathbf{0}$$

which connects them, with a, b, c not all zero. When this is true we say that **p**, **q**, **r** are *linearly dependent*; in contrast to this, if **p**, **q**, **r** are *linearly independent*, which, geometrically, would mean that they lay in three-dimensional space and were not parallel to a plane, then no such equation can be found, apart from the trivial equation with $a = b = c = 0$. We use this idea quite generally:

A set of vectors is *linearly dependent* if there is a linear non-trivial equation connecting them.

More formally:

p, **q**, **r**, ... are *linearly independent* means that

$$a\mathbf{p} + b\mathbf{q} + c\mathbf{r} + \dots = \mathbf{0} \quad \Rightarrow \quad a = b = c = \dots = 0.$$

Geometrically, it is obvious that three two-rowed column vectors such as

$$\begin{pmatrix} 5 \\ 6 \end{pmatrix}, \quad \begin{pmatrix} 3 \\ -2 \end{pmatrix}, \quad \begin{pmatrix} 4 \\ 1 \end{pmatrix}$$

lie in a plane and must be dependent, but an algebraic proof is not difficult to devise. In this case, if we label

$$\begin{pmatrix} 5 \\ 6 \end{pmatrix} \quad \text{as} \quad \mathbf{p}, \quad \begin{pmatrix} 3 \\ -2 \end{pmatrix} \quad \text{as} \quad \mathbf{q},$$

then these two vectors are independent (one is not a multiple of the other) and it is easy to find the *base vectors*

$$\begin{pmatrix} 1 \\ 0 \end{pmatrix}, \quad \begin{pmatrix} 0 \\ 1 \end{pmatrix}$$

in terms of **p** and **q**. In fact

$$\begin{pmatrix} 1 \\ 0 \end{pmatrix} = \frac{\mathbf{p} + 3\mathbf{q}}{14} \quad \text{and} \quad \begin{pmatrix} 0 \\ 1 \end{pmatrix} = \frac{3\mathbf{p} - 5\mathbf{q}}{28}.$$

This done, we can now express $\begin{pmatrix} 4 \\ 1 \end{pmatrix}$ in terms of $\mathbf{p}$ and $\mathbf{q}$, and the linear dependence is shown

$$\begin{pmatrix} 4 \\ 1 \end{pmatrix} = \tfrac{2}{7}(\mathbf{p}+3\mathbf{q})+\tfrac{1}{28}(3\mathbf{p}-5\mathbf{q}).$$

Furthermore, such an expression is unique (provided $\mathbf{p}$ and $\mathbf{q}$ are independent). For if it were possible to have two different expressions

$$\mathbf{r} = a\mathbf{p}+b\mathbf{q}$$
$$= a'\mathbf{p}+b'\mathbf{q},$$

then by subtraction $\qquad (a-a')\mathbf{p}+(b-b')\mathbf{q} = \mathbf{0}$

with $(a-a')$ and $(b-b')$ not both zero, so that $\mathbf{p}$ and $\mathbf{q}$ would be linearly dependent, contrary to hypothesis.

Exactly similar considerations apply to three-rowed vectors in three-dimensional space; any four of them must be linearly dependent, and if three of them are independent, then the fourth can be expressed uniquely in terms of these three. These geometrically obvious facts are by no means trivial when considered in algebraic terms: in fact, much of the rest of the chapter is concerned with this.

Exercise A

1. Solve by the echelon process

$$\begin{cases} x+2y+\ z = 1, \\ x-2y-\ z = 3, \\ 2x+8y+pz = q, \end{cases}$$

where $\quad$ (a) $p = 5, q = 1$; $\quad$ (b) $p = 4, q = 1$; $\quad$ (c) $p = 4, q = 0$.

2. Solve by the echelon process expressed in matrix form:

$$\begin{cases} 3x-\ y+2z = 1, \\ 2x\ \ \ \ +3z = 1, \\ -x+3y+6z = 1, \end{cases}$$

and find a linear relationship between these equations.

3. Solve by the echelon process:

$$\begin{cases} 17x+\ y-\ 19z = \ \ -2, \\ 119x+7y-133z = -14, \\ -51x-3y+\ 57z = \ \ \ \ 6. \end{cases}$$

4. Show that the three column-vectors comprising the matrix

$$\begin{pmatrix} 2 & 7 & 5 \\ 3 & -6 & 2 \\ 1 & 17 & 7 \end{pmatrix}$$

are linearly dependent; and so also are its three row-vectors.

5. Are

$$\begin{pmatrix} a \\ b \end{pmatrix}, \quad \begin{pmatrix} c \\ d \end{pmatrix}, \quad \begin{pmatrix} e \\ f \end{pmatrix}$$

always linearly dependent for all values of a, b, c, d, e, f? Are the vectors (a, c, e) and (b, d, f) always linearly dependent?

6. Find k if the three vectors

$$\begin{pmatrix} 1 \\ -1 \\ 3 \end{pmatrix}, \quad \begin{pmatrix} 2 \\ 1 \\ -1 \end{pmatrix}, \quad \begin{pmatrix} k \\ 0 \\ 2 \end{pmatrix}$$

are linearly dependent. In this case find a linear combination of the row-vectors $(1\ 2\ k)$, $(3\ -1\ 2)$ which has its third component zero, and hence show that the three row-vectors $(1\ 2\ k)$, $(-1\ 1\ 0)$, $(3\ -1\ 2)$ are also linearly dependent.

7. State whether the following pairs of equations have a unique solution, no solution, or an infinity of solutions. (You are *not* asked to solve them.)

(i) $\begin{cases} 3x - y = 11, \\ x - 3y = 8; \end{cases}$
   (ii) $\begin{cases} 7x + 4y = 3, \\ 21x + 12y = 10; \end{cases}$

(iii) $\begin{cases} 17x - 19y = 31, \\ 51x - 57y = 93; \end{cases}$
   (iv) $\begin{cases} 76x + 247y = 189, \\ 92x + 299y = 288. \end{cases}$

In (i) consider the linear dependence of each pair of

$$\begin{pmatrix} 3 \\ 1 \end{pmatrix}, \quad \begin{pmatrix} -1 \\ -3 \end{pmatrix}, \quad \begin{pmatrix} 11 \\ 8 \end{pmatrix};$$

do likewise for the other sets of equations. If possible formulate a rule in terms of the linear dependence of pairs of the vectors

$$\begin{pmatrix} a \\ c \end{pmatrix}, \quad \begin{pmatrix} b \\ d \end{pmatrix}, \quad \begin{pmatrix} p \\ q \end{pmatrix}$$

under which the equations $\quad \begin{cases} ax + by = p \\ cx + dy = q \end{cases}$

have (*a*) a unique solution, (*b*) no solution, (*c*) an infinity of solutions.

8. Show that the equations $3x + 4y = 5$ and $6x + 8y = 10$ have a solution $x = a + bt$, $y = c + dt$ for all values of t, where a, b, c, d are *integers* to be found.

9. Show that the equations $3x + 2y = 1$ and $2x + 3y = 2$ have no solution in the field of integers modulo 5; and find λ, μ such that $\lambda(3x + 2y) + \mu(2x + 3y) = 0$.

1274

1.3   Determinants in 2×2 equations. As a basis for the development of future ideas we look at the simple case of two equations in two unknowns. These have the general form

$$\begin{cases} ax+by = p. \\ cx+dy = q. \end{cases}$$

When $p = q = 0$ the equations are said to be 'homogeneous', and we shall start by considering the existence of solutions of the homogeneous set of equations

$$\begin{cases} ax+by = 0, \\ cx+dy = 0. \end{cases}$$

These clearly have a solution: $(x, y) = (0, 0)$. This solution is known as a 'trivial' solution; any other solutions which may exist are then called 'non-trivial' solutions. We shall show that non-trivial solutions exist if, and only if, $ad-bc = 0$. The number '$ad-bc$', whose vanishing or non-vanishing determines the existence or otherwise of solutions is called the 'determinant' of the matrix of coefficients $\begin{pmatrix} a & b \\ c & d \end{pmatrix}$ and is written $\begin{vmatrix} a & b \\ c & d \end{vmatrix}$.

Our theorem can now be stated:

The pair of equations $\begin{cases} \text{(i)} \ \ ax+by = 0 \\ \text{(ii)} \ cx+dy = 0 \end{cases}$ **has non-trivial solutions** $\Leftrightarrow \begin{vmatrix} a & b \\ c & d \end{vmatrix} = 0.$

We can see in a rough and ready way that it is reasonable:

$$\frac{x}{y} = -\frac{b}{a} \ \text{ from (i), and } \ \frac{x}{y} = -\frac{d}{c} \ \text{ from (ii);}$$

so $b/a = d/c$, or $ad = bc$. Furthermore, the relation $b/a = d/c$ suggests equations like

$$\begin{cases} 2x+3y = 0, \\ 4x+6y = 0, \end{cases}$$

which really amount to only one equation, $2x+3y = 0$, and this has for its solution all the points on the line $2x+3y = 0$; that is the single infinity of solutions which can be written $(x, y) = (3\lambda, -2\lambda)$.

$b/a = d/c$ also might suggest equations like

$$\begin{cases} 2x+0y = 0, \\ 5x+0y = 0, \end{cases} \ \text{ where } \ b = d = 0,$$

and these have the single infinity of solutions $(x, y) = (0, \lambda)$. We might ask what happens if $a = b = 0$, but our rough and ready method breaks down here with zeros in the denominator. So we must deal with the

1275

theorem properly, proving the implication both ways and considering all possible cases.

We start by supposing there are non-trivial solutions and that one of the coefficients in the equations is not zero. Without loss of generality we may suppose $a \neq 0$. Then

$$ax + by = 0 \quad \Rightarrow \quad x = -by/a,$$

where y can take any non-zero value;

and
$$cx + dy = 0 \quad \Rightarrow \left(-\frac{cb}{a} + d\right) y = 0$$

$$\Rightarrow \quad -\frac{cb}{a} + d = 0, \quad \text{since } y \neq 0,$$

$$\Rightarrow \quad \begin{vmatrix} a & b \\ c & d \end{vmatrix} = 0, \quad \text{since } a \neq 0.$$

If $a = b = c = d = 0$, then again $\begin{vmatrix} a & b \\ c & d \end{vmatrix} = 0.$

Hence in all cases

The existence of non-trivial solutions implies $\begin{vmatrix} a & b \\ c & d \end{vmatrix} = 0.$

Conversely, $\begin{vmatrix} a & b \\ c & d \end{vmatrix} = 0 \Rightarrow$

either $a = b = c = d = 0$, when the equations have a double infinity of solutions $(x, y) = (\lambda, \mu)$ for all λ and μ;

or one of the coefficients is not zero—suppose it is a—when the equations have the non-trivial solution $(x, y) = (-b, a)$, and indeed any multiple of this, as is easily verified.

Note. For the immediate purpose it is rather meaningless even to contemplate equations
$$\begin{cases} 0x + 0y = 0, \\ 0x + 0y = 0, \end{cases}$$

but the result in its full form is needed for situations where these possibilities arise within the general solution of 3×3 equations.

The theorem we have proved can usefully be interpreted in terms of the dependence of vectors, by writing the equations as

$$\begin{pmatrix} a \\ c \end{pmatrix} x + \begin{pmatrix} b \\ d \end{pmatrix} y = \begin{pmatrix} 0 \\ 0 \end{pmatrix}.$$

When non-trivial solutions of this equation exist the vectors

$$\begin{pmatrix} a \\ c \end{pmatrix}, \quad \begin{pmatrix} b \\ d \end{pmatrix}$$

are linearly dependent, and when they do not exist they are independent. We can therefore restate the theorem:

$$\begin{pmatrix} a \\ c \end{pmatrix} \quad \text{and} \quad \begin{pmatrix} b \\ d \end{pmatrix} \quad \text{are linearly dependent} \quad \Leftrightarrow \quad \begin{vmatrix} a & b \\ c & d \end{vmatrix} = 0.$$

We shall use this idea in discussing the existence of solutions for the pair of non-homogeneous equations:

$$\left. \begin{cases} ax + by = p, \\ cx + dy = q, \end{cases} \right\} \quad \text{where} \quad p, q \text{ are not both zero.}$$

If $\begin{vmatrix} a & b \\ c & d \end{vmatrix} = 0$, we know that $\begin{pmatrix} a \\ c \end{pmatrix}, \begin{pmatrix} b \\ d \end{pmatrix}$ are linearly dependent, and therefore our equations, which can be written as

$$\begin{pmatrix} a \\ c \end{pmatrix} x + \begin{pmatrix} b \\ d \end{pmatrix} y = \begin{pmatrix} p \\ q \end{pmatrix},$$

will have solutions if, and only if, $\begin{pmatrix} p \\ q \end{pmatrix}$ is a scalar multiple of either $\begin{pmatrix} a \\ c \end{pmatrix}$ or $\begin{pmatrix} b \\ d \end{pmatrix}$ (which allows for the possibility of one of these vectors being zero). When there are solutions, there are an infinite number of them and this is consistent with the fact that one equation is merely a multiple of the other and is therefore redundant.

If $\begin{vmatrix} a & b \\ c & d \end{vmatrix} \neq 0$, then $\begin{pmatrix} a \\ c \end{pmatrix}, \begin{pmatrix} b \\ d \end{pmatrix}$ are linearly independent and the vector $\begin{pmatrix} p \\ q \end{pmatrix}$ is expressible as a unique linear combination of them; and conversely. Hence

$$\left. \begin{matrix} ax + by = p, \\ cx + dy = q, \end{matrix} \right\} \quad (p, q \text{ not both zero}) \text{ have a unique solution} \quad \Leftrightarrow \quad \begin{vmatrix} a & b \\ c & d \end{vmatrix} \neq 0.$$

1.4 Determinants in 3×3 homogeneous equations. We consider a numerical case first.

Example 2. Solve
$$\begin{cases} x+ y+ z = 0 \\ 3x+6y+5z = 0 \\ 6x+3y+4z = 0 \end{cases}.$$

We write these as
$$\begin{pmatrix} 1 & 1 & 1 \\ 3 & 6 & 5 \\ 6 & 3 & 4 \end{pmatrix} \begin{pmatrix} x \\ y \\ z \end{pmatrix} = \begin{pmatrix} 0 \\ 0 \\ 0 \end{pmatrix}.$$

This can be reduced to the echelon form

$$\begin{pmatrix} 1 & 1 & 1 \\ 0 & 3 & 2 \\ 0 & 0 & 0 \end{pmatrix} \begin{pmatrix} x \\ y \\ z \end{pmatrix} = \begin{pmatrix} 0 \\ 0 \\ 0 \end{pmatrix},$$

so that z can have any value; y can then be determined from $3y+2z = 0$ and x from $x+y+z = 0$. Hence the solutions are: $(x, y, z) = \lambda(1, 2, -3)$, for any λ. If we change the third of the original equations to $6x+3y+5z=0$, the echelon form becomes

$$\begin{pmatrix} 1 & 1 & 1 \\ 0 & 3 & 2 \\ 0 & 0 & 1 \end{pmatrix} \begin{pmatrix} x \\ y \\ z \end{pmatrix} = \begin{pmatrix} 0 \\ 0 \\ 0 \end{pmatrix},$$

for which there exists only the trivial solution $(x, y, z) = (0, 0, 0)$.

From this example, as with some earlier ones, it can be seen that with numerical equations the echelon process leads directly to a simple analysis of the situation.

We now turn to a discussion of the general set of 3×3 homogeneous equations and will show that the condition for non-trivial solutions can be expressed simply in terms of the coefficients. Let the equations be

$$\begin{cases} a_1x+b_1y+c_1z = 0, & (1) \\ a_2x+b_2y+c_2z = 0, & (2) \\ a_3x+b_3y+c_3z = 0. & (3) \end{cases} \tag{i}$$

We start by considering the solutions of equations (2) and (3). Suppose

$$\begin{vmatrix} a_2 & b_2 \\ a_3 & b_3 \end{vmatrix} \neq 0.$$

With $z = 0$, by one of the results of Section 1.2, there are no solutions except $x = y = 0$. So we may, in our search for non-trivial solutions, assume that $z \neq 0$. Then, for any z, the equations give a unique solution for x and y (again, see Section 1.2). To find the solutions, multiply (2) by b_3 and (3) by b_2 and subtract, whence

$$(a_2b_3-a_3b_2)x = (b_2c_3-b_3c_2)z;$$

1278

and multiply (3) by a_2 and (2) by a_3 and subtract, whence

$$(a_2b_3 - a_3b_2)y = (a_3c_2 - a_2c_3)z.$$

Hence, provided
$$\begin{vmatrix} a_2 & b_2 \\ a_3 & b_3 \end{vmatrix} \neq 0,$$

we have
$$\begin{cases} a_2x + b_2y + c_2z = 0, \\ a_3x + b_3y + c_3z = 0 \end{cases}$$

$$\Rightarrow \begin{cases} (a_2b_3 - a_3b_2)x = (b_2c_3 - b_3c_2)z, \\ (a_2b_3 - a_3b_2)y = (a_3c_2 - a_2c_3)z \end{cases}$$

$$\Rightarrow (x, y, z) = \lambda \left(\begin{vmatrix} b_2 & c_2 \\ b_3 & c_3 \end{vmatrix}, \ -\begin{vmatrix} a_2 & c_2 \\ a_3 & c_3 \end{vmatrix}, \ \begin{vmatrix} a_2 & b_2 \\ a_3 & b_3 \end{vmatrix} \right) \quad (\lambda \neq 0). \tag{ii}$$

It is obvious from the symmetry of this result that we should have arrived at the same solutions if we had started from the supposition that one of the other two of these determinants was not zero. We can now verify by direct substitution that these solutions do in fact satisfy the original equations (2) and (3) for all λ, and are non-trivial provided at least one of the determinants is not zero. So, subject to the condition that not all these determinants are zero, we can see, by substituting in equation (1), that

equations (i) have a non-trivial solution $\Leftrightarrow$ $a_1\begin{vmatrix} b_2 & c_2 \\ b_3 & c_3 \end{vmatrix} - b_1\begin{vmatrix} a_2 & c_2 \\ a_3 & c_3 \end{vmatrix} + c_1\begin{vmatrix} a_2 & b_2 \\ a_3 & b_3 \end{vmatrix} = 0.$

The expression $\quad a_1\begin{vmatrix} b_2 & c_2 \\ b_3 & c_3 \end{vmatrix} - b_1\begin{vmatrix} a_2 & c_2 \\ a_3 & c_3 \end{vmatrix} + c_1\begin{vmatrix} a_2 & b_2 \\ a_3 & b_3 \end{vmatrix}$

is written
$$\begin{vmatrix} a_1 & b_1 & c_1 \\ a_2 & b_2 & c_2 \\ a_3 & b_3 & c_3 \end{vmatrix}$$

and is called the determinant of the matrix

$$\begin{pmatrix} a_1 & b_1 & c_1 \\ a_2 & b_2 & c_2 \\ a_3 & b_3 & c_3 \end{pmatrix}.$$

Its value is $\quad a_1(b_2c_3 - b_3c_2) - b_1(a_2c_3 - a_3c_2) + c_1(a_2b_3 - a_3b_2).$

It is easy to verify, by writing them out fully, that

$$\begin{vmatrix} a_2 & b_2 & c_2 \\ a_3 & b_3 & c_3 \\ a_1 & b_1 & c_1 \end{vmatrix} \quad \text{and} \quad \begin{vmatrix} a_3 & b_3 & c_3 \\ a_1 & b_1 & c_1 \\ a_2 & b_2 & c_2 \end{vmatrix}$$

also have the same value. This shows that if we had approached the problem initially by solving equations (1) and (3) and substituting (2), or solving (1) and (2) and substituting in (3), we should have arrived at the same condition,

$$\begin{vmatrix} a_1 & b_1 & c_1 \\ a_2 & b_2 & c_2 \\ a_3 & b_3 & c_3 \end{vmatrix} = 0,$$

for the existence of non-trivial solutions, subject in each case to the appropriate restrictions. We may therefore say (iii)

$$\left. \begin{array}{l} a_1 x + b_1 y + c_1 z = 0, \\ a_2 x + b_2 y + c_2 z = 0, \\ a_3 x + b_3 y + c_3 z = 0, \end{array} \right\} \quad \textbf{have a non-trivial solution} \quad \Leftrightarrow \quad \begin{vmatrix} a_1 & b_1 & c_1 \\ a_2 & b_2 & c_2 \\ a_3 & b_3 & c_3 \end{vmatrix} = 0$$

provided at least one of the nine 2×2 determinants, like

$$\begin{vmatrix} a_1 & b_1 \\ a_2 & b_2 \end{vmatrix} \quad \text{or} \quad \begin{vmatrix} b_1 & c_1 \\ b_3 & c_3 \end{vmatrix}$$

and so on, is not zero.

If all these nine determinants are zero then there are non-trivial solutions like $(x, y, z) = (b_2, -a_2, 0)$ with one of x, y, z explicitly zero (as can easily be verified), unless *all* the coefficients are zero, in which case the three equations, although rather meaningless, certainly have non-trivial solutions. In any of these cases

$$\begin{vmatrix} a_1 & b_1 & c_1 \\ a_2 & b_2 & c_2 \\ a_3 & b_3 & c_3 \end{vmatrix} = 0.$$

Hence (iii) is true in all cases.

The result we have just obtained can usefully be expressed in terms of dependence of vectors. The three equations can be written

$$\begin{pmatrix} a_1 \\ a_2 \\ a_3 \end{pmatrix} x + \begin{pmatrix} b_1 \\ b_2 \\ b_3 \end{pmatrix} y + \begin{pmatrix} c_1 \\ c_2 \\ c_3 \end{pmatrix} z = \begin{pmatrix} 0 \\ 0 \\ 0 \end{pmatrix}.$$

If this holds for values of x, y, z, not all zero, then the three vectors are linearly dependent. Hence

$$\begin{pmatrix} a_1 \\ a_2 \\ a_3 \end{pmatrix}, \quad \begin{pmatrix} b_1 \\ b_2 \\ b_3 \end{pmatrix}, \quad \begin{pmatrix} c_1 \\ c_2 \\ c_3 \end{pmatrix} \quad \textbf{are linearly dependent} \quad \Leftrightarrow \quad \begin{vmatrix} a_1 & b_1 & c_1 \\ a_2 & b_2 & c_2 \\ a_3 & b_3 & c_3 \end{vmatrix} = 0.$$

Exercise B

1. In the following equations, write down the determinant of the coefficients of x and y, and hence state which of them have unique solutions:

(a) $\begin{cases} 2x+5y = 7, \\ 8x-3y = 2; \end{cases}$ (b) $\begin{cases} 3x+2y = 5, \\ 9x+6y = 4; \end{cases}$ (c) $\begin{cases} -6x+9y = 12, \\ 4x-6y = -8; \end{cases}$

(d) $\begin{cases} 2x+8y = 5, \\ 3y = 7; \end{cases}$ (e) $\begin{cases} 3x-2y = 0, \\ -6x+4y = 0. \end{cases}$

Which of them have no solutions?

2. For what value of k are the solutions of

$$\begin{cases} 3x-2y = 5, \\ 5x+ky = 4, \end{cases}$$

not unique? When k has this value, is there an infinity of solutions or no solution?

3. Use the result of Section 1.4(ii) to write down the solutions of

(a) $\begin{cases} 4x+3y-2z = 0, \\ x-5y+ z = 0; \end{cases}$ (b) $\begin{cases} 4x+2y+z = 0, \\ 2x+ y+z = 0; \end{cases}$

(c) $\begin{cases} 5/x-3/y+1/z = 0, \\ 2/x+1/y-3/z = 0. \end{cases}$

4. Evaluate, from the definition, the determinants:

(a) $\begin{vmatrix} 1 & 0 & 0 \\ 0 & 1 & 0 \\ 0 & 0 & 1 \end{vmatrix}$; (b) $\begin{vmatrix} 0 & 1 & 0 \\ 0 & 0 & 1 \\ 1 & 0 & 0 \end{vmatrix}$; (c) $\begin{vmatrix} 1 & 0 & 0 \\ 1 & 1 & 0 \\ 1 & 1 & 1 \end{vmatrix}$;

(d) $\begin{vmatrix} 1 & 1 & 1 \\ 2 & 3 & 4 \\ 5 & 6 & 7 \end{vmatrix}$; (e) $\begin{vmatrix} 0 & 1 & 2 \\ 3 & 0 & 4 \\ 5 & 6 & 0 \end{vmatrix}$; (f) $\begin{vmatrix} 1 & 1 & 1 \\ p & q & r \\ p+\lambda & q+\lambda & r+\lambda \end{vmatrix}$.

5. (a) Decide if the vectors $\begin{pmatrix} 2 \\ 3 \\ 1 \end{pmatrix}$, $\begin{pmatrix} 4 \\ 2 \\ 0 \end{pmatrix}$, $\begin{pmatrix} 3 \\ 7 \\ 1 \end{pmatrix}$

are linearly dependent or not, by evaluating

$$\begin{vmatrix} 2 & 4 & 3 \\ 3 & 2 & 7 \\ 1 & 0 & 1 \end{vmatrix}.$$

(b) Use a determinant to find for what value of k the vectors

$$\begin{pmatrix} k \\ 0 \\ 1 \end{pmatrix}, \begin{pmatrix} 3 \\ 2 \\ 2 \end{pmatrix}, \begin{pmatrix} 1 \\ 4 \\ 3 \end{pmatrix}$$

are linearly dependent.

6. Verify by direct multiplication that if

$$A = \begin{pmatrix} a & b \\ c & d \end{pmatrix} \quad \text{and} \quad B = \begin{pmatrix} p & q \\ r & s \end{pmatrix}$$

and 'det A' means 'the determinant of A', and similarly for B, then

$$\det (AB) = (\det A) \times (\det B).$$

7. Show that

$$\begin{vmatrix} a_1 & b_1 & c_1 \\ a_2 + ka_2' & b_2 + kb_2' & c_2 + kc_2' \\ a_3 & b_3 & c_3 \end{vmatrix} = \begin{vmatrix} a_1 & b_1 & c_1 \\ a_2 & b_2 & c_2 \\ a_3 & b_3 & c_3 \end{vmatrix} + k \begin{vmatrix} a_1 & b_1 & c_1 \\ a_2' & b_2' & c_2' \\ a_3 & b_3 & c_3 \end{vmatrix}.$$

2. INVERSE OF A MATRIX

2.1 Properties of an inverse. As an alternative to the echelon process for solving equations we can use a method which, although of less practical value, has theoretical significance. We shall illustrate it in terms of the first set of equations considered in this chapter.

Example 3. Solve
$$\begin{cases} 2x + y - z = 2, \\ 4x - y - 3z = -2, \\ 2x + 2y + z = 9. \end{cases}$$

These in matrix form are:

$$\begin{pmatrix} 2 & 1 & -1 \\ 4 & -1 & -3 \\ 2 & 2 & 1 \end{pmatrix} \begin{pmatrix} x \\ y \\ z \end{pmatrix} = \begin{pmatrix} 2 \\ -2 \\ 9 \end{pmatrix}.$$

Premultiply both sides by an appropriate matrix as shown:

$$\begin{pmatrix} -0{\cdot}5 & 0{\cdot}3 & 0{\cdot}4 \\ 1 & -0{\cdot}4 & -0{\cdot}2 \\ -1 & 0{\cdot}2 & 0{\cdot}6 \end{pmatrix} \begin{pmatrix} 2 & 1 & -1 \\ 4 & -1 & -3 \\ 2 & 2 & 1 \end{pmatrix} \begin{pmatrix} x \\ y \\ z \end{pmatrix} = \begin{pmatrix} -0{\cdot}5 & 0{\cdot}3 & 0{\cdot}4 \\ 1 & -0{\cdot}4 & -0{\cdot}2 \\ -1 & 0{\cdot}2 & 0{\cdot}6 \end{pmatrix} \begin{pmatrix} 2 \\ -2 \\ 9 \end{pmatrix}$$

therefore
$$\begin{pmatrix} 1 & 0 & 0 \\ 0 & 1 & 0 \\ 0 & 0 & 1 \end{pmatrix} \begin{pmatrix} x \\ y \\ z \end{pmatrix} = \begin{pmatrix} 2 \\ 1 \\ 3 \end{pmatrix}$$

that is
$$\begin{pmatrix} x \\ y \\ z \end{pmatrix} = \begin{pmatrix} 2 \\ 1 \\ 3 \end{pmatrix}.$$

The reader will remember from Chapter 21 how the appropriate matrix can be found. It was called the inverse of the matrix of coefficients. Here we want to see by what rights it has been called *the* inverse, and this we shall do in quite general terms. At the same time we shall consider under what conditions it can exist.

The general 3×3 set of equations can be written in abbreviated matrix form as

$$\mathbf{Ax} = \mathbf{d} \tag{i}$$

where $\quad \mathbf{A} = \begin{pmatrix} a_1 & b_1 & c_1 \\ a_2 & b_2 & c_2 \\ a_3 & b_3 & c_3 \end{pmatrix}, \quad \mathbf{x} = \begin{pmatrix} x \\ y \\ z \end{pmatrix} \quad \text{and} \quad \mathbf{d} = \begin{pmatrix} d_1 \\ d_2 \\ d_3 \end{pmatrix}.$

If $\mathbf{A}$ has a 'left'-inverse $\mathbf{B}$, so that $\mathbf{BA} = \mathbf{I}$, then

$$\mathbf{Ax} = \mathbf{d}$$
$$\Rightarrow \mathbf{BAx} = \mathbf{Bd}$$
$$\Rightarrow \quad \mathbf{x} = \mathbf{Bd}. \tag{ii}$$

These implications show that the solutions of equation (i) are contained in the solution (ii) (on the assumption that $\mathbf{A}$ has a left-inverse), so that to solve the original equations it is necessary to show that the value of $\mathbf{x}$ from (ii) does satisfy equation (i). This will be so if $\mathbf{A}(\mathbf{Bd}) = \mathbf{d}$; that is if $(\mathbf{AB})\mathbf{d} = \mathbf{d}$. For this we need to know that $\mathbf{AB} = \mathbf{I}$; that is that $\mathbf{B}$ is also a right-inverse of $\mathbf{A}$.

We shall be fully justified in calling $\mathbf{B}$ *the* inverse of $\mathbf{A}$ when we have established the facts: (i) $\mathbf{B}$ is a left-inverse $\Leftrightarrow \mathbf{B}$ is a right inverse, and (ii) the left-inverse and right-inverse are unique. This will be done soon.

2.2 Singular and non-singular forms. At this stage we need to define some terms. A matrix of the form

$$\begin{pmatrix} 1 & * & * \\ 0 & 1 & * \\ 0 & 0 & 1 \end{pmatrix}$$

with 1's on the diagonal, 0's below and the other elements unrestricted, will be said to be of 'non-singular echelon' form. If any of the 1's on the diagonal are replaced by 0's, it will be said to be of 'singular echelon' form.

We know that any matrix $\mathbf{A}$ under elementary row-operations (each one corresponding to premultiplication by an elementary matrix) can be reduced to a non-singular or singular echelon form.

Now suppose $\mathbf{A}$ reduces to a non-singular echelon form $\mathbf{N}$; then

$$\mathbf{Ax} = \mathbf{0} \quad \Leftrightarrow \quad \mathbf{Nx} = \mathbf{0}.$$

But $\mathbf{Nx} = \mathbf{0}$ has only $\mathbf{x} = \mathbf{0}$ as a solution, and therefore $\mathbf{Ax} = \mathbf{0}$ has only the trivial solution.

If, instead, $\mathbf{A}$ reduces to a singular echelon form $\mathbf{S}$; let it be

$$\begin{pmatrix} 1 & h & k \\ 0 & 0 & l \\ 0 & 0 & 1 \end{pmatrix}.$$

Then

$$\mathbf{Ax} = \mathbf{0} \iff \mathbf{Sx} = \mathbf{0} \iff \begin{pmatrix} 1 & h & k \\ 0 & 0 & l \\ 0 & 0 & 1 \end{pmatrix} \begin{pmatrix} x \\ y \\ z \end{pmatrix} = \begin{pmatrix} 0 \\ 0 \\ 0 \end{pmatrix}$$

for which there is a non-trivial solution $(x, y, z) = (-h, 1, 0)$ for any k. Similar non-trivial solutions exist for other forms of S. Hence $\mathbf{Ax} = \mathbf{0}$ has non-trivial solutions.

The echelon form of reduction of a matrix is not unique (for example, any row can be added to a higher row), but the equation $\mathbf{Ax} = \mathbf{0}$ has either non-trivial or only trivial solutions, so in whatever way the reduction to echelon form is made it will produce either a non-singular form always or a singular form always. We shall call A itself a singular or non-singular matrix according as it reduces to a singular or non-singular echelon form.

2.3 A condition for non-singularity. A matrix A is non-singular if it has a left-inverse.

For suppose B is a left-inverse of A, then $\mathbf{BA} = \mathbf{I}$. Now, using the steps for solving an equation by means of an inverse matrix, we have

$$\mathbf{Ax} = \mathbf{0} \Rightarrow \mathbf{BAx} = \mathbf{B0} \Rightarrow \mathbf{Ix} = \mathbf{0} \Rightarrow \mathbf{x} = \mathbf{0}.$$

Hence A is non-singular.

2.4 2-sided inverse as elementary matrix product. In Chapter 21 it was shown that *provided a matrix is non-singular* there exist elementary matrices $\mathbf{E}_1, \mathbf{E}_2, \ldots, \mathbf{E}_n$, such that

$$\mathbf{E}_n \ldots \mathbf{E}_2\mathbf{E}_1\mathbf{A} = \mathbf{I}. \tag{i}$$

Now, remembering the row operations associated with the three types of elementary matrix, it is clear that these matrices have left-inverses. For example, if E adds row 2 to row 1, it has a left-inverse $\mathbf{E}^{-1}$ which restores the status quo by subtracting row 2 from row 1. (It is also obvious that if E and $\mathbf{E}^{-1}$ are reversed in the order in which they operate they are still equivalent to the identity, so that we can talk about an inverse here without having to specify whether it is right or left. The fact that elementary matrices have 2-sided inverses can of course be verified immediately by writing down the actual matrices and multiplying them.)

Now
$$\mathbf{E}_n \ldots \mathbf{E}_2\mathbf{E}_1\mathbf{A} = \mathbf{I} \tag{i}$$
$$\Rightarrow (\mathbf{E}_1^{-1}\mathbf{E}_2^{-1} \ldots \mathbf{E}_n^{-1})(\mathbf{E}_n \ldots \mathbf{E}_2\mathbf{E}_1\mathbf{A}) = \mathbf{E}_1^{-1}\mathbf{E}_2^{-1} \ldots \mathbf{E}_n^{-1}$$
$$\Rightarrow \qquad\qquad\qquad \mathbf{A} = \mathbf{E}_1^{-1}\mathbf{E}_2^{-1} \ldots \mathbf{E}_n^{-1},$$
$$\Rightarrow \qquad \mathbf{A}(\mathbf{E}_n \ldots \mathbf{E}_2\mathbf{E}_1) = (\mathbf{E}_1^{-1}\mathbf{E}_2^{-1} \ldots \mathbf{E}_n^{-1})(\mathbf{E}_n \ldots \mathbf{E}_2\mathbf{E}_1)$$
$$= \mathbf{I}. \tag{ii}$$

From (i) and (ii) we see that if A is non-singular, it has a 2-sided inverse C where $\mathbf{C} = \mathbf{E}_n \ldots \mathbf{E}_2\mathbf{E}_1$.

2.5 Uniqueness of the left-inverse. If **B** is a left-inverse of **A**, then **A** is non-singular (by Section 2.3). So **A** has the 2-sided inverse **C** of the previous Section. Therefore

$$\mathbf{BAC} = \mathbf{IC} = \mathbf{C}; \quad \text{and also} \quad \mathbf{BAC} = \mathbf{BI} = \mathbf{B}.$$

Hence $\qquad\qquad\qquad\qquad \mathbf{B} = \mathbf{C}.$

That is, the left-inverse of a matrix (if it exists) is unique.

2.6 Uniqueness of the right-inverse. If **B** is a right-inverse of **A**, then $\mathbf{AB} = \mathbf{I}$. It follows that **A** is the left-inverse of **B**, so that **B** is non-singular (by Section 2.3). Hence **A** is a 2-sided inverse of **B** (by Section 2.4), so that $\mathbf{BA} = \mathbf{I}$. Now (by the previous section) this implies that $\mathbf{B} = \mathbf{C}$.

This completes the proof of the existence and uniqueness of the inverse of a non-singular matrix, and of its commutativity with that matrix.

Note also that a singular matrix cannot have any inverse. By Section 2.3 it cannot have a left-inverse, and by Section 2.6 any right-inverse must also be a left-inverse.

3. PROPERTIES OF DETERMINANTS

3.1 Determinants of elementary matrices. Elementary matrices are of three types:

$$\mathbf{K} = \begin{pmatrix} k & 0 & 0 \\ 0 & 1 & 0 \\ 0 & 0 & 1 \end{pmatrix}, \quad \text{which multiplies the first row by } k;$$

$$\mathbf{T} = \begin{pmatrix} 0 & 1 & 0 \\ 1 & 0 & 0 \\ 0 & 0 & 1 \end{pmatrix}, \quad \text{which interchanges the first two rows;}$$

$$\mathbf{S} = \begin{pmatrix} 1 & 0 & 0 \\ k & 1 & 0 \\ 0 & 0 & 1 \end{pmatrix}, \quad \text{which adds } k \text{ times the first row to the second row.}$$

Of course 'first' and 'second' in these definitions can be replaced by any other pair of numbers of rows, with corresponding changes in the matrix.

It is immediately obvious from the definition that

$$\det \mathbf{K} = k, \quad \det \mathbf{T} = -1, \quad \det \mathbf{S} = 1$$

(where det is short for determinant). Further, for the general matrix

$$\mathbf{G} = \begin{pmatrix} a_1 & b_1 & c_1 \\ a_2 & b_2 & c_2 \\ a_3 & b_3 & c_3 \end{pmatrix}$$

it is easy to verify that $\det \mathbf{KG} = k \det \mathbf{G}$, $\det \mathbf{TG} = -\det \mathbf{G}$, and $\det \mathbf{SG} = \det \mathbf{G}$. To check the last, we have by Exercise B, Question 7

$$\det \mathbf{SG} = \begin{vmatrix} a_1 & b_1 & c_1 \\ a_2+ka_1 & b_2+kb_1 & c_2+kc_1 \\ a_3 & b_3 & c_3 \end{vmatrix} = \begin{vmatrix} a_1 & b_1 & c_1 \\ a_2 & b_2 & c_2 \\ a_3 & b_3 & c_3 \end{vmatrix} + k \begin{vmatrix} a_1 & b_1 & c_1 \\ a_1 & b_1 & c_1 \\ a_3 & b_3 & c_3 \end{vmatrix}.$$

The last determinant is zero, since if $\mathbf{M}$ is the matrix

$$\begin{vmatrix} a_1 & b_1 & c_1 \\ a_1 & b_1 & c_1 \\ a_3 & b_3 & c_3 \end{vmatrix},$$

then $\det \mathbf{M} = \det (\mathbf{TM}) = -\det \mathbf{M}$; so that $\det \mathbf{M} = 0$.

In these three cases, therefore, we have for any elementary matrix $\mathbf{E}$ and any matrix $\mathbf{G}$
$$\det (\mathbf{EG}) = \det \mathbf{E} \times \det \mathbf{G}.$$

We shall use this special result to prove the following general theorem.

3.2 Product theorem for determinants. We wish to prove that $\det (\mathbf{AB}) = \det \mathbf{A} . \det \mathbf{B}$. There are two cases.

(a) If $\mathbf{A}$ is non-singular we know that there is a chain of elementary matrices $\mathbf{E}_1$, $\mathbf{E}_2$, ..., $\mathbf{E}_n$ such that $\mathbf{E}_n \ldots \mathbf{E}_2\mathbf{E}_1\mathbf{A} = \mathbf{I}$. Now, for any matrix $\mathbf{B}$,

$$\det (\mathbf{IB}) = \det \mathbf{I} . \det \mathbf{B}, \quad \text{since} \quad \det \mathbf{I} = 1.$$
Therefore
$$\det[(\mathbf{E}_n \ldots \mathbf{E}_2\mathbf{E}_1\mathbf{A})\mathbf{B}] = \det (\mathbf{E}_n \ldots \mathbf{E}_2\mathbf{E}_1\mathbf{A}) . \det \mathbf{B}. \tag{i}$$

Now, for any matrix $\mathbf{X}$, using the result at the end of the previous section repeatedly, we have

$$\det (\mathbf{E}_n \ldots \mathbf{E}_2\mathbf{E}_1\mathbf{X}) = \det \mathbf{E}_n . \det (\mathbf{E}_{n-1} \ldots \mathbf{E}_1\mathbf{X})$$
$$= \det \mathbf{E}_n . \det \mathbf{E}_{n-1} \ldots \det \mathbf{E}_1 . \det \mathbf{X}.$$

Using this on both sides of (i), and cancelling the non-zero product $\det \mathbf{E}_n . \det \mathbf{E}_{n-1} \ldots \det \mathbf{E}_1$, we have

$$\det (\mathbf{AB}) = \det \mathbf{A} . \det \mathbf{B}.$$

(b) If $\mathbf{A}$ is singular, it can be reduced to singular echelon form, so there is a chain of elementary matrices $\mathbf{F}_1$, $\mathbf{F}_2$, ..., $\mathbf{F}_m$ such that

$$\mathbf{F}_m \ldots \mathbf{F}_2\mathbf{F}_1\mathbf{A} = \begin{pmatrix} p & * & * \\ 0 & q & * \\ 0 & 0 & 0 \end{pmatrix},$$

where p, q are either 1 or 0. Hence, proceeding as before,

$$\det \mathbf{F}_m \ldots \det \mathbf{F}_2 \det \mathbf{F}_1 \det \mathbf{A} = 0;$$

and since determinants of elementary matrices are not zero, $\det \mathbf{A} = 0$. That is, *the determinant of a singular matrix is zero.* Now,

$$\mathbf{A} \text{ is singular} \Rightarrow \mathbf{AB} \text{ is singular.}$$

For if not, there is a matrix $\mathbf{C}$ such that $(\mathbf{AB})\mathbf{C} = \mathbf{I}$. Then $\mathbf{A}(\mathbf{BC}) = \mathbf{I}$, and $\mathbf{A}$ is non-singular. So $\det \mathbf{AB} = 0$ also. Therefore,

$$\det \mathbf{AB} = 0 = \det \mathbf{A} . \det \mathbf{B}.$$

Hence in all cases $\qquad \det (\mathbf{AB}) = \det \mathbf{A} . \det \mathbf{B}.$

3.3 Transpose of a matrix. The matrix obtained from a matrix $\mathbf{M}$ by interchanging the rows and columns (while preserving their order) is called the *transpose* of $\mathbf{M}$, and will be written $\mathbf{M}'$. When $\mathbf{M}$ is a square matrix, this is equivalent to a reflexion in the leading diagonal.

It is easy to show that transposing a 2×2 or a 3×3 matrix leaves the determinant unchanged. The result is true in general when $n \times n$ matrices have been defined—as may be done by an extension of the definition of 3×3 matrices in terms of 2×2 matrices, as in Section 1.3. Here we write out a proof for 3×3 matrices.

Let

$$\mathbf{M} = \begin{pmatrix} a_1 & b_1 & c_1 \\ a_2 & b_2 & c_2 \\ a_3 & b_3 & c_3 \end{pmatrix}, \quad \text{so that} \quad \mathbf{M}' = \begin{pmatrix} a_1 & a_2 & a_3 \\ b_1 & b_2 & b_3 \\ c_1 & c_2 & c_3 \end{pmatrix}.$$

$$\begin{aligned} \det \mathbf{M}' &= a_1(b_2 c_3 - b_3 c_2) - a_2(b_1 c_3 - b_3 c_1) + a_3(b_1 c_2 - b_2 c_1) \\ &= a_1(b_2 c_3 - b_3 c_2) - b_1(a_2 c_3 - a_3 c_2) + c_1(a_2 b_3 - a_3 b_2) \\ &= \det \mathbf{M}. \end{aligned}$$

It follows that in any theorem about determinants we may interchange 'rows' and 'columns'. With this in mind we now collect the properties of determinants that have been encountered so far. They have been stated in terms of 3×3 matrices, but they are, in fact, true in general.

3.4 Summary of properties of determinants

Theorem A. If two rows (or columns) of a matrix are interchanged, the sign of its determinant is changed. Hence

Theorem B. If two rows (or columns) of a matrix are the same, its determinant is zero.

Theorem C. If a row (or column) of a matrix is multiplied by a number k, its determinant is multiplied by k.

Theorem D. If to any row (or column) of a matrix is added a multiple of another row (or column), its determinant is unchanged.

Theorem E. det $(\mathbf{AB}) = \det \mathbf{A} . \det \mathbf{B}$.

We have also shown that the determinant of a singular matrix is zero; and have left it to the reader to show that the determinant of a non-singular matrix is non-zero.

Example 4. Evaluate $\begin{vmatrix} 175 & 325 \\ 375 & 700 \end{vmatrix}$.

$$\begin{vmatrix} 175 & 325 \\ 375 & 700 \end{vmatrix} = 25 \begin{vmatrix} 7 & 13 \\ 375 & 700 \end{vmatrix} = 625 \begin{vmatrix} 7 & 13 \\ 15 & 28 \end{vmatrix} \quad \text{(applying Theorem C twice)}$$

$$= 625 \begin{vmatrix} 7 & 13 \\ 1 & 2 \end{vmatrix} \qquad \begin{array}{l} \text{(using Theorem D: subtracting twice} \\ \text{row one from row two)} \end{array}$$

$$= 625.$$

Exercise C

1. (See Section 3.1.) Write out a proof that $\det (\mathbf{EA}) = \det \mathbf{E} \times \det \mathbf{A}$ in the three cases

$$(a)\ \mathbf{E} = \begin{pmatrix} 1 & 0 & 0 \\ 0 & k & 0 \\ 0 & 0 & 1 \end{pmatrix}, \qquad (b)\ \mathbf{E} = \begin{pmatrix} 0 & 0 & 1 \\ 0 & 1 & 0 \\ 1 & 0 & 0 \end{pmatrix}, \qquad (c)\ \mathbf{E} = \begin{pmatrix} 1 & 0 & 0 \\ 0 & 1 & 0 \\ k & 0 & 1 \end{pmatrix},$$

$$\text{with} \quad \mathbf{A} = \begin{pmatrix} a_1 & b_1 & c_1 \\ a_2 & b_2 & c_2 \\ a_3 & b_3 & c_3 \end{pmatrix}.$$

2. Evaluate the determinants:

$$\begin{vmatrix} 200 & 300 \\ 3 & 5 \end{vmatrix}, \quad \begin{vmatrix} 157 & -471 \\ -156 & 470 \end{vmatrix}, \quad \begin{vmatrix} p^2+pq & p^2+q^2 \\ pq+q^2 & -2pq \end{vmatrix}.$$

3. Evaluate the matrix product

$$\begin{pmatrix} a & -b \\ b & a \end{pmatrix} \begin{pmatrix} c & -d \\ d & c \end{pmatrix}$$

and deduce from Theorem E an expression for $(a^2+b^2)(c^2+d^2)$ as the sum of two squares. Express 29×13 in two ways as the sum of two squares of integers.

4. If

$$\begin{pmatrix} a \\ b \end{pmatrix} = \mathbf{p}, \quad \begin{pmatrix} d \\ c \end{pmatrix} = \mathbf{q}$$

and the angle between $\mathbf{p}$ and $\mathbf{q}$ is θ, deduce from the result of Question 3 that

$$pq \sin \theta = \pm (ac - bd).$$

5. Evaluate

$$\begin{vmatrix} 2ab & ad+bc \\ ad+bc & 2cd \end{vmatrix}$$

as the product of two determinants.

6. Prove that the determinant of a non-singular matrix is non-zero.

7. By considering the determinant

$$\begin{vmatrix} a_1 & b_1 & c_1 \\ a_1 & b_1 & c_1 \\ a_2 & b_2 & c_2 \end{vmatrix}$$

and another one like it, show that

$$(x, y, z) = \lambda\left(\begin{vmatrix} b_1 & c_1 \\ b_2 & c_2 \end{vmatrix}, \begin{vmatrix} a_1 & c_1 \\ a_2 & c_2 \end{vmatrix}, \begin{vmatrix} a_1 & b_1 \\ a_2 & b_2 \end{vmatrix} \right) \quad \text{for all } \lambda,$$

are solutions of the equations

$$\begin{cases} a_1x + b_1y + c_1z = 0, \\ a_2x + b_2y + c_2z = 0. \end{cases}$$

8. Find the values of λ for which

$$\begin{vmatrix} 5-\lambda & 3 \\ 3 & -3-\lambda \end{vmatrix} = 0.$$

Evaluate the following determinants:

9. $\begin{vmatrix} 1 & 2 & 3 \\ 4 & 5 & 6 \\ 7 & 8 & 9 \end{vmatrix}$.

10. $\begin{vmatrix} 10 & 20 & 30 \\ 40 & 50 & 60 \\ 70 & 80 & 90 \end{vmatrix}$.

11. $\begin{vmatrix} 3 & 12 & 21 \\ 5 & -4 & 28 \\ 1 & 8 & -7 \end{vmatrix}$.

12. $\begin{vmatrix} 11 & 12 & 13 \\ 14 & 15 & 16 \\ 17 & 18 & 19 \end{vmatrix}$.

13. $\begin{vmatrix} 40 & 41 & 42 \\ 43 & 46 & 49 \\ 45 & 50 & 56 \end{vmatrix}$.

14. $\begin{vmatrix} 1 & -1 & 1 \\ -1 & 1 & 1 \\ 1 & 1 & -1 \end{vmatrix}$.

15. $\begin{vmatrix} 0 & 5 & -7 \\ -5 & 0 & 11 \\ 7 & -11 & 0 \end{vmatrix}$.

16. $\begin{vmatrix} 0 & p & 0 \\ p & 0 & p \\ 0 & p & 0 \end{vmatrix}$.

17. $\begin{vmatrix} \cos\theta & -\sin\theta & 0 \\ \sin\theta & \cos\theta & 0 \\ \cos\phi & \sin\phi & 1 \end{vmatrix}$.

18. $\begin{vmatrix} 1 & 1 & 1 \\ a & b & c \\ a^2 & b^2 & c^2 \end{vmatrix}$.

19. $\begin{vmatrix} 1+p & q & r \\ p & 1+q & r \\ p & q & 1+r \end{vmatrix}$.

20. $\begin{vmatrix} 1-\lambda & 3 & 1 \\ 0 & 2-\lambda & 2 \\ 0 & 0 & -\lambda \end{vmatrix}$.

21. $\begin{vmatrix} -5 & 11 & 6 \\ 13 & -2 & 5 \\ -7 & 9 & -6 \end{vmatrix}$.

22. $\begin{vmatrix} 2 & 5j & 0 \\ -5j & 3 & -j \\ 0 & j & 4 \end{vmatrix}$.

4. GEOMETRICAL ILLUSTRATIONS

4.1 Elementary transformations. The matrix

$$\begin{pmatrix} 0 & 1 & 0 \\ 1 & 0 & 0 \\ 0 & 0 & 1 \end{pmatrix}$$

operating on the position vector $\begin{pmatrix} x \\ y \\ z \end{pmatrix}$ of a point P,

transforms it into $\begin{pmatrix} y \\ x \\ z \end{pmatrix}$, that is to say it *reflects* P in the plane $x = y$.

The other elementary matrices can also be interpreted as geometrical transformations.

$$\begin{pmatrix} k & 0 & 0 \\ 0 & 1 & 0 \\ 0 & 0 & 1 \end{pmatrix}$$

is clearly a 'one-way stretch' by a factor of k in the x-direction; while

$$\begin{pmatrix} 1 & 0 & 0 \\ k & 1 & 0 \\ 0 & 0 & 1 \end{pmatrix}$$

represents a shear parallel to the y-axis, shifting the point (a, b, c) to the point $(a, ka+b, c)$. Figure 1 shows the effect of this shear on the unit cube.

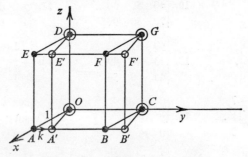

Fig. 1

We notice that the determinant of the first matrix is -1; of the second, k; and of the third, 1. The first matrix leaves the volume of the unit cube unchanged, but reverses the orientation of the cube; the second turns the cube into a cuboid and multiplies its volume by k; the third leaves the volume unchanged. In all cases, therefore, the determinant gives the factor by which the volume of the unit cube is multiplied, the volume being counted negative when the orientation is reversed.

1290

Since any non-singular matrix **A** can be resolved into a product of elementary matrices, as we have seen in Section 2.4, and its determinant is the product of the elementary determinants, it follows that det **A** is the factor by which the volume of the unit cube is multiplied by the corresponding chain of elementary transformations, that is, by the single transformation given by **A**. We thus have

Theorem F. The matrix **A**, acting on the position vectors of points in space, transforms the unit cube into a parallelepiped of volume det **A**.

If the whole space is partitioned, by sets of planes parallel to the coordinate axes, into cubes each congruent to the unit cube, then under the linear transformations considered, these cubes will all be mapped into parallelepipeds congruent to one another. So the volume within any region will be multiplied by det **A** under the transformation.

Exercise D

1. What is the geometrical transformation corresponding to each of the following matrices, and what is the factor by which it multiplies volume?

$$(a) \begin{pmatrix} 0 & 0 & 1 \\ 0 & 1 & 0 \\ 1 & 0 & 0 \end{pmatrix};$$
$$(b) \begin{pmatrix} 1 & 2 & 0 \\ 0 & 1 & 0 \\ 0 & 0 & 1 \end{pmatrix};$$

$$(c) \begin{pmatrix} 1 & 0 & 0 \\ 0 & 3 & 0 \\ 0 & 0 & 1 \end{pmatrix};$$
$$(d) \begin{pmatrix} 2 & 0 & 0 \\ 0 & 3 & 0 \\ 0 & 0 & \frac{1}{6} \end{pmatrix};$$

Illustrate the effect of each on a unit cube with edges along the axes of coordinates.

2. $A(a_1, a_2, a_3)$, $B(b_1, b_2, b_3)$, and $C(c_1, c_2, c_3)$ are three points of space. What is the matrix which transforms $(1, 0, 0)$, $(0, 1, 0)$, $(0, 0, 1)$ into A, B, C respectively? (Remember, a matrix premultiplies *column*-vectors.)

3. With the notation of Question 2, what is the volume of the parallelepiped which has OA, OB, OC as edges? Is this parallelepiped unique for fixed A, B, C?

4. A parallelepiped has the origin as one corner, and its three vertices nearest the origin are $(0, 1, 3)$, $(2, -1, 5)$, $(-1, 3, -1)$. Find its remaining vertices and its volume.

5. If A^{-1} is the inverse of a matrix **A**, what is the connection between det (A^{-1}) and det (A)?

6. Find a chain of elementary transformations which will transform the vectors

$$\begin{pmatrix} 1 \\ 0 \\ 0 \end{pmatrix}, \begin{pmatrix} 0 \\ 1 \\ 0 \end{pmatrix}, \begin{pmatrix} 0 \\ 0 \\ 1 \end{pmatrix} \text{ into } \begin{pmatrix} 2 \\ 1 \\ 0 \end{pmatrix}, \begin{pmatrix} 0 \\ 3 \\ -4 \end{pmatrix}, \begin{pmatrix} 0 \\ 0 \\ 5 \end{pmatrix}.$$

Verify that the determinants of these elementary matrices have a product equal to 30.

1291

4.2 Singular matrices. A matrix with a zero row, like

$$\begin{pmatrix} 2 & 1 & 2 \\ 0 & 1 & 1 \\ 0 & 0 & 0 \end{pmatrix},$$

reduces all vectors to vectors whose third component is zero, that is, to vectors in the plane $z = 0$. It maps all points of three-dimensional space onto a two-dimensional space.

Any singular matrix can be reduced by the echelon process to a matrix with at least one row of zeros. None of the elementary transformations of the echelon process reduces the dimensions; the only possibility therefore is that the original matrix was of this type. We state this result as a theorem.

Theorem G. A singular $n \times n$ matrix transforms n-dimensional space into a space of fewer dimensions.

We notice that if $\mathbf{A}$ is singular, det $\mathbf{A} = 0$, so that in this case also det $\mathbf{A}$ gives the ratio of volume change, for the unit cube is flattened onto a plane region, or onto a line or onto a point, and is therefore of zero volume.

Example 5. Interpret the matrix $\begin{pmatrix} 6 & 2 \\ 3 & 1 \end{pmatrix}$ as a geometrical transformation.

Under this transformation the corners of the unit square map into the

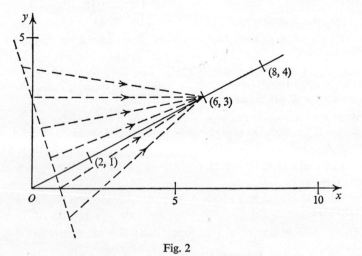

Fig. 2

collinear points $(0, 0)$, $(6, 3)$, $(2, 1)$, $(8, 4)$ on the line $2y = x$. This mapping from two-dimensions to one-dimension is what we would expect from a singular matrix (where the top row is twice the bottom row). To see more

1292

precisely what the matrix does we shall find all the points which map onto one particular point, say (6, 3). These are the solutions of

$$\begin{pmatrix} 6 & 2 \\ 3 & 1 \end{pmatrix} \begin{pmatrix} x \\ y \end{pmatrix} = \begin{pmatrix} 6 \\ 3 \end{pmatrix},$$

that is, of $6x+2y = 6$, and $3x+y = 3$, so they lie on the line $3x+y = 3$. This line is shown in Figure 2 as a broken line from which arrowed lines indicate the mapping of points on it onto the point (6, 3). In the same way the mapping onto any other point of the line $2y = x$ will be from the points of a line parallel to $3x+y = 3$, and could be shown by an enlargement from the origin with a suitable scale factor of the part of the figure which is in broken lines.

Example 6. What is the matrix that projects points of space parallel to the x-axis onto the plane $x-2y+3z = 0$? (see Figure 3).

Since the projection is parallel to the x-axis, the y- and z-coordinates are unchanged. Since P' is on $x-2y+3z = 0$,

$$x' = 2y'-3z' = 2y-3z.$$

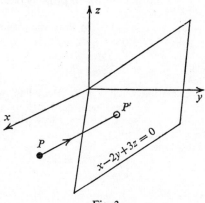

Fig. 3

The matrix is therefore

$$\begin{pmatrix} 0 & 2 & -3 \\ 0 & 1 & 0 \\ 0 & 0 & 1 \end{pmatrix}.$$

Note that it is singular, with a zero column.

Exercise E

1. Show that
$$\begin{pmatrix} 3 & 1 \\ 6 & 2 \end{pmatrix} \begin{pmatrix} 1 & 3 \\ -3 & -9 \end{pmatrix} = \begin{pmatrix} 0 & 0 \\ 0 & 0 \end{pmatrix}.$$

What does this mean geometrically?

2. What are the products **AB** and **BA** when
$$\mathbf{A} = \begin{pmatrix} p & q \\ 0 & 0 \end{pmatrix} \quad \text{and} \quad \mathbf{B} = \begin{pmatrix} 0 & r \\ 0 & s \end{pmatrix}?$$

Explain your results in terms of the geometrical significance of the matrices **A, B** applied to vectors in a plane.

3. If **A, B** are two 3×3 matrices such that **AB** = **0**, prove that either det **A** or det **B** must be zero.

If neither **A** nor **B** is the zero matrix, must they *both* be singular? Either give a (geometrical) proof, or a counter-example.

4. What is the matrix of the transformation which projects points (x, y) of a plane orthogonally
   (a) onto the x-axis;   (b) onto the line $x = y$;
   (c) onto the line $3x+4y = 0$?

5. Give the matrix of a transformation which projects points of space parallel to the z-axis
   (a) onto the x-y plane;   (b) onto the plane $y = 2z$;
   (c) onto the plane $px+qy+rz = 0$.

6. Interpret the matrix
$$\mathbf{A} = \begin{pmatrix} 2k & 2 \\ 3k & 3 \end{pmatrix}$$

as a geometrical transformation when $k = 2$. What line maps into the point $(6, 9)$? For what value of k is the line which maps into the point $(6, 9)$ perpendicular to $2y = 3x$? Does $(6, 9)$ lie on this line? For what value of k does the line which maps into $(6, 9)$ pass through $(6, 9)$?
   Find a matrix **B** of the form
$$\begin{pmatrix} 2p & 2q \\ 3p & 3q \end{pmatrix}$$

such that $(6, 9)$ lies on the line which maps into $(6, 9)$ and such that this line is perpendicular to $2y = 3x$. Give a simple description of the transformation effected by **B**.
   Show that **BB** = **B**, but **AA** $\neq$ **A** for any value of k except $k = -1$, and explain geometrically why this should be so.

5. LINEAR DEPENDENCE

5.1 Homogeneous equations.
We saw in Section 1.3 that
$$\Delta = \begin{vmatrix} a_1 & b_1 & c_1 \\ a_2 & b_2 & c_2 \\ a_3 & b_3 & c_3 \end{vmatrix} = 0$$

is the condition for

$$a_1 x + b_1 y + c_1 z = 0,$$
$$a_2 x + b_2 y + c_2 z = 0,$$
$$a_3 x + b_3 y + c_3 z = 0,$$

to have non-trivial solutions. It is interesting to look at this in the context of geometrical transformations.

If $\Delta = 0$, the matrix

$$\begin{pmatrix} a_1 & b_1 & c_1 \\ a_2 & b_2 & c_2 \\ a_3 & b_3 & c_3 \end{pmatrix}$$

is singular, and therefore as a transformation matrix it reduces the dimensions of three-dimensional space. Hence the three vectors

$$\begin{pmatrix} a_1 \\ a_2 \\ a_3 \end{pmatrix}, \quad \begin{pmatrix} b_1 \\ b_2 \\ b_3 \end{pmatrix}, \quad \begin{pmatrix} c_1 \\ c_2 \\ c_3 \end{pmatrix},$$

which are the images of **i**, **j**, **k**, cannot be linearly independent, so there are numbers x_0, y_0, z_0, not all zero, such that

$$x_0 \begin{pmatrix} a_1 \\ a_2 \\ a_3 \end{pmatrix} + y_0 \begin{pmatrix} b_1 \\ b_2 \\ b_3 \end{pmatrix} + z_0 \begin{pmatrix} c_1 \\ c_2 \\ c_3 \end{pmatrix} = 0.$$

Note that if x_0, y_0, z_0 satisfy the equations, then so do $\lambda x_0, \lambda y_0, \lambda z_0$ for all values of λ. So there is a whole line of points $(\lambda x_0, \lambda y_0, \lambda z_0)$ which the matrix transforms into the origin; this is the *annihilated line* of the transformation. A singular matrix may of course annihilate a whole plane, or, if it is the zero matrix, the whole space.

We may call this key result Theorem H, and write it in the following form, with a corollary which follows from the fact that the transposed matrix has the same determinant as the original:

Theorem H.

$$\begin{vmatrix} a_1 & b_1 & c_1 \\ a_2 & b_2 & c_2 \\ a_3 & b_3 & c_3 \end{vmatrix} = 0$$

$\Leftrightarrow$ there exist numbers x, y, z not all zero such that

$$x \begin{pmatrix} a_1 \\ a_2 \\ a_3 \end{pmatrix} + y \begin{pmatrix} b_1 \\ b_2 \\ b_3 \end{pmatrix} + z \begin{pmatrix} c_1 \\ c_2 \\ c_3 \end{pmatrix} = 0$$

$\Leftrightarrow$ the vectors $\begin{pmatrix} a_1 \\ a_2 \\ a_3 \end{pmatrix}, \quad \begin{pmatrix} b_1 \\ b_2 \\ b_3 \end{pmatrix}, \quad \begin{pmatrix} c_1 \\ c_2 \\ c_3 \end{pmatrix}$ are linearly dependent.

1295

Corollary.

$$\begin{vmatrix} a_1 & b_1 & c_1 \\ a_2 & b_2 & c_2 \\ a_3 & b_3 & c_3 \end{vmatrix} = \begin{vmatrix} a_1 & a_2 & a_3 \\ b_1 & b_2 & b_3 \\ c_1 & c_2 & c_3 \end{vmatrix} = 0$$

⟺ there exist numbers λ, μ, ν not all zero such that

$$\lambda(a_1, b_1, c_1) + \mu(a_2, b_2, c_2) + \nu(a_3, b_3, c_3) = 0.$$

⟺ the linear forms

$$a_1 x + b_1 y + c_1 z,$$
$$a_2 x + b_2 y + c_2 z,$$
$$a_3 x + b_3 y + c_3 z,$$

are linearly dependent.

5.2 Non-homogeneous equations. As we have said before, in numerical cases the echelon process reduces the equations to a simple form from which the solutions can be found if they exist; and from which, in any case, it is immediately clear whether solutions, unique or otherwise, exist or there are no solutions. Nevertheless, it is of some interest to see the variety of possibilities by expressing the equations in the form

$$\begin{pmatrix} a_1 \\ a_2 \\ a_3 \end{pmatrix} x + \begin{pmatrix} b_1 \\ b_2 \\ b_3 \end{pmatrix} y + \begin{pmatrix} c_1 \\ c_2 \\ c_3 \end{pmatrix} z = \begin{pmatrix} d_1 \\ d_2 \\ d_3 \end{pmatrix},$$

or more briefly, $\mathbf{a}x + \mathbf{b}y + \mathbf{c}z = \mathbf{d}$, where $\mathbf{d} \neq \mathbf{0}$, and using the language of linear dependence while thinking of geometrical vectors. We shall not attempt a thorough analysis but merely look at some particular possibilities.

Clearly, if $\mathbf{a}, \mathbf{b}, \mathbf{c}$ are linearly independent, the values of x, y, z are unique. That is, if

$$\Delta = \begin{vmatrix} a_1 & b_1 & c_1 \\ a_2 & b_2 & c_2 \\ a_3 & b_3 & c_3 \end{vmatrix} \neq 0,$$

there is a unique solution to the equations.

If $\Delta = 0$, then $\mathbf{a}, \mathbf{b}, \mathbf{c}$ are linearly dependent and therefore lie in a plane. A variety of things can now happen. The most obvious is that if $\mathbf{d}$ is not in this plane, there is no solution. Now suppose $\mathbf{a}, \mathbf{b}, \mathbf{c}$ lie in a plane in which $\mathbf{d}$ also lies (see Figure 4(i)); then $\mathbf{d}$ can be expressed as a linear combination

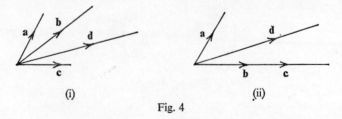

(i)   (ii)

Fig. 4

1296

of **a**, **b**, **c** in a single infinity of ways: we can choose a multiple of any one of **a**, **b**, **c** and then the multiples of the other two to be added depend on that choice. This would arise, for example, with the equations:

$$\begin{aligned} x+3y+4z &= 5, \\ x+2y+3z &= 4, \\ x+\ y+2z &= 3, \end{aligned} \quad \text{or} \quad \begin{pmatrix}1\\1\\1\end{pmatrix}x+\begin{pmatrix}3\\2\\1\end{pmatrix}y+\begin{pmatrix}4\\3\\2\end{pmatrix}z = \begin{pmatrix}5\\4\\3\end{pmatrix}.$$

Choosing $x = \lambda$, we will find $y = \lambda-1$, $z = 2-\lambda$; that is,

$$(x, y, z) = (\lambda, \lambda-1, 2-\lambda).$$

If instead we had chosen $z = \mu$ we would find $x = 2-\mu$, $y = 1-\mu$. These solutions are in fact the same, as is seen by putting $\mu = 2-\lambda$.

Next suppose **b** is a scalar multiple of **c**, so that **a**, **b**, **c** are necessarily coplanar (see Figure 4(ii)). Then if **d** is in this plane it can be expressed as a linear combination of **a**, **b**, **c** in a single infinity of ways, but in this case always with the same multiple of **a**. That is, there is a single infinity of solutions, but with unique x. For example

$$\begin{aligned} 2x+\ y+2z &= 9 \\ 3x+2y+4z &= 17 \\ 2x+3y+6z &= 23 \end{aligned} \quad \text{have the solutions} \quad (x, y, z) = (1, 7-2\lambda, \lambda).$$

(In cases where there is an infinity of solutions, the equations are not independent. Here, if we add the last equation to five times the first, we get four times the second.) Now if **a** as well as **b** is a scalar multiple of **c**, then there is no solution unless **d** is also a scalar multiple of **c**, as will indeed be obvious from the equations themselves. Here we have either no solution or a double infinity of solutions.

Another way of looking at the general system of 3×3 equations is put forward in the next section.

5.3   Linear transformations. The general 3×3 equations can be put in the form $\mathbf{Lx} = \mathbf{d}$; where

$$\mathbf{L} = \begin{pmatrix}a_1 & b_1 & c_1\\ a_2 & b_2 & c_2\\ a_3 & b_3 & c_3\end{pmatrix}, \quad \mathbf{x} = \begin{pmatrix}x\\y\\z\end{pmatrix}, \quad \mathbf{d} = \begin{pmatrix}d_1\\d_2\\d_3\end{pmatrix}.$$

We start by showing that

if $\mathbf{x}_1$ satisfies $\mathbf{Lx} = \mathbf{d}$,

and $\mathbf{x}_0$ satisfies $\mathbf{Lx} = \mathbf{0}$,

then $\mathbf{x}_1+k\mathbf{x}_0$ satisfies $\mathbf{Lx} = \mathbf{d}$,   for all values of k.

(It is left as an exercise to the reader to show that if $Lx = d$ has *a* solution, then every solution of this equation is the sum of this solution and some solution of $Lx = 0$.)

$$L(x_1 + kx_0) = L(x_1) + L(kx_0) \quad \text{(since matrix multiplication is}$$
$$= L(x_1) + kL(x_0) \quad \text{a linear operation)}$$
$$= L(x_1) \quad \text{(since } x_0 \text{ satisfies } Lx_0 = 0)$$
$$= d \quad \text{(since } x_1 \text{ satisfies } Lx_1 = d).$$

So $x_1 + kx_0$ satisfies $Lx = d$.

Now, by Theorem H, $Lx_0 = 0 \Leftrightarrow \Delta = 0$, where Δ is the determinant of L; hence, $\Delta = 0 \Leftrightarrow Lx = d$ has infinitely many solutions if it has a solution.

This we shall now treat geometrically; and for this purpose it will be convenient if we shorten such descriptions as 'the point whose position vector is p' to 'the point p'.

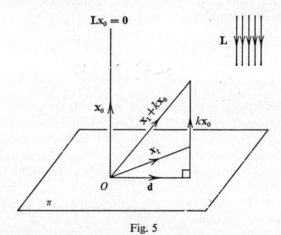

Fig. 5

L can be thought of as a linear transformation of three-dimensional space which, if $\Delta = 0$, annihilates the whole line of points kx_0 (for all k). In this case, if any point is transformed into the point d (and there may not be any), a whole family of points is so transformed. For example, in the case of orthogonal projection onto a plane π (which implies $\Delta = 0$), if the point d does not lie in π, no point is projected into d, but if the point d does lie in π, all points which lie on the normal to π at the point d are projected onto the point d.

Exercise F

1. Without solving the equations find values of p and q for which

$$\left.\begin{array}{l} x+\ y+\ z = 5 \\ 2x-\ y+3z = p \\ qx+5y+\ z = 0 \end{array}\right\}$$

have (a) an infinity of solutions, (b) no solution. In case (a), find the linear relation connecting the three equations.

2. Express as a vector equation

$$\left\{\begin{array}{l} x+\ y-z = 2, \\ 3x-5y+z = -2, \\ 4x-2y-z = 2. \end{array}\right.$$

Of the four column vectors involved, which pairs or triples are linearly dependent? What does this imply about the types of solutions to the equations? Confirm this by solving the equations. Find the linear relation connecting the three equations.

3. Show that there are three values of a for which the equations

$$\left\{\begin{array}{l} ap+\ q+2r = 0, \\ p-aq\ \ \ \ \ = 0, \\ 4p-3q+ar = 0, \end{array}\right.$$

have a non-trivial solution, and find them. In each case find the non-trivial solution for which $r = 1$.

4. Show that the planes

$$8x-5y+3z = 11, \quad 3x+4y-z = 2, \quad 5x-9y+4z = 9$$

have a line in common and find its equations in standard form.

5. If x_1 satisfies $Lx = d$, show that any solution of $Lx = d$ is x_1+x_2, where x_2 is some solution of $Lx = 0$.

6. Show that a, b, c linearly dependent and a, b, d linearly dependent does not imply a, c, d linearly dependent. Invent a set of 3×3 numerical non-homogeneous equations to which this is relevant. Have they a solution?

7. Show that it is possible to have a set of 3×3 non-homogeneous equations $a_i x+b_i y+c_i z = d_i$ ($i = 1, 2, 3$), for which all three 3×3 determinants, formed from the matrix

$$\begin{pmatrix} a_1 & b_1 & c_1 & d_1 \\ a_2 & b_2 & c_2 & d_2 \\ a_3 & b_3 & c_3 & d_3 \end{pmatrix}$$

by omitting each column in turn, are zero, and such that there is (i) no solution, (ii) an infinity of solutions.

8. What set of points is annihilated under the transformation

$$\begin{pmatrix} x' \\ y' \\ z' \end{pmatrix} = \begin{pmatrix} 2 & 1 & 3 \\ 3 & 1 & 4 \\ 1 & -2 & -1 \end{pmatrix} \begin{pmatrix} x \\ y \\ z \end{pmatrix}?$$

Find a solution of

$$\left. \begin{aligned} 2x + y + 3z &= 6, \\ 3x + y + 4z &= 9, \\ x - 2y - z &= 3, \end{aligned} \right\} \quad \text{with } y = z = 0,$$

and hence write down the general solution of these equations.

9. Show that the following equations, for R, S, T in terms of W, have a solution but are not independent.

$$R - T = W \cos \theta; \quad S = W \sin \theta; \quad 2R \sin \alpha = W \sin (\alpha + \theta);$$

$$R \sin \alpha - S \cos \alpha + T \sin \alpha = 0.$$

10. Solve the equations for x, y, z, where p, q, r are all distinct:

$$p^2 x + py + z = qr,$$

$$q^2 x + qy + z = rp,$$

$$r^2 x + ry + z = pq.$$

11. Show that the following equations have a unique solution in the field of rational numbers, but no solution in the field of integers modulo 3 unless a has a definite value. If a has this value, find their general solution.

$$x + y + z = 1,$$

$$2x - y + z = -1,$$

$$x + y = a.$$

12. Show that

the points (x_1, y_1), (x_2, x_2), (x_3, y_3) are collinear $\Leftrightarrow$ $\begin{vmatrix} x_1 & y_1 & 1 \\ x_2 & y_2 & 1 \\ x_3 & y_3 & 1 \end{vmatrix} = 0.$

13. Show that the equation of the line joining (x_1, y_1) to (x_2, y_2) is

$$\begin{vmatrix} x & y & 1 \\ x_1 & y_1 & 1 \\ x_2 & y_2 & 1 \end{vmatrix} = 0.$$

Find the equations of the lines joining the following pairs of points:

(a) $(5, 11)$, $(10, 21)$;   (b) (p^2, p), (q^2, q);

(c) $(at_1^2, 2at_1)$, $(at_2^2, 2at_2)$;   (d) $(cp, c/p)$, $(cq, c/q)$.

14. What is the condition for the lines

$$a_1 x + b_1 y + c_1 = 0, \quad a_2 x + b_2 y + c_2 = 0, \quad a_3 x + b_3 y + c_3 = 0$$

to have (a) one common point; (b) two common points?

1300

15. What is the condition that the planes

$$p_1x+q_1y+r_1z = 0, \quad p_2x+q_2y+r_2z = 0, \quad p_3x+q_3y+r_3z = 0$$

have a common line?

16. There is a finite geometry with nine points whose two coordinates are integers in the field of integers modulo 3. They can be taken to be either 0, $+1$, or -1. Write down the coordinates of the nine points, and find the equations of the twelve lines joining them. Verify that exactly three points lie on each line and four lines pass through each point.

17. Consider the extensions to three dimensions of the results of Questions 12, 13, 16. You will need to consider how to define a 4×4 determinant.

*6. COFACTORS

Here we shall develop an idea of general importance with a particular application to the evaluation of the inverse of a matrix by a method which does not involve row operations. It is based directly on our definition of a 3×3 determinant in terms of 2×2 determinants.

Let Δ be the determinant of the matrix

$$\begin{pmatrix} a_1 & b_1 & c_1 \\ a_2 & b_2 & c_2 \\ a_3 & b_3 & c_3 \end{pmatrix}.$$

Then

$$\Delta = \begin{vmatrix} a_1 & b_1 & c_1 \\ a_2 & b_2 & c_2 \\ a_3 & b_3 & c_3 \end{vmatrix} = a_1 \begin{vmatrix} b_2 & c_2 \\ b_3 & c_3 \end{vmatrix} - b_1 \begin{vmatrix} a_2 & c_2 \\ a_3 & c_3 \end{vmatrix} + c_1 \begin{vmatrix} a_2 & b_2 \\ a_3 & b_3 \end{vmatrix}.$$

The determinants

$$\begin{vmatrix} b_2 & c_2 \\ b_3 & c_3 \end{vmatrix}, \quad -\begin{vmatrix} a_2 & c_2 \\ a_3 & c_3 \end{vmatrix}, \quad \begin{vmatrix} a_2 & b_2 \\ a_3 & b_3 \end{vmatrix},$$

are called, respectively, the 'cofactors' of a_1, b_1, c_1 in Δ, and are written A_1, B_1, C_1. Hence we can write:

$$\Delta = a_1 A_1 + b_1 B_1 + c_1 C_1.$$

If we bring the second row to the top by interchanging the first two rows, we shall have a determinant numerically equal to Δ but with the opposite sign. We can then expand this determinant in terms of 2×2 determinants. Thus

$$\Delta = -\begin{vmatrix} a_2 & b_2 & c_2 \\ a_1 & b_1 & c_1 \\ a_3 & b_3 & c_3 \end{vmatrix} = -a_2 \begin{vmatrix} b_1 & c_1 \\ b_3 & c_3 \end{vmatrix} + b_2 \begin{vmatrix} a_1 & c_1 \\ a_3 & c_3 \end{vmatrix} - c_2 \begin{vmatrix} a_1 & b_1 \\ a_3 & b_3 \end{vmatrix};$$

and we call

$$-\begin{vmatrix} b_1 & c_1 \\ b_3 & c_3 \end{vmatrix}, \quad \begin{vmatrix} a_1 & c_1 \\ a_3 & c_3 \end{vmatrix}, \quad -\begin{vmatrix} a_1 & b_1 \\ a_3 & b_3 \end{vmatrix}$$

the cofactors of a_2, b_2, c_2 in Δ, and write them A_2, B_2, C_2. This provides us with another form of expansion for the determinant:

$$\Delta = a_2 A_2 + b_2 B_2 + c_2 C_2.$$

Similarly, using the elements of the third row, we have

$$\Delta = a_3 A_3 + b_3 B_3 + c_3 C_3$$

where

$$A_3 = \begin{vmatrix} b_1 & c_1 \\ b_2 & c_2 \end{vmatrix}, \quad B_3 = -\begin{vmatrix} a_1 & c_1 \\ a_2 & c_2 \end{vmatrix}, \quad C_3 = \begin{vmatrix} a_1 & b_1 \\ a_2 & b_2 \end{vmatrix}.$$

It will be seen that in each case the cofactor of an element is the determinant of the 2×2 matrix left when the row and column in which the element occurs in the original matrix are removed, prefixed by $+$ or $-$, according to the following rule: the sign for each element is the corresponding one in the array

$$\begin{pmatrix} + & - & + \\ - & + & - \\ + & - & + \end{pmatrix}.$$

Thus we have

$$\Delta = a_i A_i + b_i B_i + c_i C_i \quad \text{for} \quad i \dots 1, 2, 3.$$

Interchanging rows and columns, we shall also have:

$$\Delta = a_1 A_1 + a_2 A_2 + a_3 A_3$$
$$= b_1 B_1 + b_2 B_2 + b_3 B_3$$
$$= c_1 C_1 + c_2 C_2 + c_3 C_3.$$

Hence any 3×3 determinant can be expanded by adding serially the products of the elements of a row or column and their cofactors.

Example 7. Evaluate the determinant

$$\begin{vmatrix} 1 & 2 & 3 \\ 4 & 5 & 6 \\ 7 & 8 & 9 \end{vmatrix}.$$

We choose to do this using the elements of the middle column and their cofactors. Its value is

$$-2\begin{vmatrix} 4 & 6 \\ 7 & 9 \end{vmatrix} + 5\begin{vmatrix} 1 & 3 \\ 7 & 9 \end{vmatrix} - 8\begin{vmatrix} 1 & 3 \\ 4 & 6 \end{vmatrix} = (-2)(-6) + (5)(-12) - (8)(-6) = 0.$$

Theorem I.

$$a_i A_j + b_i B_j + c_i C_j \begin{cases} = \Delta & \text{if} \quad i = j \\ = 0 & \text{if} \quad i \neq j \end{cases} \quad (i, j = 1, 2, 3).$$

The first part has already been proved. For the second part, as an example, consider the determinant

$$\begin{vmatrix} a_1 & b_1 & c_1 \\ a_2 & b_2 & c_2 \\ a_2 & b_2 & c_2 \end{vmatrix}.$$

When this is expanded by the elements of the third row, we get,

$$a_2 \begin{vmatrix} b_1 & c_1 \\ b_2 & c_2 \end{vmatrix} - b_2 \begin{vmatrix} a_1 & c_1 \\ a_2 & c_2 \end{vmatrix} + c_2 \begin{vmatrix} a_1 & b_1 \\ a_2 & b_2 \end{vmatrix} = a_2 A_3 + b_2 B_3 + c_2 C_3,$$

where A_3, B_3, C_3 have the meanings assigned to them from the original matrix. But this determinant has two equal rows, and is therefore zero.

In general, $a_i A_j + b_i B_j + c_i C_j$ is the expansion by the elements of the jth row of the determinant formed from the original matrix by repeating in the jth row the elements of the ith row. This determinant, having two rows the same if $i \neq j$, is zero.

Corollary. Similar results hold for expansions by columns.

Example 8. (i) Simplify

$$\begin{pmatrix} a_1 & b_1 & c_1 \\ a_2 & b_2 & c_2 \\ a_3 & b_3 & c_3 \end{pmatrix} \begin{pmatrix} A_1 & A_2 & A_3 \\ B_1 & B_2 & B_3 \\ C_1 & C_2 & C_3 \end{pmatrix};$$

(ii) Evaluate

$$\begin{pmatrix} 1 & 2 & 3 \\ 3 & 4 & 5 \\ 5 & 7 & 10 \end{pmatrix} \begin{pmatrix} 5 & 1 & -2 \\ -5 & -5 & 4 \\ 1 & 3 & -2 \end{pmatrix}.$$

(i) Using the theorem the product can be written down directly as

$$\begin{pmatrix} \Delta & 0 & 0 \\ 0 & \Delta & 0 \\ 0 & 0 & \Delta \end{pmatrix}.$$

(ii) The product is found, in the ordinary way, to be

$$\begin{pmatrix} -2 & 0 & 0 \\ 0 & -2 & 0 \\ 0 & 0 & -2 \end{pmatrix}.$$

In this numerical example the simplicity of the result arises because the second matrix has been formed, as in (i), by evaluating the cofactors of all the elements of the determinant of the first matrix, writing them down in the corresponding positions as a matrix, and then transposing it. It should now be clear that we have a method for writing down the inverse of a matrix. Thus, the inverse of

$$\begin{pmatrix} 1 & 2 & 3 \\ 3 & 4 & 5 \\ 5 & 7 & 10 \end{pmatrix} \quad \text{is} \quad \begin{pmatrix} -\frac{5}{2} & -\frac{1}{2} & 1 \\ \frac{5}{2} & \frac{5}{2} & -2 \\ -\frac{1}{2} & -\frac{3}{2} & 1 \end{pmatrix}.$$

In general, the inverse of

$$\begin{pmatrix} a_1 & b_1 & c_1 \\ a_2 & b_2 & c_2 \\ a_3 & b_3 & c_3 \end{pmatrix} \text{ is } \begin{pmatrix} A_1/\Delta & A_2/\Delta & A_3/\Delta \\ B_1/\Delta & B_2/\Delta & B_3/\Delta \\ C_1/\Delta & C_2/\Delta & C_3/\Delta \end{pmatrix},$$

or (more conveniently written)

$$1/\Delta \begin{pmatrix} A_1 & A_2 & A_3 \\ B_1 & B_2 & B_3 \\ C_1 & C_2 & C_3 \end{pmatrix},$$

provided $\Delta \neq 0$. If $\Delta = 0$, there is no inverse.

In numerical work, the method of finding an inverse given in Chapter 21, p. 594, is usually quicker, and certainly so for larger matrices.

Exercise G

1. Invert the following matrices:

(a) $\begin{pmatrix} 1 & -4 & 2 \\ 2 & 1 & 4 \\ 4 & 3 & -2 \end{pmatrix}$;

(b) $\begin{pmatrix} 0 & j & 1+j \\ -j & 0 & j \\ 1-j & j & 0 \end{pmatrix}$;

(c) $\begin{pmatrix} 1 & 2 & 3 \\ 4 & 5 & 6 \\ 7 & 8 & 10 \end{pmatrix}$;

(d) $\begin{pmatrix} a & 1 & 0 \\ 1 & b & 1 \\ 0 & 1 & c \end{pmatrix}$;

(e) $\begin{pmatrix} 1 & 0 & p \\ p & 1 & 0 \\ 0 & p & 1 \end{pmatrix}$;

(f) $\begin{pmatrix} a & 0 & c \\ 0 & 1 & 0 \\ d & 0 & b \end{pmatrix}$.

2. Write down the matrix of the cofactors of

$$\begin{pmatrix} 2 & 5 & 0 \\ -3 & 7 & -1 \\ 5 & -3 & 1 \end{pmatrix}$$

and use it to solve the equations:

$$\begin{aligned} 2x+5y &= 8, \\ -3x+7y-z &= 5, \\ 5x-3y+z &= 3. \end{aligned}$$

3. Find a matrix X such that $\mathbf{AX} = \mathbf{B}$, where

$$\mathbf{A} = \begin{pmatrix} 0 & 1 & 2 \\ 1 & 2 & 0 \\ 2 & 0 & 1 \end{pmatrix} \text{ and } \mathbf{B} = \begin{pmatrix} 3 & 4 & 5 \\ 4 & 5 & 3 \\ 5 & 3 & 4 \end{pmatrix}.$$

Does $\mathbf{XA} = \mathbf{B}$?

1304

4. Express

$$\begin{vmatrix} p^4+p^2+1 & p^2q^2+pq+1 & p^2r^2+pr+1 \\ p^2q^2+pq+1 & q^4+q^2+1 & q^2r^2+qr+1 \\ p^2r^2+pr+1 & q^2r^2+qr+1 & r^4+r^2+1 \end{vmatrix}$$

as the product of two determinants, and hence show that its value is

$$(p-q)^2(q-r)^2(r-p)^2.$$

5. Prove, by expressing it as the product of two determinants, or otherwise, that

$$\begin{vmatrix} ap+bq & aq+br & ar+bp \\ bp+cq & bq+cr & br+cp \\ cp+aq & cq+ar & cr+ap \end{vmatrix} = 0.$$

Miscellaneous Exercise

1. Verify that

$$\begin{pmatrix} 1 & -1 & 3 \\ 5 & -3 & 11 \\ 3 & -4 & 5 \end{pmatrix} = \begin{pmatrix} 1 & 0 & 0 \\ 5 & 2 & 0 \\ 3 & -1 & -6 \end{pmatrix} \begin{pmatrix} 1 & 1 & 3 \\ 0 & 1 & -2 \\ 0 & 0 & 1 \end{pmatrix}.$$

Hence solve the equations

$$x-\ y+\ 3z =\ 2,$$
$$5x-3y+11z =\ 8,$$
$$3x-4y+\ 5z = 11,$$

by first putting

$$\begin{pmatrix} 1 & -1 & 3 \\ 0 & 1 & -2 \\ 0 & 0 & 1 \end{pmatrix} \begin{pmatrix} x \\ y \\ z \end{pmatrix} = \begin{pmatrix} u \\ v \\ w \end{pmatrix},$$

and solving an intermediate set of equations for u, v, w.

2. Solve the equations:

$$x-2y-3z = 2,$$
$$3x-4y+2z = 1,$$
$$5x+\ y-7z = 5,$$

by expressing the matrix

$$\begin{pmatrix} 1 & -2 & -3 \\ 3 & -4 & 2 \\ 5 & 1 & -7 \end{pmatrix}$$

as a product of the form

$$\begin{pmatrix} * & 0 & 0 \\ * & * & 0 \\ * & * & * \end{pmatrix} \begin{pmatrix} 1 & * & * \\ 0 & 1 & * \\ 0 & 0 & 1 \end{pmatrix}$$

and proceeding as in Question 1.

3. Consider what happens when the process of the preceding question is applied to the equations

$$x-2y-3z = 2,$$
$$3x-4y+2z = 1,$$
$$5x-6y+7z = 0.$$

4. By applying *Theorem E* to the product of the matrices

$$\begin{pmatrix} a & b & c \\ d & e & f \\ g & h & i \end{pmatrix} \begin{pmatrix} 1 & D & G \\ 0 & E & H \\ 0 & F & I \end{pmatrix},$$

where D is the cofactor of d, etc., in the first matrix, show that $EI - HF = a\Delta$, where Δ is the determinant of the first matrix.

5. Verify that

$$\begin{pmatrix} a & 0 & 0 \\ d & I/a & 0 \\ g & -F/a & \Delta/I \end{pmatrix} \begin{pmatrix} 1 & b/a & c/a \\ 0 & 1 & -H/I \\ 0 & 0 & 1 \end{pmatrix} = \begin{pmatrix} a & b & c \\ d & e & f \\ g & h & i \end{pmatrix}.$$

What light does this throw on the process of Questions 1–3?

(Questions 1–5 refer to *Choleski's process*, which can be used both for solving equations and for testing a matrix for singularity. The process is systematic and completely general, and well suited for a computer.)

6. What is the inverse of the matrix,

$$\begin{pmatrix} a & 0 & 0 \\ d & k & 0 \\ g & l & m \end{pmatrix}, \quad \text{where} \quad akm \neq 0?$$

7. What is the inverse of the matrix

$$\begin{pmatrix} 1 & p & q \\ 0 & 1 & r \\ 0 & 0 & 1 \end{pmatrix}?$$

8. Use the results of Questions 1, 6 and 7 to write down two matrices whose product is the inverse of the matrix

$$\begin{pmatrix} 1 & -1 & 3 \\ 5 & -3 & 11 \\ 3 & -4 & 5 \end{pmatrix}$$

and find this inverse.

9. Show that if the matrix

$$\begin{pmatrix} a & h & g \\ h & b & f \\ g & f & c \end{pmatrix}$$

is non-singular, the cofactors of the *adjoint* matrix

$$\begin{pmatrix} A & H & G \\ H & B & F \\ G & F & C \end{pmatrix}$$

are the elements of the original matrix multiplied by its determinant. (See Question 4.)

1306

10. Find the values of k for which

$$\begin{pmatrix} 3 & 2 \\ 1 & 4 \end{pmatrix} \begin{pmatrix} x \\ y \end{pmatrix} = k \begin{pmatrix} x \\ y \end{pmatrix}.$$

Find vectors $\begin{pmatrix} x \\ y \end{pmatrix}$ corresponding to these values of k. If these vectors are **u** and **v**, what is the image of $a\mathbf{u} + b\mathbf{v}$ under the transformation given by the matrix $\begin{pmatrix} 3 & 2 \\ 1 & 4 \end{pmatrix}$? Illustrate this geometrically. (**u** and **v** are called *eigenvectors* of the matrix.)

43

CONVERGENCE

1. CONVERGENCE OF A SEQUENCE

Throughout this course we have repeatedly used iterative processes to approximate to certain numbers: for example, we have used the Newton–Raphson method to approximate to the root of an equation; we have used step-by-step methods to solve a differential equation, and relaxation methods to solve simultaneous equations. Usually a few repetitions of such processes have been sufficient to provide us with an answer which we have confidently assumed to be correct within prescribed limits of accuracy. We have also assumed that if we continued the process further we should obtain steadily closer approximations to the true answer. But are these assumptions justified? This question we now proceed to examine.

There are two basic assumptions that we make in any process of this kind. The first is that there *is* an answer; that is to say that if, for example, we are trying to solve the equation $x^2 = 2$, then there is a 'number' (which we call $\sqrt{2}$) which satisfies this. The second assumption is that the process we use yields a sequence of numbers which steadily approach the answer; more precisely, that if we wish to approximate to the answer to any given degree of accuracy, we can find a number of times to repeat the process which will ensure our doing so. Of these two assumptions the first is the more fundamental, but we shall leave it aside for the moment. In fact, as we shall see, it will be necessary to take as an axiom the idea that, for suitably restricted sequences, there is a number to which they converge.

The second assumption needs to be made more precise, and to be examined more critically, since it is obviously not always true. This we shall now do.

1.1 Challenge and response. We begin with a very simple example where our intuition tells us that the sequence steadily approaches a well-known number. Consider the sequence of numbers

$$\tfrac{1}{2}, \tfrac{1}{4}, \tfrac{1}{8}, \ldots, (\tfrac{1}{2})^i,$$

which will be generated by the following flow diagram.

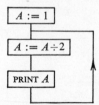

No term of this sequence is zero, but if we programmed a computer to evaluate them, the terms would soon be printed as zeros, since they would be smaller than the smallest number that the machine could handle. Furthermore, this would be true however many decimal places the output could print. Challenged to produce a number N which will enable us to say 'all terms from the Nth onwards will be zero to the first 50 decimal places', we can certainly find such a number; and we can do so whatever number the challenger puts in the place of 50.

Notice two things: we are not committed to produce the *smallest* such number N, but only one suitable N; secondly, we cannot produce a single number N for all time, which will dispose of the challenge no matter what number is put in the place of 50. Our response depends on the challenge with which we are faced. Formally, we can express the situation like this:

Given any number p, there can be found a number N such that

$$\left|\frac{1}{2^i}\right| < 10^{-p} \quad \text{for all} \quad i > N.$$

When this is true, we say that the *limit* of $1/2^i$ is zero, or that $1/2^i$ *converges* to zero, as i increases without limit. This is written

$$\lim_{i \to \infty} \frac{1}{2^i} = 0.$$

There is, of course, no particular virtue in decimal representation; from the mathematical point of view all that is necessary is to say that

For every positive number k, there is a number N such that

$$\left|\frac{1}{2^i}\right| < k \quad \text{for all} \quad i > N.$$

Notice again that although in this case the flow diagram

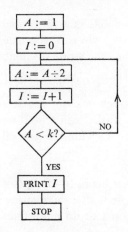

will print out the smallest value of N, yet this would not always be the case for more general sequences, and the fact that the computer stops does not guarantee convergence. There *are* sequences which give a very close approximation after, say, 1000 terms but which give increasingly bad approximations from then on.

Exercise A

1. Find a value of N for which you can be sure that

$$\frac{1}{2^i} < k \quad \text{for all} \quad i > N$$

(*a*) when $k = 10^{-6}$;   (*b*) when $k = 10^{-12}$;   (*c*) when $k = 10^{-6p}$. (You are not asked for the smallest value of N.)

2. Prove by induction that $(1+x)^i > 1 + ix$ for integral $i \geqslant 2$, if $x > -1$.

3. Use the result of Question 2 to find a value of N such that

$$(\tfrac{4}{3})^i > 10^6 \quad \text{for all} \quad i > N.$$

4. Use the result of Question 3 to find a value of N such that

(*a*) $(\tfrac{3}{4})^i < 10^{-6}$ for all $i > N$;
(*b*) $(\tfrac{3}{4})^i < k$ for all $i > N$ $(k > 0)$.

What does this tell you about the sequence $\{(\tfrac{3}{4})^i\}$?

5. For what values of i is $\dfrac{i}{i+2}$

(*a*) greater than 0·99;   (*b*) greater than 0·9999?

6. Can you find a value of N for which

$$|(\tfrac{1}{2})^i + (\tfrac{3}{4})^i \sin \tfrac{1}{2} i\pi| < k \quad \text{for all} \quad i > N?$$

(Use Questions 1 and 4.)

1.2 Limits of sequences. We now give some formal definitions.

If f is a function whose domain is N, the set of natural numbers (sometimes with zero added), then the string of numbers

$$f(1), f(2), f(3), \dots, f(i), \dots$$

is called a *sequence*. Although it is not necessarily a set (since there may well be repetitions), no confusion will arise if we write $\{f(i)\}$ to denote the sequence as a whole. Before giving the general definition of a limit, we consider two further examples.

Example 1. Consider the sequence $\{(-1)^i/i\}$ (see Figure 1).

The figure certainly suggests that the sequence converges to the limit 0. But it is not enough by itself to do more than suggest it to us. Helpful though a graph may be—and visual pictures of this sort are almost indispensable—it can by its nature only show a finite number of terms. This could equally well be the graph of the sequence defined by

$$\begin{cases} f(i) = (-1)^i/i & \text{if} \quad 1 \leqslant i \leqslant 10; \\ f(i) = 10^i & \text{if} \quad i > 10. \end{cases}$$

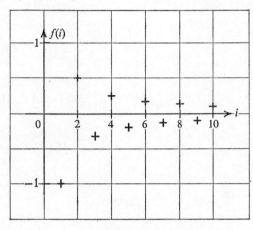

Fig. 1

The first few terms are not really relevant to the behaviour of the sequence in the long run; indeed, if we replace the first million terms of a sequence by zeros, it makes no difference to the existence or otherwise of the limit.

A graph is also very insensitive to small numbers. Think how hard it was to draw Figure 1 accurately—or indeed to check its accuracy. It would not be possible to draw graphs to distinguish between $\{(-1)^i/i\}$ and $\{(-1)^i(1/i+10^{-6})\}$; and yet the first sequence has a limit of zero, and the second has no limit. This possibility also reminds us that no finite size of interval can ever be small enough to test the existence of limits for all sequences; it is easy to devise sequences like the one above which will elude any given test.

And yet, although the part of a graph which we can see is of no use (on these two counts) for testing convergence, our imagination can often make a graph suggest an accurate result. Consider how easy it is to picture the behaviour of the three sequences suggested in this example, although any actual graph we drew would have to be heavily distorted to show it up.

Example 2. Is there a limit to the sequence $\{(2+(-1)^i)/i\}$? (see Figure 2).

In this case, although the terms of the sequence are alternately greater and less than their predecessors, the sequence has a perfectly good limit.

1311

In fact, if we take a standard of k, all subsequent terms of the sequence will lie between 0 and k after about $[3/k]$ terms. Some terms (in fact, all the alternate ones) will lie between 0 and k after about $[1/k]$ terms; but it is of no use to us until all the terms do so. Thus, if $k = 0.1$, the 11th, 13th, 15th... terms are less than k, but not until the 31st term do they all become less than k.

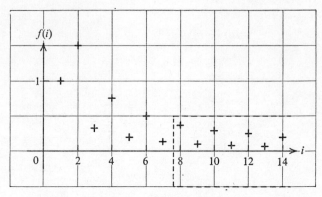

Fig. 2

The 'box' drawn on Figure 2 illustrates this well. In graphical terms, we are given the height k of the box, and we want to be sure that we can place the left-hand end of it so that the box includes all the points to the right of it which represent terms of the sequence. If we can do this for any named height k, the sequence has a limit; we are not concerned with getting the left-hand end of the box as far left as possible, merely with finding some such end. This suggests the definition we need:

Definition. If for every positive number k there is a number N such that

$$i > N \Rightarrow |f(i) - c| < k,$$

the sequence $\{f(i)\}$ has the *limit* c, and we write

$$f(i) \to c \quad \text{as} \quad i \to \infty, \quad \text{or} \quad \lim_{i \to \infty} f(i) = c.$$

1.3 Sequences without limits.

Example 3. Discuss the behaviour of $\{x^i\}$, for different values of x.

Although many sequences behave less regularly than this one, the four main types of behaviour can be seen clearly.

(*a*) Convergence to a limit:

$$|x| < 1 \Rightarrow x^i \to 0; \quad x = 1 \Rightarrow x^i \to 1.$$

(*b*) Finite oscillation: $x = -1$ gives a sequence whose terms remain bounded, but do not approach a limit.

1312

(c) Divergence to $\pm \infty$: $x > 1 \Rightarrow x^i \to +\infty$, which simply means that a term can be found of any size we care to name, and all subsequent terms exceed it; similarly $-(x^i) \to -\infty$.

(d) Infinite oscillation: $x < -1$ gives a sequence which does not fall into any of the other three categories, and we say that it oscillates infinitely. It is not necessary for terms to approach both $+\infty$ and $-\infty$; $\{x^i + (-x)^i\}$ still oscillates infinitely, though alternate terms are zero.

Every sequence falls into one of these categories, though it is not always obvious which it will be. But the sequences which will be most important to us are those which have limits.

Exercise B

Discuss the behaviour of the sequences whose ith terms are given in Questions 1, 2, 3:

1. (a) $i^2/1000$;   (b) 2^i;   (c) $(-1)^i$;
   (d) $(-1)^i/i$;   (e) $i/2^i$;   (f) $(1 \cdot 01)^i/1000$.

2. (a) $i + 1/i$;   (b) $1/(i^2 - 1)$;   (c) $1/i + 1/i^2$;
   (d) $(i-1)/(i+1)$;   (e) $(2-3i)/(i+2)$;   (f) $i^{-\frac{1}{2}}$.

3. (a) $\sin \pi i$;   (b) $\cos \frac{1}{2}\pi i$;   (c) $(\cos \pi i)/i$.

2. ITERATIVE PROCESSES

2.1 Square root by iteration. We can best discuss the practical question of the convergence of sequences obtained as a result of iterative processes by considering a simple example.

Example 4. Discuss the convergence of the process defined by

$$x_1 = 1, \quad x_{i+1} = \frac{1}{2}\left(x_i + \frac{A}{x_i}\right) \quad (i \geqslant 1).$$

(a) What is the limit of this sequence, if it has one?

It is clear that if the sequence has a limit l, and at any stage $x_n = l$ within the prescribed limits of accuracy, then $x_{n+1} = l$ also, within those limits. Hence

$$l = \frac{1}{2}\{l + (A/l)\}$$

$$\Rightarrow l = A/l$$

$$\Rightarrow l^2 = A$$

$$\Rightarrow l = \pm\sqrt{A}.$$

Since every x_i is clearly positive, $l = +\sqrt{A}$.

(b) Can we prove that $x_i \to \sqrt{A}$?

Let us examine the difference $|x_i - \sqrt{A}|$.

For every $i \in N$,
$$x_{i+1} - \sqrt{A} = \tfrac{1}{2}\{x_i + (A/x_i)\} - \sqrt{A}$$
$$= \frac{(x_i - \sqrt{A})^2}{2x_i} > 0.$$

Hence $x_{i+1} > \sqrt{A}$ for every $i \in N$, and
$$0 < x_{i+1} - \sqrt{A} < K(x_i - \sqrt{A})^2,$$

where K can be taken either as $\tfrac{1}{2}$ if $A \geqslant 1$ or as $1/2\sqrt{A}$ if $A < 1$. It follows at once that $x_i - \sqrt{A}$ is either less than 1 at the start, or rapidly becomes so; and as soon as this happens,
$$|x_{i+1} - \sqrt{A}| < r|x_i - \sqrt{A}|, \quad \text{where} \quad 0 < r < 1.$$

Thus, for some m,
$$|x_{m+n} - \sqrt{A}| < r^n|x_m - \sqrt{A}|$$

and clearly tends to 0. In practice, convergence is very rapid. Thus, if $A = 4$, $x_1 = 1$, $x_2 = 2 \cdot 5$, $x_3 = 2 \cdot 05$, $x_4 = 2 \cdot 0006$, and the number of accurate decimal places roughly doubles with each iteration.

2.2   A more general iteration.

Example 5. Discuss the sequence defined by $x_{n+1} = 4 - 1/x_n$, for various values of x_1.

Figure 3 shows the graphs of $y = x$ and of $y = 4 - 1/x$. If $x_1 = 1$, as marked, $y_1 = 4 - 1/x_1 = x_2$, so that the procedure for passing from $(x_1, 0)$ to $(x_2, 0)$ is

go up to $y = 4 - 1/x$,
|
go across to $y = x$
|
go down to the axis.

The procedure for going from (x_1, x_1) to (x_2, x_2) is even simpler, and the reader should convince himself how it works and what will happen to the sequence for this and other values of x_1.

The graph suggests that if a point is chosen between A and B to represent (x_1, x_1) all its successors will remain between A and B, and that it will steadily approach A from below; if the point is above A, it will steadily approach A from above; and if it is below B, (x_3, x_3) at least will be above A, so that the sequence will still converge. The only exceptions to this rule are when (x_1, x_1) is at 0 or at B. (What happens then, and why can we be sure that no subsequent point lies at 0 or at B if the initial point does not?)

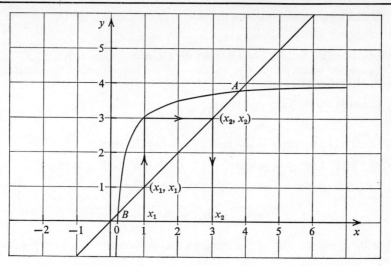

Fig. 3

The limit, if any, of the sequence must satisfy $c = 4-1/c$, and is therefore $2+\sqrt{3}$, which is the larger root of this equation.

Further,

$$x_{n+1} = 4-\frac{1}{x_n} \quad \text{and} \quad c = 4-\frac{1}{c}$$

$$\Rightarrow \quad x_{n+1}-c = \frac{1}{c}-\frac{1}{x_n} = \frac{x_n-c}{cx_n},$$

and once again it is clear that x_n converges to c provided that at some stage $cx_n > 1$.

Exercise C

1. $\sqrt{2}$ may be determined by the Newton–Raphson process by defining

$$x_1 = 2, \quad x_{i+1} = \tfrac{1}{2}(x_i+2/x_i).$$

Show that x_i is a decreasing sequence, and that

$$\left(\frac{x_{i+1}-\sqrt{2}}{2\sqrt{2}}\right) < \left(\frac{x_i-\sqrt{2}}{2\sqrt{2}}\right)^2.$$

and estimate what error in x_5 this allows.

2. For the sequence defined by $x_{n+1} = 4-1/x_n$, work out the first four terms, with $x_1 = 4, 3, 2, 1, 0, -1$ respectively, and confirm that they behave as Example 5 suggests.

3. Sketch a graph, and calculate the limit of the sequence given by

$$u_1 = 1, \quad u_{i+1} = 1 + 1/u_i.$$

What connection has this sequence with the Fibonacci numbers $1, 1, 2, 3, 5, 8, \ldots$? Compare the values of the first six terms of the sequence with the calculated limit. How do they approach it?

4. Consider the sequence defined by

$$u_1 = 2, \quad u_{i+1} = \tfrac{1}{2}(u_i + 2/u_i).$$

Illustrate its convergence to the limit by drawing the graphs

(a) $y = x$ and $y = \tfrac{1}{2}x + 1/x$;   (b) $y = x$ and $y = 2/x$.

5. Calculate the first six terms of the sequence defined by

$$u_1 = 1; \quad u_{i+1} = 1 + \frac{2}{1 + u_i}.$$

Find the presumed limit of the sequence, and show that if this limit is a, then

$$\frac{u_{i+1} - a}{u_i - a} = \frac{-2}{(1+a)(1+u_i)}.$$

Hence show that the sequence does indeed converge to this limit.

2.3   The real numbers. The sequences discussed in Exercise C show clearly that within the system of rational numbers we have not enough equipment to define the limits properly. For it is clear that we there had sequences of rational numbers whose limits were definitely not rational numbers; indeed, in that system no limits exist, for the definition of Section 1.2 depends on the existence of c. Although there are rational numbers which lie as close as we please to these limits, nevertheless there are gaps where the limits should be, which can only be filled by extending the system of rational numbers.

Unfortunately in this course we have not yet made clear what we mean by 'real numbers', although our name 'measuring numbers' and our experience of handling such numbers may by this time have given us quite a fair idea of how they must behave.

There must be a subset of them—the rational real numbers—which correspond exactly to the rational numbers; they must, like the rational numbers, obey the field laws; and they should have no property that the rationals do not, except those that arise from the extension we are going to make. This extension will ensure that all sequences (of real numbers as well as of rational real numbers) will have limits if they 'should' have limits.

We have several times pointed out that certain sequences appear intuitively to have limits; and the types which we intuitively feel should approach a limit are (a) sequences like that in Exercise C, Question 3, whose alternate members rise and fall, bracketing the limit more closely each time; (b) increasing sequences which do not tend to infinity (e.g. Example 5 with $x_1 = 1$); and (c) decreasing sequences which do not tend to $-\infty$ (e.g. Example 4).

It is not difficult to see that if sequences of type (b) have a limit, it follows that sequences of types (a) and (c) have a limit as well provided in case (a) that the 'brackets' are sufficiently small; we therefore examine (b) more closely.

If a sequence $\{a_i\}$ is *increasing*, that is, if $a_{i+1} \geqslant a_i$ for all i, there appear to be only two possibilities. We say that $\{a_i\}$ tends to infinity if for every number A the members of the sequence exceed A from some point on. If this is not the case, there must be a number A which exceeds or is equal to all the members of the sequence; for with an increasing sequence, if any member exceeds A, all subsequent members will. This number A may then be called an *upper bound* of the sequence, and the sequence will be described as *bounded above*. If a sequence is bounded above, there will (intuitively) be a least number A_{min} which bounds it, and when the sequence is increasing, intuitively, its limit will be A_{min}. We cannot justify this intuition without defining the real numbers; this is not easy, and we shall be content to assume this result as a fundamental axiom:

Every bounded increasing sequence of real numbers has a limit.

This will not only provide familiar 'numbers' such as $\sqrt{2}$ as limits of sequences, but also many other numbers which can be approached by methods of successive approximation.

3. CONVERGENCE OF SERIES

3.1   Sequences of partial sums. So far we have only defined sequences by means of explicit functions. But one very important type of sequence is defined in terms of the finite series of Chapter 11 (see p. 314). The GP (geometrical progression) of Example 6 is a particularly simple case.

Example 6. Discuss the sequence of partial sums of the series

$$\tfrac{1}{2} + \tfrac{1}{3} + \tfrac{2}{9} + \tfrac{4}{27} + \dots,$$

where each term is two-thirds of the previous one.

We may write the ith term as $\tfrac{1}{2}(\tfrac{2}{3})^{i-1}$, and the sum of the first n terms as $\sum_1^n \tfrac{1}{2}(\tfrac{2}{3})^{i-1}$, which we shall call $f(n)$, since each natural number n gives this a unique value.

If we draw a graph of $\{f(n)\}$, as in Figure 4, we can see that the sequence is steadily increasing, and in decreasing steps. This is not enough to ensure that the sequence has a limit, but in this particular case it should be possible to guess from the figure what the limit is, though it is not very obvious how the sequence continues: $\frac{1}{2}, \frac{5}{6}, \frac{19}{18}, \frac{65}{54}, \frac{211}{162}, \dots$

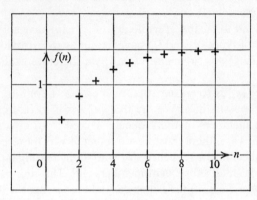

Fig. 4

We have, however, a general formula for partial sums of GPs (see p. 314):

$$\sum_1^n ar^{i-1} = a\left(\frac{1-r^n}{1-r}\right),$$

and, writing $a = \frac{1}{2}$, $r = \frac{2}{3}$, we have an explicit formula for $f(n)$

$$f(n) = \frac{1}{2}\left(\frac{1-(\frac{2}{3})^n}{1-\frac{2}{3}}\right) = \frac{3}{2}-(\tfrac{2}{3})^{n-1},$$

after simplification.

Now, by taking n to be large enough, we can make $(\frac{2}{3})^{n-1}$ as small as we please; so the sequence tends to the limit $\frac{3}{2}$, (sometimes called the *sum to infinity* of the series).

Unfortunately, however, it is often far from easy to find an explicit formula for the nth partial sum; and sometimes sequences which appear superficially similar may behave entirely differently. Examples 7 and 8 illustrate this.

Example 7. Discuss the sequence of partial sums $\sum_1^n i^{-2}$.

There is no explicit algebraic formula for the nth partial sum, and since the terms decrease rather slowly a numerical approach is not particularly enlightening.

On the other hand,

$$\sum_1^n \frac{1}{i(i+1)} = \sum_1^n \left(\frac{1}{i}-\frac{1}{i+1}\right)$$
$$= 1-\frac{1}{n+1},$$

and this sequence tends to the limit 1.

1318

But $1/(i(i+1)) < 1/i^2 < 1/((i-1)i)$, so that

$$\sum_1^n \frac{1}{i(i+1)} < \sum_1^n \frac{1}{i^2} < \sum_2^n \frac{1}{(i-1)i} + 1$$

$$\Rightarrow \quad 1 - \frac{1}{n+1} < \sum_1^n \frac{1}{i^2} < 2 - \frac{1}{n},$$

and it is intuitively obvious (though not yet proved) that the sequence has a limit between 1 and 2. The limit is, in fact, $\frac{1}{6}\pi^2$.

Example 8. Discuss the sequence of partial sums $\sum_1^n i^{-1}$.

Again, there is no explicit algebraic formula for the nth partial sum, and a numerical approach is inconclusive. But the terms are respectively larger than those of the series

$$1 + \tfrac{1}{2} + \tfrac{1}{4} + \tfrac{1}{4} + \tfrac{1}{8} + \tfrac{1}{8} + \tfrac{1}{8} + \tfrac{1}{8} + \tfrac{1}{16} + \ldots$$

in which two terms are equal to $\frac{1}{4}$, four equal to $\frac{1}{8}$, eight to $\frac{1}{16}$, and so on. Each time the number of terms is doubled, $\frac{1}{2}$ is added to the sum, so that $f(2^n) = 1 + \frac{1}{2}n$. This sequence tends to infinity, and therefore so does the original sequence of partial sums.

This is a very surprising result, and becomes even more surprising when we reflect that even if the first million terms were replaced by zeros, the partial sums would still diverge to $+\infty$, even though every term of the series is less than 10^{-6}.

3.2   Convergence and the behaviour of terms. We say that a series *converges* if the sequence of its partial sums converges to a limit. Suppose we write a general series in the form

$$u_1 + u_2 + u_3 + u_4 + \ldots$$

and its nth partial sum

$$f(n) = u_1 + u_2 + u_3 + u_4 + \ldots + u_n.$$

Now if the sequence $f(n)$ tends to a limit l, then from some point on the values of $f(n)$ will be within k of l, where k is as small as we like. Since both $f(n)$ and $f(n+1)$ are within k of l, their difference

$$u_{n+1} = f(n+1) - f(n) < 2k.$$

Since this can be made as small as we please, we have that $u_{n+1} \to 0$.

The terms of a convergent series tend to zero.

Example 8 is very important because it shows us that

The converse of this statement is not true.

It is a much more difficult problem to establish conditions on the terms of a series to ensure that it will be convergent; we shall content ourselves with one or two simple tests which can be derived from our basic assumption that a bounded increasing sequence has a limit.

1. If we can show that the partial sums of a series of positive terms are all less than a fixed number A, then the series converges.

Proof. $u_i > 0$ for all $i \Rightarrow f(n)$ is an increasing sequence.

It is given that $f(n)$ is a bounded sequence.

Hence $f(n)$ tends to a limit.

2. If a series is convergent when every term is positive, it is also convergent when the signs of any number of terms are changed.

Proof. Let $p(n)$ be the sum of the terms that remain positive in the first n terms of the series. Let $q(n)$ be the sum of the terms that have their signs made negative in these n terms.

Then $f(n) = p(n) + q(n) \Rightarrow p(n) < f(n)$ and $q(n) < f(n)$.

Since the series is convergent, $f(n)$ is bounded; hence $p(n)$ and $q(n)$ are bounded and increasing and tend to limits p and q. When the signs are changed, the partial sum of the first n terms is

$$g(n) = p(n) - q(n) \to p - q.$$

3. If Σu_i and Σv_i are two series of positive terms, and (except possibly for a finite number of terms at the beginning)

$$u_i < v_i \quad \text{for all } i,$$

then Σu_i is convergent if Σv_i is convergent.

For Σu_i is increasing and bounded, since it is less than the limit of Σv_i.

3.3   Taylor approximations. We shall now apply these results to some familiar Taylor approximations that we have met during the course.

The exponential series. We know (Chapter 29, Section 8) that a Taylor approximation for e^x is

$$f(n) = 1 + \frac{x}{1!} + \frac{x^2}{2!} + \frac{x^3}{3!} + \frac{x^4}{4!} + \ldots + \frac{x^n}{n!}.$$

There are two questions that we naturally ask: (a) as n increases, does $f(n)$ tend to a limit? (b) is this limit e^x? To answer (a), we first note that by (2) above it is sufficient to prove that $f(n)$ tends to a limit when x is positive; if so, it will also tend to a limit when the sign of x is changed.

Now, whatever value x has, ultimately we shall have $n > 2x$. From then on, each term will be less than half its predecessor, and

$$f(n+k) < 1 + \frac{x}{1!} + \frac{x^2}{2!} + \frac{x^3}{3!} + \frac{x^4}{4!} + \ldots + \frac{x^n}{n!} (1 + \tfrac{1}{2} + \tfrac{1}{4} + \tfrac{1}{8} + \ldots + (\tfrac{1}{2})^k).$$

The series in brackets is a GP whose sum is infinity to 2. Hence $f(n+k)$ is bounded, and increasing (since all the terms are positive), and therefore, by our basic assumption, it tends to a limit. This is, in fact, a particular case of (3) above.

To prove that this limit is e^x we need a more sophisticated approach. Integration by parts gives

$$I_k = \int_0^x \frac{t^k}{k!} e^{-t} dt = \frac{-x^k}{k!} e^{-x} + \int_0^x \frac{t^{k-1}}{(k-1)!} e^{-t} dt,$$

so that
$$\frac{x^k}{k!} = e^x(I_{k-1} - I_k).$$

Hence, by addition,

$$f(n) = 1 + e^x\{(I_0 - I_1) + (I_1 - I_2) + \ldots + (I_{n-1} - I_n)\} = 1 + e^x(I_0 - I_n).$$

Now
$$I_0 = \int_0^x e^{-t} dt = 1 - e^{-x},$$

so that we have
$$f(n) = e^x - e^x . I_n.$$

But
$$\int_0^x \frac{t^n}{n!} dt < e^x . I_n < \int_0^x e^x \frac{t^n}{n!} dt,$$

since $e^{-x} \leqslant e^{-t} \leqslant 1$ over the range of integration, $(x > 0)$.

Hence
$$\frac{x^{n+1}}{(n+1)!} < e^x - f(n) < \frac{x^{n+1}}{(n+1)!} . e^x.$$

But $x^{n+1}/\{(n+1)\}!$, being the $(n+2)$th term of the Taylor approximation which we have just proved to be convergent, must tend to zero. This means that $e^x - f(n)$ must tend to zero, which is to say that $f(n)$ converges to e^x. The reader can supply the modifications when $x < 0$. We may therefore write

$$e^x = 1 + \frac{x}{1!} + \frac{x^2}{2!} + \frac{x^3}{3!} + \frac{x^4}{4!} + \ldots + \frac{x^n}{n!} + \ldots \quad \text{for all values of } x,$$

where the *infinite series* on the right-hand side means the limit of the partial sums $f(n)$ as $n \to \infty$.

From (2) above we can deduce immediately that the Taylor approximations

$$\sin x = x - \frac{x^3}{3!} + \frac{x^5}{5!} - \frac{x^7}{7!} + \ldots,$$

$$\cos x = 1 - \frac{x^2}{2!} + \frac{x^4}{4!} - \frac{x^6}{6!} + \ldots,$$

$$\sinh x = x + \frac{x^3}{3!} + \frac{x^5}{5!} + \frac{x^7}{7!} + \ldots,$$

$$\cosh x = 1 + \frac{x^2}{2!} + \frac{x^4}{4!} + \frac{x^6}{6!} + \ldots$$

are convergent, and a similar argument can be used to show that the limits are in fact the stated functions of x for all values of x. Such infinite series are usually called *Taylor series*, or Taylor expansions; they are usually convergent only for restricted domains of x, as the following example shows.

3.4 The logarithmic series. In Chapter 29, p. 894, we obtained the Taylor approximation of degree n to $\log(1+x)$ in the form

$$\log(1+x) = x - \frac{x^2}{2} + \frac{x^3}{3} - \frac{x^4}{4} + \dots + (-1)^n \frac{x^n}{n}.$$

Does the series on the right converge to a limit as $n \to \infty$?

To begin with, (2) of Section 3.2 assures us that we need only consider the series when every term is positive

$$f(n) = x + \frac{x^2}{2} + \frac{x^3}{3} + \frac{x^4}{4} + \dots + \frac{x^n}{n} \quad (x > 0).$$

Next, it is clear that each term of $f(n)$ is less than the corresponding term of the GP
$$x + x^2 + x^3 + x^4 + \dots + x^n,$$

which is convergent so long as $x < 1$. Hence, by (3), the series converges when $-1 < x < 1$. Example 8 shows that the series for $\log(1+x)$ diverges when $x = -1$, and it obviously diverges for any numerically greater value of x. It can be shown that it actually converges when $x = 1$, but more subtle arguments are required to show this, and also to prove that the limit of the series is in fact $\log(1+x)$ in all cases when it converges; we shall not go into these. In point of fact the series is quite useless for practical computation unless $|x|$ is appreciably less than 1.

Summarizing these results, we have

$$\log(1+x) = x - \frac{x^2}{2} + \frac{x^3}{3} - \frac{x^4}{4} + \dots \quad \text{for} \quad |x| < 1,$$

$$-\log(1-x) = x + \frac{x^2}{2} + \frac{x^3}{3} + \frac{x^4}{4} + \dots \quad \text{for} \quad |x| < 1,$$

and
$$\log 2 = 1 - \tfrac{1}{2} + \tfrac{1}{3} - \tfrac{1}{4} + \dots;$$

this last series is a somewhat academic curiosity. From the first two we can derive a series which is sometimes useful:

$$\tfrac{1}{2} \log \frac{1+x}{1-x} = x + \frac{x^3}{3} + \frac{x^5}{5} + \dots, \quad \text{for} \quad |x| < 1.$$

Exercise D

1. In Example 6, how many terms must be taken before the partial sum is within (a) 10^{-3}, (b) 10^{-6} of its limit? Repeat with the first term $\frac{1}{2}$, and the multiplier (i) $\frac{1}{2}$, (ii) $\frac{1}{3}$, (iii) $\frac{19}{20}$.

2. Can you derive a general result for the GP $a + ar + ar^2 + \dots$ to indicate after how many terms the sum is within (a) 1 %, (b) 0·01 % of its limit? How does this formula break down when $r \geqslant 1$?

Apply the result to the series of Question 1.

3. Use partial fractions, as in Example 7, to find the sums

$$\sum_{1}^{n} \frac{1}{i(i+1)(i+2)} \quad \text{and} \quad \sum_{1}^{n} \frac{1}{i(i+1)(i+2)(i+3)}$$

and to find after how many terms they approach within 10^{-3} of their limits. Evaluate the first six partial sums of each series from the original definitions.

4. By differentiation, by multiplication by $(1-r)^2$, or otherwise, guess a formula for $\sum_{1}^{n} ir^{i-1}$.

Verify that your formula gives the correct result for the first six partial sums of the sequence $1 + \frac{2}{10} + \frac{3}{100} + \frac{4}{1000} + \dots$; find out when the series with $r = \frac{1}{2}$ approaches within 10^{-3} of its limit; and prove the formula by induction.

4. LIMITS OF FUNCTIONS

From time to time we have had occasion to make such statements as

$$\frac{1}{x} \to 0 \quad \text{as} \quad x \to \infty,$$

or

$$\frac{x^2 - 1}{x - 1} \to 2 \quad \text{as} \quad x \to 1;$$

it is time to look into the matter a little more closely. We have written these two statements as

$$\lim_{x \to \infty} \frac{1}{x} = 0 \quad \text{and} \quad \lim_{x \to 1} \frac{x^2 - 1}{x - 1} = 2.$$

In both cases we are dealing with functions of x; in the first case we want to know what happens to $f(x)$ when x is large; in the second case we are interested in the behaviour of $f(x)$ near a point where it happens to be undefined.

4.1 Behaviour of functions of x for large x. The characteristic of $1/x$ as x becomes large is that it can be made as small as we like by taking x sufficiently large. If we wish $1/x$ to be smaller than 10^{-6}, we have only to take x larger than 10^6, and so on. Clearly this is a 'challenge and response' situation once again: we may write

For every positive number h there is a number A such that

$$x > A \quad \Rightarrow \quad 0 < 1/x < h.$$

Now $1/x$ happens always to be positive for large positive x; this is not a necessary part of the behaviour of a function which tends to a limit for large x. The function $(\sin x)/x$, for example, oscillates between positive and negative values in successive intervals of π, but it still settles down to zero quite happily for large x. We therefore frame the general definition as follows:

Definition. If for every positive number h there is a number A such that

$$x > A \quad \Rightarrow \quad |f(x)-c| < h,$$

then we say that $f(x)$ tends to c as x tends to infinity, and write

$$f(x) \to c \quad \text{as} \quad x \to \infty, \quad \text{or} \quad \lim_{x \to \infty} f(x) = c.$$

From the discussion in Chapter 5, it is clear that, for example,

$$\frac{2x+1}{x-1} \to 2 \quad \text{as} \quad x \to \infty,$$

whereas $x^2/(x-1)$ increases without limit and

$$\lim_{x \to \infty} \frac{x^2}{x-1}$$

does not exist. It is obvious how the definition should be modified for the case which x tends to $-\infty$. In many cases the two limits are the same: we could write

$$\lim_{|x| \to \infty} 1/x = 0,$$

by which we mean that, for every positive number h there is a number A such that

$$|x| > A \quad \Rightarrow \quad \left|\frac{1}{x}\right| < h.$$

4.2 Behaviour of functions as x tends to a. In many cases we are not interested so much in the behaviour of a function as x tends to infinity, as in its behaviour in the neighbourhood of a point a. Functions such as

$$f: x \to \frac{x^2-1}{x-1}$$

arise when we try to find the derivative of x^2 at $x = 1$. This function is not defined for $x = 1$, but, when x is near 1, $f(x)$ is certainly near 2, and $f(x)$ can be made as near to 2 as we please by taking x sufficiently near 1. The 'challenge and response' situation has appeared once again: we write

$$f(x) \to 2 \quad \text{as} \quad x \to 1, \quad \text{or} \quad \lim_{x \to 1} f(x) = 2,$$

meaning that:

For every positive number h, there is a number k, such that

$$|x-1| < k \quad \Rightarrow \quad |f(x)-2| < h.$$

Given any standard or nearness h, we can ensure that $f(x)$ is within h of 2 for *all* x within a certain neighbourhood of 1, whose half-width k is determined for us by the choice of h. If, whenever challenged with an h, we can always respond with a k, then $f(x)$ tends to a limit as $x \to 1$. Generally we may give the following definition:

Definition. If for every positive number h there is a number k, such that

$$|x-a| < k \quad \Rightarrow \quad |f(x)-c| < h,$$

then we write

$$f(x) \to c \quad \text{as} \quad x \to a, \quad \text{or} \quad \lim_{x \to a} f(x) = c.$$

5. CONTINUITY

All the analysis we have used hitherto has been concerned primarily with the ideas of *derivative* and *integral*, and for these we have thought in terms of *continuous* functions; and although there was a short discussion of continuity on pp. 155–9 we have been more concerned with the ideas which lie behind the three italicized words in their simplest form, without asking many questions about when difficulties may arise.

The reader should work Exercise E, thinking how the ideas of Section 4 can help towards an understanding of what is happening.

Exercise E

1. Find if possible $\lim_{x \to 0} f(x)$, and $f(0)$ for the following functions. Which are continuous at 0?

(a) $f: x \to [x]$; (b) $f: x \to [1-x^2]$;
(c) $f: x \to [x^2]$; (d) $f: x \to 1-|x|$;
(e) $f: x \to 1+x.|x|$; (f) $f: x \to x/x$.

2. How is the question of continuity connected with the rest of the answer in each part of Question 1?

3. What can you say about $\lim_{x \to a} f(x)$ for each value of a for the following functions? Where are they continuous?

(a) $f: x \to 1/x$; (b) $f: x \to x/(x^2+1)$; (c) $f: x \to [x]/x$;
(d) $f(x) = 0$ if x is rational, $f(x) = 1$ otherwise;
(e) $f(x) = 0$ if x is rational, $f(x) = x$ otherwise.

4. Where is the following function continuous, and where has it a derivative? Where is the derivative continuous?

$$f(x) = 0 \quad \text{if} \quad x < 0; \quad f(x) = 2-x^2 \quad \text{if} \quad 0 \leqslant x < 1;$$

$$f(x) = (x-2)^2 \quad \text{if} \quad 1 \leqslant x < 3; \quad f(x) = 2 \quad \text{if} \quad 3 \leqslant x < 4;$$

$$f(x) = 6-x \quad \text{if} \quad 4 \leqslant x < 6; \quad f(x) = 0 \quad \text{if} \quad x \geqslant 6.$$

5. Show that, if
$$\lim_{h \to 0} \frac{f(a+h)-f(a)}{h}$$
exists and is equal to $f'(a)$, then
$$\lim_{h \to 0} \frac{f(a+h)-f(a-h)}{2h}$$
exists and is equal to $f'(a)$; but give an example to show that the converse is not true.

5.1   Redefining continuity. Exercise E gives a number of examples of discontinuities, and should have made it clear that $\lim\limits_{x \to a} f(x)$ may be entirely different from $f(a)$, and that either may exist independently of the other. This, in fact, is the essence of a discontinuity, and we may provisionally redefine continuity as follows:

Definition. f is said to be *continuous* at a if
$$\lim_{x \to a} f(x) = f(a).$$

This can immediately be rewritten in 'challenge and response' form, from our knowledge of limits:

Theorem. f is continuous at a if and only if for every positive number h there is a number k such that
$$|x-a| < k \Rightarrow |f(x)-f(a)| < h.$$

The theorem follows at once from the definition of a limit.

That this is a redefinition only can be seen from the fact that the expression on the right in the statement of the theorem is the condition that $f(x)$ is a member of a general neighbourhood of $f(a)$; the expression on the left is the condition that x should belong to a particular neighbourhood of a, chosen by ourselves; and the implication sign leads us to the statement in its original terms:

If the inverse image of every neighbourhood of the point $f(a)$ of the range of a function f includes a neighbourhood of a, then f is continuous at a (see p. 157).

Note that the word 'neighbourhood' here simply means a symmetrical interval centred on the point.

5.2   Derivatives. In Chapter 7 we took as our definition of a derivative one of the equivalent forms
$$\lim_{h \to 0} \frac{f(a+h)-f(a)}{h} \quad \text{or} \quad \lim_{b \to a} \frac{f(b)-f(a)}{b-a}$$
provided that they exist. (Notice that the existence of the third form of the limit given on p. 201 is not enough to ensure that the others exist; thus,
$$\lim_{h \to 0} \frac{f(a+h)-f(a-h)}{2h}$$

exists and is equal to zero for the function $f: x \to |x|$ at $x = 0$, though clearly the derivative does not exist there.)

When we find the derivative of $f: x \to x^2$ at $x = 2$, say, we have now defined it as

$$\lim_{b \to 2} \frac{b^2 - 4}{b - 2}.$$

The function
$$g: x \to \frac{x^2 - 4}{x - 2}$$

cannot include 2 in its domain; elsewhere, its images are the same as those of $h: x \to x + 2$. Its graph (see Figure 5) is therefore that of the latter function, with a point missing at $(2, 4)$.

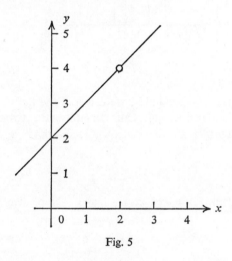

Fig. 5

There is therefore no image $g(2)$ for this function, but $\lim\limits_{x \to 2} g(x)$ exists and is equal to 4. This number, 4, is the derivative $f'(2)$; it is simply the number which plugs the gap so as to make $g(x)$ continuous at $x = 2$; it is therefore the natural value to supply for the local scale factor.

5.3   Integrals. Our definition of an integral in Chapter 22 can also be examined more carefully rather in the light of our axiom. For our definition is that $\int_a^b f(x)\,dx$ is the limit of what we have called $\overset{x=b}{\underset{x=a}{\mathbf{S}}} f(x).\delta x$, that is, the sum of rectangles as shown in Figure 6. Confining our attention to the part of the curve for which f is continuous and increasing, if we divide the base δx of a rectangle into two parts we shall either increase the sum or leave it unchanged. If therefore we keep dividing each interval into two equal parts, we shall generate a bounded increasing sequence. Now if we extended our definition by taking the lower bound of the function over each interval, we should still be able to generate such a sequence for *any* function defined over (x, b); and by our fundamental axiom this sequence has a limit.

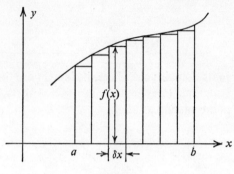

Fig. 6

Similarly, using the upper bounds, we can find the limit of another such sequence, this time decreasing. Unfortunately, the two limits may be different, but when they are the same, we have a possible wider definition of an integral.

Exercise F

1. Prove that if $f(x) \to +\infty$ and $g(x) \to 1$ as $x \to +\infty$, then $f(x).g(x) \to +\infty$ as $x \to +\infty$.

2. Prove that if $f(x) \to 0$ and $g(x) \to k$ as $x \to 0$, $f(x).g(x) \to 0$ as $x \to 0$.

3. Prove that if $f(x) \to +\infty$ and $g(x) \to 0$ as $x \to +\infty$, $f(x).g(x)$ may, by suitable choice of f and g:

    (*a*) tend to $+\infty$,   (*b*) tend to 0,
    (*c*) tend to any finite limit,   (*d*) oscillate finitely, **or**
    (*e*) oscillate infinitely.

4. Prove that if $f(x) \to k$ as $x \to a$, $(f(x))^2 \to k^2$ as $x \to a$.

5. Justify the statements

    (*a*) $\displaystyle \int_1^\infty \frac{1}{x^2}\, dx = 1;$ (*b*) $\displaystyle \int_0^1 x^{-\frac{1}{2}}\, dx = 2.$

Give careful definitions which will cover similar cases.

6. Show that $f_n : x \to x^n/(1+x^n)$ is continuous for all $x \geqslant 0$. Show also that

$$f : x \to \lim_{n \to \infty} x^n/(1+x^n)$$

is not. Sketch the graph of f_{100}.

1328

7. Show how the definition of an integral may be extended to cover functions like $[x]$; hence show how (by defining a suitable function g) $\sum_{1}^{n} f(i)$ may always be replaced by $\int_{0}^{n} g(x)\,dx$.

Show that $\sum_{1}^{n} 1/n$ lies between $(1+\log n)$ and $\log(n+1)$, and hence that the series diverges.

8. Use the definition suggested in Question 7 to show that the definitions of mean, variance and so on could all be expressed in terms of integrals rather than of sums.

9. Use the properties of limits to show that if $f'(a) = 0$ and $f''(a) < 0$ then there is an interval $(a-h, a+h)$ such that

$$x \in (a-h, a+h) \Rightarrow f(x) < f(a).$$

Is the converse true?

10. Investigate the existence of the derivative at 0 of $f: x \to x\sin(1/x)$.

REVISION EXERCISES

41. RATIONAL FORMS

1. Express
$$\frac{x^3+x^2-5}{x(x-1)(x+2)}$$
as a polynomial together with a set of partial fractions.

2. Evaluate
$$\int_{\sqrt{3}}^{2+\sqrt{3}} \frac{dx}{(x-1)^2(x^2+1)}.$$

3. By expressing
$$\frac{1}{(x^2+x+1)(x^3+x+1)}$$
in partial fractions, or otherwise, find polynomials P and Q so that
$$P(x^2+x+1)+Q(x^3+x+1) = 1.$$
Hence find a solution in integers of the equation $111p+1011q = 3$, and explain why there can be no solution of $111p+1011q = 1$.

4. Find the condition for
$$f: x \to \frac{x-a}{(x-b)(x-c)}$$
to have a gap in its range. If $a = b+c$, show that the gap extends from
$$\frac{1}{(\sqrt{b}-\sqrt{c})^2} \quad \text{to} \quad \frac{1}{(\sqrt{b}+\sqrt{c})^2} \quad (b, c > 0).$$

5. Prove that the sum of the first k terms of the series
$$\frac{2}{1.3}+\frac{2}{3.5}+\frac{2}{5.7}+\dots+\frac{2}{(2n-1)(2n+1)}+\dots \quad \text{is} \quad 1-\frac{1}{2k+1}.$$
How many terms of this series must be taken to bring the sum within 10^{-6} of its limiting value?

6. Decompose the rational function
$$\frac{x-1}{x(x+1)(x^2+1)}$$
into real partial fractions.

By setting $y = x-1$ in your decomposition, or otherwise, show that, if $0 < x < \sqrt{3}$, the function can be expanded as a convergent series of ascending powers of $(x-1)$:
$$\frac{x-1}{x(x+1)(x^2+1)} = a_0+a_1(x-1)+a_2(x-1)^2+a_3(x-1)^3+\dots,$$
where $\quad a_0 = 0, \quad a_1 = \frac{1}{4}, \quad a_2 = -\frac{5}{8} \quad$ and $\quad a_3 = \frac{15}{16}.$

(A correct argument will be accepted if it leads to a number other than $\sqrt{3}$ in the inequalities $0 < x < \sqrt{3}$.) (OC)

1330

42. LINEAR DEPENDENCE

1. Reduce to echelon form and solve the equations $x - 3y = 2$, $2x - 3y = 7$. For what value of p does this solution satisfy $3x + 4y = p$? Interpret this in terms of the lines in a plane given by the above three equations, and also in terms of the points in space $(1, 2, 3)$, $(-3, -3, 4)$ and $(2, 7, p)$.

2. Find a if the three equations:

$$x - y + z = 0,$$
$$3x - y + 2z = 0,$$
$$ax + y + z = 0,$$

have a solution other than the trivial solution $x = y = z = 0$.

Show that in this case the vectors

$$\begin{pmatrix} 1 \\ -1 \\ 1 \end{pmatrix}, \quad \begin{pmatrix} 3 \\ -1 \\ 2 \end{pmatrix}, \quad \begin{pmatrix} a \\ 1 \\ 1 \end{pmatrix}$$

are linearly dependent, and exhibit the linear relation connecting them.

3. Show that the planes

$$x - 2y + 2z = 17, \quad 3x + 15y - z = -12, \quad 2x + 5y + z = 7$$

have a line in common, and find parametric equations for it. What does this tell you about the vectors

$$\begin{pmatrix} 1 \\ 3 \\ 2 \end{pmatrix}, \quad \begin{pmatrix} -2 \\ 15 \\ 5 \end{pmatrix}, \quad \begin{pmatrix} 2 \\ -1 \\ 1 \end{pmatrix}, \quad \begin{pmatrix} 17 \\ -12 \\ 7 \end{pmatrix}?$$

What can you say about the space into which three-dimensional space is transformed by the matrix

$$\begin{pmatrix} 1 & -2 & 2 \\ 3 & 15 & -1 \\ 2 & 5 & 1 \end{pmatrix}?$$

Does the vector $\begin{pmatrix} 17 \\ -12 \\ 7 \end{pmatrix}$ lie in the transformed space?

4. (a) Are the three-dimensional Euclidean vectors

$$\begin{pmatrix} 4 \\ 2 \\ 1 \end{pmatrix}, \quad \begin{pmatrix} 2 \\ 0 \\ 1 \end{pmatrix}, \quad \begin{pmatrix} 3 \\ 1 \\ 1 \end{pmatrix}$$

linearly dependent or independent?

Interpret your answer geometrically.

(b) Discuss the solution of the equations

$$x - y + z = 1,$$
$$x + (\lambda^2 - \lambda - 1)y + (\lambda + 1)z = 2,$$
$$2x + (\lambda^2 - \lambda - 2)y + 2(\lambda + 1)z = 3,$$

for all real values of λ.

(OC)

5. P, Q, R, S are coplanar, but no three of them are collinear. Prove
(a) that there is a relation

$$a\mathbf{p} + b\mathbf{q} + c\mathbf{r} + d\mathbf{s} = \mathbf{0}$$

between their position vectors, with a, b, c, d not all zero;
(b) that, apart from a constant multiplier, there is only one.

6. Prove by induction that in a space of n dimensions (that is, one in which any vector can be expressed in terms of a *basis* of n independent vectors), any $n+1$ vectors are linearly dependent.

(To establish the inductive step, suppose it true for $n = k$ and consider $k+2$ vectors $\mathbf{r}_i$ in a space with a basis $\mathbf{e}_1, \mathbf{e}_2, ..., \mathbf{e}_k, \mathbf{e}_{k+1}$. Unless they all fall in a k-space (and are dependent), one (say $\mathbf{r}_{k+2}$) contains $\mathbf{e}_{k+1}$. By expressing $\mathbf{e}_{k+1}$ in terms of $\mathbf{r}_{k+2}$ and $\mathbf{e}_1 ... \mathbf{e}_k$ we can now obtain $k+1$ vectors of the form $\mathbf{r}_k + \alpha . \mathbf{r}_{k+2}$ which lie in k-space and are dependent.)

43. CONVERGENCE

1. $g_1(t) = \frac{1}{6}(1 - \frac{5}{6}t)^{-1}$ generates the probabilities of throwing a six with a fair die on the 1st, 2nd, 3rd, ... throw. Verify that the sum of this sequence converges to 1. Repeat for $g_2(t) = \frac{1}{36}(1 - \frac{5}{6}t)^{-2}$, and for $g_1'(t)$; what is the limit in the latter case, and what does it represent?

2. If $u_n = (1 + (1/n))^n$, show by using the Binomial Theorem that

$$u_n < 1 + 1 + \frac{1}{2!} + \frac{1}{3!} + ... + \frac{1}{n!}.$$

Use test 3, p. 1320, to show that $\{u_n\}$ converges to a limit less than 3.

3. Prove that $\sqrt[3]{3}$ is irrational. (Suppose it equal to p/q, a fraction in its lowest terms, and prove a contradiction.)

4. Investigate the following promotion scheme. Grades 1, 2 and 3 are allotted to each member of the Popular Democratic Army at the half-yearly elections. Long experience shows that a soldier graded 1 is invariably re-graded 2; a soldier graded 2 has a $\frac{1}{6}$ chance of promotion and a $\frac{1}{2}$ chance of demotion; a soldier graded 3 has a $\frac{1}{3}$ chance of promotion, to grade 2 only.

5. $a_1 + \cfrac{1}{a_2 + \cfrac{1}{a_3 + ... \cfrac{1}{a_n}}}$ is a *continued fraction*. Its value is equal to p_n/q_n, where

$$p_i = a_i p_{i-1} + p_{i-2}, \quad q_i = a_i q_{i-1} + q_{i-2}.$$

Prove this statement. Prove also that

$$p_i/q_i - p_{i-1}/q_{i-1} = (-1)^i/q_i q_{i-1}.$$

Hence prove that if (a) $a_i = 1$ for all i, (b) $a_i = 2$ for all i, the sequence converges, and find the limits.

6. A sequence of numbers x_0, x_1, x_2 is governed by the following equations:

$$x_0 = 1, \quad x_1 = 2, \quad 3x_n = x_{n-1} + 2x_{n-2} \quad (n = 2, 3, \ldots).$$

If x_n is represented by the point P_n on the real number line, describe geometrically the position of P_n in relation to P_{n-1} and P_{n-2}. Hence or otherwise give an intuitive argument to indicate that the sequence has a limit l.

Suggest, with reasons, either two inequalities governing l, or, preferably, a value of l.

You wish to compute l to an accuracy of 10^{-12}. Construct a flow diagram for a computer programme which you hope will achieve this. Explain, with reasons, why your programme would, or would not, give *with certainty* the value of l to the required accuracy.

Make an estimate of the number of terms of the sequence which the programme will calculate to obtain the specified accuracy. (OC)

44

REVISION PROJECTS

This chapter contains a set of questions on each of 18 different topics. The topics are outside the Advanced Level syllabus; some of them belong more properly to Further Mathematics. But the techniques that are employed are those covered in the advanced course, so that the process of working through a project will provide useful revision. We have tried to give as wide a coverage as possible, but there are, of course, a great many other topics which might have been included.

Some of the questions are deliberately open-ended, to encourage your own research. A good mathematical library will contain many books dealing with the topics here. Some of them are well-worked fields, and fuller treatment will easily be found. Others, however, after only a little further investigation, will be found to involve questions that are as yet completely unanswered. We hope this rather random sample will be found useful and stimulating, and that it will give you some idea of the flavour and fascination of more advanced mathematics.

1. FINITE ARITHMETIC

1. Show that, if p is a prime, and a is any integer, then no two of $a, 2a, ..., (p-1)a$ can be equivalent modulo p.

2. Deduce that $a.2a.3a ... (p-1)a = (p-1)!(\mod p)$, and hence that

$$a^{p-1} = 1(\mod p) \quad \text{(Fermat's Theorem)}.$$

3. Now consider a possible converse. If $a^n = 1 \ (\mod p)$, does it follow that $n = p-1$? Show, by considering $p = 7$, $a = 2$, that there are cases, other than the trivial $a = \pm 1$, for which it does not.

4. If, for a given a, n is the *smallest* index for which $a^n = 1$, show, by writing $p-1 = nb+k$, $k < n$, that n divides $p-1$.

5. Show that the groups $\{Z_p^*, \times\}$ and $\{Z_{p-1}, +\}$ are isomorphic, provided an a can be found so that $n = p-1$ is the smallest n for which $a^n = 1 \ (\mod p)$. Such an a is called a *primitive root* in Z_p.

6. Consider in detail the isomorphism for $p = 13$, $a = 2$. For which elements x in $\{Z_{12}, +\}$ will it be true that $n = p-1$ is the smallest n for which $nx = 0 \ (\mod p-1)$? Deduce which are the primitive roots in Z_{13}.

7. Show that 10 is a primitive root in Z_7, but not in Z_{13}. What does this tell you about the decimal expressions for $\frac{1}{7}$ and $\frac{1}{13}$? Investigate other decimal expressions similarly.

1334

8. Use the isomorphism in Question 6 to solve the equation

$$x^3 = 5$$

in Z_{13}.

2. QUADRATICS

1. Show, by completing the square, that $x^2+4x+13$ is positive for all values of x.

2. Evaluate $$\int \frac{dx}{x^2+4x+13} \quad \text{and} \quad \int \frac{dx}{\sqrt{(x^2+4x+13)}}.$$

3. Show that $$f: x \to \frac{2x+7}{x^2+4x+13}$$

is everywhere continuous and find the greatest and least values of $f(x)$. Sketch the graph of $y = f(x)$.

4. The curve whose equation is

$$x^2+2xy+4y^2-2x+2y+6 = 0$$

lies wholly within the rectangle $a \leqslant x \leqslant b$, $c \leqslant y \leqslant d$, whose sides it touches. Find a, b, c and d.

5. Find the solution set for the inequality $5x^2-7x-6 \leqslant 0$.

6. Express the equation

$$4x^2+9y^2+4x-24y-8 = 0$$

in the form $$\lambda(x-p)^2+\mu(y-q)^2 = 1.$$

What is the relation of the point (p, q) to the locus given by this equation?
    Show that a suitable combination of transformations will map this locus onto the circle $x^2+y^2 = 1$, and hence sketch it.

3. OUTER PRODUCT

If **a**, **b** are two vectors in a plane, we define their *outer product* [ab] to be the area of the parallelogram formed by **a** and **b**, counted positive when the shortest rotation from **a** to **b** is counter-clockwise, and negative when it is clockwise.

1. Prove that [ab] $= |$a$| \,.\, |$b$| \sin \theta$, where θ is the angle from **a** to **b**.

2. Prove that [ab] $= -$[ba], [aa] $= 0$, and [ab] $= 0 \Leftrightarrow$ **a**$=$**0**, or **b** $= \lambda$**a** for some scalar λ.

3. Prove that [a(b$+$c)] $=$ [ab]$+$[ac] and [a(λb)] $= \lambda$[ab].

4. Prove from 2 and 3 that [(a$-$b)(a$+$b)] $= 2$[ab], and explain the meaning of this in terms of area.

5. Prove from the definition that [ij] $= 1$.

6. Use 3 and 5 to show that if $\mathbf{a} = a_1\mathbf{i} + a_2\mathbf{j}, \mathbf{b} = b_2\mathbf{i} + b_2\mathbf{j}$, then $[\mathbf{ab}] = a_1 b_2 - a_1 b_2$.

7. Interpret geometrically $[\mathbf{a}(\mathbf{b} + \lambda\mathbf{a})] = [\mathbf{ab}]$.

8. Prove that the area of a triangle ABC is $\frac{1}{2}\{[\mathbf{bc}] + [\mathbf{ca}] + [\mathbf{ab}]\}$, where $\mathbf{a}$, $\mathbf{b}$, $\mathbf{c}$ are the position vectors of A, B, C.

9. Given a triangle ABC, take points D, E, F on its sides such that

$$BD/DC = CE/EA = AF/FB = 2.$$

Let BE, CF meet at P; CF, AD at Q; AD, BE at R.
  (*a*) Take origin at A; show that

$$\mathbf{q} = \lambda(\mathbf{b} + 2\mathbf{c}) = \mu\mathbf{c} + (1 - \mu).\tfrac{2}{3}\mathbf{b}$$

for some λ, μ, and hence express $\mathbf{q}$ in terms of $\mathbf{b}$ and $\mathbf{c}$.
  (*b*) Find $\mathbf{r}$ and $\mathbf{p}$ similarly.
  (*c*) Express the area of the triangle PQR in terms of $[\mathbf{bc}]$ and hence find $\triangle PQR/\triangle ABC$.

10. Generalize 9 if $BD/DC = CE/EA = AF/FB = n$.
  (PQR has been called the *nedian* triangle of ABC.)

4. NON-SQUARE MATRICES

1. If
$$A = \begin{pmatrix} 3 & 4 \\ 2 & 3 \\ 1 & 2 \end{pmatrix} \quad \text{and} \quad B = \begin{pmatrix} 3 & -4 & 0 \\ -2 & 3 & 0 \end{pmatrix},$$

evaluate the products AB and BA. What do you notice?

2. Find a matrix C of the form
$$\begin{pmatrix} 0 & a & b \\ 0 & c & d \end{pmatrix}$$

so that $CA = I$. Show that $(pB + qC)A = I$ for certain values of p and q, and say what is the restriction on p and q for this to be true.

3. If we call B and C 'left-inverses' of A, show that

$$D = \begin{pmatrix} 6 & -10 & 3 \\ -4 & 7 & -2 \end{pmatrix}$$

is also a left-inverse, and express D in terms of B and C.

4. Show that
$$A \begin{pmatrix} x \\ y \end{pmatrix} = \begin{pmatrix} 1 \\ 2 \\ 1 \end{pmatrix} \Rightarrow \begin{pmatrix} x \\ y \end{pmatrix} = B \begin{pmatrix} 1 \\ 2 \\ 1 \end{pmatrix},$$

but that the implication sign cannot be reversed. Does the 'solution' obtained in this way satisfy the original equations? Explain the result.

5. For what values of a do the equations

$$\left.\begin{array}{l} 3x+4y = 1, \\ 2x+3y = 2, \\ x+2y = a, \end{array}\right\} \quad \text{have a solution?}$$

What does this mean in terms of the vectors

$$\begin{pmatrix} 3 \\ 2 \\ 1 \end{pmatrix}, \quad \begin{pmatrix} 4 \\ 3 \\ 2 \end{pmatrix}, \quad \begin{pmatrix} 1 \\ 2 \\ a \end{pmatrix}?$$

6. Show that

$$\begin{pmatrix} x \\ y \\ z \end{pmatrix} = \mathbf{A} \begin{pmatrix} 1 \\ 2 \end{pmatrix} \Rightarrow \mathbf{D} \begin{pmatrix} x \\ y \\ z \end{pmatrix} = \begin{pmatrix} 1 \\ 2 \end{pmatrix},$$

but that, once again, the implication sign cannot be reversed.
Do the equations

$$\left.\begin{array}{l} 6x-10y+3z = 1 \\ -4x+ 7y-2z = 2 \end{array}\right\} \quad \text{have a solution?}$$

7. Show that $\mathbf{D} \begin{pmatrix} x \\ y \\ z \end{pmatrix} = \begin{pmatrix} 0 \\ 0 \end{pmatrix} \Rightarrow y = 0 \quad \text{and} \quad 2x+z = 0.$

Use this to write down
  (a) the most general solution of the equations

$$\left.\begin{array}{l} 6x-10y+3z = 1, \\ -4x+ 7y-2z = 2, \end{array}\right\}$$

  (b) the most general 'right-inverse' of $\mathbf{D}$.

8. Give examples of situations, and interpret them geometrically, in which two equations in three unknowns have:
  (a) no solutions;   (b) an infinity of solutions.
  Can they ever have a unique solution?

9. Repeat Question 8 for three equations in two unknowns.

10. Consider the matrices corresponding to the cases you have written down in Questions 8 and 9, and examine their maximum number of independent rows and columns in each case. State any conclusions you think might be drawn.

5. NETWORKS AND SQUARES

1. Find the currents in each arm of the network shown, if the resistance in each arm is 1 ohm.

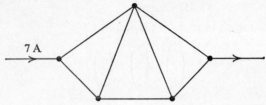

2. Represent a wire carrying a current of x amperes through a potential difference of y volts by a rectangle x units wide and y units long.

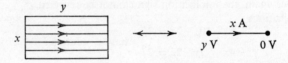

Show that for each link in the above network the corresponding rectangle is a square.

3. Explain why the network corresponds to this dissection of a rectangle into squares, and give the number of units in the side of each square.

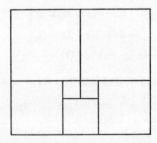

4. What is the equivalent resistance of this network?

5. Now consider this network, each link again having resistance 1 Ω. Find the currents and draw the corresponding rectangle dissected into squares. Show that this solves the problem of dissecting a rectangle into a set of *different* integral-sided squares. (It is the smallest such rectangle.)

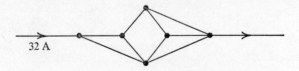

6. Complete the dimensions of this pattern of squares, and draw the corresponding network.

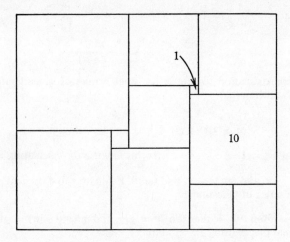

What corresponds to the area of each square, and of the whole rectangle?
What is the equivalent resistance of the network?

7. Now consider links of different resistances. Show that we now have a dissection of a rectangle into rectangles, and explain the connection between the resistance of each link and the rectangle that represents it. What do the following represent, in general?

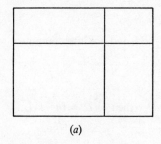

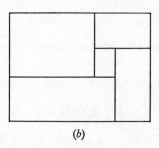

(a)   (b)

8. Investigate:
  (a) the possible uses of such diagrams in the solution of network problems;
  (b) the use of networks in the solution of dissection problems.
Find out how the problem of dividing a square into unequal squares was solved. (See, e.g. Gardner, *More Mathematical Puzzles and Diversions*; Bell, 1963.)

6. π

1. Prove that
$$\frac{1}{1+x^2} = 1 - x^2 + x^4 - x^6 + \dots + x^{4n} - \frac{x^{4n+2}}{1+x^2}.$$

Deduce that
$$x - \frac{x^3}{3} + \frac{x^5}{5} - \frac{x^7}{7} + \dots + \frac{x^{4n+1}}{4n+1}$$

is a good approximation to $\tan^{-1}x$ for small values of x. Estimate the error involved by showing that

$$\frac{x^{4n+3}}{(4n+3)(1+x^2)} < \int_0^x \frac{t^{4n+2}}{1+t^2} \, dt < \frac{x^{4n+3}}{4n+3}.$$

2. Show that $\frac{1}{4}\pi = 1 - \frac{1}{3} + \frac{1}{5} - \frac{1}{7} + \dots$. Is this any use for calculating π?

3. If $\theta + \phi = \frac{1}{4}\pi$, and $\tan\theta = \frac{2}{3}$, find $\tan\phi$. Evaluate π to 4 decimal places using this and the series of Question 1.

4. Prove that if $\tan\theta = \frac{1}{5}$, then $\tan 4\theta = \frac{120}{119}$, and $\tan(4\theta - \frac{1}{4}\pi) = \frac{1}{239}$. Evaluate π to 4 decimal places using $\frac{1}{4}\pi = 4\tan^{-1}\frac{1}{5} - \tan^{-1}\frac{1}{239}$.

5. Find π as the area of a circle of radius 1, using Simpson's rule with ten strips to find the area between $x = 0$ and $x = \frac{1}{2}$. Explain why it will not give a very good result if we use Simpson's Rule to find the area of a quadrant.

6. Prove that $2\cos\frac{1}{2}\theta = \sqrt{(2 + 2\cos\theta)} = \sin\theta / \sin\frac{1}{2}\theta$.

Prove by induction that if $u_1 = 0 \ (= 2\cos\frac{1}{2}\pi)$ and $u_{r+1} = \sqrt{(2 + u_r)}$, then $u_n = 2\cos(\pi/2^n)$. Now show that

$$u_2 u_3 \dots u_n = \frac{\sin\frac{1}{2}\pi}{\sin(\pi/2^n)} \to \frac{2^n}{\pi}.$$

Write a flow diagram to evaluate π by this method, and use it to compute π to 4 decimal places.

7. By integrating by parts, prove that if

$$I_n = \int_0^{\frac{1}{2}\pi} \sin^n\theta \, d\theta = \int_0^{\frac{1}{2}\pi} \sin^{n-1}\theta . \sin\theta \, d\theta, \quad \text{then} \quad nI_n = (n-1)I_{n-2}.$$

Prove that $I_0 = \frac{1}{2}\pi$, $I_1 = 1$, and, if we write

$$V_n = \frac{I_{2n+1}}{I_{2n}}, \quad \text{then} \quad 1 > V_n > \frac{2n}{2n+1},$$

so that $V_n \to 1$.
    Show that

$$\frac{V_n}{V_{n-1}} = \frac{2n.2n}{(2n+1)(2n-1)};$$

and, using this, that

$$\frac{1}{2}\pi = V_n \times \frac{2.2}{1.3} \times \frac{4.4}{3.5} \times \dots \times \frac{2n.2n}{(2n-1)(2n+1)}.$$

Write a flow diagram based on this formula for computing π. (It converges very slowly.)

8. Show that the result of Question 7 can be written in the form

$$\pi = \lim_{n \to \infty} \frac{2^{4n+1}(n!)^4}{(2n+1)[(2n)!]^2}.$$

9. Show, using 8, that the probability of tossing exactly n heads and n tails in $2n$ tosses of a coin is approximately $1/\sqrt{(\pi n)}$.

10. Look up Buffon's needle, and carry out a statistical experiment to determine the value of π.

11. It can be proved that

$$\frac{1}{1^4} + \frac{1}{2^4} + \frac{1}{3^4} + \cdots = \frac{\pi^4}{90}.$$

Deduce the value of $\qquad \dfrac{1}{1^4} - \dfrac{1}{2^4} + \dfrac{1}{3^4} - \cdots.$

and write a flow diagram for computing π^4 by this method.

12. Prove that $\qquad \displaystyle\int_0^1 \frac{t^4(1-t)^4}{1+t^2}\, dt = \tfrac{22}{7} - \pi.$

Show that the integral is between $\tfrac{1}{2}I$ and I, where

$$I = \int_0^1 t^4(1-t)^4 dt.$$

Evaluate I, and find bounds for the value of π.

7. CONICS

1. A conic can be defined as the locus of a point P whose distance from a fixed point S is a constant (e) times its distance from a fixed line. Construct the loci for $e = \tfrac{1}{3}, \tfrac{1}{2}, \tfrac{2}{3}, 1, \tfrac{3}{2}, 2, 3$ by the following method. Draw the fixed line down the centre of a sheet of squared paper. Take S 2 cm from it. Draw circles, centre S, with radii $\tfrac{1}{2}$ cm, 1 cm, $1\tfrac{1}{2}$ cm, 2 cm, and so on up to 8 cm, and locate points on the loci at the intersection of these circles and the lines of the squared paper.

2. Prove that the points A, A' on the axis of symmetry farthest from and nearest to S are at distances $e/(1+e)$ and $e/(e \sim 1)$ inches from S.

3. If $e \neq 1$, denote the distance AA' by $2a$, and show that the distance of S (the focus) from the fixed line (the directrix) is $a(1 \sim e^2)/e$.

4. Take the origin at the mid-point of AA', and AA' as the x-axis. Show that S is $(ae, 0)$ and the directrix $x = a/e$. Obtain the equation of the conic $(e \neq 1)$, and show that it has symmetry about both axes.

5. When $e = 1$, obtain the equation with S as origin and show that the curve is a parabola.

6. Obtain the polar equation with S as origin and SA as initial line in the form $l/r = 1 + e \cos \theta$.
  l is the length of half the chord through S perpendicular to SA.

7. A particle P moves on a conic with focus S in such a way that SP sweeps out area at a constant rate. Show that this means that $r^2\dot{\theta}$ is constant.

8. If $r^2\dot{\theta} = h$, prove that $\dot{r} = (eh/l)\sin\theta$.

Find the acceleration along PS, and show that it is proportional to $1/r^2$. Give physical examples of motion of this kind.

9. Does it make sense to say that a circle is a conic for which $e = 0$?

10. Deduce from symmetry that when $e \neq 1$ there must be a second focus S'. Prove that for the ellipse $(e < 1)$ $SP + PS' = 2a$, and for the hyperbola $(e > 1)$ $SP \sim PS' = 2a$.

11. Find the gradients of the directions in which the hyperbola $x^2 - y^2/(e^2 - 1) = a^2$ 'disappears to infinity', and show that when $e = \sqrt{2}$ they are at right-angles.

12. In this last case, find a transformation which will change the equation of the locus into $xy = c^2$ for a suitable value of c.

8. CONICS AND POLARS

The locus of a point (x, y) subject to the condition

$$(x \quad y \quad 1)\begin{pmatrix} a & h & g \\ h & b & f \\ g & f & c \end{pmatrix}\begin{pmatrix} x \\ y \\ 1 \end{pmatrix} = 0,$$

where the determinant of the square matrix is not zero, is called a *conic*. Show that, provided $\begin{vmatrix} a & h \\ h & b \end{vmatrix} \neq 0$, the mapping $(x, y) \to (x^*, y^*)$ where $x = kx^* + \alpha$, $y = ky^* + \beta$, with a suitable choice of k, α, β, will reduce this to the form

$$(x^* \quad y^*)\begin{pmatrix} a & h \\ h & b \end{pmatrix}\begin{pmatrix} x^* \\ y^* \end{pmatrix} = 1.$$

(Choose α, β so that $\begin{cases} a\alpha + h\beta + g = 0, \\ h\alpha + b\beta + f = 0. \end{cases}$ Why is this possible?)

Conics for which this is possible are called *central* conics. Show that a half-turn about the new origin leaves the locus unchanged.

The line

$$(x \quad y)\begin{pmatrix} a & h \\ h & b \end{pmatrix}\begin{pmatrix} x' \\ y' \end{pmatrix} = 1$$

is called the *polar of* (x', y') with respect to $(x \quad y)\begin{pmatrix} a & h \\ h & b \end{pmatrix}\begin{pmatrix} x \\ y \end{pmatrix} = 1$.

1. Show that the equation can also be written

$$(x' \quad y')\begin{pmatrix} a & h \\ h & b \end{pmatrix}\begin{pmatrix} x \\ y \end{pmatrix} = 1.$$

2. Hence show that if P_1 is on the polar of P_2 then P_2 is on the polar of P_1.

3. Prove that P_1 is on its own polar $\Leftrightarrow P_1$ is on the conic.

4. Prove that, if P_1 and P_2 are on the conic, then

$$(x \quad y)\begin{pmatrix} a & h \\ h & b \end{pmatrix}\begin{pmatrix} x_1+x_2 \\ y_1+y_2 \end{pmatrix} = 1 + (x_1 \quad y_1)\begin{pmatrix} a & h \\ h & b \end{pmatrix}\begin{pmatrix} x_2 \\ y_2 \end{pmatrix}$$

is the equation of the chord P_1P_2.

5. Deduce from 4 that when P_1 is on the conic, its polar is the tangent at P_1.

6. Deduce from 5 and 2 that when P_1 is outside the conic, its polar contains the points of contact of the tangents from P_1 to the conic.

7. Consider the mapping

$$\begin{pmatrix} l \\ m \end{pmatrix} \leftrightarrow \text{the line } lx+my = 1.$$

Show that under this mapping

$$\begin{pmatrix} a & h \\ h & b \end{pmatrix}\begin{pmatrix} x' \\ y' \end{pmatrix} \leftrightarrow \text{the polar of } (x', y').$$

8. Suppose that $A = \begin{pmatrix} a & h \\ h & b \end{pmatrix}$ is non-singular, and A^{-1} is its inverse. Show that if

$$\begin{pmatrix} l \\ m \end{pmatrix} \leftrightarrow \text{polar of } \begin{pmatrix} x \\ y \end{pmatrix}$$

then

$$(l \quad m)A^{-1}\begin{pmatrix} l \\ m \end{pmatrix} = (x \quad y)AA^{-1}A\begin{pmatrix} x \\ y \end{pmatrix}$$

$$= (x \quad y)A\begin{pmatrix} x \\ y \end{pmatrix};$$

deduce that $lx+my = 1$ touches the conic $\Leftrightarrow (l \quad m)A^{-1}\begin{pmatrix} l \\ m \end{pmatrix} = 1$.

9. Use 8 to write down the condition that $lx+my = 1$ is a tangent to

(a) the ellipse $\dfrac{x^2}{a^2}+\dfrac{y^2}{b^2} = 1$;

(b) the hyperbola $x^2-y^2 = a^2$;

(c) the hyperbola $xy = c^2$.

10. Investigate the results corresponding to 1–9 above for the conic

$$(x \quad y \quad 1)\begin{pmatrix} a & h & g \\ h & b & f \\ g & f & c \end{pmatrix}\begin{pmatrix} x \\ y \\ 1 \end{pmatrix} = 0.$$

1343

9. THE SPIROGRAPH

[The Spirograph is manufactured by Denys Fisher Ltd., Boston Spa, Yorks, and one should be obtained for this project.]

1. The numbers of teeth on the outside of the various discs are 24, 30, 32, 36, 40, 42, 45, 48, 50, 52, 56, 60, 63, 64, 72, 75, 80, 84, 144, 150. Show that gear ratios m/n can be obtained from these, including all values for which $m < n \leqslant 10$ and $\frac{1}{6} \leqslant m/n < 1$ (as well as many others) with the single exception of $\frac{7}{9}$. The numbers of teeth on the *inside* of the two rings are 96 and 105. Show that for a disc rolling inside a ring all values m/n are obtainable with $\frac{1}{4} \leqslant m/n \leqslant \frac{5}{6}$ and $m < n \leqslant 7$.

2. Find one disc which does not enter into any of these ratios. (a) Suggest a reason why it is included. (b) Suggest a replacement which would enable the ratio $\frac{7}{9}$ to be obtained.

3. It can in fact be proved that the curves obtained by rolling a circle of radius b on the outside of a circle of radius a, are similar to those obtained by rolling a circle of radius $a+b$ *around* the circle of radius a, so as to enclose it. Show that the ratio $\frac{7}{9}$ is obtainable by this method.

Experiment with the spirograph to show the truth of this. Show also that curves obtained by rolling circles of radii a or b inside a circle of radius $a+b$ are similar.

4. Now consider a circle of radius b rolling on the inside of a fixed circle of radius $a+b$.

(a) Show that when the point of contact has moved through an angular distance θ, the circle b has turned through an angle $a\theta/b$ in the opposite sense.

(b) Deduce equations for the path of a point at distance c from the centre of the rolling circle in the form

$$x = a \cos \theta + c \cos a\theta/b,$$

$$y = a \sin \theta - c \sin a\theta/b.$$

5. By putting $\phi = a\theta/b$, show that reflection and enlargement will transform this curve into the curve given by

$$x = b \cos \phi + c' \cos b\phi/a,$$

$$y = b \sin \phi - c' \sin b\phi/a,$$

and give the value of c'. Does this prove the last statement in Question 3? (These curves are called *hypotrochoids*.)

6. Obtain parametric equations for the curve traced by a point at distance c from the centre of a circle of radius b which rolls on the outside of a fixed circle of radius a, in the form

$$x = (a+b) \cos \theta + c \cos \frac{a+b}{b} \, \theta,$$

$$y = (a+b) \sin \theta + c \sin \frac{a+b}{b} \, \theta.$$

(This curve is an *epitrochoid*.)

7. Find suitable transformations which show the truth of the first statement in Question 3. $\left(\text{Put } \dfrac{a+b}{b}\, \theta = \phi \text{ for a start.} \right)$

8. Consider the hypotrochoid of Question 5 when $b = a$. What sort of curve is it? What is the ratio of the radii of the circles? If $c = b$, what does it become? Demonstrate with the spirograph. ($c = b$ cannot be quite obtained.)

9. If we use the straight racks, trochoids will be drawn. They differ from the cycloid of Chapter 17, Section 4.2, in that the point is not on the rim of the rolling circle. Find parametric equations for them.

10. LISSAJOUS'S FIGURES

1. It is a simple matter to make the spot on a cathode ray oscilloscope move so that its x-coordinate is given by a sine wave of the form $x = a \sin mt$, while its y-coordinate is given by $y = b \sin (nt + \phi)$, where a, b, m, n, ϕ are constants. The curves traced out by the spot in these circumstances are called Lissajous's figures. If $a = b$ and $m = n$, show that
    (*a*) the curve repeats after a time $2\pi/m$;
    (*b*) the curve lies in the square $|x| \leqslant a$, $|y| \leqslant a$, and touches its sides;
    (*c*) there is a value of ϕ for which the curve is a circle, and another for which it is a straight line. Sketch some intermediate cases.

2. Sketch the curves given by

$$x = 5 \cos t,$$

$$y = 5 \cos (2t + \phi)$$

for $\qquad\qquad \phi = 0,\ \dfrac{\pi}{3},\ \dfrac{\pi}{2},\ \dfrac{2\pi}{3}.$

Prove that the one which appears to be part of a parabola is in fact so.

3. Sketch the curves
$$x = 5 \cos 2t,$$

$$y = 5 \cos (3t + \phi)$$

for a few different values of ϕ.

4. A continuous Lissajous's figure has loops touching the top and bottom edges of the square each four times and the side edges each three times. Can you suggest equations for it and sketch a possible curve?

5. The curves can be described mechanically with the aid of two pendulums vibrating in two perpendicular planes. Devise an apparatus for doing this.

6. What will happen:
    (*a*) if m and n have a common factor?
    (*b*) if m/n is irrational?

7. Suppose now we made one or both of the wave forms of the inputs to the c.r.o. a sawtooth or square wave, given by graphs as in the figure:

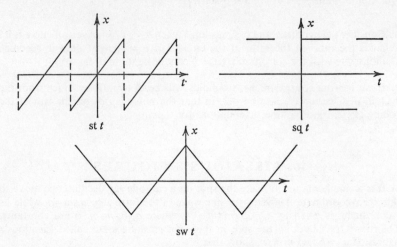

st t

sq t

sw t

Discuss the effect of combining these with one another, or with a sine wave, in different phases.

11. FOURIER SERIES

1. Draw with the same axes, from $x = -\pi$ to $+\pi$, the graphs of (a) $\sin x$, (b) $\sin x + \frac{1}{3} \sin 3x$, (c) $\sin x + \frac{1}{3} \sin 3x + \frac{1}{5} \sin 5x$. If this series were continued, what do you think the graphs would be like?

2. Show that, if m and n are integers,

$$\int_0^\pi \sin mx \sin nx \, dx \begin{cases} = 0 \;\; (m \neq n) \\ = \tfrac{1}{2}\pi \;\; (m = n). \end{cases}$$

Deduce from this that if a function whose domain is $\{x : 0 \leqslant x \leqslant \pi\}$ can be represented by a series of the form

$$f(x) = a_1 \sin x + a_2 \sin 2x + a_3 \sin 3x + \dots$$

then

$$\int_0^\pi f(x) \sin mx \, dx = \tfrac{1}{2}\pi a_m.$$

3. Show that, for such a function, $f(0) = f(\pi) = 0$ always. Suppose that for $0 < x < \pi$, $f(x) = k$; use the result of 2 to show that $a_m = (4k/\pi).(1/m)$, and hence confirm your guess in Question 1. What happens to $f(x)$ outside the domain $0 < x < \pi$? Sketch its graph.

4. Find a_m if $f(x) = x$, $0 \leqslant x < \pi$, and hence discover a similar series which might be expected to approach the saw-tooth wave-form $f(x) = x \pmod{2\pi}$, where $-\pi < x < \pi$.

   Sketch the graphs of the sums of the first few terms of this series, as in Question 1.

1346

5. Consider the same problem for the see-saw wave-form for which

$$f(x) \begin{cases} = x & 0 \leqslant x \leqslant \tfrac{1}{2}\pi \\ = \pi - x & \tfrac{1}{2}\pi \leqslant x \leqslant \pi. \end{cases}$$

What form will the series give for the continuation of $f(x)$ outside this domain?

It can be proved that, under certain rather mild conditions, any finite function $f(x)$ can be expanded in this way over the domain $(0, \pi)$; the series will give $f(-x) = -f(x)$ and $f(x+2\pi) = f(x)$. This analyses an odd periodic function of this kind into *harmonics* which combine to form the original function. The human ear possesses a remarkable power of analysis of this kind, resolving a complex periodic vibration of the air into its component musical notes.

For a general (not odd) function, cosine terms must also be added, but the principle is the same.

6. Study the wave-forms produced by various musical instruments, and obtain the first few coefficients a_m by numerical integration. Certain electronic organs allow the performer to mix the different harmonics (i.e. to vary $a_m, m \leqslant 6$ usually) at will, and thus to produce a tolerable imitation of various instruments.

12. GENERAL BINOMIAL SERIES

1. Show that the Taylor Series for $(a+x)^n$ is

$$a^n + na^{n-1}x + \frac{n(n-1)}{2}a^{n-2}x^2 + \frac{n(n-1)(n-2)}{2.3}a^{n-3}x^3 + \dots.$$

2. Find the error in taking r terms only of this series as an approximation to $(a+x)^{-1}$, by using the results of Chapter 11.

3. If $n = -2$, find the error in taking r terms only by multiplying the series by $(a+x)^2$.

4. Simplify the first four terms of the Taylor Series for $(a+x)^{\frac{1}{2}}$. Show that $6\sqrt{3} = (100+8)^{\frac{1}{2}}$, and $58\sqrt{3} = (10000+92)^{\frac{1}{2}}$; use each relation to obtain a value of $\sqrt{3}$ correct to 5 s.f.

5. Find an integer k such that $k^2 \times 7 \simeq 10000$. Hence find $\sqrt{7}$ to 5 s.f.

6. Solve $x^2 - 7 = 0$ by the Newton–Raphson method. Is this quicker than using the method of Question 5?

7. Find an integer k such that $k^3 \times 3 \simeq 1000$. Hence find $\sqrt[3]{3}$ to 5 s.f.

8. Find $\sqrt[3]{7}$ to 5 s.f., using any method you like.

9. Can you write a flow diagram to find $\sqrt{b}$ using the method of Questions 4 and 5?

10. Find:

(a) $\displaystyle\int_0^1 \sqrt{(100+x^2)}\,dx$; (b) $\displaystyle\int_0^1 \frac{1}{10+x^3}\,dx$; (c) $\displaystyle\int_{-0.1}^{0.1} \sqrt[3]{(1-x^2)}\,dx$.

Assess the accuracy of your answers.

11. Write down the first five terms of the Binomial Series for $(1-x^2)^{-\frac{1}{2}}$, and hence obtain a polynomial approximation for $\sin^{-1} x$.

17-2

13. COIN-TOSSING

Suppose we toss a coin a large number of times, keeping a running count of our score of heads and tails. Is it more likely that the count of heads will always exceed that of the tails, or that it will do so for just half the time?

Conduct a few experiments and see if you can make an estimate of the probabilities. (Count a throw which equalizes the scores as an excess of heads if it was preceded by an excess of heads, and vice versa.)

It can be proved that for a long run the probability of heads being in excess for a total fraction x of the time is given approximately by the density function

$$\phi(x) = \frac{1}{\pi\sqrt{(x-x^2)}}.$$

That is to say, the probability of the fraction lying between x and $x+\delta x$ is about $\phi(x)\delta x$.

1. Plot the graph of $\phi(x)$ for $0 < x < 1$ and comment on it.

2. What is $\int_0^1 \phi(x)\,dx$?

3. What is the probability of heads being in excess for less than a fraction t of the time?

4. Show that, under the rule about zero excess, in an even number of tosses the number of occasions when heads are in excess must always be even. What would you use as an estimate of the probability of this number being zero in a total of 20 tosses?

5. Using $\int_{9/20}^{11/20} \phi(x)\,dx$ as an estimate, evaluate the probability of heads being in excess on just 10 occasions out of 20 tosses.

(The actual probabilities are: for zero excess, 0·176; for half-time excess, 0·061.)

6. In a number of trials, each of 100 tosses, what is the number of occasions when heads are in excess which will not be exceeded on about one trial in every five?

14. TRINOMIAL FREQUENCIES

The chapter on Binomial Frequencies was concerned with repeated independent trials in each of which *two* outcomes were possible. We saw the important part played by the binomial coefficients which can be displayed in Pascal's triangle, and the connection between sets of probabilities and the coefficients in the expansion of $(a+bt)^n$. Here we extend all these ideas to three dimensions.

1. $(1+t+u)^1 = 1+t+u,$

$(1+t+u)^2 = 1+2t+2u+t^2+2tu+u^2,$

$(1+t+u)^3 = 1+3t+3u+3t^2+6tu+3u^2+t^3+3t^2u+3tu^2+u^3.$

The coefficients of these expansions can be written as follows:

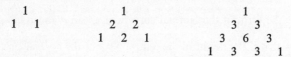

```
        1                 1                      1
     1     1           2     2              3        3
        1   2   1         1   2   1         3    6    3
                                         1    3    3    1
```

These can usefully be thought of as layers in a pyramid.
  Obtain the next two layers of the pyramid.

2. Show how a number of one layer can be found by adding together three numbers from the previous layer, and explain why this should always be correct.

3. Show that the sixth layer is

```
                  1
               6     6
            15    30    15
         20    60    60    20
      15    60    90    60    15
    6    30    60    60    30    6
  1    6    15    20    15    6    1
```

Comment on the numbers in each row, the sum of the numbers in each row, and the sum of the numbers in the whole layer. Generalize.

4. Explain where to find the coefficient of $t^i u^j$ in the expansion of $(1+t+u)^n$ in the pyramid. Give a formula (in factorials) for this number.

5. A large constituency has 50 % Socialist, 30 % Conservative and 20 % Liberal supporters. What is the probability that a random sample of six electors should be 3 Liberals, 2 Conservatives, and 1 Socialist?

6. Explain why the probability that a random sample of n electors (from the constituency of Question 5) gives i Socialists, j Conservatives and k Liberals, is approximately

$$\frac{n!}{(i!\,j!\,k!)}a^i b^j c^k \quad \text{where} \quad i+j+k = n, \quad a = 0.5, \quad b = 0.3, \quad c = 0.2.$$

7. Prove, by induction or otherwise, that the general term in Pascal's pyramid is

$$\frac{n!}{i!\,j!\,(n-i-j)!}.$$

8. What values of i, j, k give the greatest probability in Question 6
  (a) if $n = 20$,   (b) if $n = 15$?

9. Write down simplified forms of

(a) $\displaystyle\sum_{j=0}^{j=n-i} \frac{n!}{i!\,j!\,(n-i-j)!}$;

(b) $\displaystyle\sum_{j=0}^{j=n-i} \frac{n!}{i!\,j!\,(n-i-j)!} a^i b^j c^k.$

15. THE NORMAL CURVE

1. In Chapter 37 we have shown that as $n \to \infty$, the binomial probability function

$$f_{2n}(r) = \binom{2n}{r} (\tfrac{1}{2})^{2n}$$

approaches the form of the Normal curve with mean n and standard deviation $\frac{1}{2}\sqrt{(2n)}$.

(a) Show that if the height of the central peak of the normal curve is K and σ is the standard deviation, then

$$K \int_{-\infty}^{\infty} e^{-x^2/2\sigma^2} dx = 1.$$

(b) Express this integral in terms of

$$\int_{-\infty}^{\infty} e^{-\frac{1}{2}v^2} dy = I.$$

(c) By using the result of Question 9 in Section 6: $\{K = 1/\sqrt{(\pi n)}\}$, and $\sigma = \sqrt{(\tfrac{1}{2}n)}$, prove that $I = \sqrt{(2\pi)}$.

We may also obtain this result as follows.

2. Describe the shape of the surface $z = \exp\{-\tfrac{1}{2}(x^2 + y^2)\}$.

3. What is the total area (expressed as an integral) of a slice of this 'hill' (above the plane $z = 0$) by a plane $x = x_1$?

4. Show, using 3, that the total volume of the hill is I^2, where

$$I = \int_{-\infty}^{\infty} e^{-\frac{1}{2}x^2} dx.$$

5. Now consider the volume of the hill between the cylinders

$$x^2 + y^2 = r^2, \quad x^2 + y^2 = (r + \delta r)^2.$$

Express the volume of the hill in the form $\int_0^{\infty} f(r) dr$.

6. Evaluate this integral by the substitution $r^2 = u$. Hence show that the volume is 2π. What value do you deduce for I?

7. What then is the equation of the Normal curve with standard deviation σ, since the total area between it and the x-axis must be 1?

16. GENETICS

1. Discs occurring in a collection, D, of discs have probabilities q, and $1-q$, of being red, and green, respectively. D is so large that the withdrawal of samples from it does not affect the probabilities of the occurrences of the 2 colours.

(a) Two of the discs are chosen at random and pasted together to form a disc of double-thickness. Find the probability of its having 2 red faces; 2 green faces; one of each.

(b) One of these randomly formed double discs is to be spun like a coin. Find the probabilities, evaluated before the result of the pasting is known, that the upper face is red; is green.

(c) Two such randomly formed double discs are spun; their lower halves are discarded and their upper halves pasted together to form a new double disc. Show that the probabilities of having 2 red faces; 2 green faces; one of each on the new double disc are respectively equal to the probabilities of these events on the original double discs, and that $p(\textbf{a given face will be red}) = q$, as in the original collection.

(This trial provides a mathematical model of inheritance by genes. The single discs represent genes and the double discs represent gene-types or genotypes which can occur when each gene has the possibility of being of one of 2 sorts, here represented as red or green. The first double disc represents the gene-pair of one parent and the two double discs represent the gene-pairs of both parents. When mating occurs one gene is chosen at random from each parent and this is represented by spinning 2 double discs and selecting their upper faces. The two genes (one from each parent) go to form the gene-pair of the offspring and this is represented by the formation of the new double-disc. The results of this question so far show that with mating which is independent of the genotype of the parents (called random mating) the probabilities of the occurrences of each gene remain fixed from generation to generation and may be calculated as if the genes were *not* paired off in the same way that the original collection D consisted of discs not paired off.)

In 3 collections of men the following frequencies of different genotypes of blood groups were observed:

	MM	MN	NN
American Indian (Pueblo)	83	46	11
From Brooklyn U.S.A.	541	903	405
Australian Aboriginal	3	44	55

(From Boyd, *Tabulae Biologicae*, 17: 230, 235, 1939.)

(d) For each collection calculate the probability of the occurrences of the genes, M, N; assuming them to be exactly equal to the relative frequency of the occurrence of the given gene in the collection.

(e) For each collection calculate the expected numbers of the different genotypes, assuming them to be proportional to the probability of the occurrences of the genotypes when random mating occurs, with the calculated probabilities of the 2 genes. (The degree of agreement between the observed and hypothetically-calculated (called *expected*) frequencies is a matter which is treated in the Further Mathematics course.)

2. The 2 genes in a certain gene-pair are each either A or a. The individuals with genotypes Aa or AA can be distinguished by appearance from those with genotype aa, but not from each other. (The characteristic produced by gene A is said to be dominant.)

(a) In a collection K of plants, $p(\textbf{given gene is } a) = \frac{1}{2}$. What is $p(\textbf{given gene is } A)$? Assuming that the collection K had been formed by random mating calculate $p(\textbf{genotype of a given plant is } aa)$.

(b) In a collection L of plants of the same species, $p(\textbf{gene is } A) = \frac{2}{3}$, what are the probabilities of the occurrences of each genotype if the mating that formed L was random?

1351

(c) In a collection M of plants of the same species, the relative frequency of the individuals of genotypes either Aa or AA can be found by appearances and is 19 %. Estimate p(**gene is A**) if the mating that formed M was random and estimate the probabilities of each genotype.

3. (See Question 2.)

A botanist takes samples of 52, 189 and 200 plants from the collections K, L, M respectively and, without realizing the different genetic constitutions of the collections, he bulks them.

(a) If one of the 441 plants is chosen at random from the bulked collection calculate p(**gene is a**), p(**gene is A**) and the probabilities of the occurrence of each genotype.

(b) In a hypothetical collection arising from random mating what value of p(**gene is a**) would give rise to the actual value of p (**genotype is aa**) that the botanist observes in his bulked collection? With this value of p (**gene is a**) calculate the probabilities of the occurrences of each of the other two genotypes in the hypothetical collection. Calculate also the expected proportions of the frequencies of individuals of the two distinguishable appearances.

(c) With the actual value of p(**gene is a**) that exists in the bulked collection and with random mating now being carried out by the botanist in his laboratory what are the probabilities of the occurrences of the 3 different genotypes among the offspring? What are the expected proportion of frequencies of individuals of the two distinguishable appearances?

4. Repeat Question 3 if the botanist's samples from K, L, M were of sizes 12, 144, 100 respectively.

5. The 2 genes of one of the many gene-pairs of a man can each be either gene B or gene b. A child receives at random one gene from each of its parents. If both parents are of genotype bb then the children are also of genotype bb (and we are said to have a true-breeding line). If a child receives one gene B in its gene-pair it is resistant to malaria, but if it has 2 genes B it suffers from sickle-cell-anaemia and there is a probability θ that it will die before having any children. Thus a true-breeding malaria-resistant line is impossible if $\theta = 1$. Starting from a population of parents all of whom are of type Bb and taking $\theta = 1$ calculate successively p(**gene is b**) in the adult stage of the children, grandchildren, great grandchildren, assuming that mating among the adult stage is independent of the genotype then existing. (This is not *strictly* random mating among the offspring since no offspring of type BB are mated.)

6. There is a probability θ that a person of genotype BB will die of anaemia before having children and a probability ϕ that a person of genotype bb will die of malaria before having children.

(a) Starting from a population of parents all of whom are of type Bb and taking $\theta = \frac{3}{5}$, $\phi = \frac{1}{5}$ find p(**gene is b**) in the adult stage of the children and grandchildren, assuming the mating among the adult stage is independent of genotype then existing.

(b) Starting from a generation of parents with p(**gene is b**) $= q$ find p(**gene is b**) in the next adult stage with general values of θ and ϕ.

(c) If p(**gene is b**) $= q$ and is unchanged in 2 successive adult stages find the value of q in terms of θ and ϕ. We then have a type of equilibrium situation in terms of generations in the collection. (This is an example of Natural Selection operating to produce a certain gene ratio dependent on the differing survival values of the different genotypes; the existence of 2 or more forms in equilibrium like this is called polymorphism.)

7. If random mating is taking place show that the biggest value of p (**2 genes are different**) is $\frac{1}{2}$; and that this occurs when the two genes are equally probable.

8. In an experiment with fowls we are concerned with 2 gene-pairs, the genes being C, c in one gene-pair I, i in the other. An offspring receives at random one gene of each gene-pair from each of the parents. Fowls of genotype cc have no black pigment at all. The presence of gene C ensures black pigment in the fowl. The presence of gene I prevents the black pigment from showing in the wing feathers even if it is present. Fowls of genotype ii show the black pigment in the wing feathers if it is present in the fowl.

(*a*) Write down the various genotypes of the fowls together with the colour of their wings: for example

$$Cc \; Ii\text{—white.}$$

(*b*) If both parents are of the same genotype and if all the offspring necessarily have the same wing colour as the parents then we have a true-breeding line. Write down the genotypes that give a true breeding line with black wings; with white wings.

(*c*) If both parents have genotypes $Cc \; Ii$ and so have white wings determine the various possible genotypes of the offspring and their probabilities; what are the expected proportions of the frequencies of offspring showing black feathers; white feathers?

(*d*) If a rival theory of this phenomenon says that there is only one gene-pair controlling the wing colour the genes being, say, B and b and only the fowls of genotype BB show black wings, then prove that the cross of a fowl of genotype Bb with another of that genotype (the only cross that would have parents of the same genotype and yet would *not* breed true) would give a different proportion of offspring with black wing feathers.

17. MARKOV CHAINS

320 people use a works canteen every day. Tea and coffee are supplied as alternatives with lunch. Of those who have tea on any one day, 10 % decide next day to have coffee. Regrettably, the coffee is worse. Of those who take it on any day, 40 % change to tea for the next day.

1. If 160 people have tea and 160 people have coffee on a given Monday, how many will have each a week later? (The canteen is open 5 days a week.)

2. Will the situation become steady? What number of teas do you suggest should be provided?

3. Show that if the vector $\begin{pmatrix} t \\ c \end{pmatrix}$ gives the numbers of those opting for tea or coffee on any day, then the vector $\mathbf{P}\begin{pmatrix} t \\ c \end{pmatrix}$ gives the same information for the next day, where $\mathbf{P}$ is the matrix

$$\begin{pmatrix} 0\cdot9 & 0\cdot4 \\ 0\cdot1 & 0\cdot6 \end{pmatrix}.$$

4. Show that if

$$U = \begin{pmatrix} 4 & 1 \\ 1 & -1 \end{pmatrix}, \quad \text{then} \quad PU = U\begin{pmatrix} 1 & 0 \\ 0 & 0\cdot5 \end{pmatrix} = UD,$$

say.

5. Writing P as UDU^{-1}, what is P^n?
What is the limit of D^n as $n \to \infty$?
What then is the limit of P^n as $n \to \infty$?
Does this agree with your answer to 2?

6. If the situation reaches a steady state given by $\begin{pmatrix} T \\ C \end{pmatrix}$ then $P\begin{pmatrix} T \\ C \end{pmatrix} = \begin{pmatrix} T \\ C \end{pmatrix}$.

Use this equation to find $\begin{pmatrix} T \\ C \end{pmatrix}$, and compare with the result of 5.

7. In general, consider the matrix

$$Q = \begin{pmatrix} 1-a & b \\ a & 1-b \end{pmatrix} \quad \text{where} \quad 0 < a+b < 1.$$

(a) Find vectors v_1, v_2 for which $Qv = \lambda v$, where λ is a scalar.
(b) Show that $Q(v_1 v_2) = (v_1 v_2)D$, where D is a diagonal matrix.
(c) Show that $Q^n v$ tends to a limit for all vectors v as $n \to \infty$, and find this limit.
Suppose a system has two states (call them L and R) and can switch from one to the other at definite moments of time. Suppose also that the probability of a switch from L to R or from R to L depends only on the state the system is in and not on the time (i.e. not on previous history), then the process is called a *Markov process* and the chain of successive states a *Markov chain*. If a is the probability of a switch from L to R, and b that of a switch from R to L, then if p_n, q_n are the probabilities of the system's being in states L, R after n time-pulses, it is clear that

$$\begin{pmatrix} p_{n+1} \\ q_{n+1} \end{pmatrix} = Q\begin{pmatrix} p_n \\ q_n \end{pmatrix}.$$

So long as $a, b \neq 0, 1$, we have shown that $\begin{pmatrix} p_n \\ q_n \end{pmatrix}$ tends to a limit, and a sufficiently large number of similar systems will reach a numerically steady state.

8. The genes A and a of a certain gene-pair *mutate* (that is: change) into each other with the probabilities below

Change	Probability of occurrence in unit time
$A \to a$	10^{-6}
$a \to A$	2×10^{-6}.

Find $p(\text{gene is } A)$ after a time has passed long enough for equilibrium to be reached, and assuming no selection operates against any of the genotypes.

1354

*9. *Project Question on Markov Processes*
Take a die and operate as follows:
  (i) States L, R are having the die in the left, right hands respectively.
  (ii) Start with the die in the left hand.
  (iii) Throw the die and determine the transitions as follows:
     (A) If in state L and a *one* is thrown, change to state R.
        If in state R and a *one* or *two* is thrown, change to state L.
  (iv) Record the states, the initial one being called the state at instant $t = 0$.
  (v) Determine the state at $t = 50$.
Repeat with the following transition rules:
     (B) L to R: if *one* or *two* is thrown;
        R to L: if *one*, *two*, *three* or *four* is thrown.
     (C) L to R: if *one*, *two* or *three* is thrown;
        R to L: if anything at all is thrown.
(Note that with ingenuity the same series of 50 throws of a die can be used in all cases provided the throws are recorded. The states and changes can be interpreted afterwards by examining the sequence.)
Suggest a physical situation for which method (C) is a suitable mathematical model.
The Markov chains set up suggest various problems such as:
  (*a*) At the start of the experiment what is the probability that at the nth instant the state will be L? will be R? and how are these probabilities affected if the chain starts at state R? Take n to be large.
  (*b*) What are the probabilities of various lengths of run in each state?
  (*c*) What is the mean length of run in each state?
  (*d*) What is the mean number of changes of state occurring in a unit interval of time?
  (*e*) How are the results affected by changing the transition probabilities? (Note that in cases (A), (B), (C) above the ratios of the transition probabilities are equal.)
You may find connections between the problems but most of them are too hard to solve here. Experimental results can be obtained to suggest likely sizes for the answers. Random Number tables are preferable to dice for long runs.

18. ROTATIONAL ENERGY

1. A rod of length $2a$ revolves about its centre with angular velocity ω. What is the velocity of a part of the rod between x and $x + \delta x$ from the centre? If the total mass of the rod is M, what is the K.E. of this part?
Find by integration the total K.E. of the rod.

2. This K.E. is written $\frac{1}{2}I\omega^2$, and the quantity I is called the *moment of inertia* of the rod about its centre. What are the dimensions of I?

3. Show that if the rod is thought of as a string of small masses distributed uniformly along its length, then $I = m\sigma^2$, where σ is the standard deviation of the distance of these masses from the centre.

4. Deduce that if the rod rotates about an axis at distance b from the centre, then the new value I' of the moment of inertia is given by $I' = I + mb^2$.

5. Show that for a bicycle wheel of radius a with all its mass concentrated at the rim, $I = ma^2$.

6. Deduce from 5 by integration that for a flat disc (like a gramophone record) $I = \frac{1}{2}ma^2$.

7. A bicycle wheel and a solid disc of the same diameter both roll down the same hill. Which will be turning faster at the bottom? Can you find the ratio of their speeds if you assume that the rotational and translational K.E.'s can be added together?

8. If the radial spokes of a wheel have $\frac{1}{10}$ the mass of the rim, what fraction do they add to its moment of inertia? (Neglect the hub.)

MISCELLANEOUS EXERCISES

QUICK·REVISION TESTS

(*Arranged in sets of* 10 *questions*)

1. In three-dimensional Euclidean space with Cartesian coordinates (x, y, z),. points A and B are given by $(2, 1, 1)$ and $(1, -4, 2)$. Prove that the sphere with AB as diameter passes through the origin.

2. Sketch the curve which, in the (x, y)-plane, is given by $y(x^2 - 1) = x$.

3. The complex number $x + jy$ is mapped into the complex number $X + jY$ where X, Y are given by the equation

$$\begin{pmatrix} 2 & 1 \\ 1 & 2 \end{pmatrix} \begin{pmatrix} x \\ y \end{pmatrix} = \begin{pmatrix} X \\ Y \end{pmatrix}.$$

Which numbers are invariant under the mapping?

4. State for each of the following functions whether it is odd, even, periodic, or none of these, justifying your answers:
   (*a*) $x \sin x$;   (*b*) $\sin x + \cos x$;   (*c*) $x + \cos x$.

5. Starting from the approximation

$$\sqrt{17} \simeq 4,$$

apply Newton's method to the equation

$$x^2 = 17$$

to obtain first the approximation $x \simeq 4.125$ and then the approximation $x \simeq 4.123$.

6. If θ may take any real value, prove that the maximum value of $(3 \cos \theta - \cos^2 \theta)$ is 2.
    Explain whether, by putting $\cos \theta = x$, it is correct to deduce that the maximum value of $(3x - x^2)$, for all x, is 2.

7. A man tosses a coin six times. Find the probability that he will throw two heads and four tails
   (*a*) in any order;
   (*b*) the two heads being thrown consecutively.

8. In a class of 10 children the marks in an examination are 14, 18, 21, 25, 29, 29, 30, 31, 35, 38. Find the mean and the standard deviation, giving your answers to the nearest integer.

9. A particle of mass 3 kg travelling at 40 m/s is deflected through 60° and has its speed halved. Calculate its change in momentum.

10. A boat travelling at 4 m/s crosses a river flowing at 5 m/s. In what direction should it be steered so as to be swept the minimum distance downstream?

11. Find the general solution of the equation

$$\cos 2x = \tfrac{1}{2},$$

giving your answer in radians.

12. The roots of the equation

$$x^3 + ax^2 + bx + c = 0$$

are three times the roots of the equation

$$x^3 + 2x^2 + 3x + 4 = 0.$$

Find a and c.

13. Express in partial fractions

(a) $\dfrac{1}{(x+1)(x+2)}$;

(b) $\dfrac{1}{(x+1)(x^2+2)}$.

14. Given that

$$3x + 2y = u,$$
$$4x + 3y = v,$$

express x, y in the form

$$x = au + bv,$$
$$y = cu + dv.$$

Write down the product of the matrices

$$\begin{pmatrix} 3 & 2 \\ 4 & 3 \end{pmatrix} \begin{pmatrix} a & b \\ c & d \end{pmatrix}.$$

15. Give a rough sketch of the curve

$$y = (x-1)(x-2)(x-3).$$

Find the equation of the tangent to the curve at the point $(1, 0)$.

16. Solve the differential equation

$$\frac{ds}{dt} + s = 1,$$

given that $s = 2$ when $t = 1$.

17. How many distinct linear functions $y = f(x)$ are there which map

$$0 \leqslant x \leqslant 1 \quad \text{onto} \quad -1 \leqslant y \leqslant 3?$$

For *one* such function, find the value of x which satisfies $x = f(x)$.

18. The mean survival period of daisies after being sprayed with a certain make of weed killer is 24 days. If the probability of survival after 27 days is $\tfrac{1}{4}$, estimate the standard deviation of the survival period.

19. Evaluate $\displaystyle\int_{-2}^{2} \frac{2\,dt}{4+t^2}$ and $\displaystyle\int_{-2}^{2} \frac{2t\,dt}{4+t^2}$.

20. Find the equivalent resistance of this network, where each link has a resistance of $1\,\Omega$.

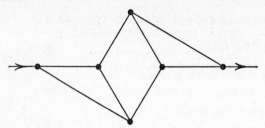

21. Express in a simpler way $\{x: x^2-7x-5 < 0\}$, and illustrate your answer with a sketch.

22. On a diagram of the complex number plane, sketch the set of points given by $|z-3j| < |z-3|$.

23. Obtain a quadratic polynomial approximation to the function sec x in the neighbourhood of $x = 0$.

24. Draw up a flow diagram for calculating, to a prescribed degree of accuracy, the real root of the equation $x^3-x^2+x+1 = 0$.

25. State carefully what is meant by the statement that '$f(x)$ is differentiable at $x = a$'. Use your definition to evaluate the derivative of $g(x)$ at $x = 1$, where

$$g(x) \begin{cases} = x -1 & (x \leqslant 1) \\ = x^2-x & (x > 1). \end{cases}$$

26. State the inverse of the matrix

$$\begin{pmatrix} 1 & 0 & 0 \\ 0 & 1 & 0 \\ 0 & 3 & 1 \end{pmatrix}$$

and explain your result geometrically.

27. Prove by induction that $\sum_{1}^{n} i^2 = n(n+1)(2n+1)/6$.

28. Use the result of Question 27 to find the standard deviation of the first 50 odd integers from their mean.

29. Solve the differential equations

(a) $\dfrac{dy}{dx} = x+3$;   (b) $\dfrac{dy}{dx} = y+3$;

given that $y = 2$ when $x = 0$ in both cases.

30. Find the area enclosed between the x-axis and one 'hump' of the curves

(a) $y = \sin x$;   (b) $y = x \sin x$.

31. Write a flow diagram to print a table of values of $n!$ from $n = 1$ to $n = 20$.

1359

32. Given that $x^3 - 2x^2 - 3x + 10 = 0$ has a zero which is an integer, find all its zeros.

33. The position vector **r** of a particle can be expressed in terms of the constant orthogonal unit vectors **i**, **j** by means of the relation

$$\mathbf{r} = \mathbf{i} \cos nt + \mathbf{j} \sin nt.$$

Find the speed of the particle at time t.
　Show that its acceleration at time t is the vector $-n^2\mathbf{r}$.

34. Express the complex number

$$2 + j\sqrt{3}$$

in the form

$$r(\cos \theta + j \sin \theta).$$

(Your value of θ may be given to the nearest degree.)

35. Differentiate
　(a) $x^2 \sin 3x$ with respect to x;
　(b) $\sin^2 2x$ with respect to u, where $u = 4x$.

36. Prove that

$$1 + \frac{1}{2} + \frac{1}{4} + \ldots + \frac{1}{2^n} = 2 - \frac{1}{2^n}.$$

Use this finite summation to explain carefully what you mean when you say that 'the sum of the infinite series

$$1 + \frac{1}{2} + \frac{1}{4} + \ldots + \frac{1}{2^n} + \ldots$$

is 2'.

37. A spherical lump of ice melts at a rate proportional to its surface area, remaining spherical throughout the process. Prove that its radius decreases at a constant rate.

38. Evaluate

$$\int_0^1 \frac{\tan^{-1} x}{1 + x^2} \, dx.$$

39. Show that there is a dimensional inconsistency in the equation

$$i = \frac{EL}{R^2 + \omega^2 L^2} \exp(-Rt/L)$$

for a current flowing in a certain electrical circuit, and suggest a suitable correction. To what kind of current does this equation refer?

40. Estimate the probability of turning up exactly ten heads in twenty tosses of a coin. (Use your tables.)

41. The position vector **r** of a particle is given by

$$\mathbf{r} = t^3\mathbf{i} - 3t\mathbf{j},$$

where **i** and **j** are constant orthogonal unit vectors. Show that its speed is never zero, and state the direction of its acceleration.

1360

42. Find the set of values of x which satisfy

$$2 \sin x + \sin 2x > 0.$$

43. Find two complex numbers whose squares are equal to

(a) $-15+8j$;   (b) $16-30j$.

Could you have deduced one pair from the other pair? How?

44. Prove that

$$\int_0^a f(x)\,dx = \int_0^a f(a-x)\,dx,$$

and hence or otherwise evaluate

$$\int_0^{\frac{1}{2}\pi} \cos^2 x\,dx.$$

Use the method to evaluate

$$\int_0^{\pi} x \sin^2 x\,dx.$$

45. a, b, c, d are the position vectors of the vertices of a tetrahedron A, B, C, D. What is the position vector of the centroid of the face BCD?

The line joining this point to A is called a *median*. Show that the four medians are concurrent, and that their point of intersection quadrisects each of them.

46. A skater A, of mass 50 kg, who is travelling at 3 m/s, crashes into a skater B of mass 75 kg, who is travelling at 2 m/s on a path at right-angles to A's. Immediately after the impact, A finds himself travelling at 1 m/s parallel to B's original path.

Sketch a vector diagram showing clearly the momentum of each skater before and after the collision. By drawing a more accurate diagram, or otherwise, estimate the magnitude and direction of B's velocity after the collision.

State briefly what assumption you make about forces between the skaters and the ice.

47. If O is the origin, and

$$\mathbf{OA} = \begin{pmatrix} 15 \\ -20 \\ 0 \end{pmatrix}, \quad \mathbf{OB} = \begin{pmatrix} 12 \\ 9 \\ -20 \end{pmatrix}, \quad \mathbf{OC} = \begin{pmatrix} 16 \\ 12 \\ 15 \end{pmatrix}$$

show that O, A, B, C are four vertices of a cube, and find the other four.

48. Manufacturers often estimate the standard deviation as follows. Observe the values in a large sample exceeded by $\frac{1}{16}$ and by $\frac{15}{16}$ of the sample; then the standard deviation is about a third of the difference between them.

Apply this to the sample given, and explain under what conditions you would expect the method to give a good estimate.

Heights (cm)	64	65	66	67	68	69	70	71	72	(nearest cm)
Frequencies	30	60	220	540	490	310	180	110	60	

49. Use your knowledge of groups of order 6 to establish the truth or falsehood

(a) of this proposition;   (b) of its converse.

'If all proper subgroups of a group G are commutative, then G is commutative.'

50. Three mutually hostile tanks A, B, C have two shells each. They fire the first shell (simultaneously) each at their more deadly opponent, and then if possible repeat the process. What is the probability that (a) all will survive, (b) none will survive, given that their chances of hitting are respectively $\frac{1}{2}$, $\frac{1}{3}$, $\frac{1}{4}$?

MISCELLANEOUS REVISION EXERCISES

(*Arranged in topics*)

A. Numbers and structure

1. In the set of real numbers, a binary operation $\sim$ is defined by

$$x \sim y = xy + x + y.$$

Prove that the set is closed under $\sim$, and that $\sim$ is associative and commutative. Show that there is a unique neutral element e for which

$$e \sim x = x \sim e = x \quad \text{for all real } x.$$

Show also that every x except -1 has a unique inverse.

2. A binary operation $*$ is defined by the following table:

$*$	i	a	b	c	d	e
i	i	a	b	c	d	e
a	a	d	c	b	e	i
b	b	c	d	e	i	a
c	c	b	e	i	a	d
d	d	e	i	a	b	c
e	e	i	a	d	c	b

Show that the equation $p * x = q$ is always soluble. Show that

$$a * (b * c) = (a * b) * c;$$

$$b * (c * d) = (b * c) * d;$$

$$c * (d * e) = (c * d) * e.$$

Is this a group table?

3. An *integer* can be written ($a \sim b$) where a, b are natural numbers, and is subject to the following laws:

(i) Equality: ($a \sim b$) = ($c \sim d$) means $a + d = b + c$.
(ii) Addition: ($a \sim b$) + ($c \sim d$) = ($a + c \sim b + d$).
(iii) Multiplication: ($a \sim b$).($c \sim d$) = ($ac + bd \sim ad + bc$).
(iv) ($a \sim a$) is written 0, and if $u = (a \sim b)$ then ($b \sim a$) is written $-u$.

Prove from these laws:

(a) that, if $u = v$, and $v = w$, then $u = w$;
(b) that $uv = vu$;
(c) that $u(v + w) = uv + uw$;
(d) that $(-u)(-v) = uv$.

4. Show that if $a/b \neq c/d$, then $(a+c)/(b+d)$ lies between them. Deduce that between any two rational numbers there are infinitely many others. Show further that if $ad-bc = 1$, then no rational number with denominator smaller than $b+d$ lies between a/b and c/d.

(*Hint*: suppose x/y does; remember that a positive non-zero integer must be at least 1, and hence prove $y \geqslant (b+d)/(ad-bc)$.)

5. Prove that $\sqrt{5}$ is not rational and deduce that if $t^2 = t+1$ then t is not rational. Express $0{\cdot}185185185\ldots$ as a rational number.

6. Invent three equations to illustrate the three possible solutions of quadratic equations and solve them. What do you notice in the case of the complex roots? Why is this?

It can be shown that in the general case of the equation (with real coefficients) of degree n, the complex roots occur in conjugate pairs (if n is odd one root, at least, must be real). Use this fact to solve completely the equation

$$2z^3 - 9z^2 + 14z - 5 = 0$$

given that $2+j$ is one root.

7. If z_1 and z_2 are two complex numbers, mark their representation on an Argand Diagram together with that of $z_1 + z_2$. Mark clearly $|z_1|$, $|z_2|$ and $|z_1 + z_2|$. What property of a triangle are we quoting if we assert that

$$|z_1 + z_2| \leqslant |z_1| + |z_2|?$$

Under what circumstances can the equality hold?
Prove this inequality without appealing to geometry.

8. Prove that

$$\left(\frac{-1}{2} + j\frac{\sqrt{3}}{2}\right)^3 = 1;$$

what are the other numbers whose cube is 1?

This complex root of unity is usually denoted by ω. Prove that *each* complex root is the square of the other and show that the three roots can be written in the form 1, ω, ω^2.

9. Show that the set of ordered pairs of real numbers (a, b) form a group under the operation $*$, where $(a, b) * (c, d) = (ac, bc+d)$. Find a set of 2×2 matrices isomorphic to this group under matrix multiplication.

10. ABC is an equilateral triangle fitting in a box PQR. If A is at P, B at Q and C at R, we can indicate this situation by the incidence matrix

$$I = \begin{pmatrix} 1 & 0 & 0 \\ 0 & 1 & 0 \\ 0 & 0 & 1 \end{pmatrix}.$$

If the triangle is put so that A is at Q, B at R, and C at P we indicate this by

$$U = \begin{matrix} & A & B & C \\ P & \\ Q & \\ R & \end{matrix} \begin{pmatrix} 0 & 0 & 1 \\ 1 & 0 & 0 \\ 0 & 1 & 0 \end{pmatrix}.$$

What operation corresponds to U: i.e. what operation will bring the triangle to this position? Answer the same question for the matrices

$$V = \begin{pmatrix} 0 & 1 & 0 \\ 0 & 0 & 1 \\ 1 & 0 & 0 \end{pmatrix}; \quad R = \begin{pmatrix} 1 & 0 & 0 \\ 0 & 0 & 1 \\ 0 & 1 & 0 \end{pmatrix}; \quad S = \begin{pmatrix} 0 & 0 & 1 \\ 0 & 1 & 0 \\ 1 & 0 & 0 \end{pmatrix}; \quad T = \begin{pmatrix} 0 & 1 & 0 \\ 1 & 0 & 0 \\ 0 & 0 & 1 \end{pmatrix}.$$

Work out the multiplication table for this set of matrices, and show that it is a group. Show, e.g. that $RV = T$ and that operation V followed by operation R brings the triangle to the same position as operation T.

B. Sequences and series

1. Simplify

$$\sum_{i=1}^{r} f(x_i) + \sum_{i=1}^{n-r} f(x_{i+r}).$$

2. Prove that

$$\sum_{i=1}^{n} f(i) + \sum_{i=1}^{n} f(n+1-i) = 2 \sum_{1}^{n} f(i),$$

and hence that

$$\sum_{i=1}^{n} f(i) = \sum_{i=1}^{n} \frac{f(i) + f(n+1-i)}{2}.$$

Use this result to find $\sum_{1}^{n} i$.

3. If $u_1, u_2, u_3, \ldots$ form a geometric progression with common ratio k, find in terms of k and u_1 the value of $\sum_{i=1}^{n} (u_i u_{i+1})$.

4. Find the value of $\sum_{r=1}^{n} r(r+2)$.

5. Find the sum of the first 20 terms and also of the first n terms of the series:
(a) $1.2 + 2.3 + 3.4 + \ldots$;
(b) $1.2.5 + 2.3.6 + 3.4.7 + \ldots$.

6. Find the sum to n terms of each of the following series:

(a) $\dfrac{1}{4.7} + \dfrac{1}{7.10} + \dfrac{1}{10.13} + \ldots$;

(b) $\dfrac{1}{2.3.4} + \dfrac{1}{3.4.5} + \dfrac{1}{4.5.6} + \ldots$.

7. Prove that, if n is even, the sum of the first n terms of the series

$$1^2 + 2 \cdot 2^2 + 3^2 + 2 \cdot 4^2 + 5^2 + 2 \cdot 6^2 + \ldots$$

is $\frac{1}{2}n(n+1)^2$, and find the sum if n is odd.

8. A solid is formed by fastening together ten solid circular cylinders, each of height one centimetre, whose radii are in A.P. The radius of the smallest is 3 cm, and that of the largest is 15 cm. The cylinders are placed with their axes coincident and each one rests on the next larger one. Find the total surface area of the solid.

9. Which of the following sequences s_n are convergent?

(a) $s_n = \dfrac{n-1}{n+1}$;

(b) $s_n = \dfrac{n^2+1}{n}$;

(c) $s_n = (-1/2)^n$;

(d) $s_n = \dfrac{1}{n}.\sin\left(\dfrac{n\pi}{2}\right)$.

10. In each case of convergence in Question 9, find the limit of the sequence, and the *first* term of the sequence which differs from the limit by less than 0·000001. Do all subsequent terms differ from the limit by less than 0·000001?

C. Vectors and matrices

1. Can you find vectors $\begin{pmatrix} x \\ y \end{pmatrix}$ whose direction is unchanged when they are pre-multiplied by the matrix $\begin{pmatrix} 4 & -1 \\ 2 & 1 \end{pmatrix}$?

(*Hint*. Put
$$\begin{pmatrix} 4 & -1 \\ 2 & 1 \end{pmatrix} \begin{pmatrix} x \\ y \end{pmatrix} = \begin{pmatrix} kx \\ ky \end{pmatrix}$$

and find k first, then x and y. Only the ratio of $x:y$ is determined.)

2. Evaluate
$$\begin{pmatrix} -7 & 1 & 10 \\ -5 & 1 & 7 \\ 6 & -1 & -8 \end{pmatrix} \begin{pmatrix} 1 & 2 & 3 \\ -2 & 4 & 1 \\ 1 & 1 & 2 \end{pmatrix}$$

and hence solve the equations
$$p+2q+3r = 11,$$
$$-2p+4q+ r = 17,$$
$$p+ q+2r = 2.$$

Write down the solution of
$$p+2q+3r = 1, \quad -2p+4q+r = 1, \quad p+q+2r = 1.$$

3. Write down the table of the smallest group under multiplication of matrices with complex elements (in terms of **A** and **B**) which includes
$$\mathbf{A} = \begin{pmatrix} 0 & j \\ j & 0 \end{pmatrix} \quad \text{and} \quad \mathbf{B} = \begin{pmatrix} j & 0 \\ 0 & -j \end{pmatrix}$$

and show that it is not isomorphic either to the symmetry group of the square or to the cyclic group of order 8.

4. (i) Decide which of the following matrices are invertible and find the inverses of the ones that are.

(a) $\begin{pmatrix} 1 & 1 \\ 0 & 1 \end{pmatrix}$;

(b) $\begin{pmatrix} 1 & 1 \\ 1 & 1 \end{pmatrix}$;

(c) $\begin{pmatrix} 0 & 1 \\ 0 & 0 \end{pmatrix}$;

(d) $\begin{pmatrix} 0 & 1 \\ 1 & 0 \end{pmatrix}$;

(e) $\begin{pmatrix} 0 & 1 & 0 \\ 0 & 0 & 1 \\ 1 & 0 & 0 \end{pmatrix}$.

(ii) For which values of p are the following matrices invertible? Find the inverses where possible.

(a) $\begin{pmatrix} p & 1 \\ 1 & 0 \end{pmatrix}$;   (b) $\begin{pmatrix} 1 & p \\ 1 & 0 \end{pmatrix}$;   (c) $\begin{pmatrix} 1 & p \\ 1 & p \end{pmatrix}$;   (d) $\begin{pmatrix} 1 & 1 \\ 1 & p \end{pmatrix}$.

5. OA, OB, OC are the unit vectors **i, j, k**. Write down the two rotation matrices which transform the tetrahedron $OABC$ into itself, besides the identity matrix. Call these matrices **W, W²**.

If **R** is a rotation matrix which transforms **OA, OB, OC** into **OD, OE, OF**, write down, in terms of **W** and **R**, the rotational symmetry transformations of $ODEF$.

Find also *one* of the reflectional symmetry transformations of $ODEF$.

6. Solve the simultaneous equations:

$$x+y+z = 3,$$
$$x+2y+3z = 6,$$
$$x+3y+kz = 4+k,$$

(a) when $k \neq 5$;
(b) when $k = 5$, giving the general solution.

7. Write down the matrix of the cofactors of A where

$$A = \begin{pmatrix} 2 & 5 & 0 \\ -3 & 7 & -1 \\ 5 & -3 & 1 \end{pmatrix}.$$

Use this matrix to solve the equations:

$$2x+5y \quad = 8,$$
$$-3x+7y-z = 5,$$
$$5x-3y+z = 3.$$

Interpret your results in terms of points, lines and planes.

8. If $x' = (x-ut)/\sqrt{(1-u^2)}$ and $t' = (t-ux)/\sqrt{(1-u^2)}$, find the matrix L_u such that

$$L_u \begin{pmatrix} x \\ jt \end{pmatrix} = \begin{pmatrix} x' \\ jt' \end{pmatrix}.$$

Hence express x and t in terms of x' and t'. Comment on the significance of your results. (This is the *Lorentz transformation* in special relativity theory. $(x',t)'$ are the space-time coordinates of an event observed by O', (x, t) those observed by O. O' is moving relative to O with velocity u along the x-axis.)

9. If, with the notation of Question 8, $L_u L_v = L_w$, prove that

$$w = \frac{u+v}{1+uv}.$$

Hence show that if $u < 1$, $v < 1$, then also $w < 1$.

10. Find the values of k for which

$$\begin{pmatrix} 4 & 2 \\ -3 & -1 \end{pmatrix} \begin{pmatrix} x \\ y \end{pmatrix} = k \cdot \begin{pmatrix} x \\ y \end{pmatrix}.$$

If these values are p and q, and

$$\begin{pmatrix} 4 & 2 \\ -3 & -1 \end{pmatrix} = \mathbf{A},$$

evaluate the matrices $\mathbf{A} - p\mathbf{I}$, $\mathbf{A} - q\mathbf{I}$, where $\mathbf{I}$ is the unit matrix, and their product. Find also the two vectors $\begin{pmatrix} x \\ y \end{pmatrix}$ corresponding to these values p and q of k, and let $\mathbf{B}$ be the matrix whose columns are these two vectors. Show that $\mathbf{AB} = \mathbf{BD}$, where $\mathbf{D}$ is a diagonal matrix, and hence that $\mathbf{A}^4\mathbf{B} = \mathbf{BD}^4$. Use this to evaluate $\mathbf{A}^4$.

D. Vector geometry and linear dependence

1. If A is $(4, 1, -8)$ and B is $(7, 4, 4)$, find:
  (a) the lengths of OA, OB;
  (b) the cosine of the angle AOB;
  (c) the coordinates of C if $OACB$ is a parallelogram;
  (d) the coordinates of the point D on AB dividing it in the ratio $3:1$.

2. A cube is placed on a horizontal table so that the vertices of its top face lie in cyclic order A, B, C, D, vertically over the respective vertices A', B', C', D' of its bottom face which is in contact with the table. A representation of this situation in terms of three-dimensional coordinate geometry is obtained by taking an origin at A' and coordinate axes $A'B'$, $A'D'$, $A'A$ so that $\mathbf{A'B'}$ is specified by a unit vector $\mathbf{i}$, $\mathbf{A'D'}$ by $\mathbf{j}$, and $\mathbf{A'A}$ by $\mathbf{k}$. What position vectors specify the points D and C'?

Find the position vectors of the mid-points of AD, DD', $D'C'$, $B'C'$, and prove that these mid-points lie in a plane perpendicular to the line $A'C$.

3. Show that the planes $x - 2y + 2z = 17$, $3x + 15y - z = -12$, $2x + 5y + z = 7$ have a line in common, and find parametric equations for it. What does this tell you about the vectors

$$\begin{pmatrix} 1 \\ 3 \\ 2 \end{pmatrix}, \quad \begin{pmatrix} -2 \\ 15 \\ 5 \end{pmatrix}, \quad \begin{pmatrix} 2 \\ -1 \\ 1 \end{pmatrix}, \quad \begin{pmatrix} 17 \\ -12 \\ 7 \end{pmatrix}?$$

What can you say about the space into which three-dimensional space is transformed by the matrix

$$\begin{pmatrix} 1 & -2 & 2 \\ 3 & 15 & -1 \\ 2 & 5 & 1 \end{pmatrix}?$$

Does the vector $\{17, -12, 7\}$ lie in the transformed space?

4. $ABCDEF$ are six points in space. The centroids of the triangles ABC, ABD, DEF, CEF are P, Q, R, S. Prove that $PQRS$ is a parallelogram.

5. In Figure 1, $BD/DC = \frac{5}{2}$, $BF/FA = \frac{2}{1}$. Write down the position vectors (in terms of **a, b, c**) in turn of D, F, P, E, and find the ratio AE/EC.

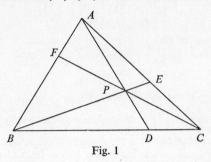

Fig. 1

6. In Figure 2, given $AD/DB = \frac{1}{1}$, $AG/GF = \frac{3}{2}$, $AE/EC = \frac{4}{1}$, find DG/GE.

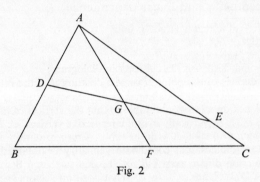

Fig. 2

7. Find a vector which is perpendicular both to $6\mathbf{i}-3\mathbf{j}-5\mathbf{k}$ and to $5\mathbf{i}+4\mathbf{j}-2\mathbf{k}$. Hence find the equation of the plane through the points $(-4, 6, 0)$, $(2, 3, -5)$ and $(1, 10, -2)$.

8. A plane meets the sides AB, BC, CD, DA of a skew quadrilateral at P, Q, R and S. Prove that $AP.BQ.CR.DS = AS.BP.CQ.DR$.

9. Find k, l, if the vector $\mathbf{p}-k\mathbf{a}-l\mathbf{b}$ is perpendicular both to **a** and **b**. Hence find the foot of the perpendicular from $(-1, 20, -11)$ onto the plane OAB, where A is $(7, 4, 4)$ and B is $(3, 2, 6)$.

10. Find a if the three equations:

$$x-y+\ z = 0,$$
$$3x-y+2z = 0,$$
$$ax+y+\ z = 0,$$

have a solution other than the trivial solution $x = y = z = 0$. Show that in this case the vectors

$$\begin{pmatrix} 1 \\ -1 \\ 1 \end{pmatrix}, \quad \begin{pmatrix} 3 \\ -1 \\ 2 \end{pmatrix}, \quad \begin{pmatrix} a \\ 1 \\ 1 \end{pmatrix}$$

are linearly dependent, and exhibit the linear relation connecting them.

E. Calculus

1. Given any real-valued function f of a real variable x, a new function g is defined by setting $g(x) = f(x)$ when $f(x) \geqslant 0$ and $g(x) = -f(x)$ when $f(x) < 0$. Sketch the graph of g for the case when f is defined in the interval $-2 \leqslant x \leqslant 5$ by

$$f(x) = -1, \qquad -2 \leqslant x < 0,$$
$$= 1 \qquad 0 \leqslant x \leqslant 1,$$
$$= 2-x, \qquad 1 \leqslant x \leqslant 3,$$
$$= -1, \qquad 3 \leqslant x \leqslant 5.$$

State for each of the following assertions whether it is true or false. Give a proof or counter-example as appropriate.

(a) If, for any function f, the function g is defined as above, then when g is continuous at a point f must also be continuous at that point.

(b) If *any* real-valued function of a real variable is continuous at a point, it is also differentiable at that point.

2. Given that $x = \frac{1}{2}(t+1/t)$ and $y = \frac{1}{2}(t-1/t)$, find dy/dx in terms of t. Find also d^2y/dx^2 in terms of t.

3. Prove that the gradient of the tangent to the curve $x = at^2$, $y = 2at$ at the point whose parameter is t is $1/t$, and hence show that the equation of the tangent at this point is $x-ty+at^2 = 0$.

The tangents at t_1 and t_2 meet at the point (h, k). What quadratic equation is satisfied by both t_1 and t_2? Use what you know about the roots of a quadratic to write down the values of h and k in terms of t_1 and t_2. Find the locus of the point of intersection of two perpendicular tangents.

4. Integrate with respect to x:

(a) $\dfrac{1}{(x+1)^2(x+2)}$;   (b) $x^2 \cos x$;   (c) $x \sin (x^2)$.

By considering the integrals

$$\int_1^{\sqrt{3}} \frac{2\,dx}{1+x^2} \quad \text{and} \quad \int_1^{\sqrt{3}} \frac{dx}{x},$$

prove that $\log_e 3 > \frac{1}{3}\pi$.

5. Sketch the graph of $y = \sin x . \sin 2x$ for $0 \leqslant x \leqslant 2\pi$.

Find the area between the graph and the x-axis for $0 \leqslant x \leqslant \frac{1}{2}\pi$, and the volume generated by rotating this area about the x-axis.

6. A cone is made from a circular filter-paper of diameter 10 cm, by folding a sector back in the usual way. Find the maximum volume of such a cone.

7. Draw the graph of the function

$$f: x \to x \left[\frac{1}{x}\right] \quad \text{for} \quad 0 < x \leqslant 2.$$

Explain when the function f' is defined, and describe it.

8. Find the length of the shortest loop of string through which a solid cone with base radius 4 cm and slant height 20 cm can just pass.

(In a general position the length of the loop is the sum of two chords: a chord of the base-circle, and a chord of the sector obtained by opening the curved surface of the cone out flat.)

9. Find a cubic polynomial which has a maximum of 4 when $x = -1$ and a minimum of -4 when $x = 1$.

Hence find a cubic polynomial which has a maximum of 7 when $x = 1$ and a minimum of -1 when $x = 3$.

If a cubic polynomial function $f: x \to f(x)$ attains its maximum value when $x = a$ and its minimum value when $x = b$, express the polynomial $f(x)$ in terms of the numbers $a, b, f(a), f(b)$. Show that

$$f\left(\frac{a+b}{2}\right) = \tfrac{1}{2}\{f(a)+f(b)\}.$$

10. Use the substitution

$$x = \frac{1}{2}\left(t+\frac{1}{t}\right)$$

to prove that

$$F(p) = \int_1^\infty \frac{dx}{(x+p)\sqrt{(x^2-1)}} = \int_1^\infty \frac{2dt}{t^2+2pt+1}.$$

Hence show that, if $|p| < 1$, $F(p) = \theta \sin \theta$, where $p = \cos \theta$, and $0 < \theta < \pi$. Evaluate $F(p)$ similarly when $|p| > 1$, and sketch the graph of $F(p)$.

F. Differential equations

1. Solve the differential equations (a) $dy/dx = x^2$, (b) $dy/dx = y^2$, giving in each case a sketch of the solution curves and the particular solution for which $y = 1$ when $x = 0$.

2. Solve the differential equation $(1-x^2)(dy/dx)-xy = x$, given $y = 1$ when $x = 0$:
  (a) by substituting $z = y\sqrt{(1-x^2)}$,
  (b) by substituting $u = y+1$.

3. What is the indefinite integral of $\cot x$ (a) if $0 < x < \pi$, (b) if $\pi < x < 2\pi$?

A family of curves is such that the angle of slope at any point is equal to the ordinate at that point.
  (i) Sketch the curves from this information in the range $0 < y < \pi$ and also in the range $\pi < y < 2\pi$.
  (ii) Write down the differential equation of the curves and solve it. (You will have to distinguish the various ranges of y.)
  (iii) What is the solution for which $y = \tfrac{3}{2}\pi$ when $x = 0$?
  (iv) Does your general solution give the solution $y = 0$ as a special case? Can you suggest why?

4. Solve $dy/dx+y(x-1) = 0$.

5. (a) A curve passes through $(2, 0)$ and its gradient is everywhere x^2-2x for all values of x. Find the equation of the curve.

(b) Show that the only family of curves, the normals at every point of which pass through the origin, are concentric circles.

1370

6. A particle moves so that its acceleration in m/s² at any time is twice its velocity in m/s. If its initial velocity is 10 m/s, find its velocity after it has gone 10 m, and the time taken to go this distance.

7. A uniform chain OA 10 cm long is being whirled round in a horizontal circle with centre O. The tension at a point x cm from O is T N. It can be proved that $dT/dx = -kx$, where k is a constant. If the tension at O is 2 N, find k and the tension at the mid-point of the chain. (N.B. the tension at A must be zero.)

8. A thermometer whose reading is θ_0 °C is placed in a vessel containing hot liquid at a temperature of T °C, which can be assumed to remain constant throughout the experiment. The temperature, θ °C, indicated by the thermometer rises at a rate proportional to the difference $T - \theta$.

Obtain and solve a differential equation for θ.

If θ_1, θ_2 and θ_3 are successive readings of θ at equal intervals of time, show that

$$T = \frac{\theta_1 \theta_3 - \theta_2^2}{\theta_1 + \theta_3 - 2\theta_2}.$$

9. A light plastic rope, 3·2 m long, whose mass is 0·5 kg per metre length and whose density is just greater than that of water, is hanging vertically submerged in a swimming bath. The upper end, which is at the water-line, is seized and pulled upwards with a steady force of 8 N. Find an expression for the velocity when x m have been raised out of the water, and show that the lower end emerges at a speed of 0·8 m/s.

10. A tank contains 600 cm³ of salt water, the mass of the dissolved salt being 123 kg. A solution of salt at a concentration of 0·08 kg/l is run into the tank at a rate of 0·40 l/s. The tank is well stirred, and the resulting mixture is drawn off at a rate of 0·20 l/s. Prove that, if m kg is the mass of salt in the tank after t s, then

$$\frac{d}{dt}(m(t+3000)) = 0 \cdot 032(t+3000).$$

Show that the mass of salt in the tank falls to a minimum and rises again. Find this minimum mass, and the time taken for it to fall to this value.

G. Mechanics

1. A model aircraft is flying at 10 m/s in a horizontal circle of radius 20 m. What is the average acceleration in the interval in which its velocity changes direction from 000° to 030°? In what direction would you expect the acceleration to be at the instant when it is flying in the direction 000°?

2. Relative to perpendicular axes, the position vector of a particle at time t is given by

$$\mathbf{r} = \begin{pmatrix} t^3 \\ 10t^2 - 20t \end{pmatrix}.$$

Find $\mathbf{r}$, $\dot{\mathbf{r}}$, and $\ddot{\mathbf{r}}$, when $t = 0, 1, 2, 3$, and hence, by drawing or calculation, obtain the magnitude and direction of the velocity and acceleration at each of these times. Show these vectors on a sketch of the path of the particle. In general, under what conditions on the path of a moving particle would you expect the velocity and acceleration vectors to be in the same direction?

3. The acceleration of a sphere falling through a liquid is $30 - 3v$ cm/s², where v is its velocity in cm/s.

(a) Sketch the graph of v against t.

(b) What is the maximum possible velocity? Is this ever reached?

(c) If the sphere starts from rest, how fast will it be travelling at time t, and how far will it then have fallen?

4. A car of mass 500 kg is travelling at 30 m/s on the banked surface of a circular track of radius 250 m. At what angle to the horizontal is the surface banked if the car has no tendency to side-slip? Investigate the maximum and minimum cornering velocities if the coefficient of friction is 0·2.

5. A chain is lying on a smooth table, half of it hanging over the edge of the table. How will the time taken for the chain to slip off the table be affected if two equal masses, each equal to the total mass of the chain, are fastened, one to each end of the chain?

If, instead, the whole chain is three times as long, half still hanging over the edge initially, how will the time be affected now?

6. A platform of mass 60 kg rests on spongy ground into which it has sunk under its own weight to a depth of 6 mm. A man of mass 75 kg jumps onto the platform from a height of 1·2 m. On the assumption that the resistance of the ground is proportional to the depth to which it is penetrated, find how much farther the platform sinks in.

7. A package of mass 15 kg is slid onto a conveyor belt running horizontally at 0·9 m/s. The package comes onto the belt with a velocity of 1·2 m/s at right-angles to the direction of motion of the belt. The coefficient of friction is 0·2.

(a) Explain why the package travels in a straight line relative to the belt.

(b) Find how long it takes to come to rest relative to the belt, and how far it moves altogether in doing so.

(c) Find the work supplied by the belt, and the energy lost in the motion.

8. A boy stands at a distance d from a smooth vertical wall. He throws a ball with velocity $\begin{pmatrix} u \\ v \end{pmatrix}$ to bounce on the wall, and catches it without moving. Show that the coefficient of restitution must be

$$e = \frac{gd}{2uv - gd}.$$

Find the minimum speed of projection for this to be possible.

9. A uniform triangular board is hung up by three strings attached to its vertices and suspended from a single hook. Prove by the use of vectors that the tensions in the strings are proportional to the lengths of the strings, provided only that each string is taut. Would this be true if the board were quadrilateral?

10. Assuming Einstein's equation $E = mc^2$ and the Newtonian definitions of momentum $\mathbf{p} = m\mathbf{v}$ and force $\mathbf{F} = d\mathbf{p}/dt$, prove the following results:

(a) $\mathbf{F}.\mathbf{v}$ = rate of change of energy $= c^2 dm/dt$;

(b) $\mathbf{p}.d\mathbf{p}/dt = (E/c^2)dE/dt$; and integrate this to obtain

(c) $c^2p^2 = E^2 - E_0^2$, where E_0 is the energy when $v = 0$ (rest energy).

(d) If $E = E_0 + T$, where T is the kinetic energy, then for small v, $T = m_0 v^2/2$, where $m_0 = E_0/c^2$, the rest mass.

(e) For large v (nearly c) $T = cp = mvc$ approximately.

(f) $m = m_0/\surd(1 - v^2/c^2)$.

H. Electricity

1. Find the r.m.s. current in a circuit carrying an a.c. $i \cos \omega t$, together with a direct current I superposed on this. What will be the r.m.s. voltage needed to drive this current through a resistance of $R\,\Omega$?

2. Find the equivalent resistance of a network of wires in the form of the edges of an octahedron, each edge having resistance R,
   (a) if the e.m.f. is connected across a pair of opposite vertices;
   (b) if the e.m.f. is connected across a pair of adjacent vertices.

3. Two normal 60-watt electric light bulbs are connected in series instead of in parallel. As a result the resistance of each falls to 75 % of its value in normal use. What power is now consumed in the pair of them?

4. Two six-volt batteries each of internal resistance $\frac{5}{6}\Omega$ are connected in parallel to two bus-bars. The contacts are corroded so that there is a resistance of 5 Ω between their positive terminals, and also the same between their negative terminals (see Figure 1).

Find the power loss in a 12-watt light bulb which is connected (without contact resistance) between A and D instead of between A and B. Assume the bulb would consume 12 W if $R_{AC} = R_{BD} = 0$.

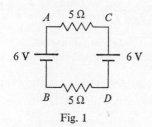

Fig. 1   Fig. 2

5. What is the maximum internal resistance of a 6 volt battery if it will light a bulb at a power of 12 W?

6. In the circuit shown in Figure 2, find the value of R for which the power consumed in it is a maximum. What then is the power
   (a) consumed in R;
   (b) consumed in the 9 Ω resistor;
   (c) wasted in the battery?

7. The circuit shown in Figure 3 includes a transformer. M is the *coefficient of mutual inductance*; that is to say that if di/dt is the rate of change of current in either coil, then a back e.m.f. of $M\,di/dt$ is induced in the other.

Show that if i_2 is the current in the right-hand coil, then

$$ME = (M^2 - L_1 L_2)\,di_2/dt - L_1 R i_2.$$

Hence show that if $M^2 = L_1 L_2$, the unit inside the box behaves like an e.m.f. of magnitude $-ME/L_1$.

1373

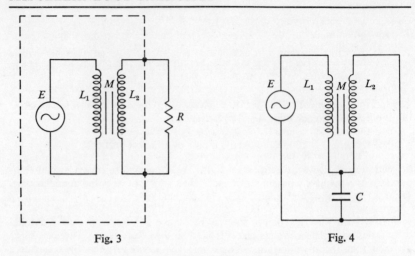

Fig. 3   Fig. 4

8. An e.m.f. of $60 \cos 100t$ V is applied to the transformer of Question 7. If $L_1 = 3M = 8L_2 = 1 \cdot 2$ H, $R = 20\,\Omega$, sketch the form of the current-time curve and find how long it takes after the transformer is switched on for the current to reach 90 % of its steady value.

9. In the circuit shown in Figure 4, the capacitance C is adjusted until no current flows in the secondary coil with inductance L_2.

Prove that if $E = E_0 \cos \omega t$, then $CM\omega^2 = 1$.

10. Show that the r.m.s. current in the primary circuit in Question 9 is

$$\frac{E}{\omega(L_1 - M)},$$

and find the mean power expended.

I. Probability and statistics

1. The local train from Bedwyn to Newbury usually has three coaches. If there are nine people on the platform at Bedwyn and they get in the train at random, find the probability
    (a) that there will be just three in each coach;
    (b) that there will be four in one coach, three in another, and two in the third.

2. The girls of Wenchcombe Pulchra decide their marriage prospects as follows: a girl takes six identical lengths of ribbon in her clenched fist. Her friend then ties together the six ends hanging down on one side in pairs and then does the same for the six ends on the other side. If the six ribbons now form one complete ring the girl who holds it will be married inside a year. Find the probability of a favourable omen.

3. A statistical toy contains a lever which operates an indicator showing either red or blue. When a ball is dropped at random through the apparatus it is twice as likely to change the indicator as to leave it alone. The indicator shows blue, and four balls are passed through; the indicator shows red at the end. What is the probability that the first ball changed it?

4. A standard pack contains 52 cards. In a defective pack, the King and Queen of Spades are missing but the King and Queen of Diamonds are duplicated. What is the probability that four cards removed one after another will produce the King of Hearts, the King of Diamonds, the Queen of Diamonds, the King of Clubs in that order?

Find the corresponding answers if (*a*) each card is replaced in the pack after identification; (*b*) cards are not replaced (as in the original problem) but the four named cards may be drawn in any order.

5. The weight of a penny in g may be regarded as a number drawn at random from an infinite Normal population with mean 9·40 and s.d. 0·16, or thereabouts. How often would a bank weighing a bag of sixty pennies to check its contents expect to let through a bag containing 59 (or fewer), if they accept anything within 5 g of the average weight?

If you wished to establish the mean weight rather more accurately—to be reasonably sure that you knew the weight to the nearest 0·01 gm—and had scales which weighed to the nearest 0·001 g available, how many pennies would you weigh, and what would you then claim for your result?

6. A small hall holds 244 people. The booking agents reckon that on the average 4 % of those who buy tickets fail to use them. If they regularly sell 250 tickets for a show, how often will they have to squeeze in extra seats?

7. A sample of n coins is drawn at random from a large collection in which a fraction p are pennies. What is the probability that just r of the coins are pennies?

If the probability that a penny is a Queen Elizabeth one is q, what is the probability that there are exactly s QE pennies among the r pennies of this sample?

Write down the probability that a sample of n coins will contain $s+k$ pennies, only s of which are QE ones, and calculate the sum of these probabilities for all possible values of k.

8. A particular large batch of sweet pea seeds is known to contain 25 % that will not germinate. Samples of 6 seeds each are sown in pots. What is:
   (*a*) the expected number of seedlings to appear in a pot?
   (*b*) the most likely number of seedlings to appear in a pot?
   (*c*) the probability of precisely this number appearing?
   (*d*) the percentage of pots in which less than half the seeds germinate?

9. A bus is due to pass the end of the road at 8.45 each weekday morning. Over a series of 15 weekdays I record (to the nearest minute) the number of minutes it is late, with the following results:

Day	1	2	3	4	5	6	7	8	9	10	11	12	13	14	15
No. of min late	3	10	0	−1	8	14	9	5	−4	0	2	−3	1	10	7

Calculate the mean time of arrival of the bus, and the standard deviation. How likely is the bus
   (*a*) to be on time or earlier?
   (*b*) to be more than 10 minutes late?
What assumptions do you make in computing these probabilities?

10. The probability that an electric-light bulb lasts between x and $x+\delta x$ hours can be taken to be

$$\phi(x).\delta x = A.\exp(-x/1200).\delta x \quad (x \geqslant 0)$$

What is the value of the constant A?

(*a*) What is the expected life of a bulb?

(*b*) If I put three bulbs in a light fitting at once, so that they all burn under identical conditions, what is the probability that I shall enjoy 900 hours service without having to replace one?

(*c*) What is the probability that at least one of the three will be burning after 1200 hours?

What assumptions have you made in computing these probabilities, and what possible causes might vitiate them?

J. Puzzles

1. What is the greatest number of subsets of a set of n elements that one can find such that no two are disjoint?

2. 15 wires, electrically conducting, and insulated from each other, run in a buried cable, the ends of which are several miles apart. It is not known which wire at one end connects with which at the other. You may join wires together at the ends in any way, and you have a means of testing electrical connection. Devise a scheme involving the minimum of journeys which will enable you to distinguish the wires.

Generalize to a cable of n wires.

3. An egg-timer is placed on a spring balance and inverted. Draw a graph of weight recorded against time from the moment the first particle of sand starts moving until the moment the last particle stops.

4. A bucket full of water is suspended, and a cork is somehow pushed down into the middle of the water. At a moment when the cork is stationary, the bucket is dropped. While the bucket is falling, does the level of the cork in relation to the bucket rise, fall or remain the same?

5. A counter is moved along a snakes and ladders board without any snakes or ladders (!) in the usual way, the number of squares moved being governed by throwing a die. The only rule is that at the end the counter must get home exactly; that is, if moving the counter on the number of squares indicated by the die would take it off the board, a turn must be missed. What is the probability of the counter landing on the last square without a turn being missed?

6. Arrange the nine digits 1, 2, ..., 9 in a 3×3 matrix so that every row and every column represents (in the scale of ten) a number divisible by 11.

7. A sheet of paper has a straight edge E, and a point P is marked on the paper, not on the edge E. The paper is then folded so that the edge E passes through the point P, and this is repeated a large number of times. Show that the creases touch a parabola.

8. If $(1+\sqrt{2})^n = a+b\sqrt{2}$, where a, b, n are positive integers, show that a is the nearest integer to $b\sqrt{2}$ and give a formula for a and b. Use this to write a flow diagram to generate successive approximations to $\sqrt{2}$.

9. An equilateral triangle ABC with side 8 units is divided into a network of small equilateral triangles by marking the points at unit intervals on its sides and joining them by lines parallel to the sides.

Show that if P is any vertex of this mesh, then

$$8\mathbf{p} = x\mathbf{a}+y\mathbf{b}+z\mathbf{c}, \quad \text{where} \quad x, y, z \in Z^+ \quad \text{and} \quad x+y+z = 8.$$

What is the locus given by $x = 3, y+z = 5$?

Indicate the region R which satisfies the inequalities

$$0 \leqslant x \leqslant 8, \quad 0 \leqslant y \leqslant 5, \quad 0 \leqslant z \leqslant 3.$$

You have three vessels with capacities 8 l, 5 l and 3 l. The 8 l vessel is full of wine, 4 l of which is to be poured into the 5 l vessel. Represent the situation with x l in the first vessel, y l in the second and z l in the third by the point P described above. Show that the operation of filling any vessel from another is represented by a path parallel to a side of the triangle, starting and ending on the boundary of the region R. Hence solve the problem.

Generalize this, showing that usually there are two solutions, but in some cases (e.g. 20 l of wine in vessels holding 20 l, 13 l, 9 l) there is only one. Can there be none?

10. $2n$ people are queueing to buy 50p tickets to enter an exhibition. n of them have only £1 notes; the other n have 50p coins. At the start the doorman has no change. If each person buys one ticket, what is the probability that no-one has to wait for change?

Show that this problem is the same as that of finding the number of ways of joining the vertices of a convex $2n$-gon in pairs by n non-intersecting line-segments.

INDEX

acceleration, dimensions and units of, 1245

algebra, of expected-value notation, 1164–7: fundamental theorem of, 1267

algebraic functions, 1249, 1250

ampere, 1245

analysis, fundamental theorem of, 1129

area, centre of, 1127; under a graph, application of integration to calculation of, 1089; under probability density graphs, 1120, 1121, 1129; under velocity-time graphs, 1096

averages, application of integration to calculation of, 1105–7

binomial probability function, 1135–9, 1148, 1150, 1152, 1167–8, 1350; limiting form of, 1135–40

binomial series, general, 1347

Buffon's needle, 1098–9

capacitance, dimensions and units of, 1245

central limit theorem, 1155–7, 1162

centre of area, 1127

centre of gravity, 1107

centre of mass, 1107; application of integration to calculation of, 1108–10, 1126–7; moment of inertia about, 1127, 1215; of a system of particles, 1214

Choleski's process, 1306

circular symmetry, integration using, 1102–5

cofactors, 1301–5

coin-tossing, 1348

collision, kinetic energy in, 1216

computer (analogue), use of simulation in, 1233

confidence limits, 1154, 1180

conics, 1341–2; central, 1342; and polars, 1342–4

conservative field of force, 1212

continuity, 1325–9

convergence, 1308–29; 1332–3; iterative processes and, 1313–17; of sequences, 1308–17; of series, 1317–25

correlation, 1166

coulomb, unit of electric charge, 1245

covariance, 1166

cover-up rule, 1252–4, 1258, 1260, 1261; formal proof of, 1265–6

criteria, two-tailed and one-tailed, 1152 n

cumulative probability functions, 1129–32

cumulative relative frequency, 1117–18

degrees of freedom, in a calculation, 1182

density, and centre of mass, 1107; dimensions and units of, 1245; *see also* population density, probability density

derivatives, 1326–7

determinants, 1270; of elementary matrices, 1285–6; linear dependence and, 1270–1307; of a non-singular matrix, 1288; product theorem for, 1286–7; properties of, 1285–8; of a singular matrix, 1287; and the solution of equations, 1270–82; in three-by-three homogeneous equations, 1277–80; in two-by-two equations, 1275–7

dimensional analysis, 1230–44, 1247–8

dimensional consistency, 1230–1

dimensionless quantities, 1235, 1237, 1239, 1242

dimensions and units, table of, 1245

directrix of a conic, 1341

discontinuity, 1326

divergence of sequences, 1313

division, synthetic, 1260

dyne, unit of force, 1245

echelon process, in solution of linear equations, 1270–1, 1278, 1296

eigenvectors, of a matrix, 1307

elastic constant, 1206

elastic strings, 1205–6

electric charge, dimensions and units of, 1245; as fundamental dimension, 1232

electric current, dimensions and units of, 1245

electric resistance, dimensions and units of, 1245

electricity, dimensions in, 1232–4

electromotive force, dimensions and units of, 1245

ellipse, 1341–2

energy, equation of, *see* equation of energy; kinetic, *see* kinetic energy; potential, 1212; principle of, 1189–90, 1199, 1200, 1208, 1213, 1216; rotational, 1355–6; work and, 1188–1229, 1246

epitrochoids, 1344

equality and equivalence, 1249–50

equation of energy, 1190, 1192; extension of, 1199, 1200, 1201; as a scalar relation, 1193; for systems of particles, 1220; for a variable force, 1209, 1210, 1211

equations, determinants and the solution of, 1270–82; homogeneous 1275, 1294–6;